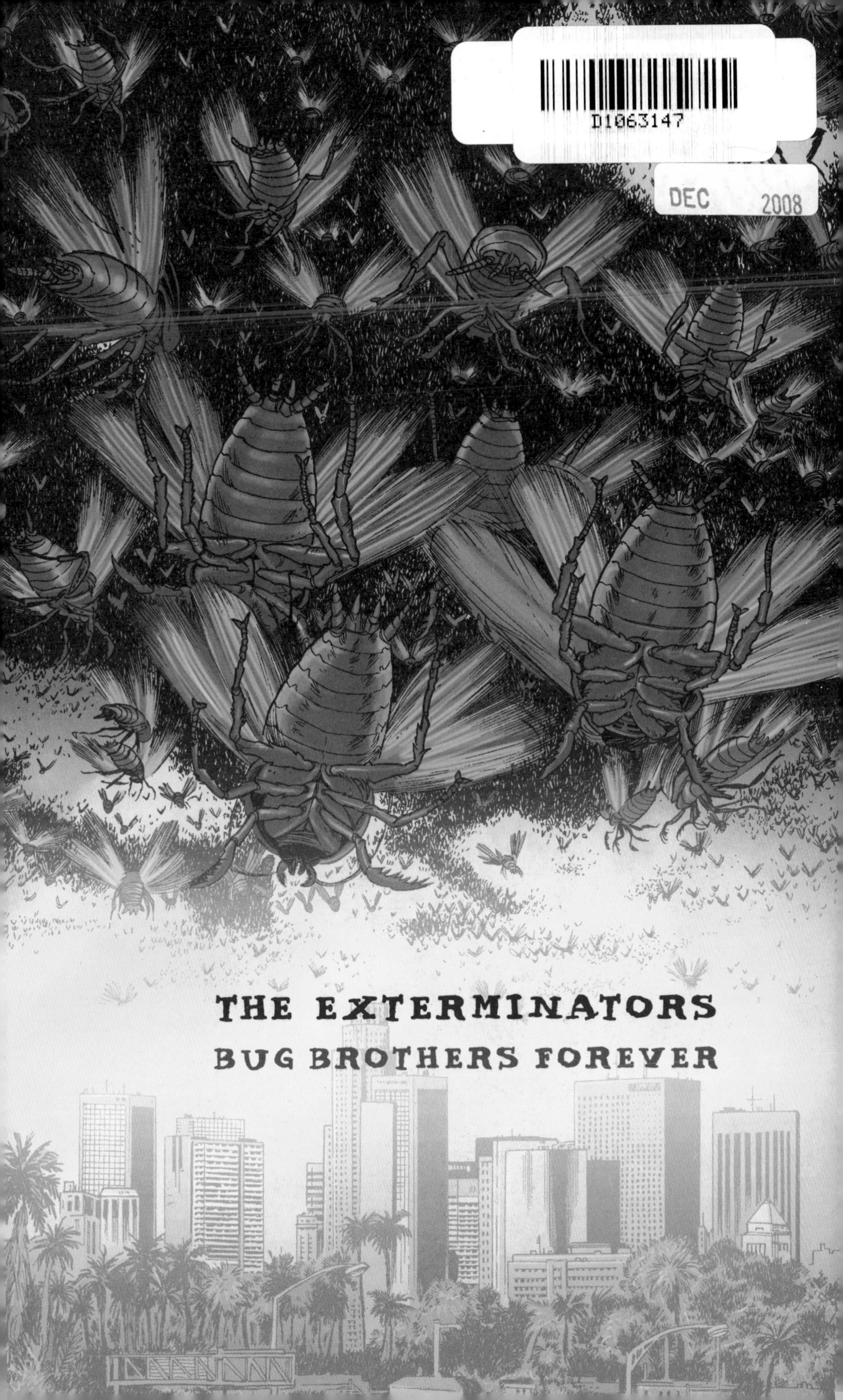
D1063147
DEC 2008
THE EXTERMINATORS
BUG BROTHERS FOREVER

Karen Berger
Senior VP-Executive Editor

Jonathan Vankin
Editor-original series

Mark Doyle
Assistant Editor-original series

Bob Harras
Editor-collected edition

Robbin Brosterman
Senior Art Director

Paul Levitz
President & Publisher

Georg Brewer
VP-Design & DC Direct Creative

Richard Bruning
Senior VP-Creative Director

Patrick Caldon
Executive VP-Finance & Operations

Chris Caramalis
VP-Finance

John Cunningham
VP-Marketing

Terri Cunningham
VP-Managing Editor

Amy Genkins
Senior VP-Business & Legal Affairs

Alison Gill
VP-Manufacturing

Hank Kanalz
VP-General Manager, WildStorm

Jim Lee
Editorial Director-WildStorm

Gregory Noveck
Senior VP-Creative Affairs

Sue Pohja
VP-Book Trade Sales

Steve Rotterdam
Senior VP-Sales & Marketing

Cheryl Rubin
Senior VP-Brand Management

Alysse Soll
VP-Advertising & Custom Publishing

Jeff Trojan
VP-Business Development, DC Direct

Bob Wayne
VP-Sales

Cover illustration by Philip Bond
Publication design by Amelia Grohman
Logo design by Ken Lopez

**THE EXTERMINATORS:
BUG BROTHERS FOREVER**

Published by DC Comics. Cover, text
and compilation Copyright © 2008 DC Comics.
All Rights Reserved. Originally published in
single magazine form as THE EXTERMINATORS 24-30.
Copyright © 2008 Simon Oliver and M. Anthony Moore.
All Rights Reserved. All characters, their distinctive
likenesses and related elements featured
in this publication are trademarks of
Simon Oliver and M. Anthony Moore.
VERTIGO is a trademark of DC Comics.
The stories, characters and incidents featured
in this publication are entirely fictional.
DC Comics does not read or accept unsolicited
submissions of ideas, stories or artwork.

DC Comics
1700 Broadway, New York, NY 10019
A Warner Bros. Entertainment Company.
Printed in Canada.
First Printing.
ISBN: 978-1-4012-1970-3

SIMON OLIVER WRITER

THE EXTERMINATORS
BUG BROTHERS FOREVER

[5]

BUFFET OF DARKNESS
ALL REDNECKS GO TO HEAVEN
BUG BROTHERS FOREVER

TONY MOORE PENCILLER

JOHN LUCAS INKER

LAURA GOES DOWN

TY TEMPLETON ARTIST

RAISING CHÉ

JOHN LUCAS ARTIST

BRIAN BUCCELLATO COLORIST
PAT BROSSEAU LETTERER
INTRODUCTION BY SIMON OLIVER

THE EXTERMINATORS CREATED BY
SIMON OLIVER & TONY MOORE

INTRODUCTION

I'd like to start by making a confession to you.

There have been a lot of mornings lately, after I've kissed my wife and young sons goodbye, taken my four-mile commute, stepped over the crackheads in my office building's doorway and taken a seat at my desk (in a office that's all in all probably a little too reminiscent of *Barton Fink*)—and that's when it hits me.

I'm gripped with this overwhelming fear, a deep sense of professional doom, that I'll never enjoy writing anything as much as I've enjoyed writing THE EXTERMINATORS.

You see, this whole thing has truly been a great ride for me. As my first piece of writing work, it's where I got to cut, and break, some of my storytelling teeth. I had the opportunity to create this seedy, nasty world of my imagination, a world where even the good guys got to have some very human failings, and bring to life a cast of strange and unsavory characters. Then I got to throw them around, and, well…

Before this, I never thought of myself as having a God complex. But I think maybe I just discovered that I do.

But that's one of the great things I discovered about writing a monthly comic, and don't ever let a jaded comic book writer tell you otherwise, it's fuck-ing fun playing with a world you create. Also you get to do something that, I think, no other medium except maybe the literary novel lets you do. You have

the luxury of spinning off on bizarre tangents and side stories that focus on supporting characters that movies and most TV shows would just pass by.

Some of my favorite EXTERMINATORS issues are the ones about supporting characters: Saloth's two-part flashback arc (see Vol. 3, *Lies of Our Fathers*), AJ in the Afterlife (in this volume), and the only truly standalone issue, a story on a tangent all its own, "Buffet of Darkness".

That's just one of the things I've learned during my time on THE EXTERMINATORS. And obviously there's a lot of other writing/story/comic book stuff that I'm not going to bore you with here. But there are other, way more unexpected things that I've learned that have to do with how people react to a comic book about bugs.

First off, when I started this I had no idea what a visceral, deep-rooted horror of bugs some people have. I knew most people may not be fans as such, and personally, I'm not too excited about physical contact with cockroaches.

But a lot of people—and I'm talking about people who watch blood and guts slasher movies, people who obviously get some pleasure in having their fear buttons pushed—told me they just couldn't bring themselves to even consider reading a comic book about pests.

Seriously, as you can imagine, it came as a big shock to me when I realized I'd picked a subject that immediately eliminated probably 25 percent of potential readers.

But that contrasts nicely with my next point, and as points go, this is a big one. For the entire history of mankind we've searched for some common thread, some element that connects us all, as a species. And outside of the obvious — sex, death and pooping—it's kind of been a bust.

Religion? Never really panned out. The United Nations—better but no cigar. And Coca Cola? Well, rotting out kids' teeth the world over…

But I think that in writing my humble piece of low-grade smut about pests and the men who hunt them, I may have stumbled on something that ties us all together regardless of any race, color, age, or sexual preference,

Everyone (and here I'm including the 25 percent with the visceral fear of bugs) has their own bug/rat/vermin/pest story to tell. And I do mean fucking *everyone*.

How do I know this? Personal experience. Any time, any place, any situation when it happened to come up in casual conversation that I was writing a book about bug exterminators, after a brief pause while that sunk in, I could literally set my watch to the time it took for the first person to share his or her pest story. Then everyone else would follow.

It's freakish, and I'll leave you with that thought. Feel free to use it in the future. You find yourself in a social situation where there's a painful lull in the conversation, or you're stuck at your sister's husband's brother's wedding and you're wondering how the fuck you're going to talk with these people you have less than zero in common with. I'm telling you, just subtly steer the conversation into the topic of pest experiences, and then silently thank me.

Of course, don't ever do it in food-related situations. And no, guys, it's probably never going to get you laid.

Simon Oliver AUGUST 2008

BUFFET OF DARKNESS

COVER ART BY PHILIP BOND

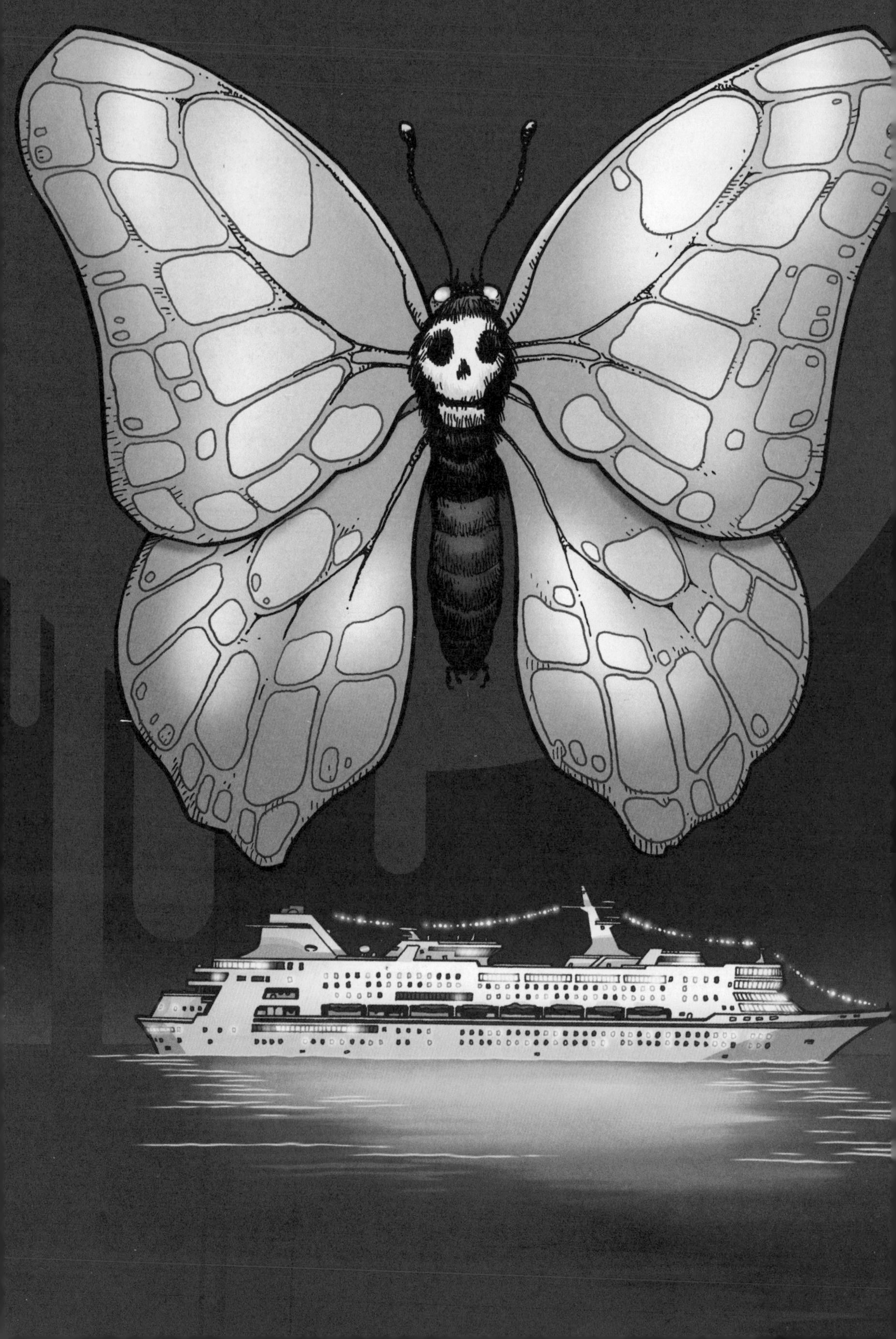

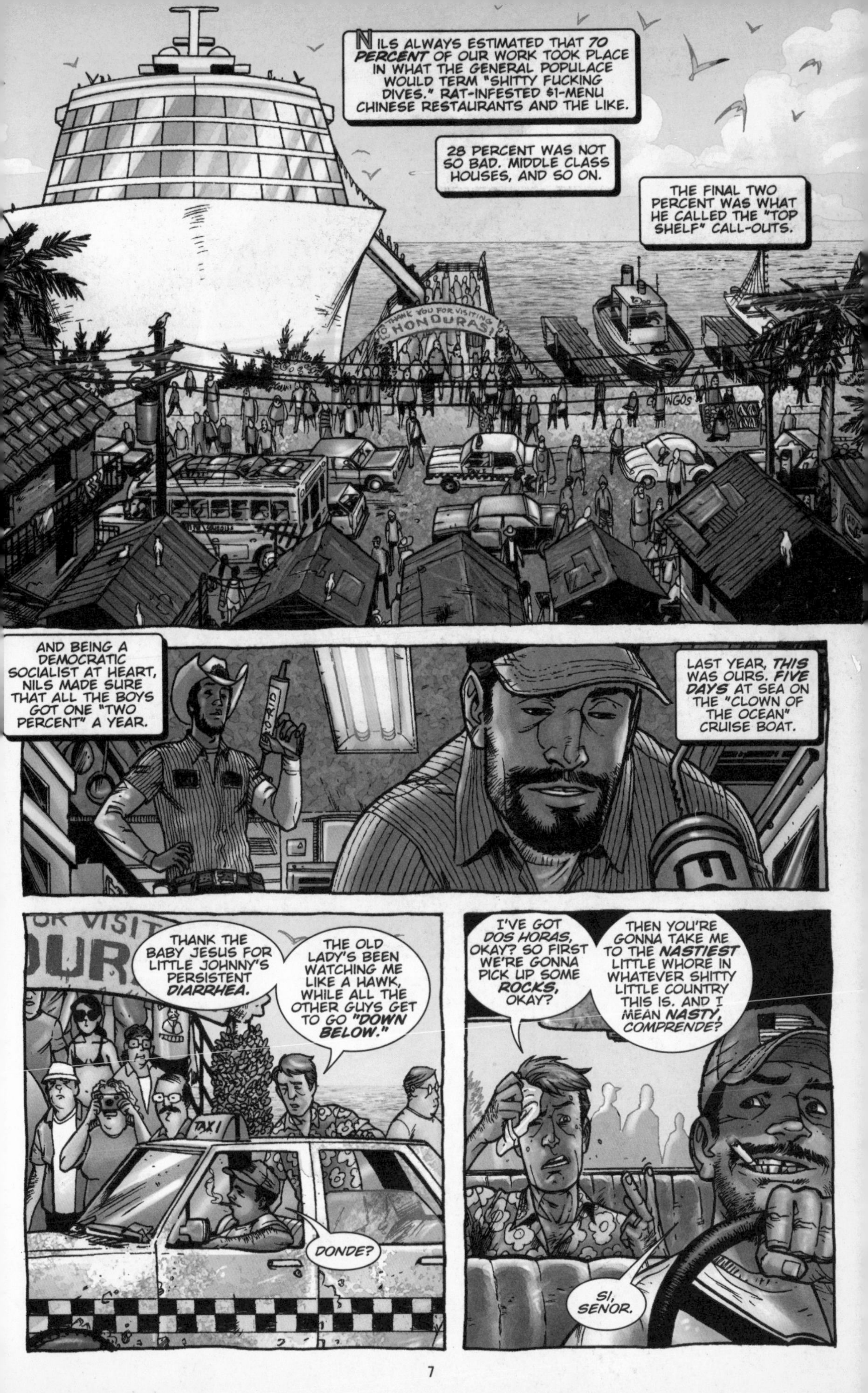
NILS ALWAYS ESTIMATED THAT 70 PERCENT OF OUR WORK TOOK PLACE IN WHAT THE GENERAL POPULACE WOULD TERM "SHITTY FUCKING DIVES." RAT-INFESTED $1-MENU CHINESE RESTAURANTS AND THE LIKE.
28 PERCENT WAS NOT SO BAD. MIDDLE CLASS HOUSES, AND SO ON.
THE FINAL TWO PERCENT WAS WHAT HE CALLED THE "TOP SHELF" CALL-OUTS.
THANK YOU FOR VISITING HONDURAS!
AND BEING A DEMOCRATIC SOCIALIST AT HEART, NILS MADE SURE THAT ALL THE BOYS GOT ONE "TWO PERCENT" A YEAR.
LAST YEAR, THIS WAS OURS. FIVE DAYS AT SEA ON THE "CLOWN OF THE OCEAN" CRUISE BOAT.
THANK THE BABY JESUS FOR LITTLE JOHNNY'S PERSISTENT DIARRHEA.
THE OLD LADY'S BEEN WATCHING ME LIKE A HAWK, WHILE ALL THE OTHER GUYS GET TO GO "DOWN BELOW."
TAXI
DONDE?
I'VE GOT DOS HORAS, OKAY? SO FIRST WE'RE GONNA PICK UP SOME ROCKS, OKAY?
THEN YOU'RE GONNA TAKE ME TO THE NASTIEST LITTLE WHORE IN WHATEVER SHITTY LITTLE COUNTRY THIS IS. AND I MEAN NASTY, COMPRENDE?
SI, SENOR.

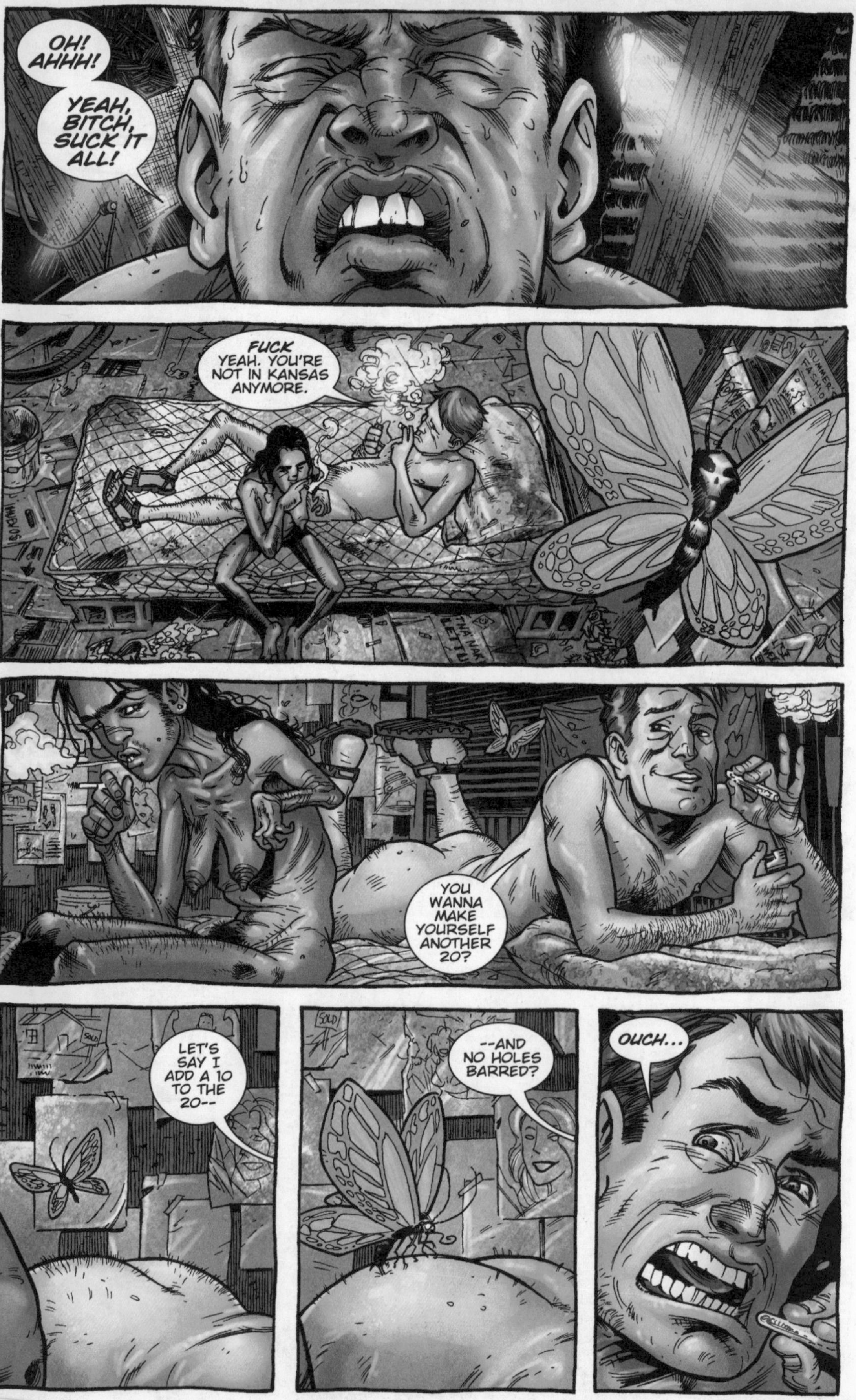
OH! AHHH!
YEAH, BITCH, SUCK IT ALL!
FUCK YEAH. YOU'RE NOT IN KANSAS ANYMORE.
YOU WANNA MAKE YOURSELF ANOTHER 20?
LET'S SAY I ADD A 10 TO THE 20--
--AND NO HOLES BARRED?
OUCH...

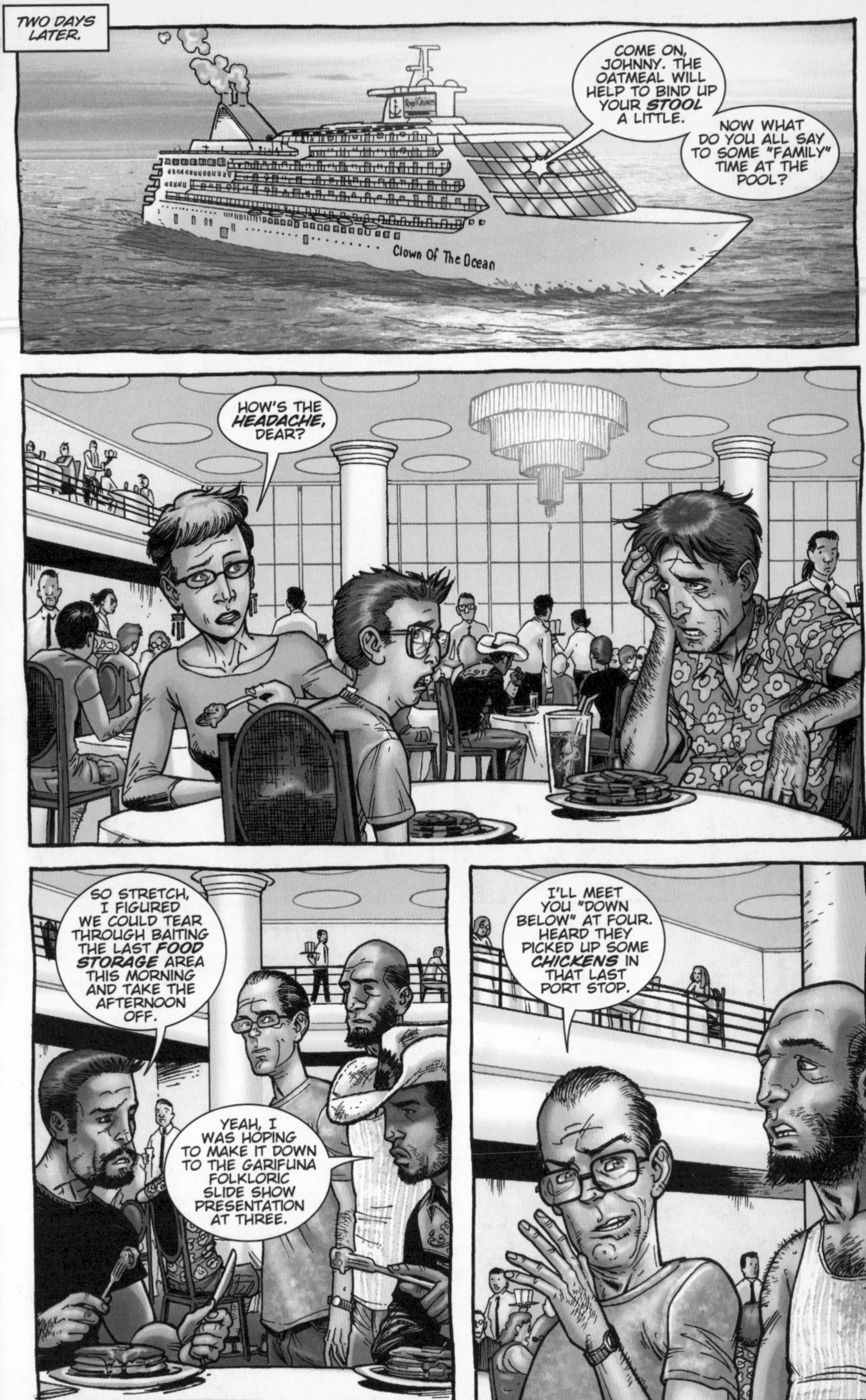
TWO DAYS LATER.
COME ON, JOHNNY. THE OATMEAL WILL HELP TO BIND UP YOUR STOOL A LITTLE.
NOW WHAT DO YOU ALL SAY TO SOME "FAMILY" TIME AT THE POOL?
Clown Of The Ocean
HOW'S THE HEADACHE, DEAR?
SO STRETCH, I FIGURED WE COULD TEAR THROUGH BAITING THE LAST FOOD STORAGE AREA THIS MORNING AND TAKE THE AFTERNOON OFF.
YEAH, I WAS HOPING TO MAKE IT DOWN TO THE GARIFUNA FOLKLORIC SLIDE SHOW PRESENTATION AT THREE.
I'LL MEET YOU "DOWN BELOW" AT FOUR. HEARD THEY PICKED UP SOME CHICKENS IN THAT LAST PORT STOP.

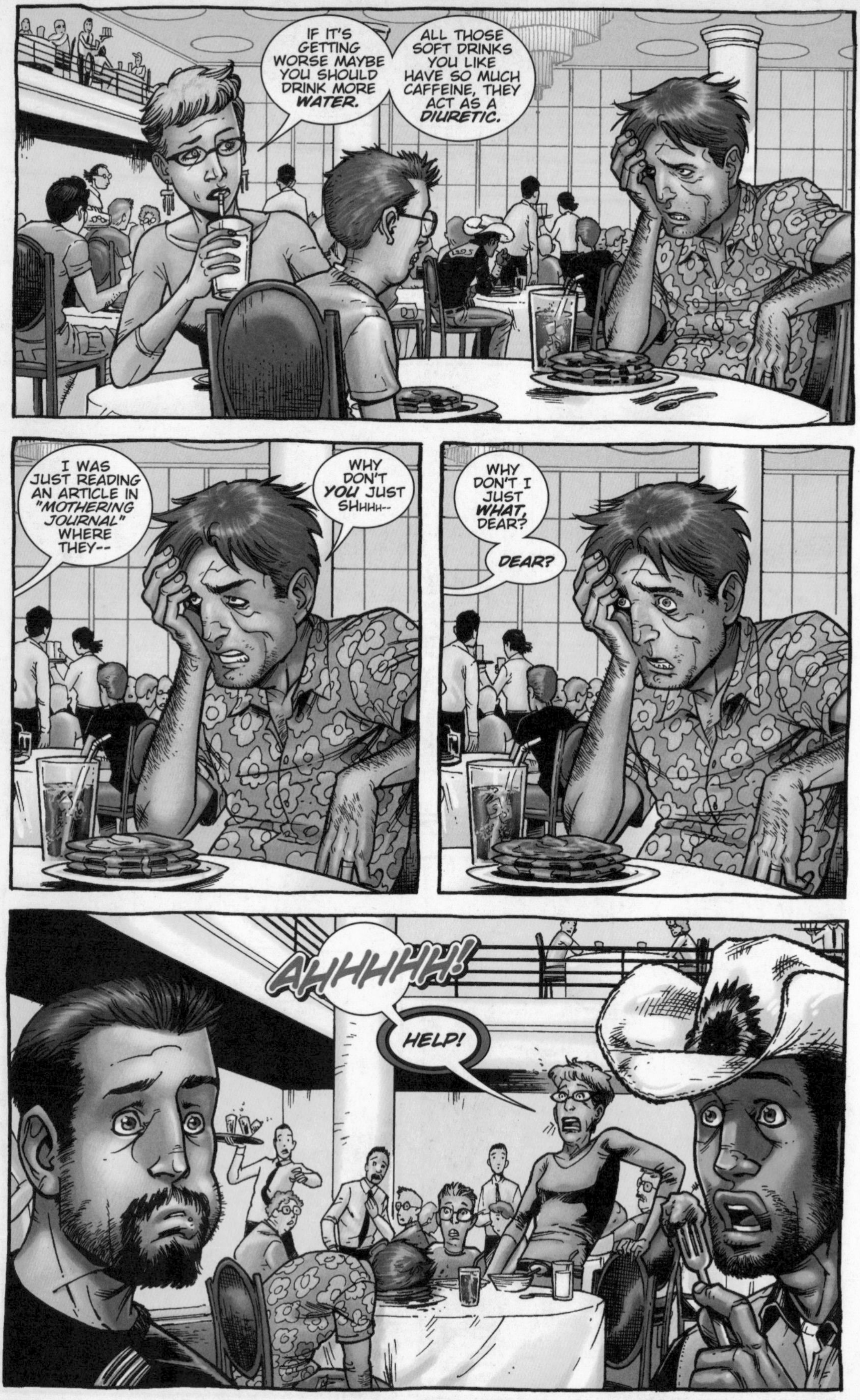
IF IT'S GETTING WORSE MAYBE YOU SHOULD DRINK MORE *WATER.*
ALL THOSE SOFT DRINKS YOU LIKE HAVE SO MUCH CAFFEINE, THEY ACT AS A *DIURETIC.*
I WAS JUST READING AN ARTICLE IN *"MOTHERING JOURNAL"* WHERE THEY--
WHY DON'T *YOU* JUST SHHHH--
WHY DON'T I JUST *WHAT,* DEAR?
DEAR?
AHHHHH!
HELP!

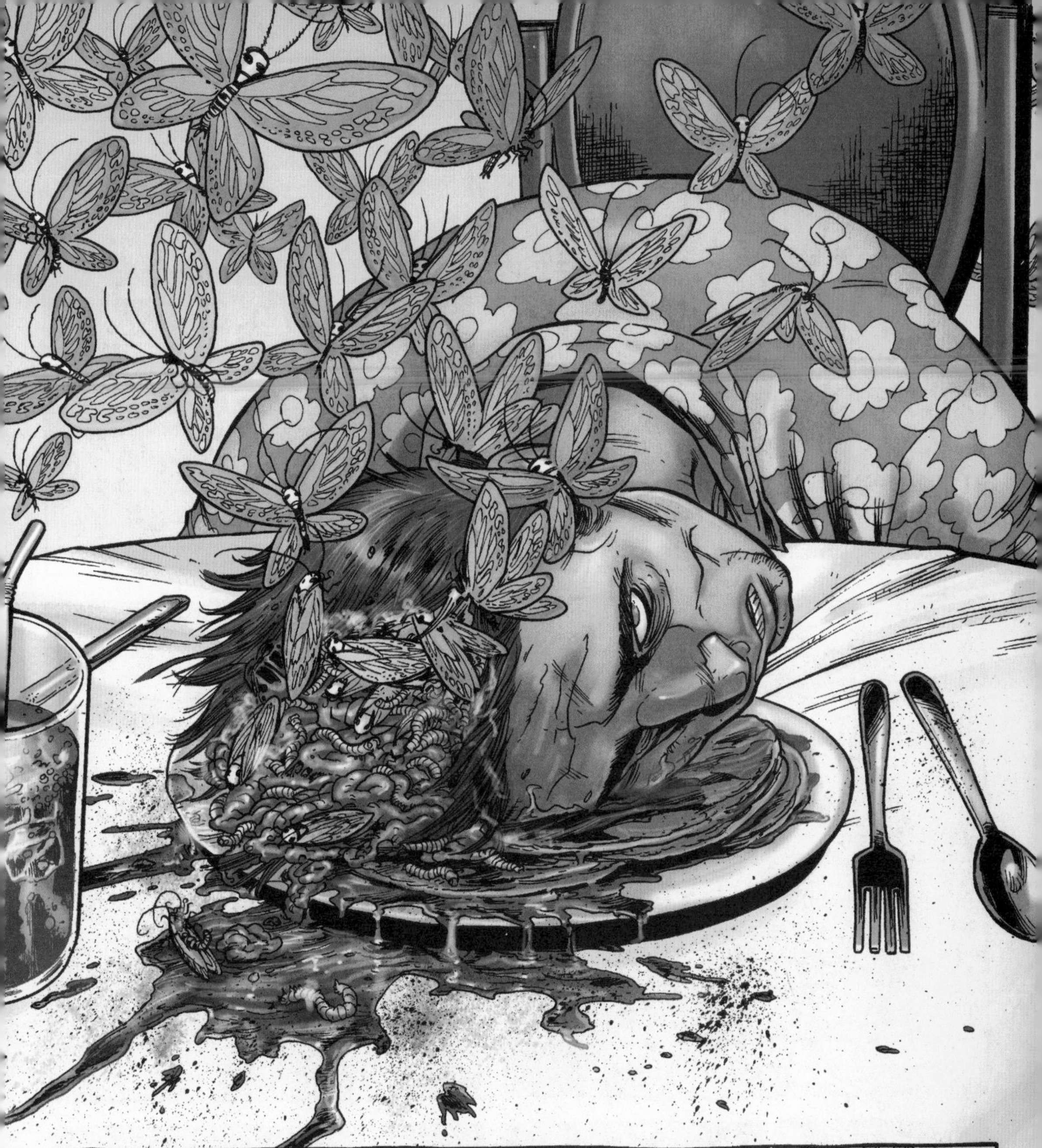

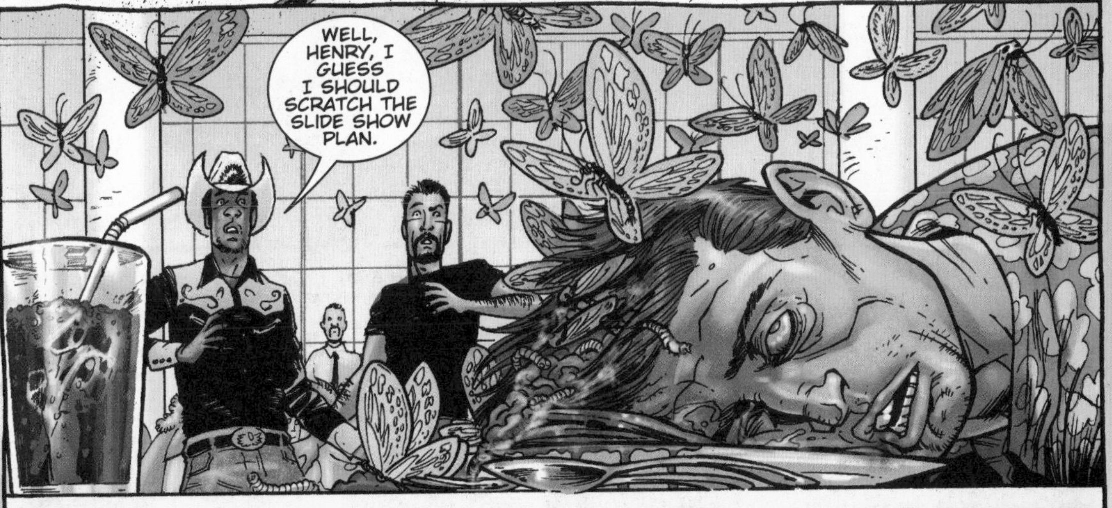
WELL, HENRY, I GUESS I SHOULD SCRATCH THE SLIDE SHOW PLAN.

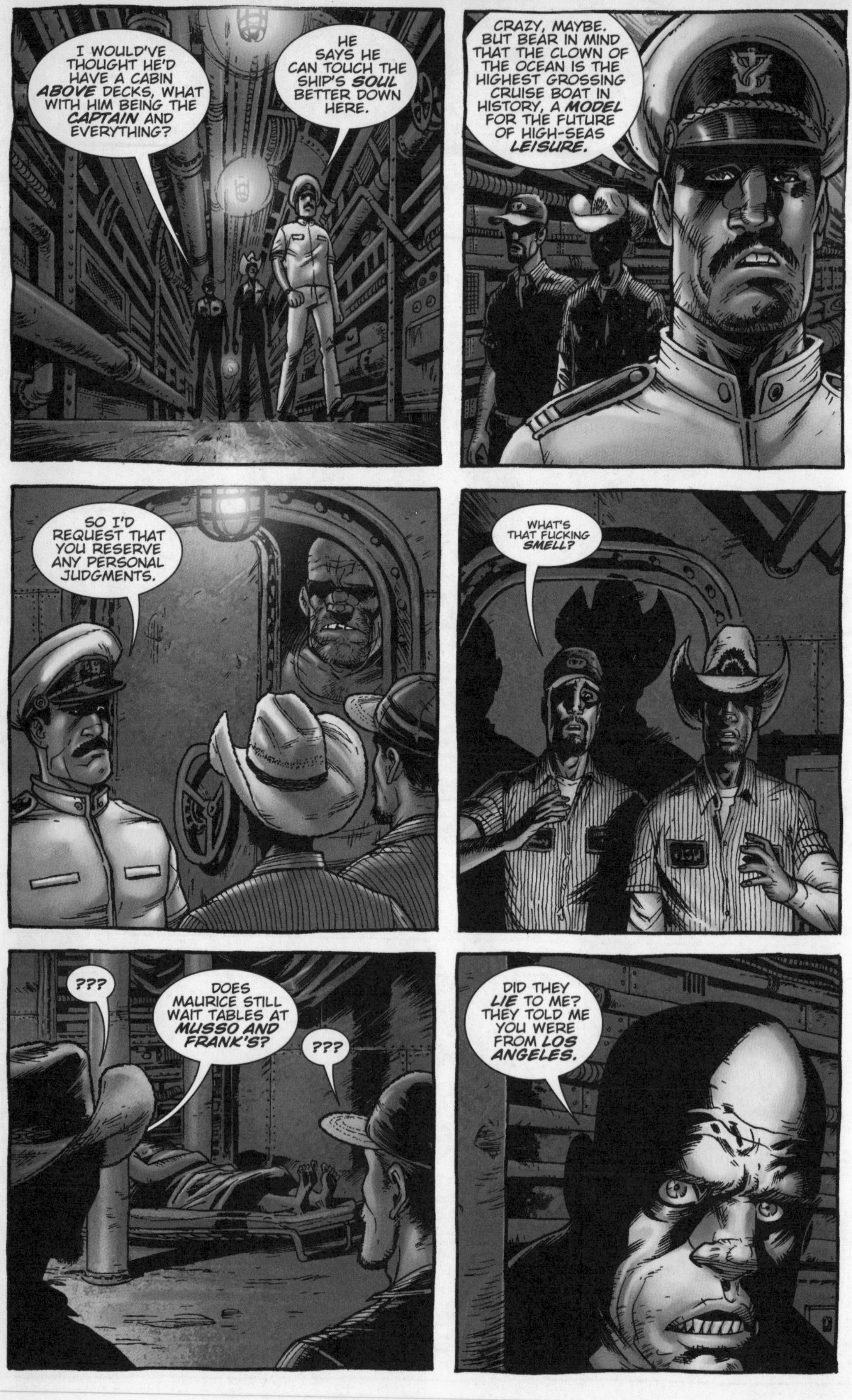
I WOULD'VE THOUGHT HE'D HAVE A CABIN ABOVE DECKS, WHAT WITH HIM BEING THE CAPTAIN AND EVERYTHING?
HE SAYS HE CAN TOUCH THE SHIP'S SOUL BETTER DOWN HERE.
CRAZY, MAYBE. BUT BEAR IN MIND THAT THE CLOWN OF THE OCEAN IS THE HIGHEST GROSSING CRUISE BOAT IN HISTORY, A MODEL FOR THE FUTURE OF HIGH-SEAS LEISURE.
SO I'D REQUEST THAT YOU RESERVE ANY PERSONAL JUDGMENTS.
WHAT'S THAT FUCKING SMELL?
???
DOES MAURICE STILL WAIT TABLES AT MUSSO AND FRANK'S?
???
DID THEY LIE TO ME? THEY TOLD ME YOU WERE FROM LOS ANGELES.

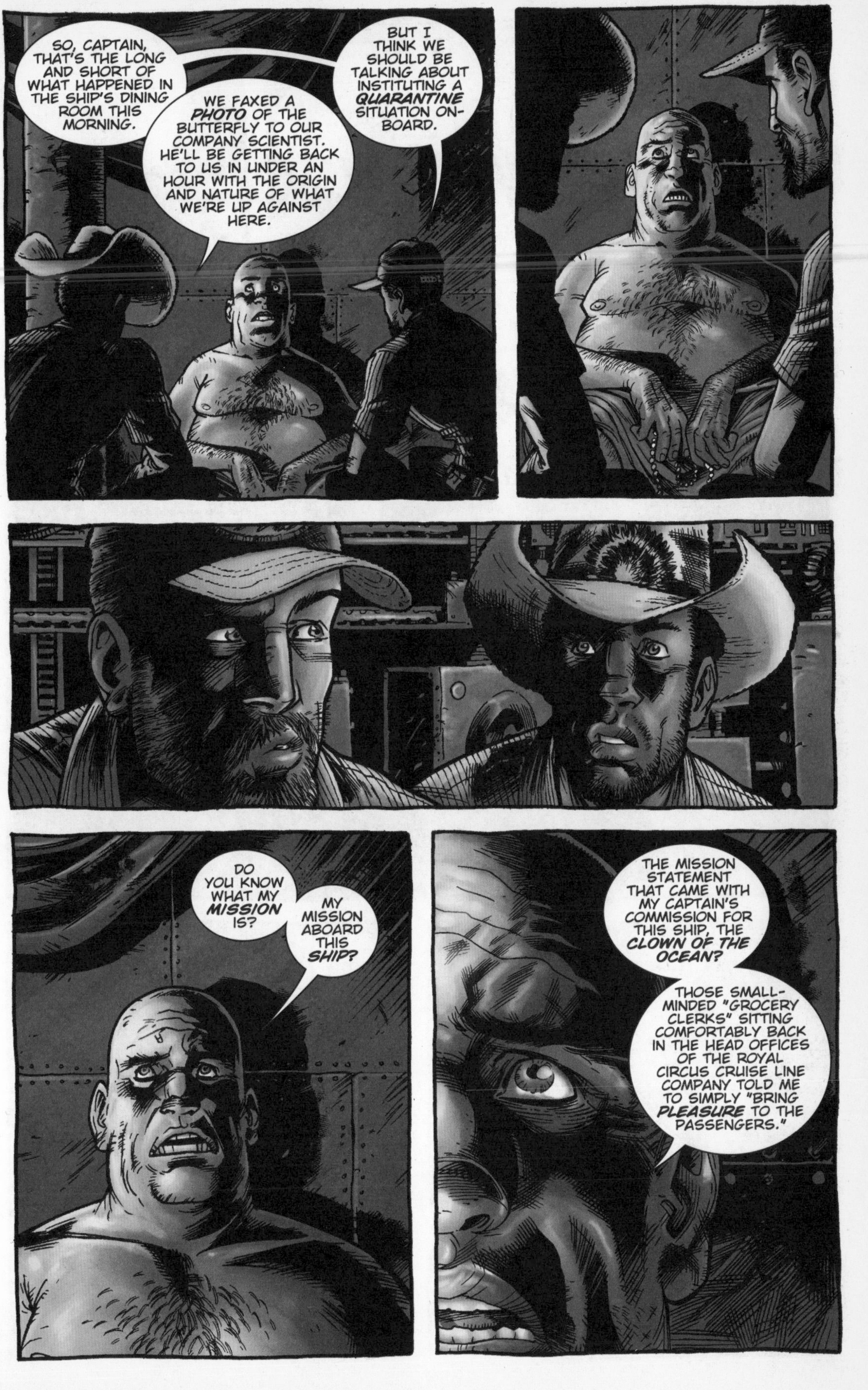
SO, CAPTAIN, THAT'S THE LONG AND SHORT OF WHAT HAPPENED IN THE SHIP'S DINING ROOM THIS MORNING.
WE FAXED A PHOTO OF THE BUTTERFLY TO OUR COMPANY SCIENTIST. HE'LL BE GETTING BACK TO US IN UNDER AN HOUR WITH THE ORIGIN AND NATURE OF WHAT WE'RE UP AGAINST HERE.
BUT I THINK WE SHOULD BE TALKING ABOUT INSTITUTING A QUARANTINE SITUATION ON-BOARD.
DO YOU KNOW WHAT MY MISSION IS?
MY MISSION ABOARD THIS SHIP?
THE MISSION STATEMENT THAT CAME WITH MY CAPTAIN'S COMMISSION FOR THIS SHIP, THE CLOWN OF THE OCEAN?
THOSE SMALL-MINDED "GROCERY CLERKS" SITTING COMFORTABLY BACK IN THE HEAD OFFICES OF THE ROYAL CIRCUS CRUISE LINE COMPANY TOLD ME TO SIMPLY "BRING PLEASURE TO THE PASSENGERS."

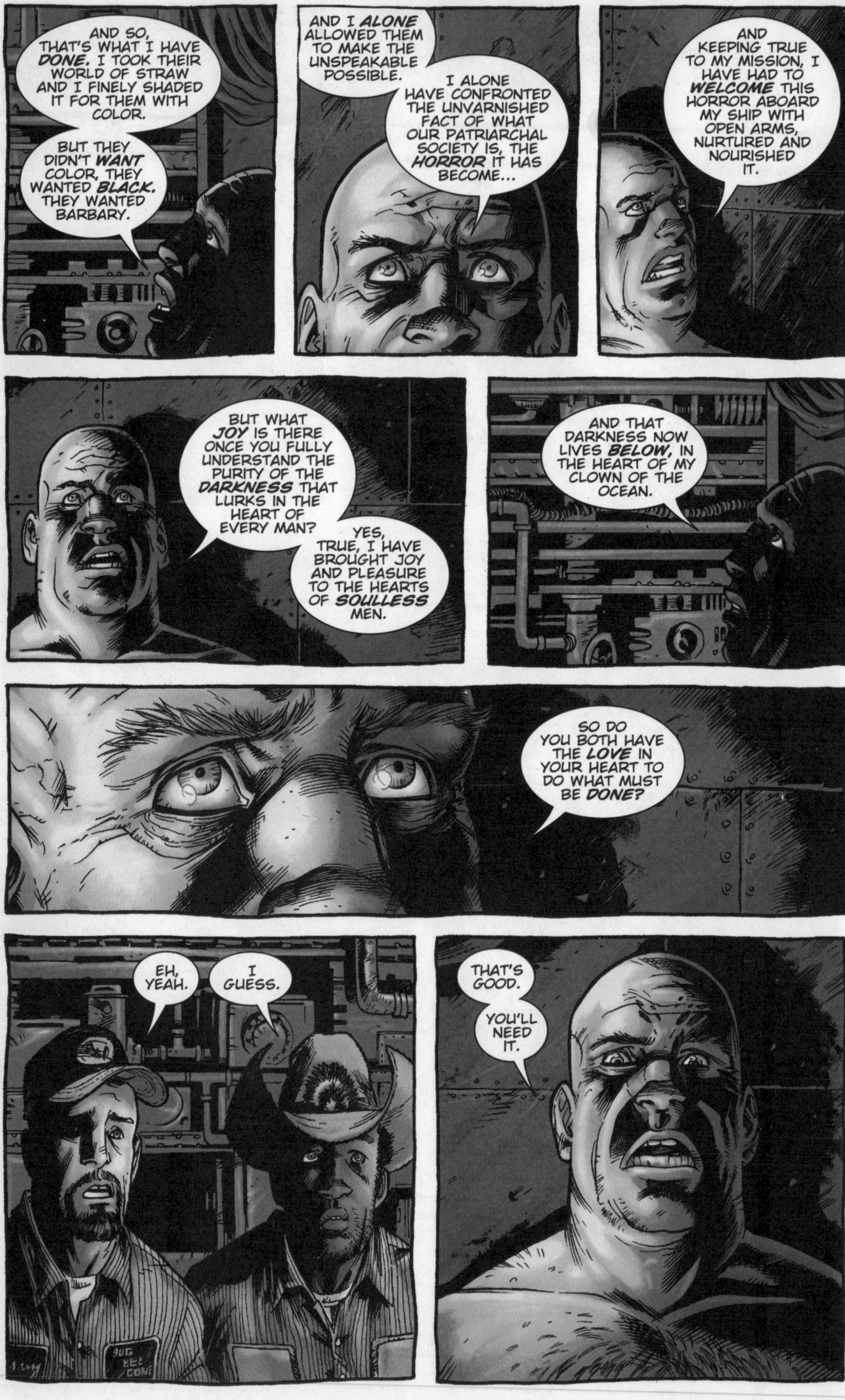
AND SO, THAT'S WHAT I HAVE DONE. I TOOK THEIR WORLD OF STRAW AND I FINELY SHADED IT FOR THEM WITH COLOR.
BUT THEY DIDN'T WANT COLOR, THEY WANTED BLACK. THEY WANTED BARBARY.
AND I ALONE ALLOWED THEM TO MAKE THE UNSPEAKABLE POSSIBLE.
I ALONE HAVE CONFRONTED THE UNVARNISHED FACT OF WHAT OUR PATRIARCHAL SOCIETY IS, THE HORROR IT HAS BECOME...
AND KEEPING TRUE TO MY MISSION, I HAVE HAD TO WELCOME THIS HORROR ABOARD MY SHIP WITH OPEN ARMS, NURTURED AND NOURISHED IT.
BUT WHAT JOY IS THERE ONCE YOU FULLY UNDERSTAND THE PURITY OF THE DARKNESS THAT LURKS IN THE HEART OF EVERY MAN?
YES, TRUE, I HAVE BROUGHT JOY AND PLEASURE TO THE HEARTS OF SOULLESS MEN.
AND THAT DARKNESS NOW LIVES BELOW, IN THE HEART OF MY CLOWN OF THE OCEAN.
SO DO YOU BOTH HAVE THE LOVE IN YOUR HEART TO DO WHAT MUST BE DONE?
EH, YEAH.
I GUESS.
THAT'S GOOD.
YOU'LL NEED IT.

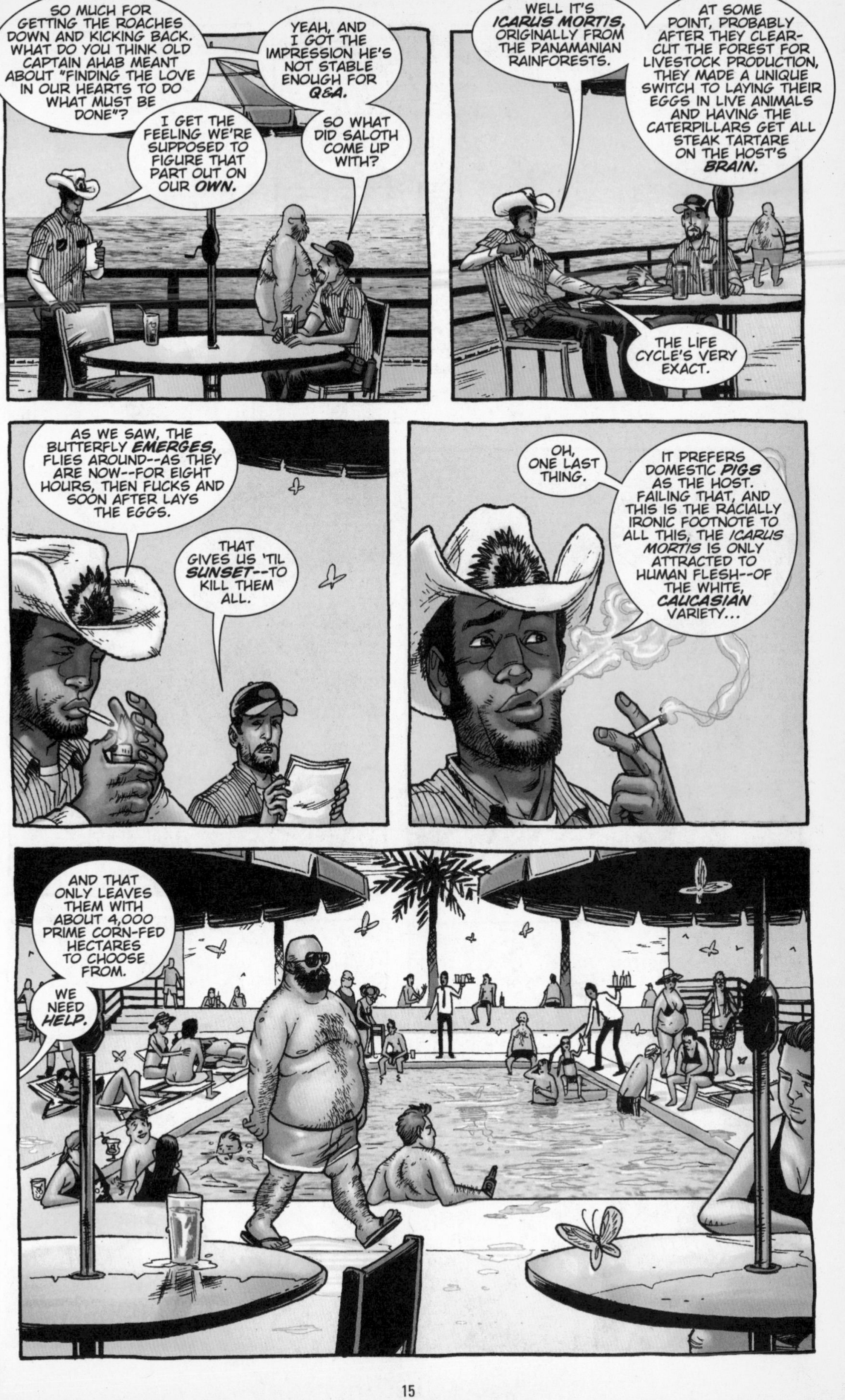
SO MUCH FOR GETTING THE ROACHES DOWN AND KICKING BACK. WHAT DO YOU THINK OLD CAPTAIN AHAB MEANT ABOUT "FINDING THE LOVE IN OUR HEARTS TO DO WHAT MUST BE DONE"?
YEAH, AND I GOT THE IMPRESSION HE'S NOT STABLE ENOUGH FOR Q&A.
I GET THE FEELING WE'RE SUPPOSED TO FIGURE THAT PART OUT ON OUR OWN.
SO WHAT DID SALOTH COME UP WITH?
WELL IT'S ICARUS MORTIS, ORIGINALLY FROM THE PANAMANIAN RAINFORESTS.
AT SOME POINT, PROBABLY AFTER THEY CLEAR-CUT THE FOREST FOR LIVESTOCK PRODUCTION, THEY MADE A UNIQUE SWITCH TO LAYING THEIR EGGS IN LIVE ANIMALS AND HAVING THE CATERPILLARS GET ALL STEAK TARTARE ON THE HOST'S BRAIN.
THE LIFE CYCLE'S VERY EXACT.
AS WE SAW, THE BUTTERFLY EMERGES, FLIES AROUND--AS THEY ARE NOW--FOR EIGHT HOURS, THEN FUCKS AND SOON AFTER LAYS THE EGGS.
THAT GIVES US 'TIL SUNSET--TO KILL THEM ALL.
OH, ONE LAST THING.
IT PREFERS DOMESTIC PIGS AS THE HOST. FAILING THAT, AND THIS IS THE RACIALLY IRONIC FOOTNOTE TO ALL THIS, THE ICARUS MORTIS IS ONLY ATTRACTED TO HUMAN FLESH--OF THE WHITE, CAUCASIAN VARIETY...
AND THAT ONLY LEAVES THEM WITH ABOUT 4,000 PRIME CORN-FED HECTARES TO CHOOSE FROM.
WE NEED HELP.

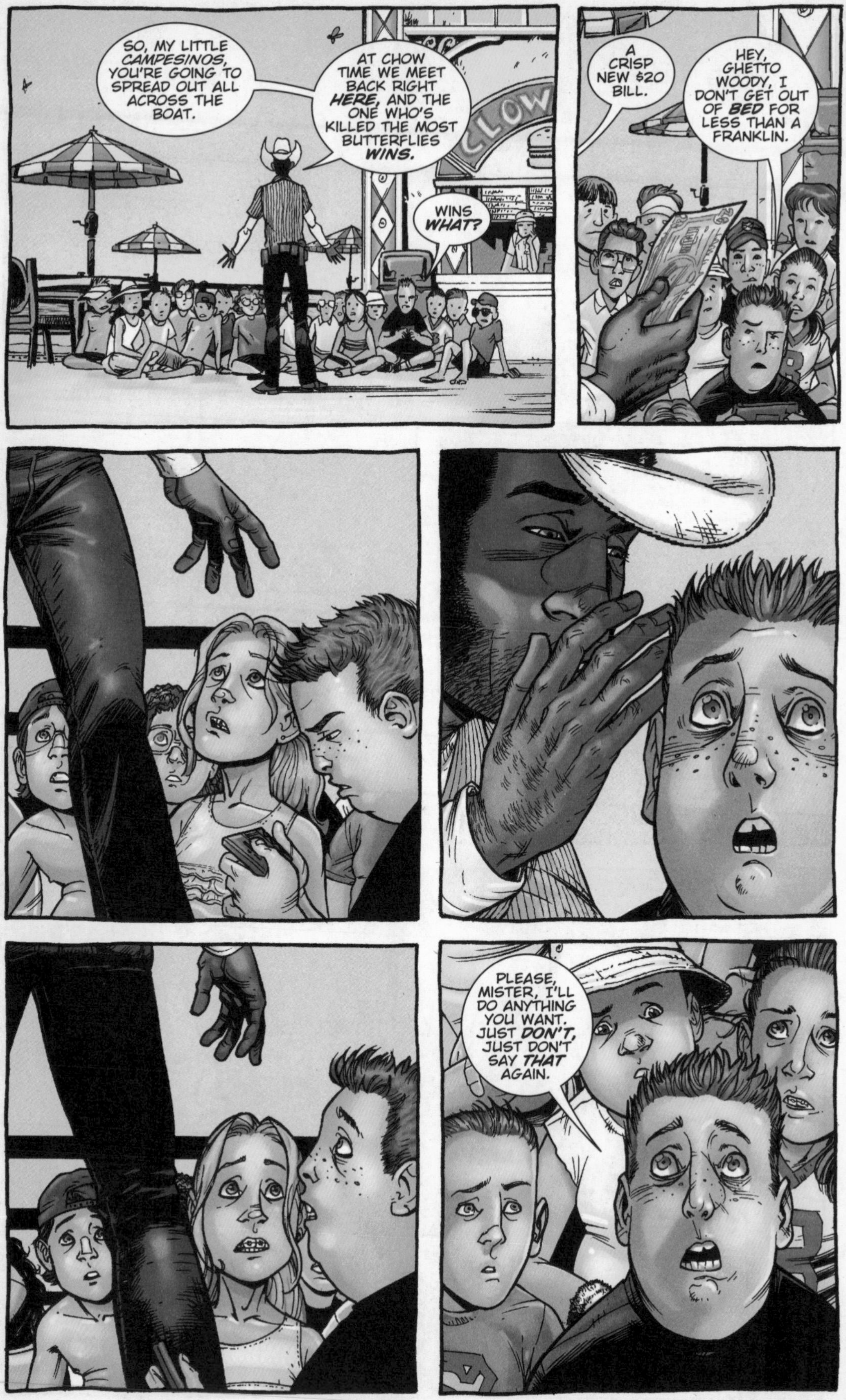
SO, MY LITTLE CAMPESINOS, YOU'RE GOING TO SPREAD OUT ALL ACROSS THE BOAT.
AT CHOW TIME WE MEET BACK RIGHT HERE, AND THE ONE WHO'S KILLED THE MOST BUTTERFLIES WINS.
WINS WHAT?
A CRISP NEW $20 BILL.
HEY, GHETTO WOODY, I DON'T GET OUT OF BED FOR LESS THAN A FRANKLIN.
PLEASE, MISTER, I'LL DO ANYTHING YOU WANT. JUST DON'T, JUST DON'T SAY THAT AGAIN.

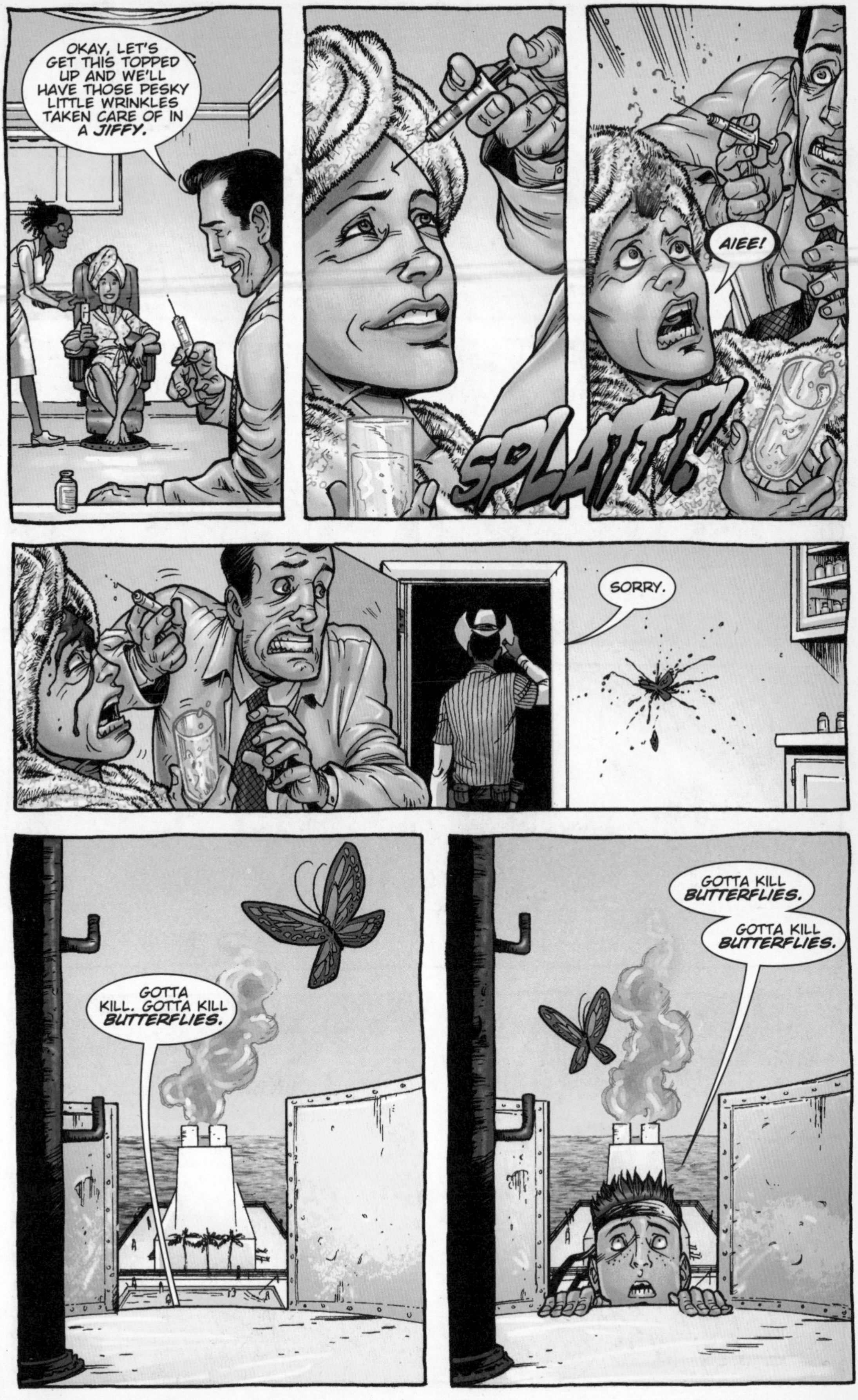
OKAY, LET'S GET THIS TOPPED UP AND WE'LL HAVE THOSE PESKY LITTLE WRINKLES TAKEN CARE OF IN A *JIFFY*.
AIEE!
SPLATT!
SORRY.
GOTTA KILL. GOTTA KILL *BUTTERFLIES*.
GOTTA KILL *BUTTERFLIES*.
GOTTA KILL *BUTTERFLIES*.

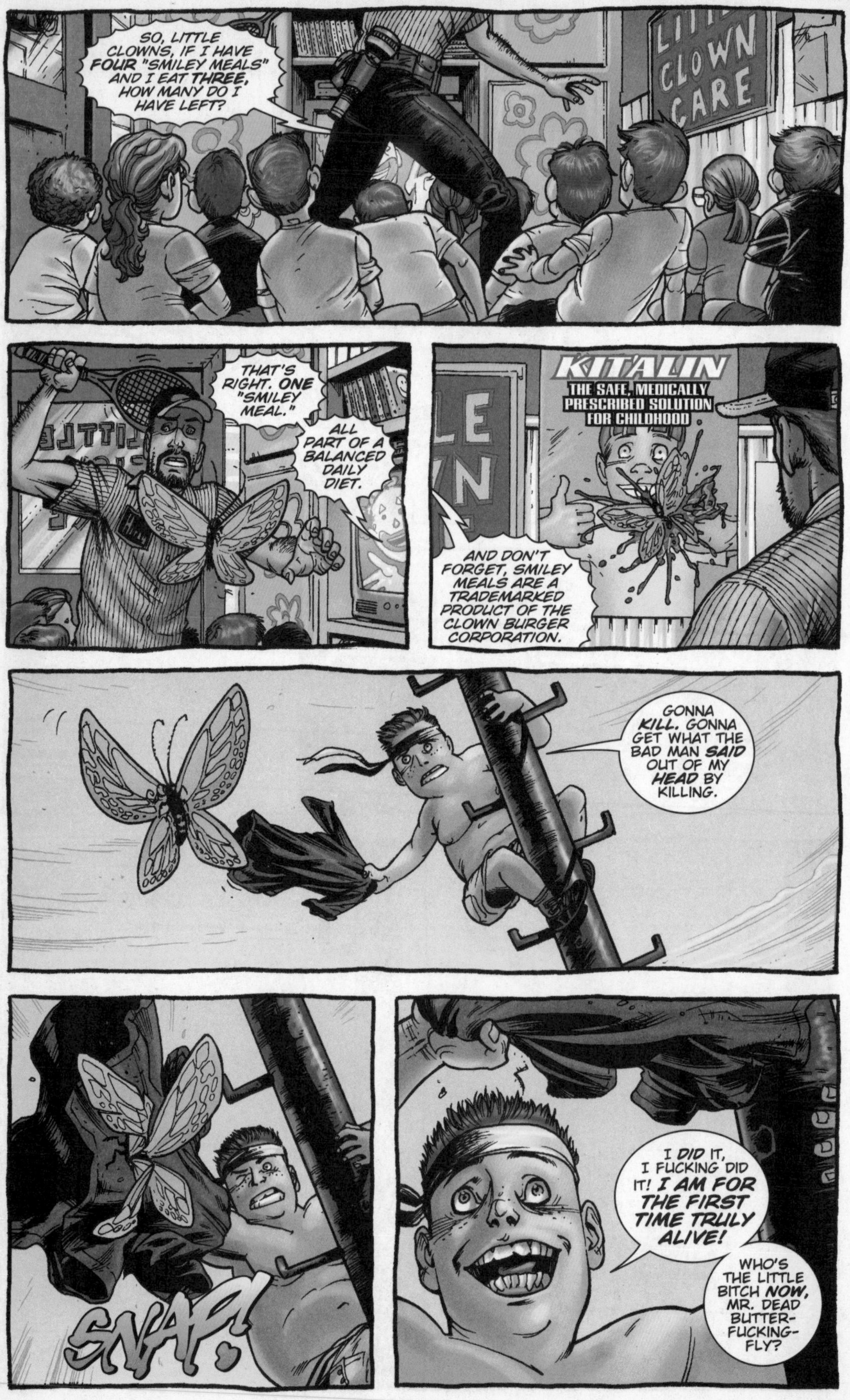

SO, LITTLE CLOWNS, IF I HAVE FOUR "SMILEY MEALS" AND I EAT THREE, HOW MANY DO I HAVE LEFT?
LITTLE CLOWN CARE
THAT'S RIGHT. ONE "SMILEY MEAL."
ALL PART OF A BALANCED DAILY DIET.
KITALIN
THE SAFE, MEDICALLY PRESCRIBED SOLUTION FOR CHILDHOOD
AND DON'T FORGET, SMILEY MEALS ARE A TRADEMARKED PRODUCT OF THE CLOWN BURGER CORPORATION.
GONNA KILL. GONNA GET WHAT THE BAD MAN SAID OUT OF MY HEAD BY KILLING.
SNAP!
I DID IT, I FUCKING DID IT! I AM FOR THE FIRST TIME TRULY ALIVE!
WHO'S THE LITTLE BITCH NOW, MR. DEAD BUTTER-FUCKING-FLY?

MADE OUT PRETTY GOOD TOO, BUT I FIGURE THERE MUST STILL BE QUITE A FEW HIDING OUT. WE'VE GOT ABOUT TWO HOURS LEFT FOR SEARCH AND DESTROY.

SO WHERE NOW?

YOU KNOW, I'VE BEEN ALL OVER THIS SHIP, AND SOCIALLY BANKRUPT AS IT IS--

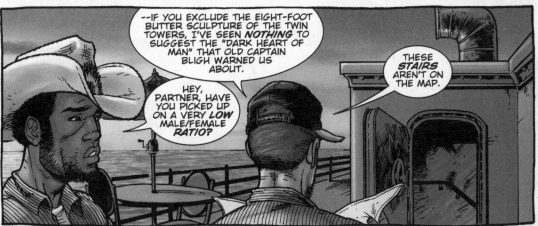

--IF YOU EXCLUDE THE EIGHT-FOOT BUTTER SCULPTURE OF THE TWIN TOWERS, I'VE SEEN *NOTHING* TO SUGGEST THE "DARK HEART OF MAN" THAT OLD CAPTAIN BLIGH WARNED US ABOUT.

HEY, PARTNER, HAVE YOU PICKED UP ON A VERY *LOW* MALE/FEMALE *RATIO?*

THESE *STAIRS* AREN'T ON THE MAP.

BUG BEE GONE

WELL, HE'S CERTAINLY GIVEN WHITE, MIDDLE-CLASS, MIDDLE-AMERICAN, MARITALLY AND SEXUALLY FRUSTRATED SUBURBAN DADS ALL THE "COLORING IN" THEY CAN POSSIBLY HANDLE.

AND MAYBE MORE.

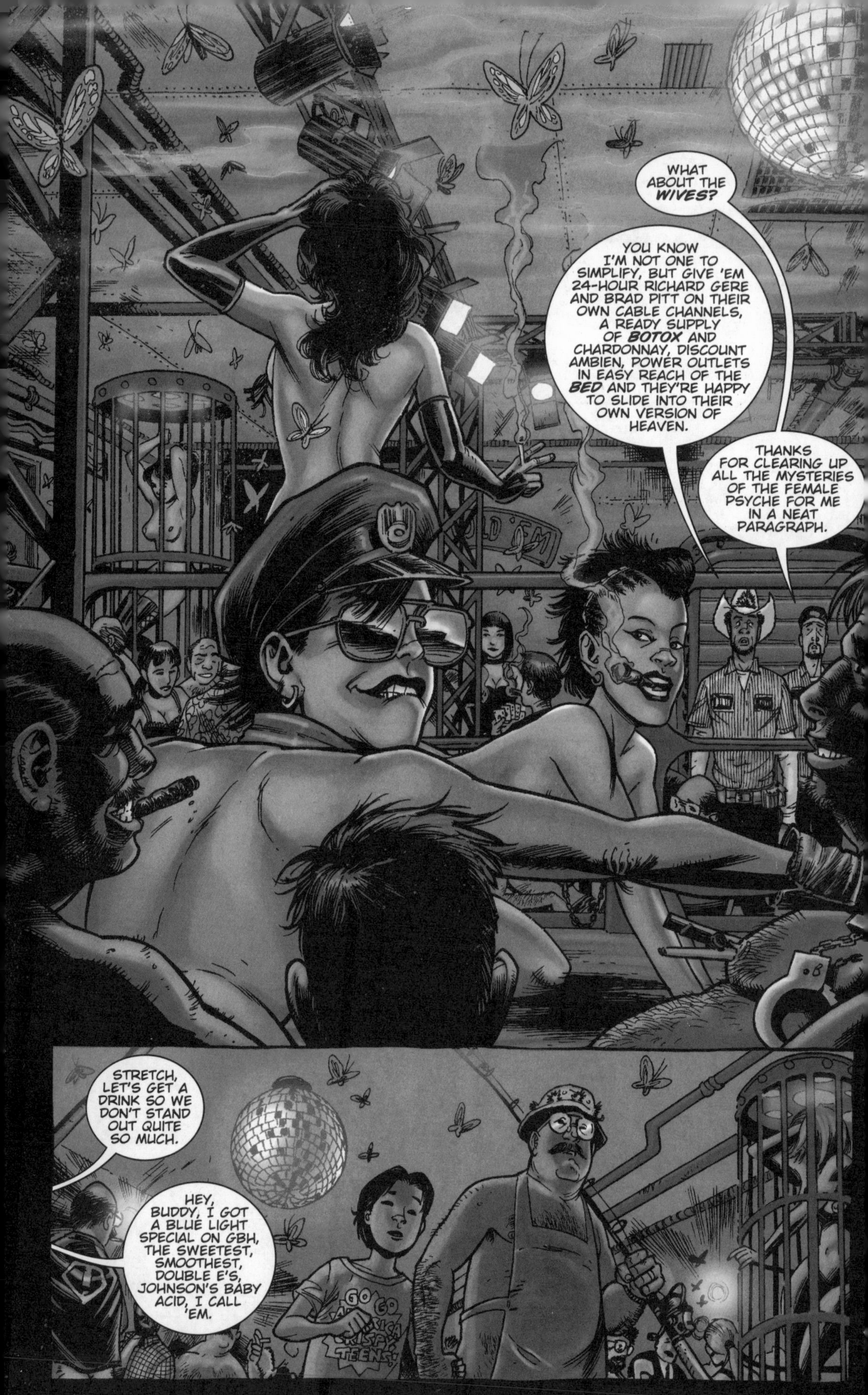
WHAT ABOUT THE WIVES?
YOU KNOW I'M NOT ONE TO SIMPLIFY, BUT GIVE 'EM 24-HOUR RICHARD GERE AND BRAD PITT ON THEIR OWN CABLE CHANNELS, A READY SUPPLY OF BOTOX AND CHARDONNAY, DISCOUNT AMBIEN, POWER OUTLETS IN EASY REACH OF THE BED AND THEY'RE HAPPY TO SLIDE INTO THEIR OWN VERSION OF HEAVEN.
THANKS FOR CLEARING UP ALL THE MYSTERIES OF THE FEMALE PSYCHE FOR ME IN A NEAT PARAGRAPH.
STRETCH, LET'S GET A DRINK SO WE DON'T STAND OUT QUITE SO MUCH.
HEY, BUDDY, I GOT A BLUE LIGHT SPECIAL ON GBH, THE SWEETEST, SMOOTHEST, DOUBLE E'S, JOHNSON'S BABY ACID, I CALL 'EM.

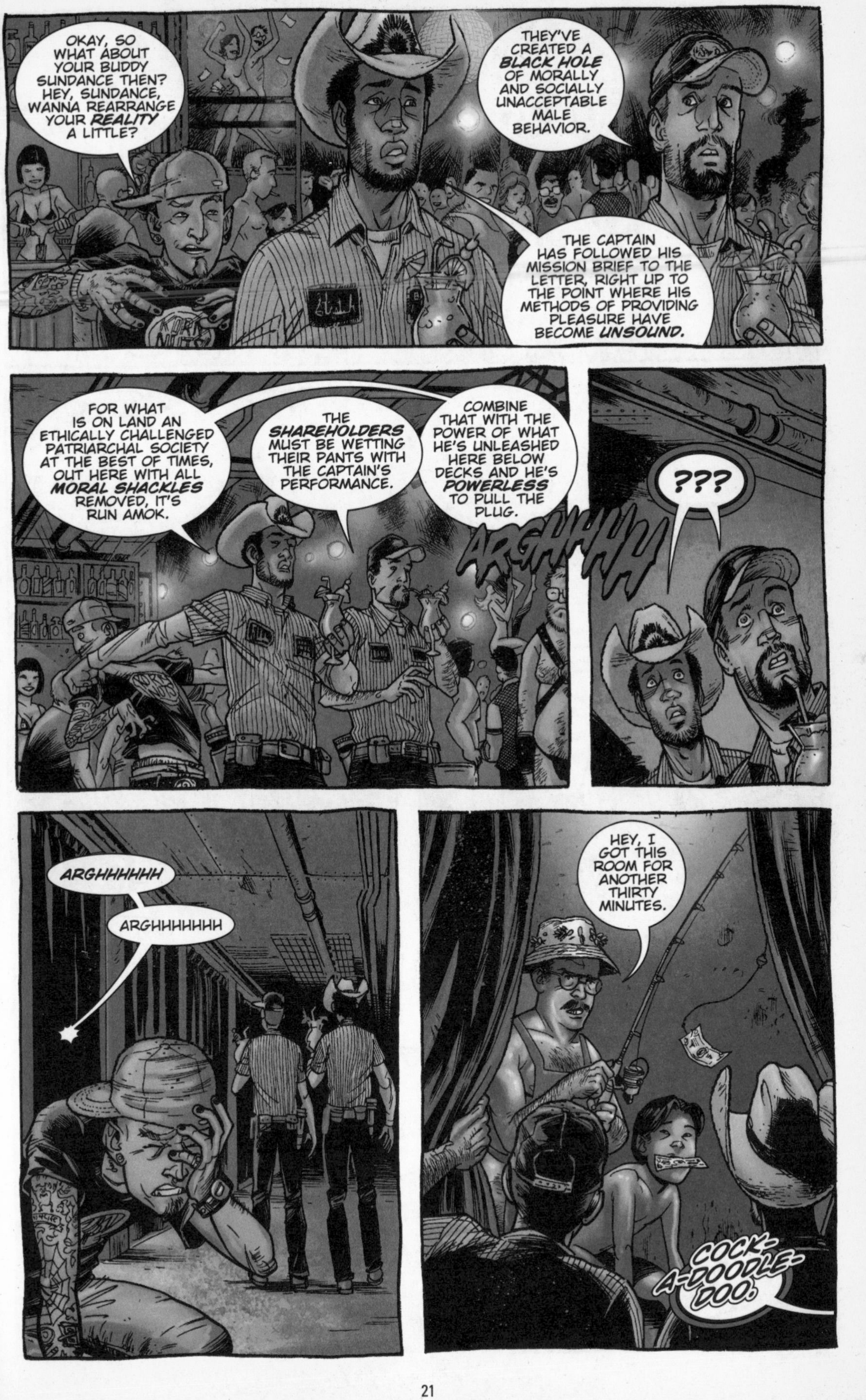

OKAY, SO WHAT ABOUT YOUR BUDDY SUNDANCE THEN? HEY, SUNDANCE, WANNA REARRANGE YOUR REALITY A LITTLE?
THEY'VE CREATED A BLACK HOLE OF MORALLY AND SOCIALLY UNACCEPTABLE MALE BEHAVIOR.
THE CAPTAIN HAS FOLLOWED HIS MISSION BRIEF TO THE LETTER, RIGHT UP TO THE POINT WHERE HIS METHODS OF PROVIDING PLEASURE HAVE BECOME UNSOUND.
FOR WHAT IS ON LAND AN ETHICALLY CHALLENGED PATRIARCHAL SOCIETY AT THE BEST OF TIMES, OUT HERE WITH ALL MORAL SHACKLES REMOVED, IT'S RUN AMOK.
THE SHAREHOLDERS MUST BE WETTING THEIR PANTS WITH THE CAPTAIN'S PERFORMANCE.
COMBINE THAT WITH THE POWER OF WHAT HE'S UNLEASHED HERE BELOW DECKS AND HE'S POWERLESS TO PULL THE PLUG.
ARGHHHH
???
ARGHHHHHH
ARGHHHHHHH
HEY, I GOT THIS ROOM FOR ANOTHER THIRTY MINUTES.
COCK-A-DOODLE-DOO.

THESE TWO--

SUN'S GOING DOWN.

WHAT'S WITH ALL THESE BUTTERFLIES DOING THIS, LIKE, *PIGGY-BACK* THING?

WHATEVER! LIKE, INSECTS ARE *SOOOO* INTERESTING.

I WAS THINKING WE SHOULD HIT THE STARZ LOUNGE AT SEVEN, 3-FOR-2 PITCHERS OF MOJITOS, THEN MAYBE *HOOK UP* WITH THAT WAITER AGAIN.

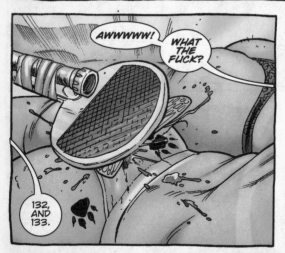

AWWWWW!

WHAT THE FUCK?

132, AND 133.

I HAVE TO *DO* THIS.

I HAVE TO KILL *BUTTERFLIES.*

YOU LITTLE *SHIT,* DO YOU HAVE ANY FUCKING IDEA HOW *TACKY* ASS-BRUISES LOOK ON NIGHT-VISION VIDEO?

I DON'T GIVE A *SHIT* WHAT YOU CONSIDER RIGHT AND WRONG.

AND I DON'T GIVE A SHIT ABOUT *DISCUSSING* IT IN THE FORM OF AN INTELLIGENT AND CIVILIZED DEBATE.

FUCK TALKING WITH THESE TWO PINKO, FAGGOT LIBERALS. THIS IS 21st-CENTURY *AMERICA* GODDAM IT! THEY'RE EITHER WITH US OR *AGAINST* US.

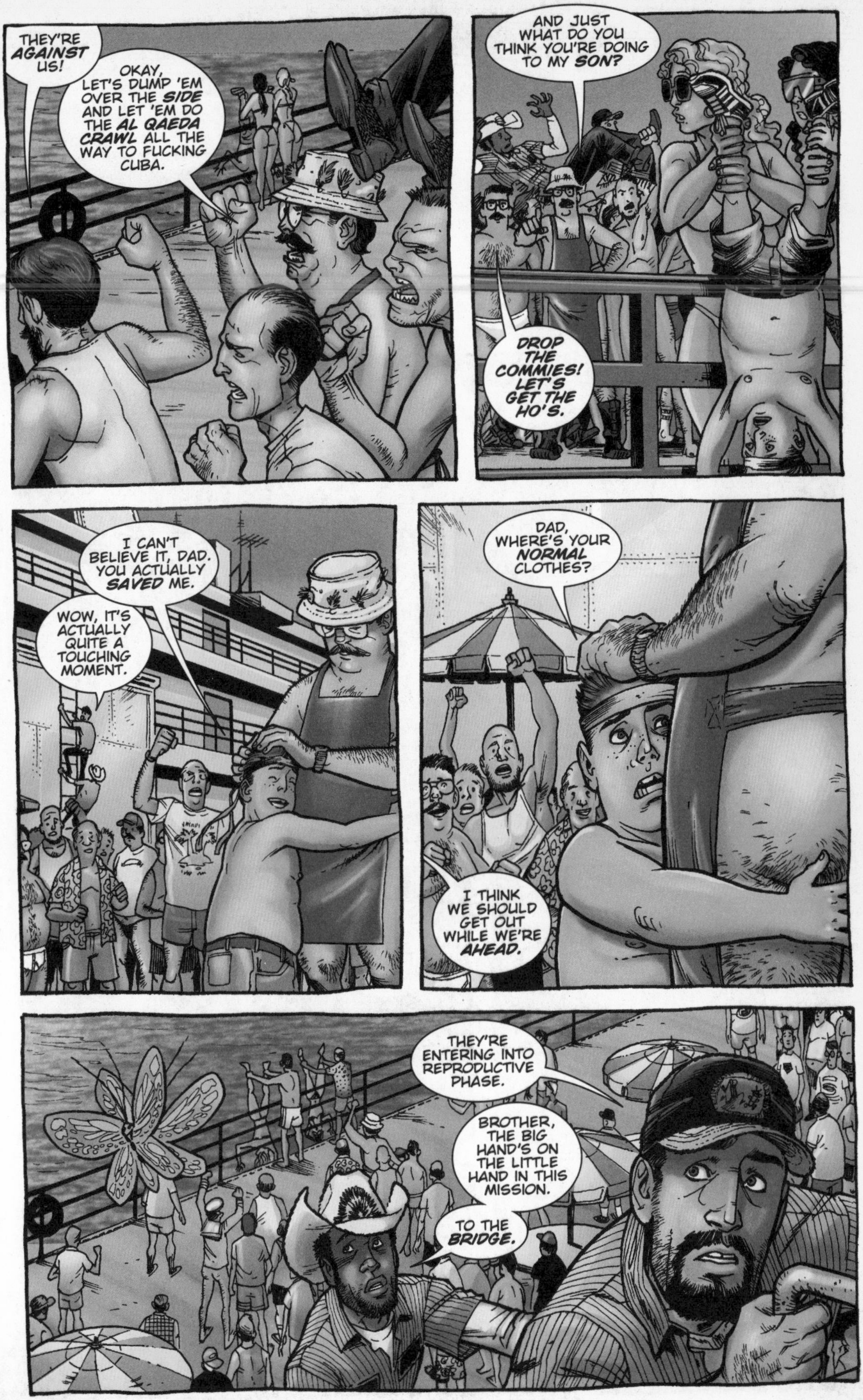
THEY'RE AGAINST US!
OKAY, LET'S DUMP 'EM OVER THE SIDE AND LET 'EM DO THE AL QAEDA CRAWL ALL THE WAY TO FUCKING CUBA.
AND JUST WHAT DO YOU THINK YOU'RE DOING TO MY SON?
DROP THE COMMIES! LET'S GET THE HO'S.
I CAN'T BELIEVE IT, DAD. YOU ACTUALLY SAVED ME.
WOW, IT'S ACTUALLY QUITE A TOUCHING MOMENT.
DAD, WHERE'S YOUR NORMAL CLOTHES?
I THINK WE SHOULD GET OUT WHILE WE'RE AHEAD.
THEY'RE ENTERING INTO REPRODUCTIVE PHASE.
BROTHER, THE BIG HAND'S ON THE LITTLE HAND IN THIS MISSION.
TO THE BRIDGE.

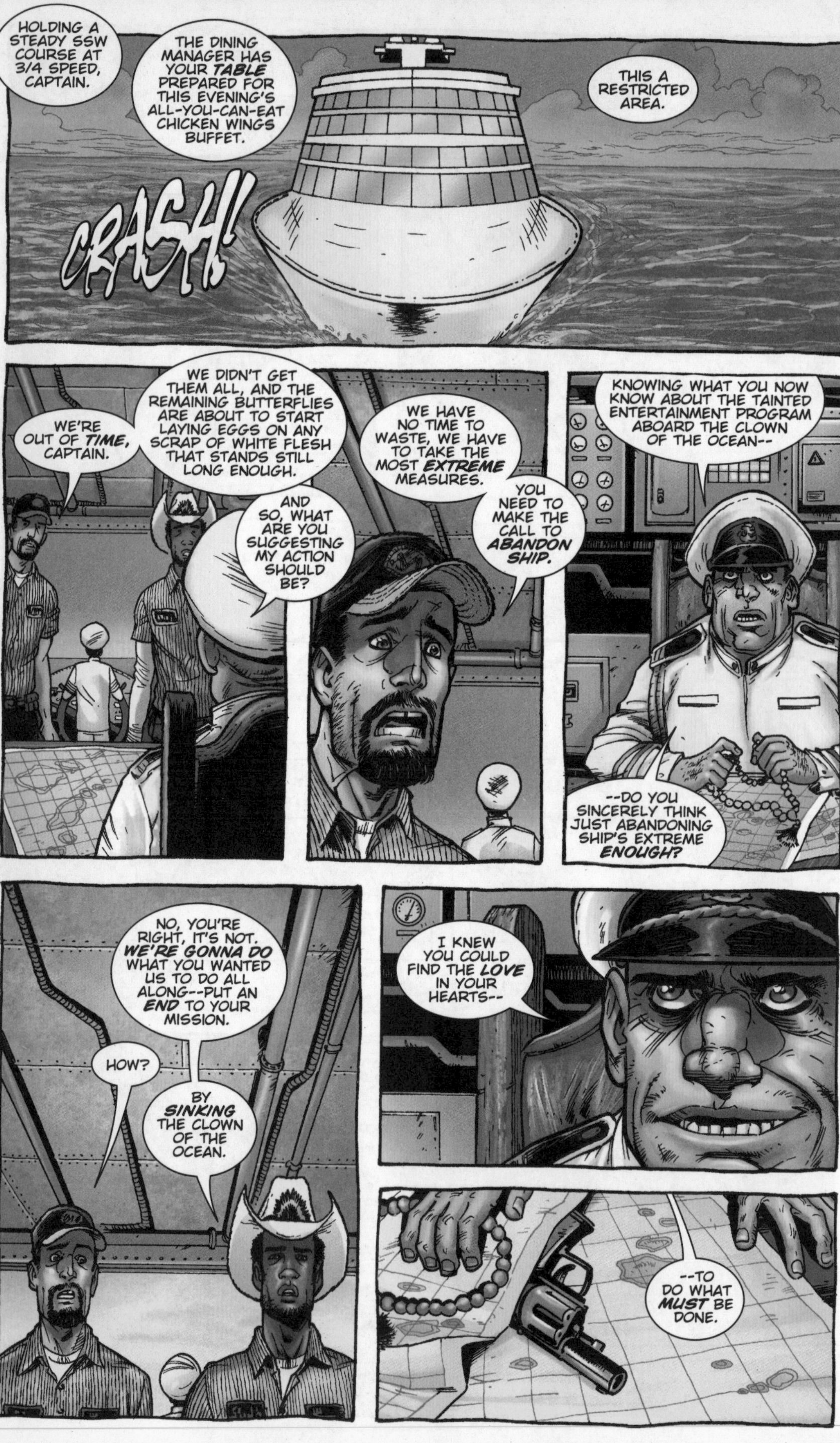
HOLDING A STEADY SSW COURSE AT 3/4 SPEED, CAPTAIN.
THE DINING MANAGER HAS YOUR TABLE PREPARED FOR THIS EVENING'S ALL-YOU-CAN-EAT CHICKEN WINGS BUFFET.
THIS A RESTRICTED AREA.
CRASH!
WE'RE OUT OF TIME, CAPTAIN.
WE DIDN'T GET THEM ALL, AND THE REMAINING BUTTERFLIES ARE ABOUT TO START LAYING EGGS ON ANY SCRAP OF WHITE FLESH THAT STANDS STILL LONG ENOUGH.
AND SO, WHAT ARE YOU SUGGESTING MY ACTION SHOULD BE?
WE HAVE NO TIME TO WASTE, WE HAVE TO TAKE THE MOST EXTREME MEASURES.
YOU NEED TO MAKE THE CALL TO ABANDON SHIP.
KNOWING WHAT YOU NOW KNOW ABOUT THE TAINTED ENTERTAINMENT PROGRAM ABOARD THE CLOWN OF THE OCEAN--
--DO YOU SINCERELY THINK JUST ABANDONING SHIP'S EXTREME ENOUGH?
NO, YOU'RE RIGHT, IT'S NOT. WE'RE GONNA DO WHAT YOU WANTED US TO DO ALL ALONG--PUT AN END TO YOUR MISSION.
HOW?
BY SINKING THE CLOWN OF THE OCEAN.
I KNEW YOU COULD FIND THE LOVE IN YOUR HEARTS--
--TO DO WHAT MUST BE DONE.

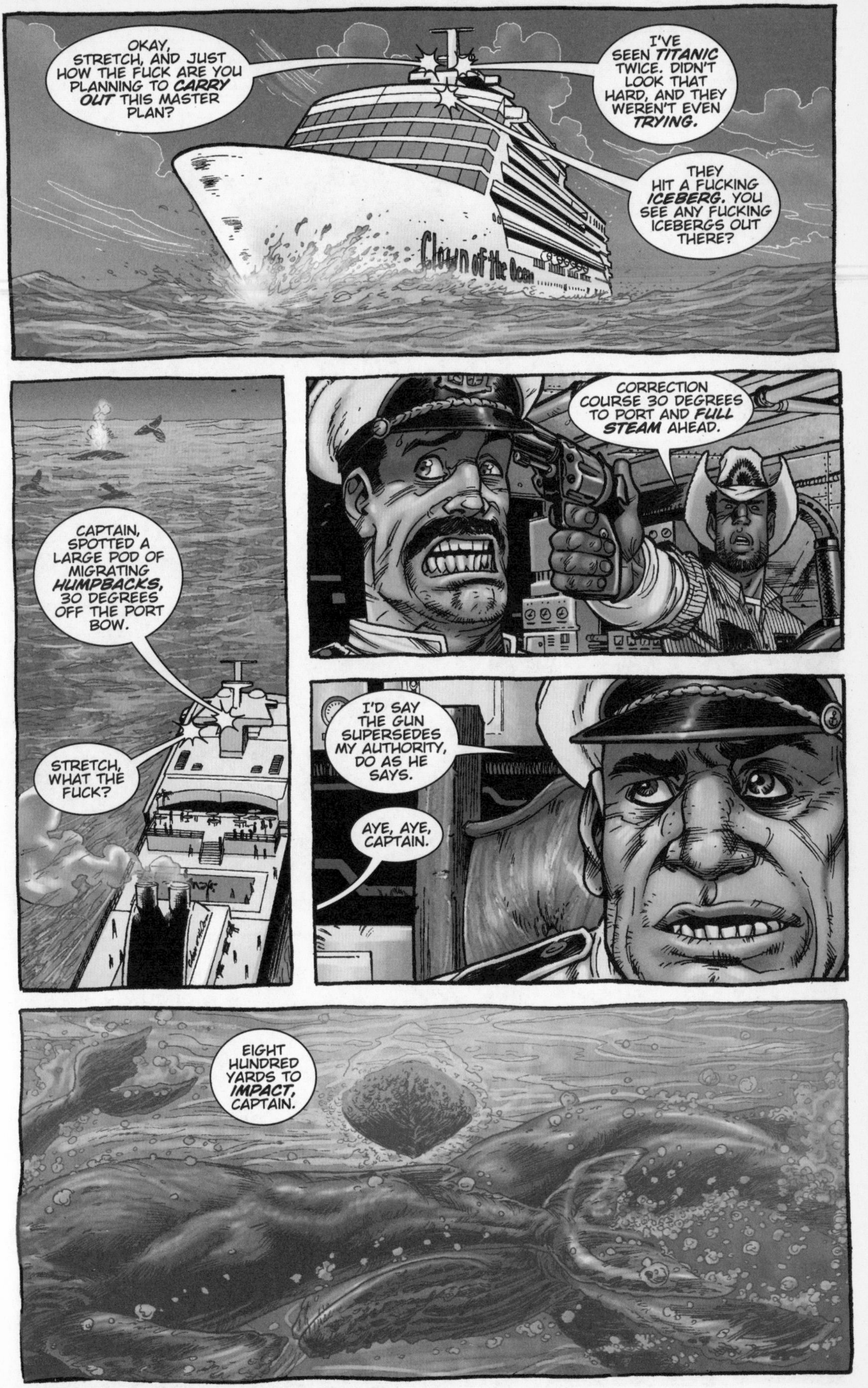
OKAY, STRETCH, AND JUST HOW THE FUCK ARE YOU PLANNING TO CARRY OUT THIS MASTER PLAN?
I'VE SEEN TITANIC TWICE. DIDN'T LOOK THAT HARD, AND THEY WEREN'T EVEN TRYING.
THEY HIT A FUCKING ICEBERG. YOU SEE ANY FUCKING ICEBERGS OUT THERE?
Clown of the Ocean
CAPTAIN, SPOTTED A LARGE POD OF MIGRATING HUMPBACKS, 30 DEGREES OFF THE PORT BOW.
STRETCH, WHAT THE FUCK?
CORRECTION COURSE 30 DEGREES TO PORT AND FULL STEAM AHEAD.
I'D SAY THE GUN SUPERSEDES MY AUTHORITY, DO AS HE SAYS.
AYE, AYE, CAPTAIN.
EIGHT HUNDRED YARDS TO IMPACT, CAPTAIN.

THREE HUNDRED AND CLOSING *FAST.*

DOES GREENPEACE HAVE DEATH SQUADS?

MINIMAL DAMAGE, SIR.

SO WE'RE BACK TO "ABANDON SHIP" VS. "PAINFUL DEATH BY CATERPILLARS," THEN?

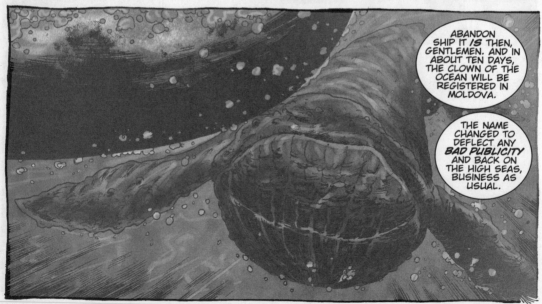

ABANDON SHIP IT *IS* THEN, GENTLEMEN. AND IN ABOUT TEN DAYS, THE CLOWN OF THE OCEAN WILL BE REGISTERED IN MOLDOVA.

THE NAME CHANGED TO DEFLECT ANY *BAD PUBLICITY* AND BACK ON THE HIGH SEAS, BUSINESS AS USUAL.

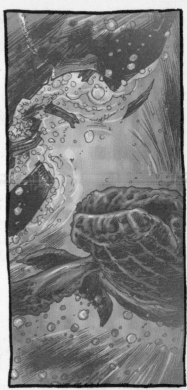

DAMAGE REPORT.

THE SECOND IMPACT OPENED A MASSIVE HOLE IN THE HULL, PORT AMIDSHIPS.

SHE'S GOING *DOWN*.

THANK YOU, GENTLEMEN, FOR COMPLETING WHAT I COULD NEVER HAVE BROUGHT *MYSELF* TO DO AND ENDING MY MISSION.

IT SEEMS THAT ONCE AGAIN, ONE WAY OR ANOTHER, NATURE HAS AIDED MAN IN REMOVING HIS MOST PUTRID STAINS.

NOW IF YOU WOULD EXCUSE ME, I HAVE ONE LAST TASK AHEAD OF ME.

CALL THE ABANDON SHIP.

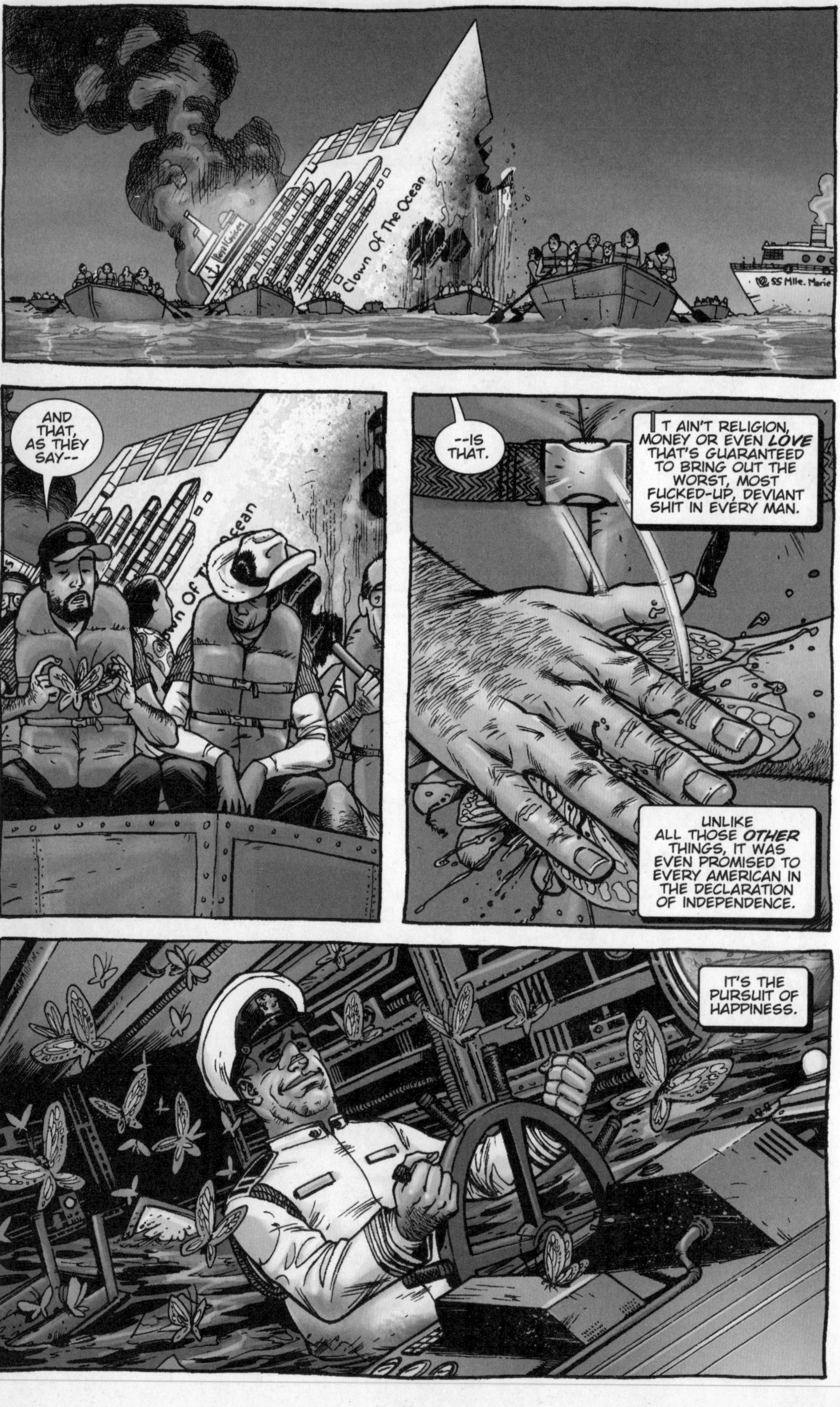
Royal Cruises
Clown Of The Ocean
SS Mlle. Marie
AND THAT, AS THEY SAY--
Clown Of The Ocean
--IS THAT.
T AIN'T RELIGION, MONEY OR EVEN LOVE THAT'S GUARANTEED TO BRING OUT THE WORST, MOST FUCKED-UP, DEVIANT SHIT IN EVERY MAN.
UNLIKE ALL THOSE OTHER THINGS, IT WAS EVEN PROMISED TO EVERY AMERICAN IN THE DECLARATION OF INDEPENDENCE.
IT'S THE PURSUIT OF HAPPINESS.

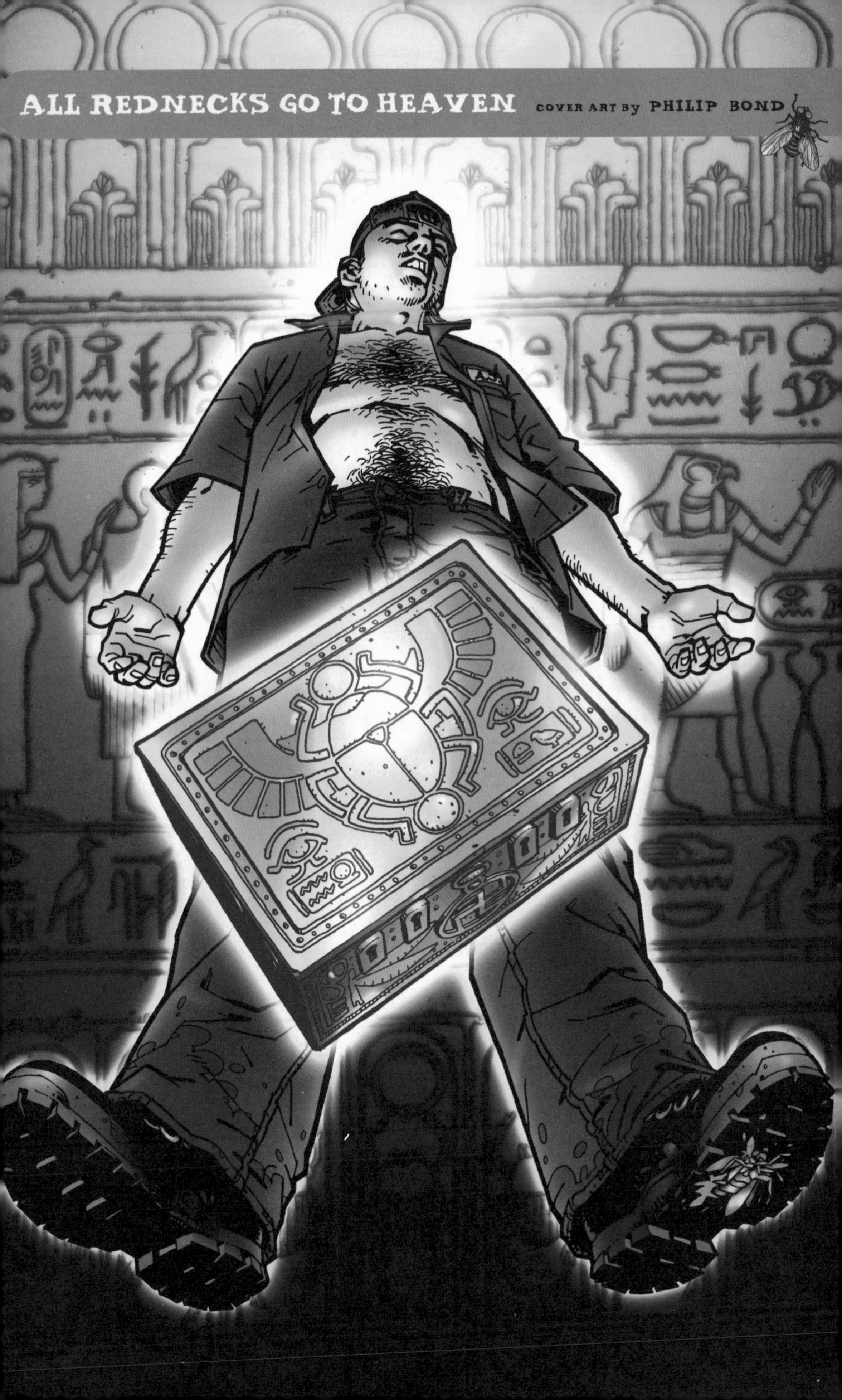
ALL REDNECKS GO TO HEAVEN
COVER ART BY PHILIP BOND

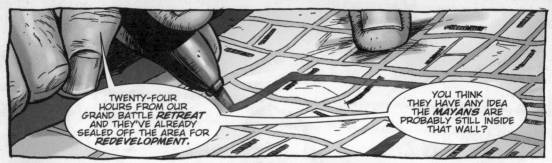

TWENTY-FOUR HOURS FROM OUR GRAND BATTLE *RETREAT* AND THEY'VE ALREADY SEALED OFF THE AREA FOR *REDEVELOPMENT.*

YOU THINK THEY HAVE ANY IDEA THE *MAYANS* ARE PROBABLY STILL INSIDE THAT WALL?

OCRAN TOWERS DEVELOPMENT? WELL, HENRY, I'M GUESSING IT'S PROBABLY HARD FOR LAURA TO JUSTIFY A MAYAN *BREEDING SANCTUARY* AS A LEGITIMATE TAX WRITE-OFF.

SO WHAT'S LAURA'S AND OCRAN'S CONNECTION TO THE MAYAN HISSERS, THEN?

I DON'T KNOW. BUT I KNOW I'M NOT BUYING INTO *COINCIDENCE* ON THIS, NOT ON THIS SCALE.

ABSOLUTELY -NO- TRESPASSING

FUTURE SITE OF THE OCRAN TOWERS DEVELOPMENT

BEE-GONE -BUG GONE

IF OCRAN'S TEAMED UP WITH AJ MARK II, HIS MAYAN HISSER ARMY AND A TEAM OF SOUTH SEAS KUNG FU DUDES TO DESTROY MANKIND--WHERE'S THE *PROFIT* ANGLE?

MAYBE IT'S *NOT* MONEY THIS TIME, BUT THERE'S A CONNECTION SOMEWHERE. AND SOMEONE WITHIN OCRAN HAS A REASON OTHER THAN REAL ESTATE DEVELOPMENT FOR THIS *WALL.*

WELL, IF THE MAYANS HAVE A HUMAN FIFTH COLUMN WITH THIS MUCH *POWER,* WE'RE GOING TO NEED TO CUT THEM OFF FAST.

SECURITY

I'M GONNA HAVE TO ASK YOU GOOD FOLKS TO *MOVE ON* NOW.

IT'S A *PUBLIC* STREET, ISN'T IT?

AS A GOVERNMENT-CONTRACTED CORPORATION, OCRAN HAS CERTAIN SECURITY RIGHTS GRANTED THEM UNDER THE PATRIOT ACT.

WHATEVER'S GOING ON, FOR SURE IT'S GOING TO BE FUCKED UP.

YEAH, SO, PAGE, WHO THE FUCK IS THIS *ATAN* GUY AGAIN?

ATAN'S BAD NEWS, A CERTIFIABLY RUTHLESS BUG-WORSHIPPING MOTHERFUCKER A GOOD 1,000 YEARS BEFORE *CHRIST* SOILED HIS FIRST SWADDLING CLOTH DIAPER.

BUT BACK IN HIS BUG BEE DAYS, *AJ* WAS *AJ*, JUST A REGULAR RUN-OF-THE-MILL DICKWAD.

SO WHEN YOU GET BEHIND YOU GRABS BOTH *NIPPLES* AND GIVE 'EM THE OLD FUCKIN' *VICE-CLAMP.*

SEE, IT'S GOTTA HURT 'EM SO FUCKIN' *MUCH* IT DISTRACTS 'EM.

AND THAT'S WHEN YOU MAKE YOUR *MOVE*, FROM THE PINK TO THE STINK.

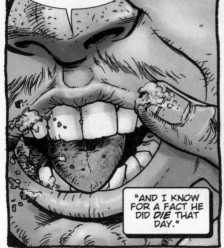

"AND I KNOW FOR A FACT HE DID *DIE* THAT DAY."

NEVER FAILS TO GET OLD AJ *BALLS-DEEP* INTO THE CHOCOLATE STARFISH.

PLEASE, HAVE THE REST.

"I KNOW I DIDN'T *DREAM* IT 'CAUSE A MONTH LATER I FOUND HIS *GALL BLADDER* LODGED IN THE TRUCK'S *AIR VENT.*"

"SO HOW COME HE'S BACK AS *ATAN* THIS TIME?"

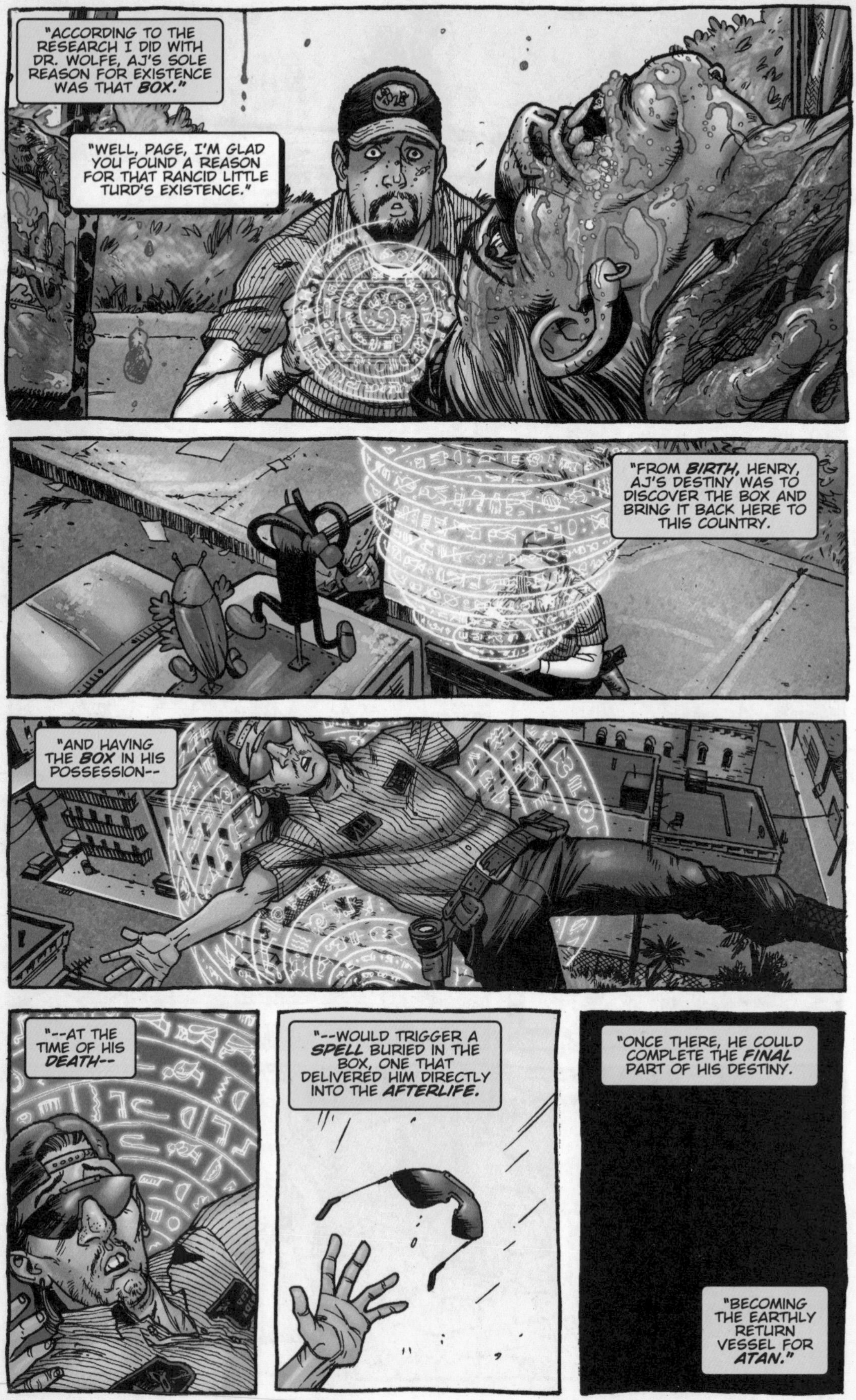
"ACCORDING TO THE RESEARCH I DID WITH DR. WOLFE, AJ'S SOLE REASON FOR EXISTENCE WAS THAT BOX."
"WELL, PAGE, I'M GLAD YOU FOUND A REASON FOR THAT RANCID LITTLE TURD'S EXISTENCE."
"FROM BIRTH, HENRY, AJ'S DESTINY WAS TO DISCOVER THE BOX AND BRING IT BACK HERE TO THIS COUNTRY.
"AND HAVING THE BOX IN HIS POSSESSION--
"--AT THE TIME OF HIS DEATH--
"--WOULD TRIGGER A SPELL BURIED IN THE BOX, ONE THAT DELIVERED HIM DIRECTLY INTO THE AFTERLIFE.
"ONCE THERE, HE COULD COMPLETE THE FINAL PART OF HIS DESTINY.
"BECOMING THE EARTHLY RETURN VESSEL FOR ATAN."

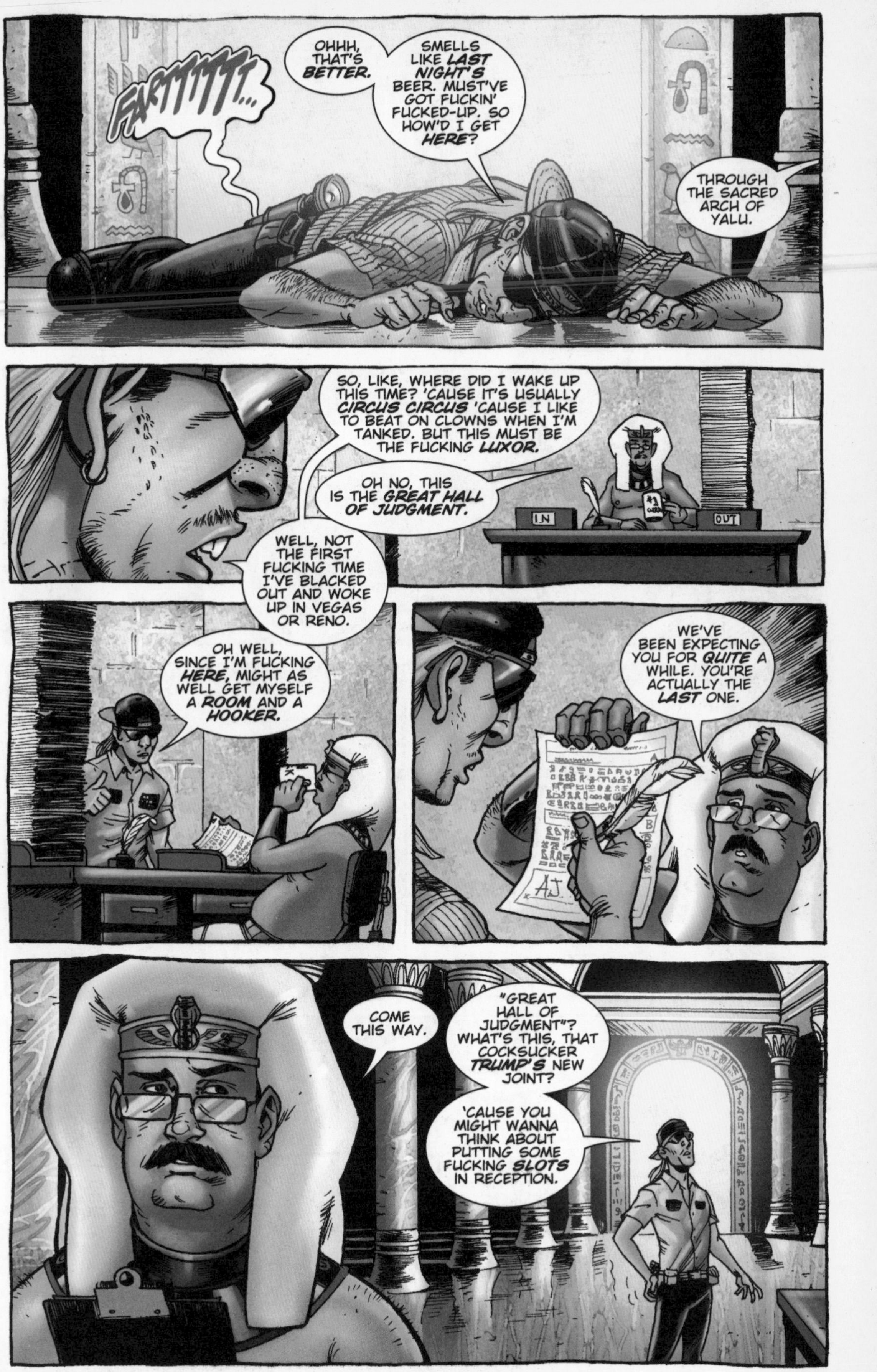
FARTTTTTT...
OHHH, THAT'S BETTER.
SMELLS LIKE LAST NIGHT'S BEER. MUST'VE GOT FUCKIN' FUCKED-UP. SO HOW'D I GET HERE?
THROUGH THE SACRED ARCH OF YALU.
SO, LIKE, WHERE DID I WAKE UP THIS TIME? 'CAUSE IT'S USUALLY CIRCUS CIRCUS 'CAUSE I LIKE TO BEAT ON CLOWNS WHEN I'M TANKED. BUT THIS MUST BE THE FUCKING LUXOR.
OH NO, THIS IS THE GREAT HALL OF JUDGMENT.
IN
OUT
WELL, NOT THE FIRST FUCKING TIME I'VE BLACKED OUT AND WOKE UP IN VEGAS OR RENO.
OH WELL, SINCE I'M FUCKING HERE, MIGHT AS WELL GET MYSELF A ROOM AND A HOOKER.
WE'VE BEEN EXPECTING YOU FOR QUITE A WHILE. YOU'RE ACTUALLY THE LAST ONE.
COME THIS WAY.
"GREAT HALL OF JUDGMENT"? WHAT'S THIS, THAT COCKSUCKER TRUMP'S NEW JOINT?
'CAUSE YOU MIGHT WANNA THINK ABOUT PUTTING SOME FUCKING SLOTS IN RECEPTION.

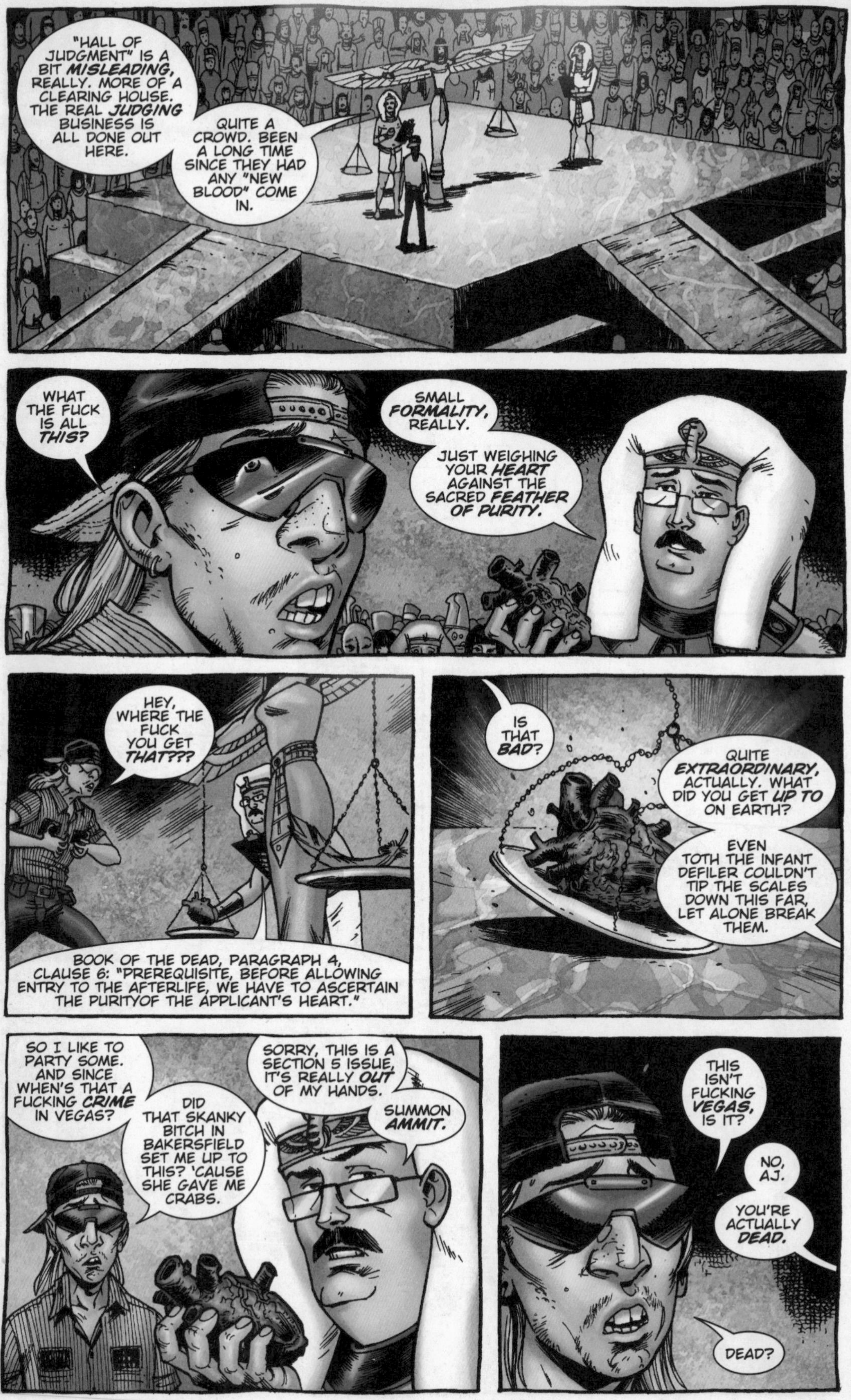

"HALL OF JUDGMENT" IS A BIT MISLEADING, REALLY. MORE OF A CLEARING HOUSE. THE REAL JUDGING BUSINESS IS ALL DONE OUT HERE.
QUITE A CROWD. BEEN A LONG TIME SINCE THEY HAD ANY "NEW BLOOD" COME IN.
WHAT THE FUCK IS ALL THIS?
SMALL FORMALITY, REALLY.
JUST WEIGHING YOUR HEART AGAINST THE SACRED FEATHER OF PURITY.
HEY, WHERE THE FUCK YOU GET THAT???
BOOK OF THE DEAD, PARAGRAPH 4, CLAUSE 6: "PREREQUISITE, BEFORE ALLOWING ENTRY TO THE AFTERLIFE, WE HAVE TO ASCERTAIN THE PURITYOF THE APPLICANT'S HEART."
IS THAT BAD?
QUITE EXTRAORDINARY, ACTUALLY. WHAT DID YOU GET UP TO ON EARTH?
EVEN TOTH THE INFANT DEFILER COULDN'T TIP THE SCALES DOWN THIS FAR, LET ALONE BREAK THEM.
SO I LIKE TO PARTY SOME. AND SINCE WHEN'S THAT A FUCKING CRIME IN VEGAS?
DID THAT SKANKY BITCH IN BAKERSFIELD SET ME UP TO THIS? 'CAUSE SHE GAVE ME CRABS.
SORRY, THIS IS A SECTION 5 ISSUE, IT'S REALLY OUT OF MY HANDS.
SUMMON AMMIT.
THIS ISN'T FUCKING VEGAS, IS IT?
NO, AJ.
YOU'RE ACTUALLY DEAD.
DEAD?

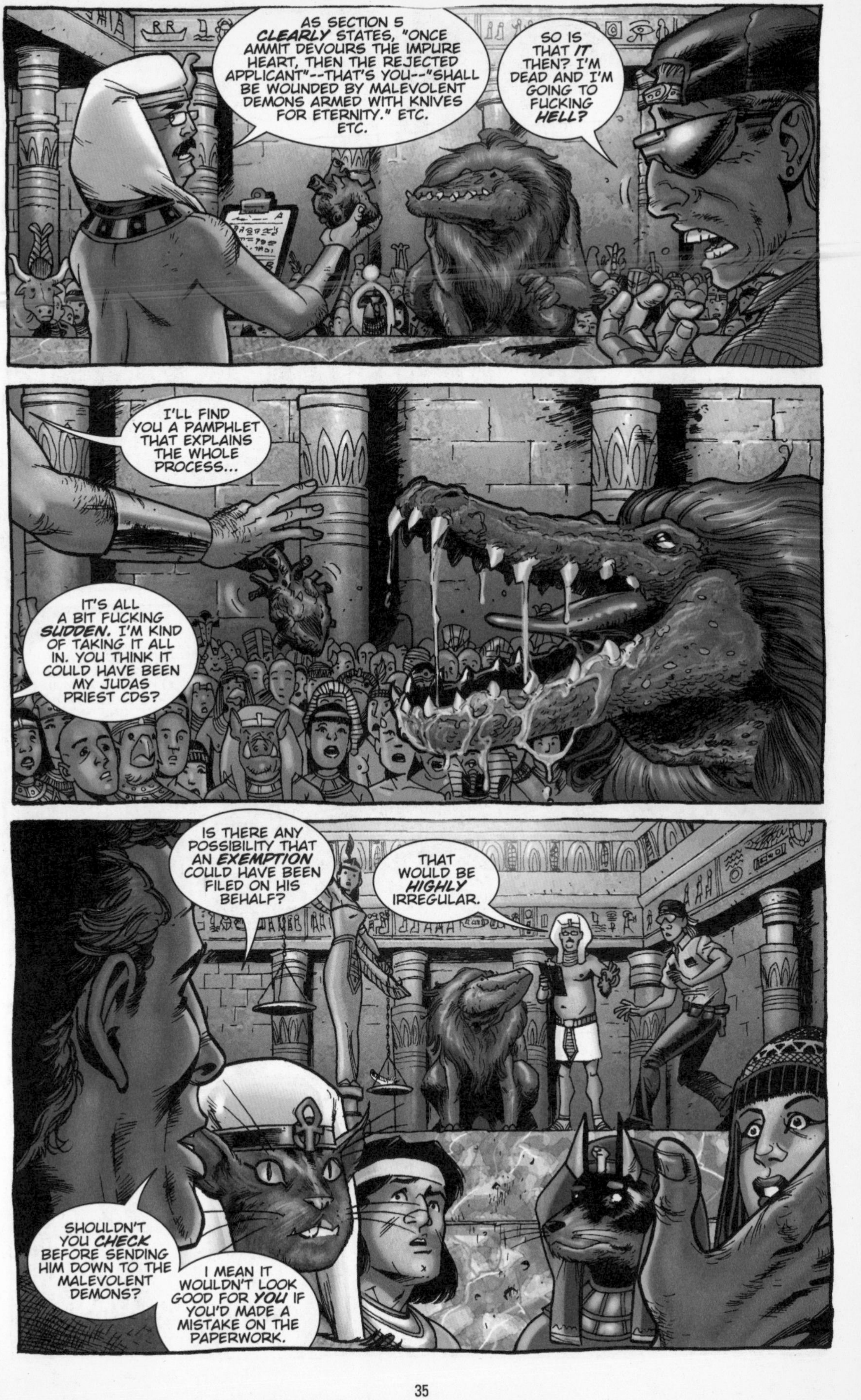
AS SECTION 5 CLEARLY STATES, "ONCE AMMIT DEVOURS THE IMPURE HEART, THEN THE REJECTED APPLICANT"--THAT'S YOU--"SHALL BE WOUNDED BY MALEVOLENT DEMONS ARMED WITH KNIVES FOR ETERNITY." ETC. ETC.
SO IS THAT IT THEN? I'M DEAD AND I'M GOING TO FUCKING HELL?
I'LL FIND YOU A PAMPHLET THAT EXPLAINS THE WHOLE PROCESS...
IT'S ALL A BIT FUCKING SUDDEN. I'M KIND OF TAKING IT ALL IN. YOU THINK IT COULD HAVE BEEN MY JUDAS PRIEST CDS?
IS THERE ANY POSSIBILITY THAT AN EXEMPTION COULD HAVE BEEN FILED ON HIS BEHALF?
THAT WOULD BE HIGHLY IRREGULAR.
SHOULDN'T YOU CHECK BEFORE SENDING HIM DOWN TO THE MALEVOLENT DEMONS?
I MEAN IT WOULDN'T LOOK GOOD FOR YOU IF YOU'D MADE A MISTAKE ON THE PAPERWORK.

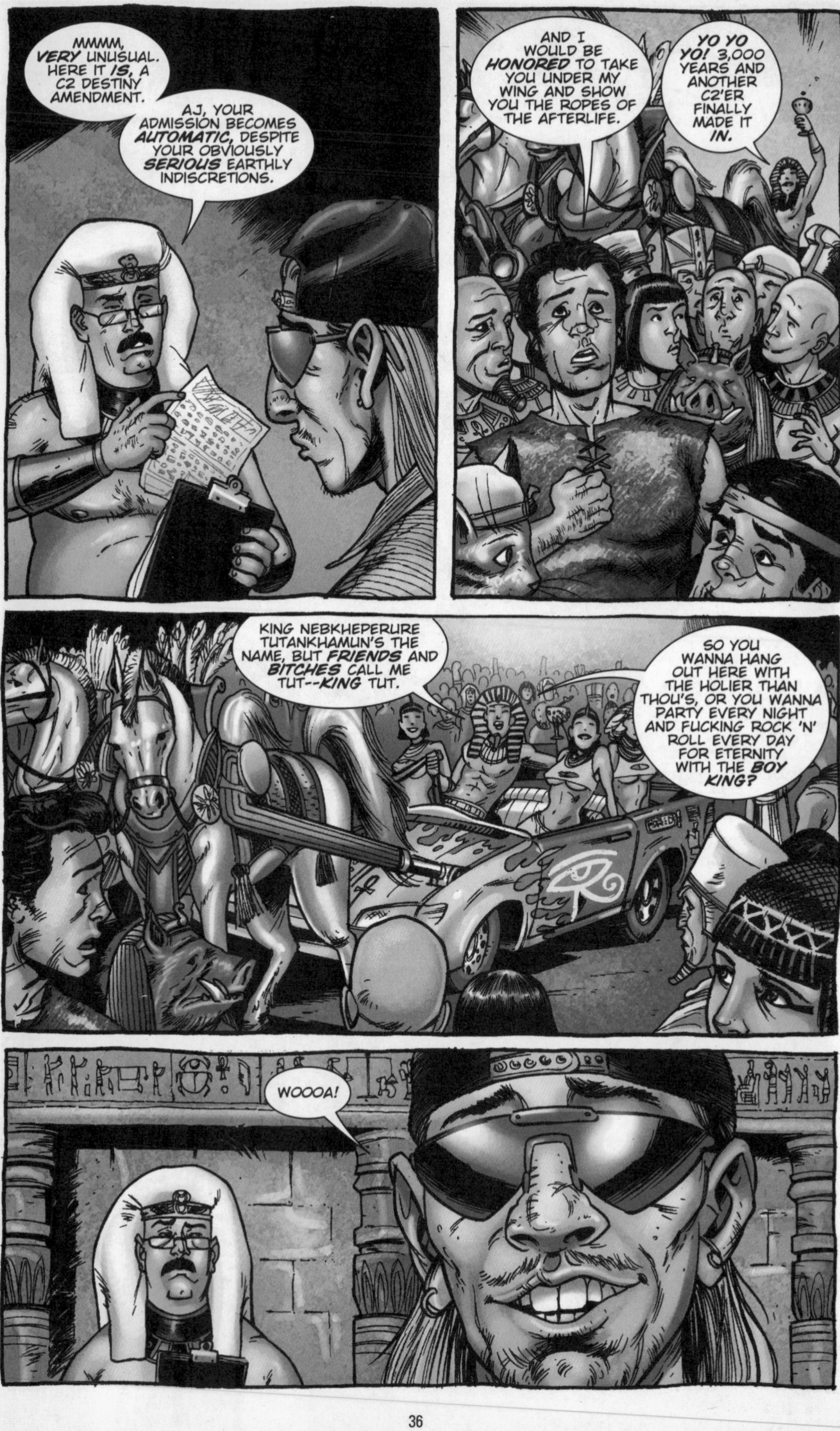
MMMM, VERY UNUSUAL. HERE IT IS, A C2 DESTINY AMENDMENT.
AJ, YOUR ADMISSION BECOMES AUTOMATIC, DESPITE YOUR OBVIOUSLY SERIOUS EARTHLY INDISCRETIONS.
AND I WOULD BE HONORED TO TAKE YOU UNDER MY WING AND SHOW YOU THE ROPES OF THE AFTERLIFE.
YO YO YO! 3,000 YEARS AND ANOTHER C2'ER FINALLY MADE IT IN.
KING NEBKHEPERURE TUTANKHAMUN'S THE NAME, BUT FRIENDS AND BITCHES CALL ME TUT--KING TUT.
SO YOU WANNA HANG OUT HERE WITH THE HOLIER THAN THOU'S, OR YOU WANNA PARTY EVERY NIGHT AND FUCKING ROCK 'N' ROLL EVERY DAY FOR ETERNITY WITH THE BOY KING?
WOOOA!

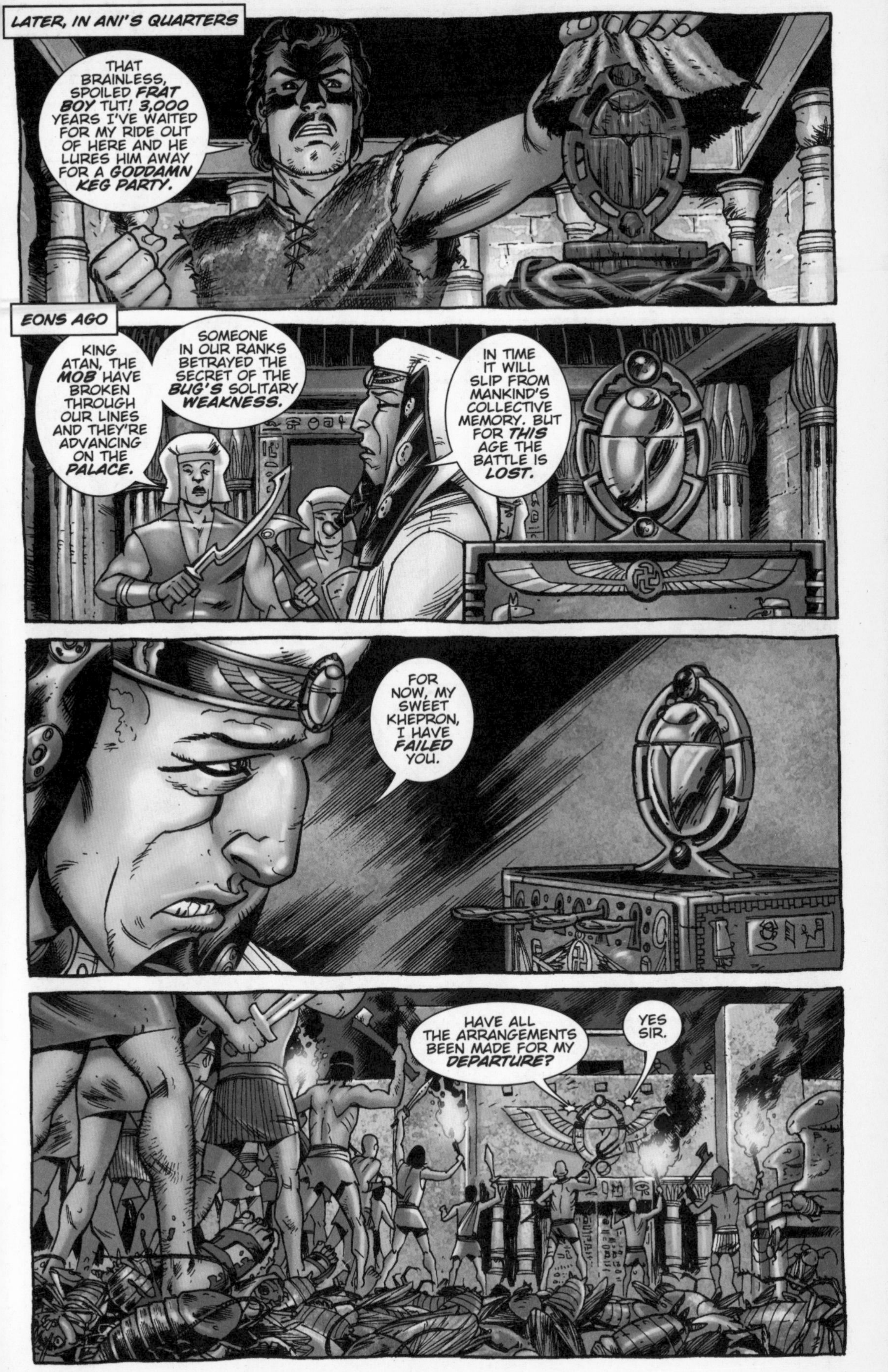
LATER, IN ANI'S QUARTERS
THAT BRAINLESS, SPOILED FRAT BOY TUT! 3,000 YEARS I'VE WAITED FOR MY RIDE OUT OF HERE AND HE LURES HIM AWAY FOR A GODDAMN KEG PARTY.
EONS AGO
KING ATAN, THE MOB HAVE BROKEN THROUGH OUR LINES AND THEY'RE ADVANCING ON THE PALACE.
SOMEONE IN OUR RANKS BETRAYED THE SECRET OF THE BUG'S SOLITARY WEAKNESS.
IN TIME IT WILL SLIP FROM MANKIND'S COLLECTIVE MEMORY. BUT FOR THIS AGE THE BATTLE IS LOST.
FOR NOW, MY SWEET KHEPRON, I HAVE FAILED YOU.
HAVE ALL THE ARRANGEMENTS BEEN MADE FOR MY DEPARTURE?
YES SIR.

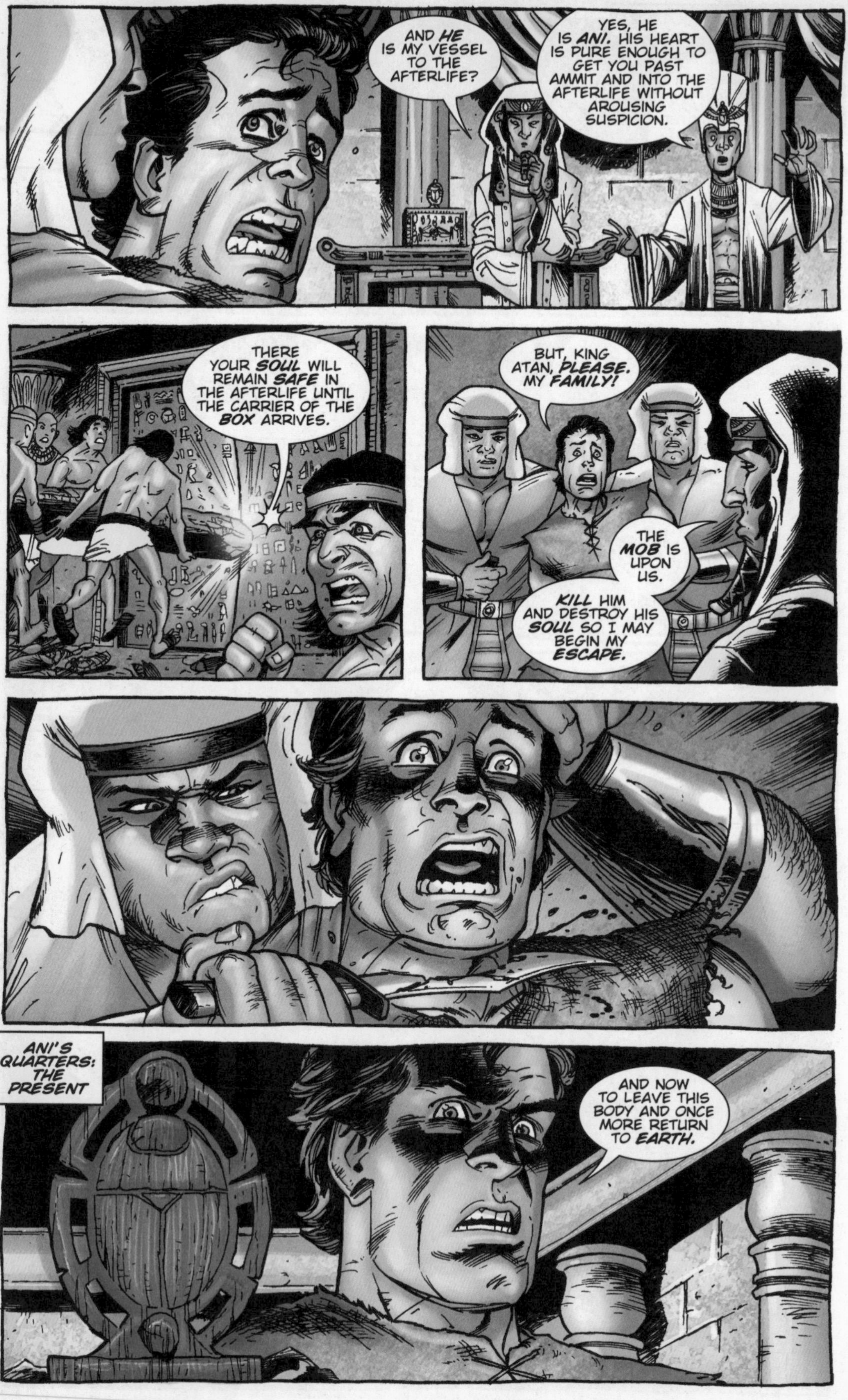
AND HE IS MY VESSEL TO THE AFTERLIFE?
YES, HE IS ANI. HIS HEART IS PURE ENOUGH TO GET YOU PAST AMMIT AND INTO THE AFTERLIFE WITHOUT AROUSING SUSPICION.
THERE YOUR SOUL WILL REMAIN SAFE IN THE AFTERLIFE UNTIL THE CARRIER OF THE BOX ARRIVES.
BUT, KING ATAN, PLEASE. MY FAMILY!
THE MOB IS UPON US.
KILL HIM AND DESTROY HIS SOUL SO I MAY BEGIN MY ESCAPE.
ANI'S QUARTERS: THE PRESENT
AND NOW TO LEAVE THIS BODY AND ONCE MORE RETURN TO EARTH.

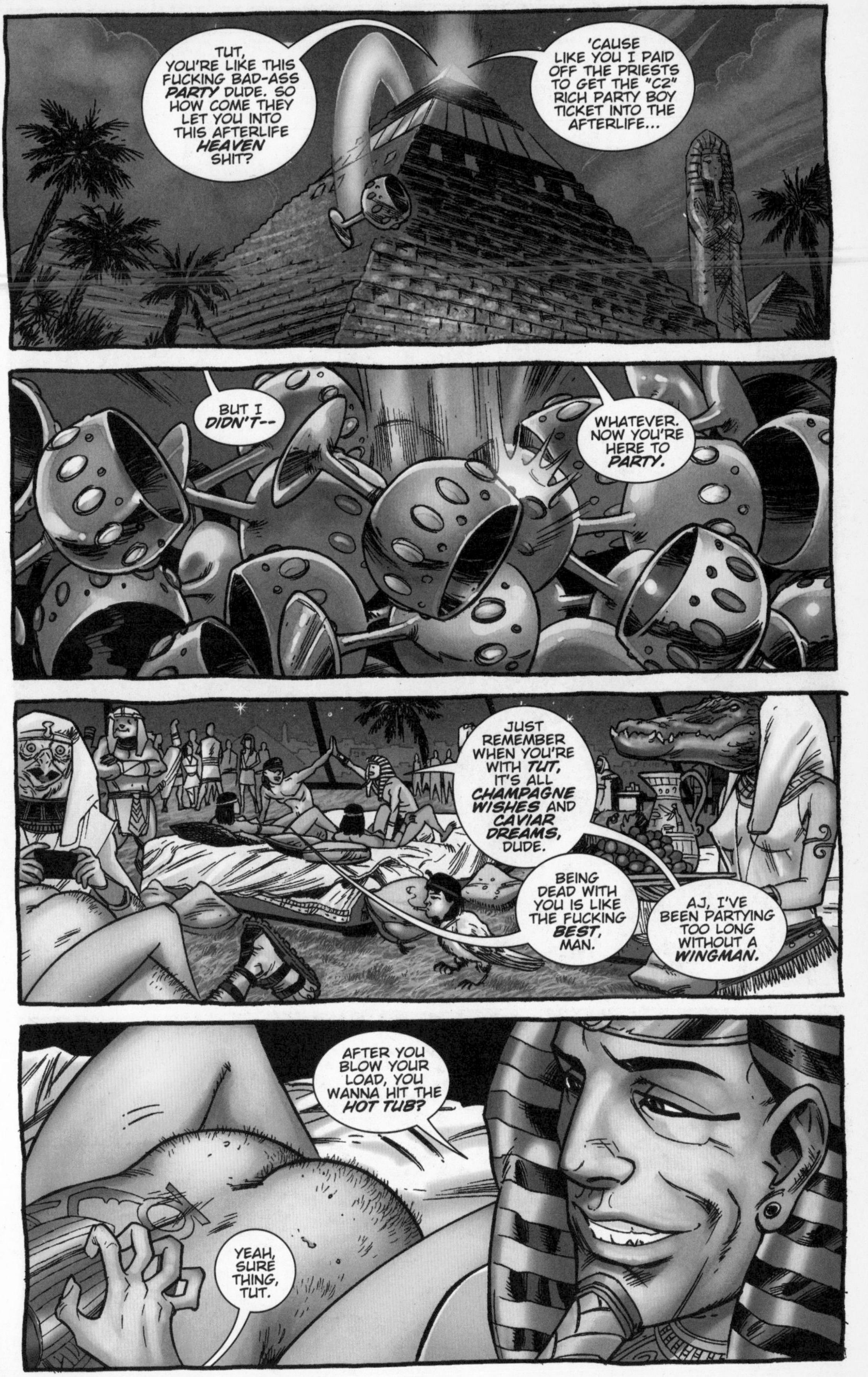
TUT, YOU'RE LIKE THIS FUCKING BAD-ASS PARTY DUDE. SO HOW COME THEY LET YOU INTO THIS AFTERLIFE HEAVEN SHIT?
'CAUSE LIKE YOU I PAID OFF THE PRIESTS TO GET THE "C2" RICH PARTY BOY TICKET INTO THE AFTERLIFE...
BUT I DIDN'T--
WHATEVER. NOW YOU'RE HERE TO PARTY.
JUST REMEMBER WHEN YOU'RE WITH TUT, IT'S ALL CHAMPAGNE WISHES AND CAVIAR DREAMS, DUDE.
BEING DEAD WITH YOU IS LIKE THE FUCKING BEST, MAN.
AJ, I'VE BEEN PARTYING TOO LONG WITHOUT A WINGMAN.
AFTER YOU BLOW YOUR LOAD, YOU WANNA HIT THE HOT TUB?
YEAH, SURE THING, TUT.

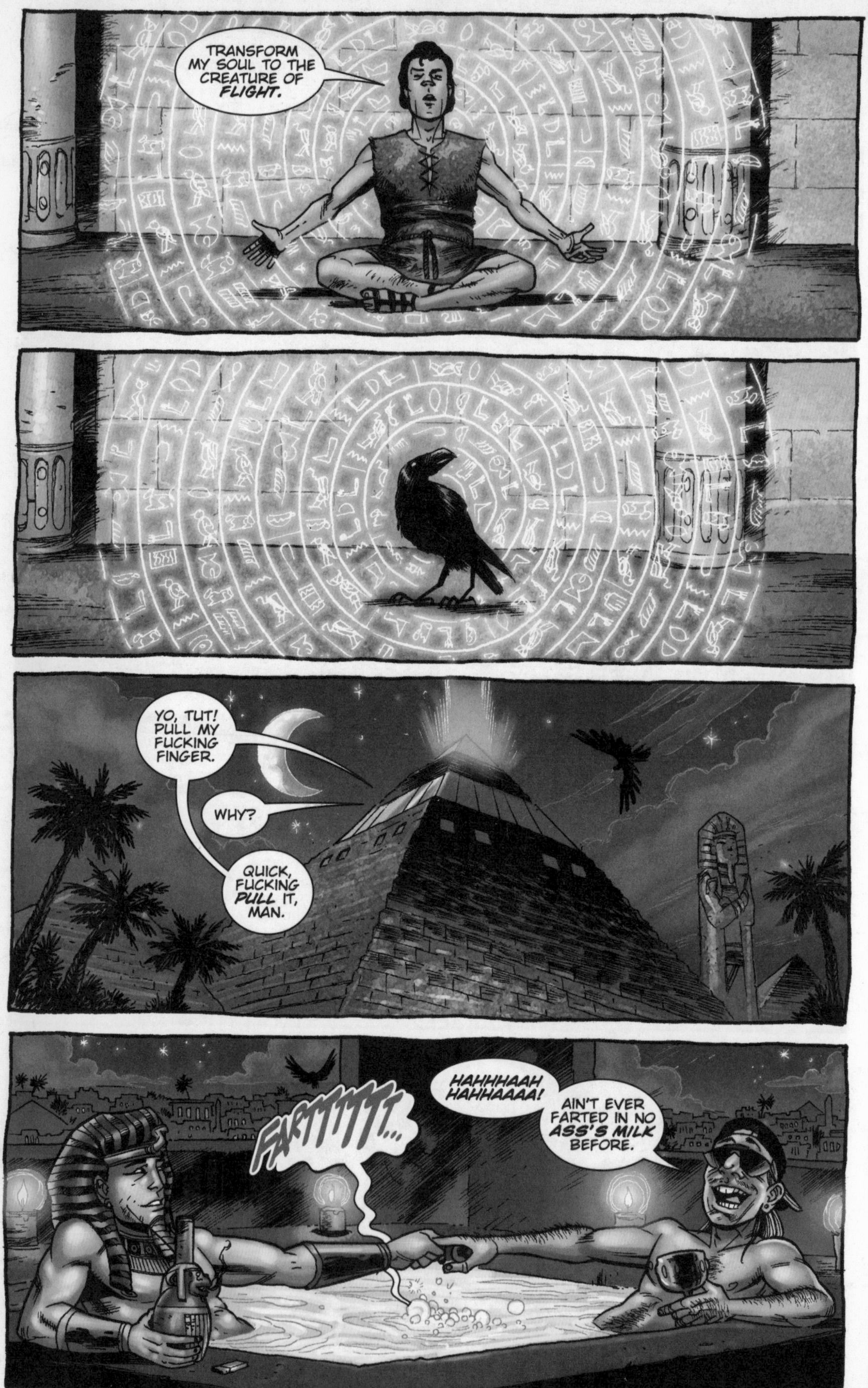
TRANSFORM MY SOUL TO THE CREATURE OF FLIGHT.
YO, TUT! PULL MY FUCKING FINGER.
WHY?
QUICK, FUCKING PULL IT, MAN.
FARTTTTTT...
HAHHHAAH HAHHAAAA!
AIN'T EVER FARTED IN NO ASS'S MILK BEFORE.

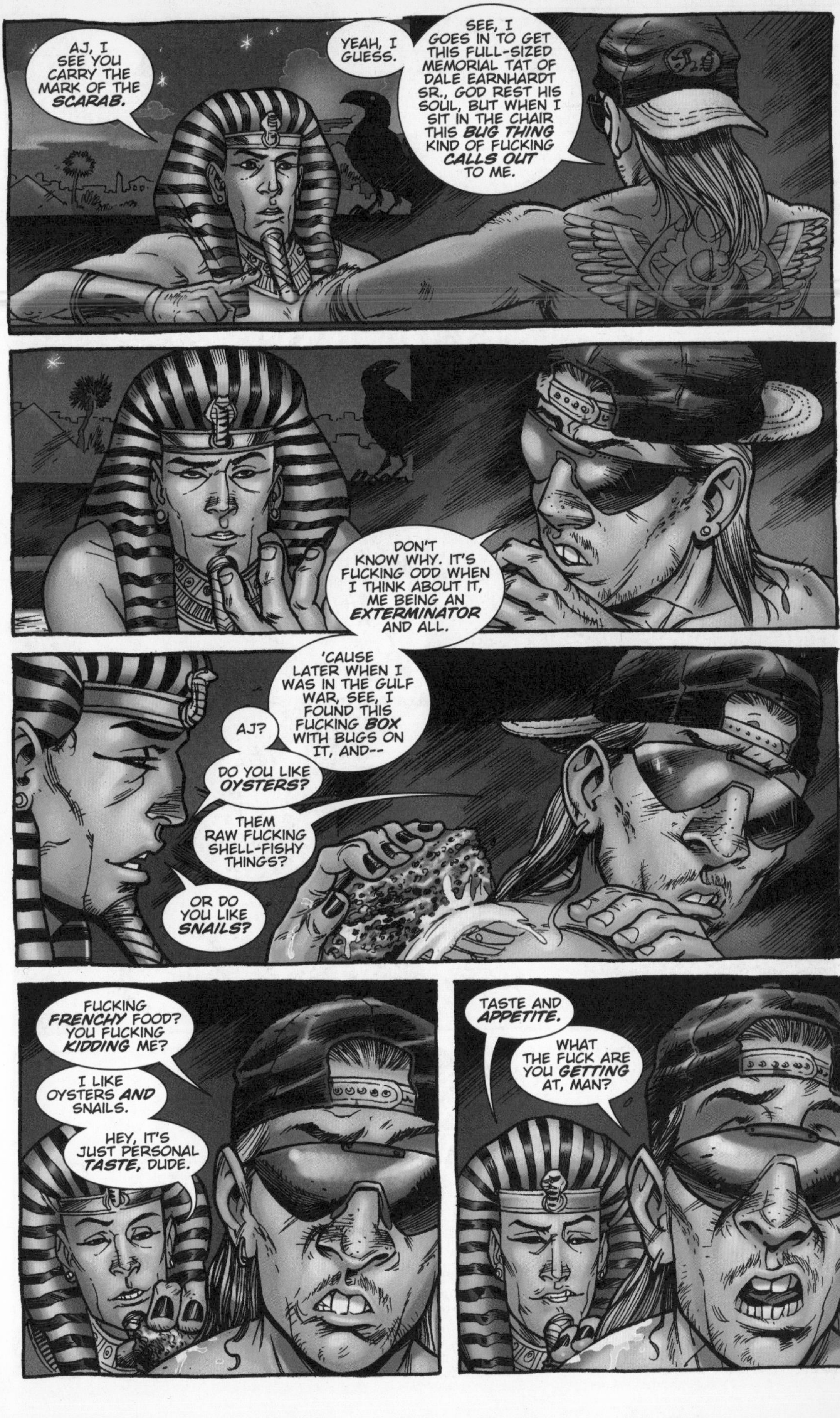
AJ, I SEE YOU CARRY THE MARK OF THE SCARAB.
YEAH, I GUESS.
SEE, I GOES IN TO GET THIS FULL-SIZED MEMORIAL TAT OF DALE EARNHARDT SR., GOD REST HIS SOUL, BUT WHEN I SIT IN THE CHAIR THIS BUG THING KIND OF FUCKING CALLS OUT TO ME.
DON'T KNOW WHY. IT'S FUCKING ODD WHEN I THINK ABOUT IT, ME BEING AN EXTERMINATOR AND ALL.
'CAUSE LATER WHEN I WAS IN THE GULF WAR, SEE, I FOUND THIS FUCKING BOX WITH BUGS ON IT, AND--
AJ?
DO YOU LIKE OYSTERS?
THEM RAW FUCKING SHELL-FISHY THINGS?
OR DO YOU LIKE SNAILS?
FUCKING FRENCHY FOOD? YOU FUCKING KIDDING ME?
I LIKE OYSTERS AND SNAILS.
HEY, IT'S JUST PERSONAL TASTE, DUDE.
TASTE AND APPETITE.
WHAT THE FUCK ARE YOU GETTING AT, MAN?

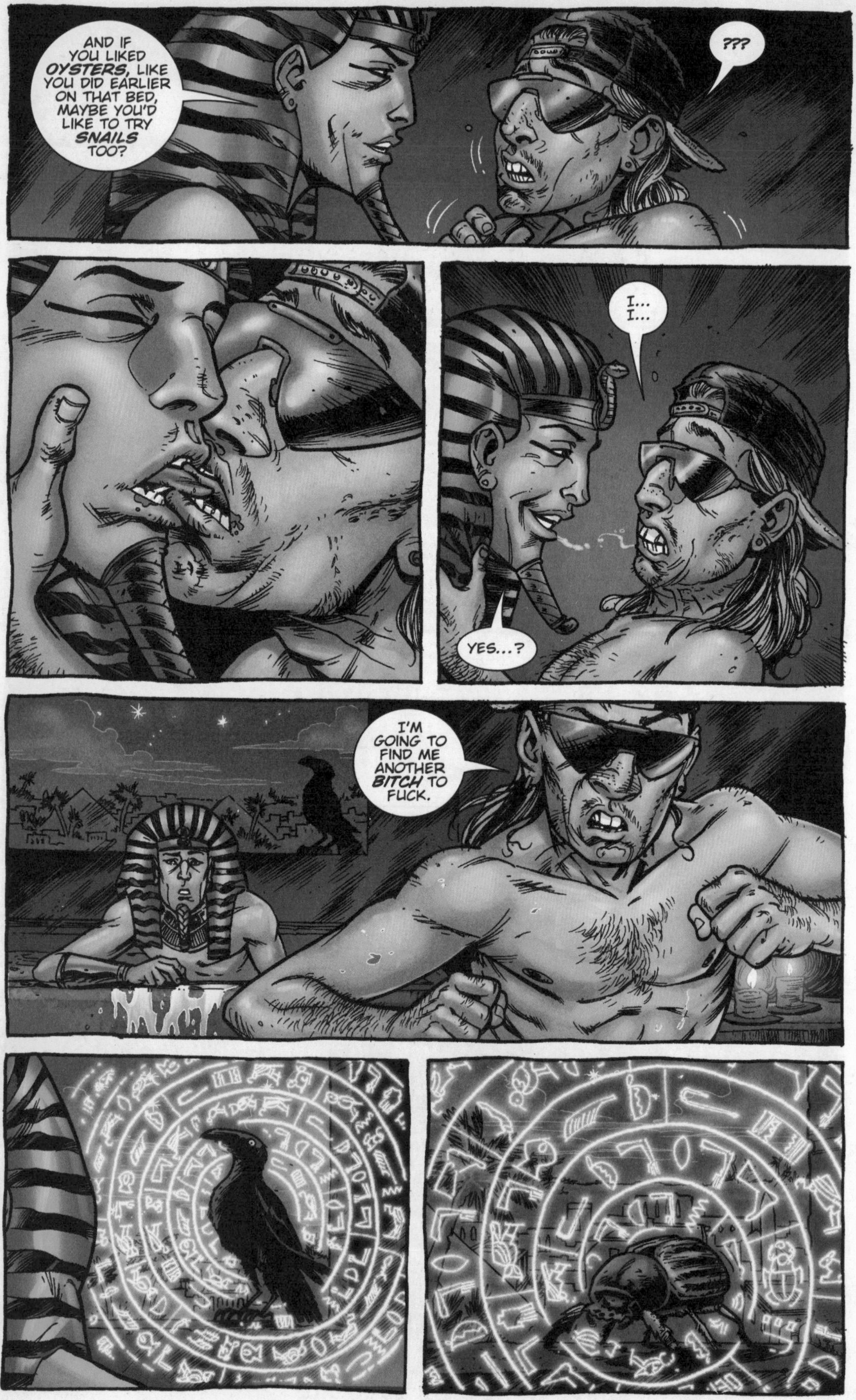
AND IF YOU LIKED OYSTERS, LIKE YOU DID EARLIER ON THAT BED, MAYBE YOU'D LIKE TO TRY SNAILS TOO?
???
I... I...
YES...?
I'M GOING TO FIND ME ANOTHER BITCH TO FUCK.

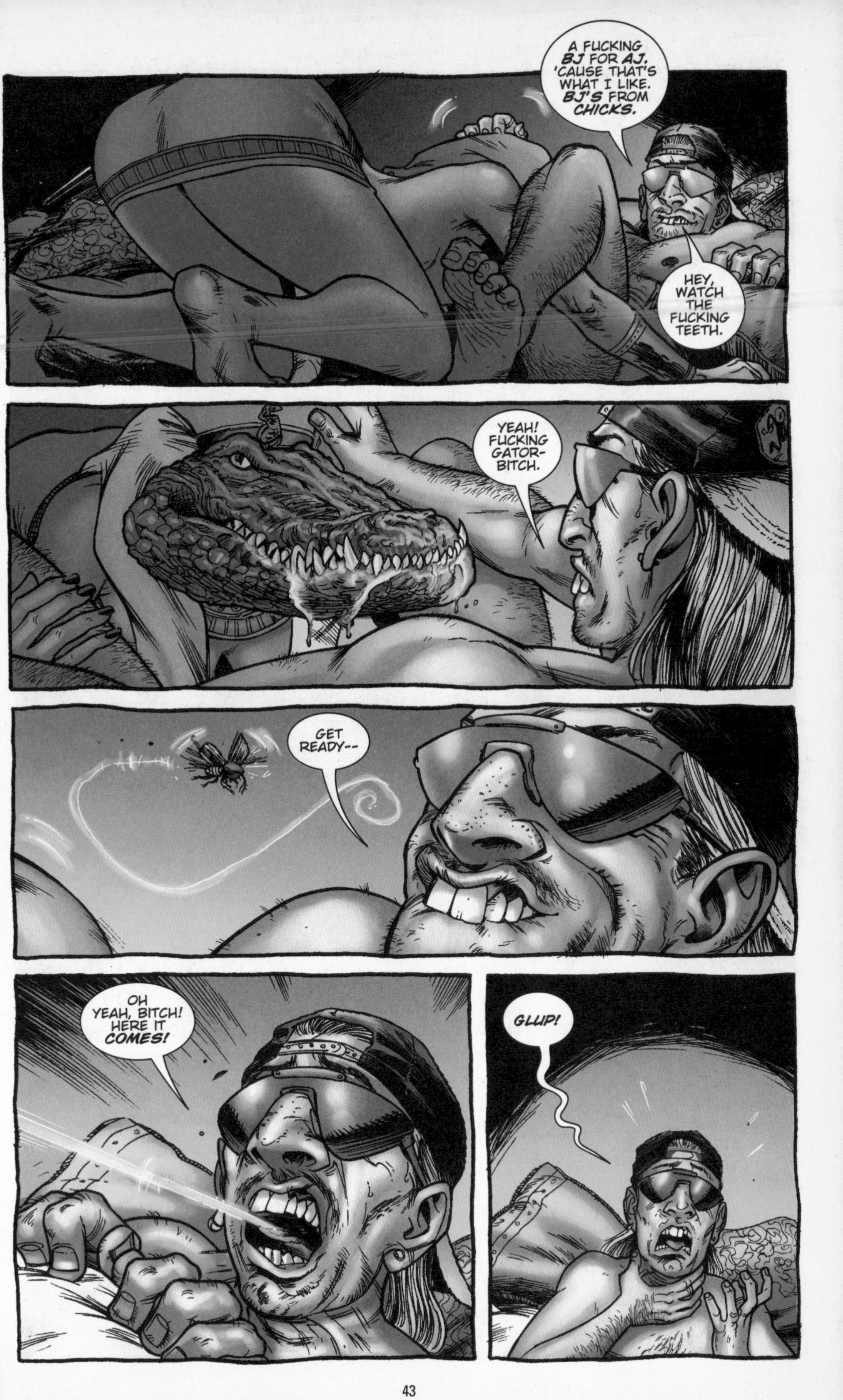

A FUCKING BJ FOR AJ. 'CAUSE THAT'S WHAT I LIKE. BJ'S FROM CHICKS.
HEY, WATCH THE FUCKING TEETH.
YEAH! FUCKING GATOR-BITCH.
GET READY--
OH YEAH, BITCH! HERE IT COMES!
GLUP!

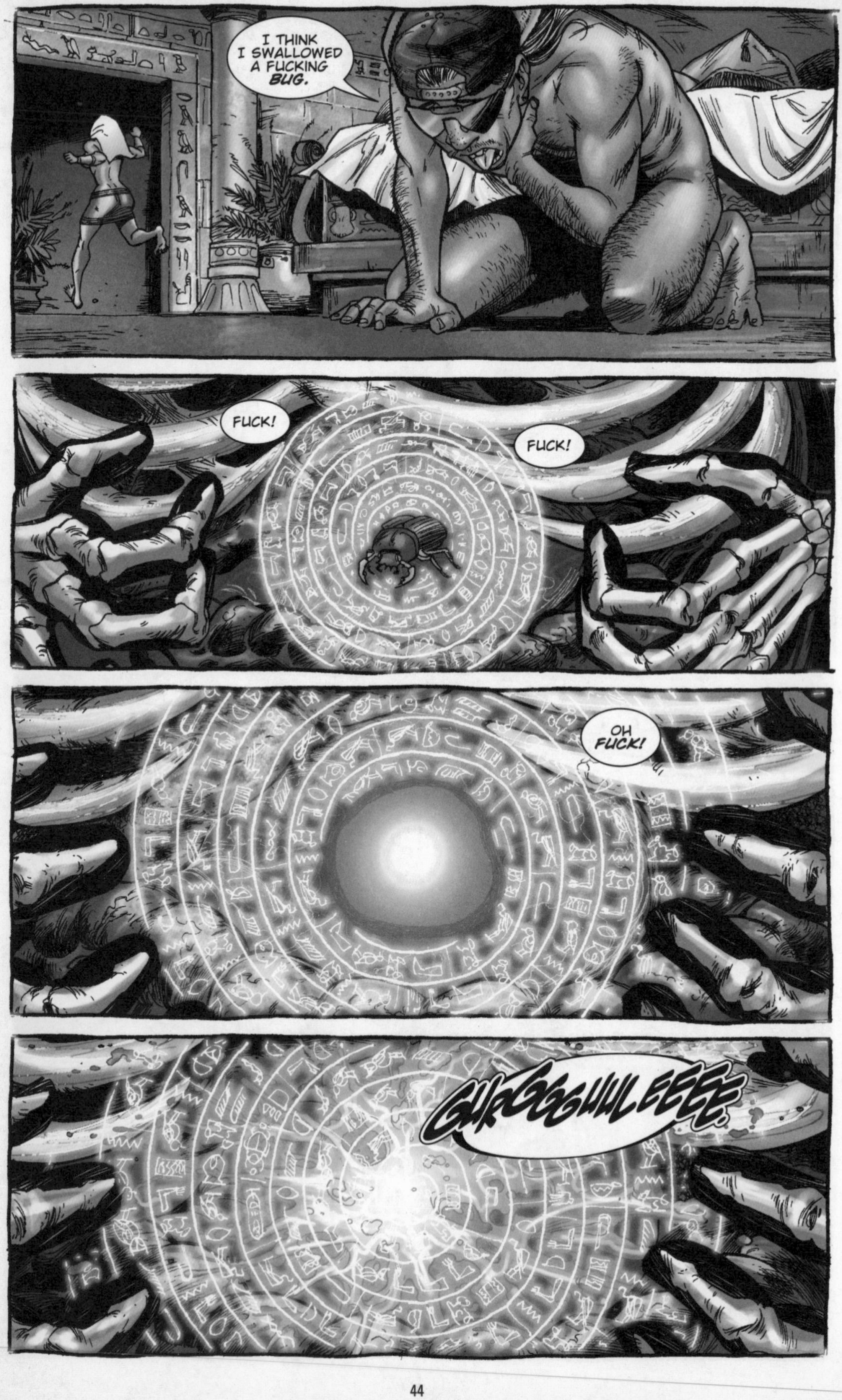
I THINK I SWALLOWED A FUCKING BUG.
FUCK!
FUCK!
OH FUCK!
GURGGGUUULEEEE.

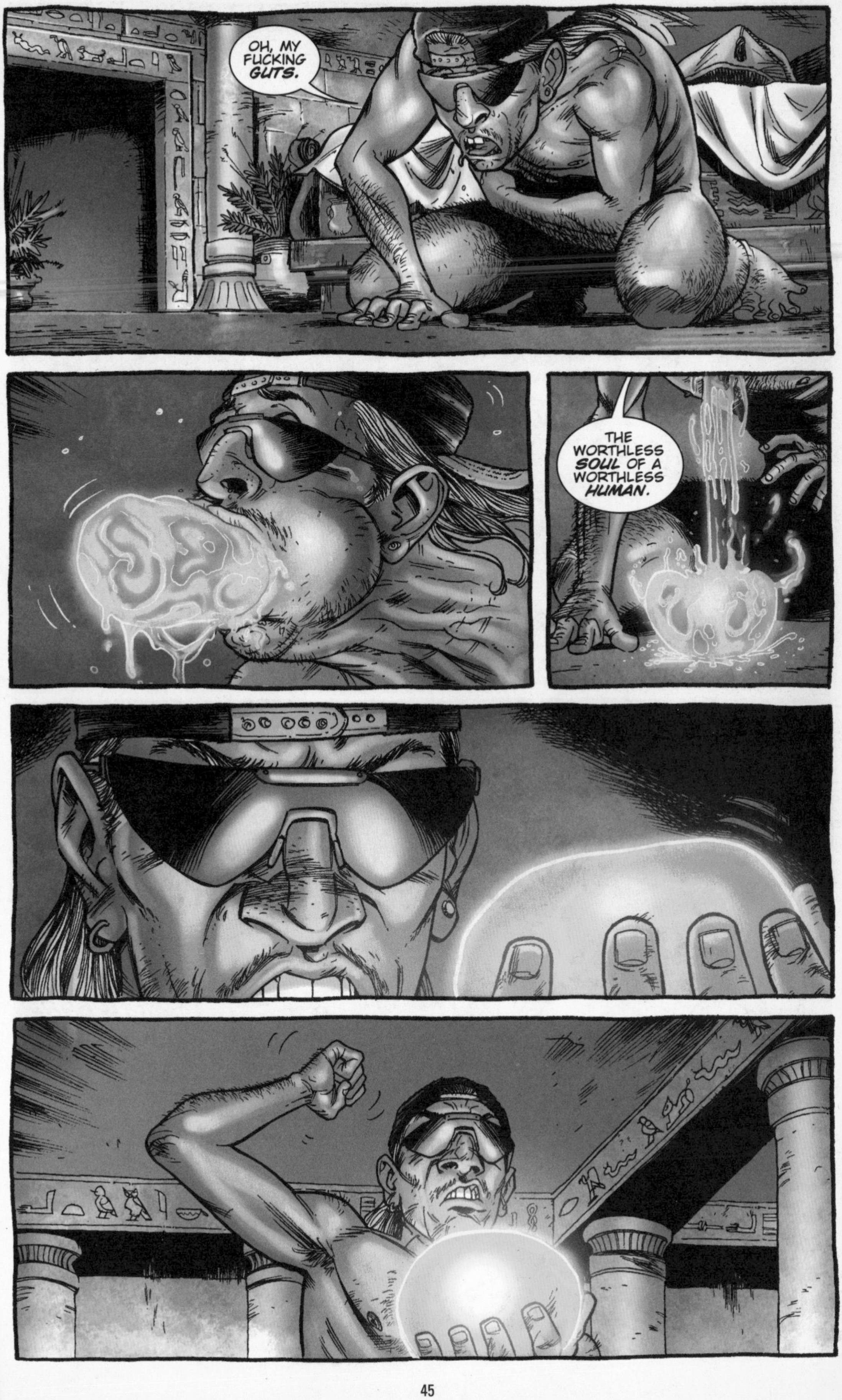
OH, MY FUCKING GUTS.
THE WORTHLESS SOUL OF A WORTHLESS HUMAN.

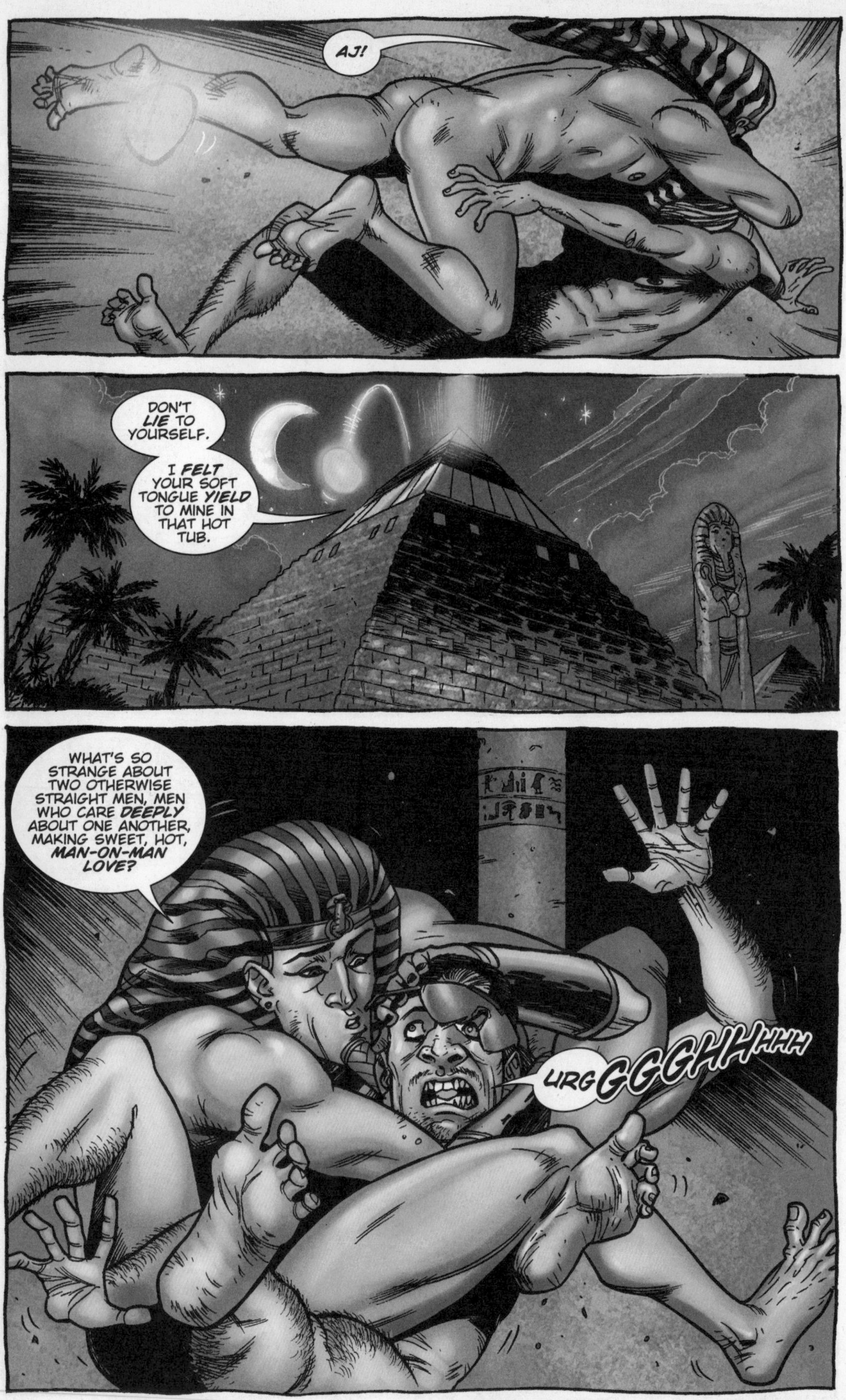
AJ!
DON'T *LIE* TO YOURSELF.
I *FELT* YOUR SOFT TONGUE *YIELD* TO MINE IN THAT HOT TUB.
WHAT'S SO STRANGE ABOUT TWO OTHERWISE STRAIGHT MEN, MEN WHO CARE *DEEPLY* ABOUT ONE ANOTHER, MAKING SWEET, HOT, *MAN-ON-MAN LOVE?*
URGGGGHHHHH

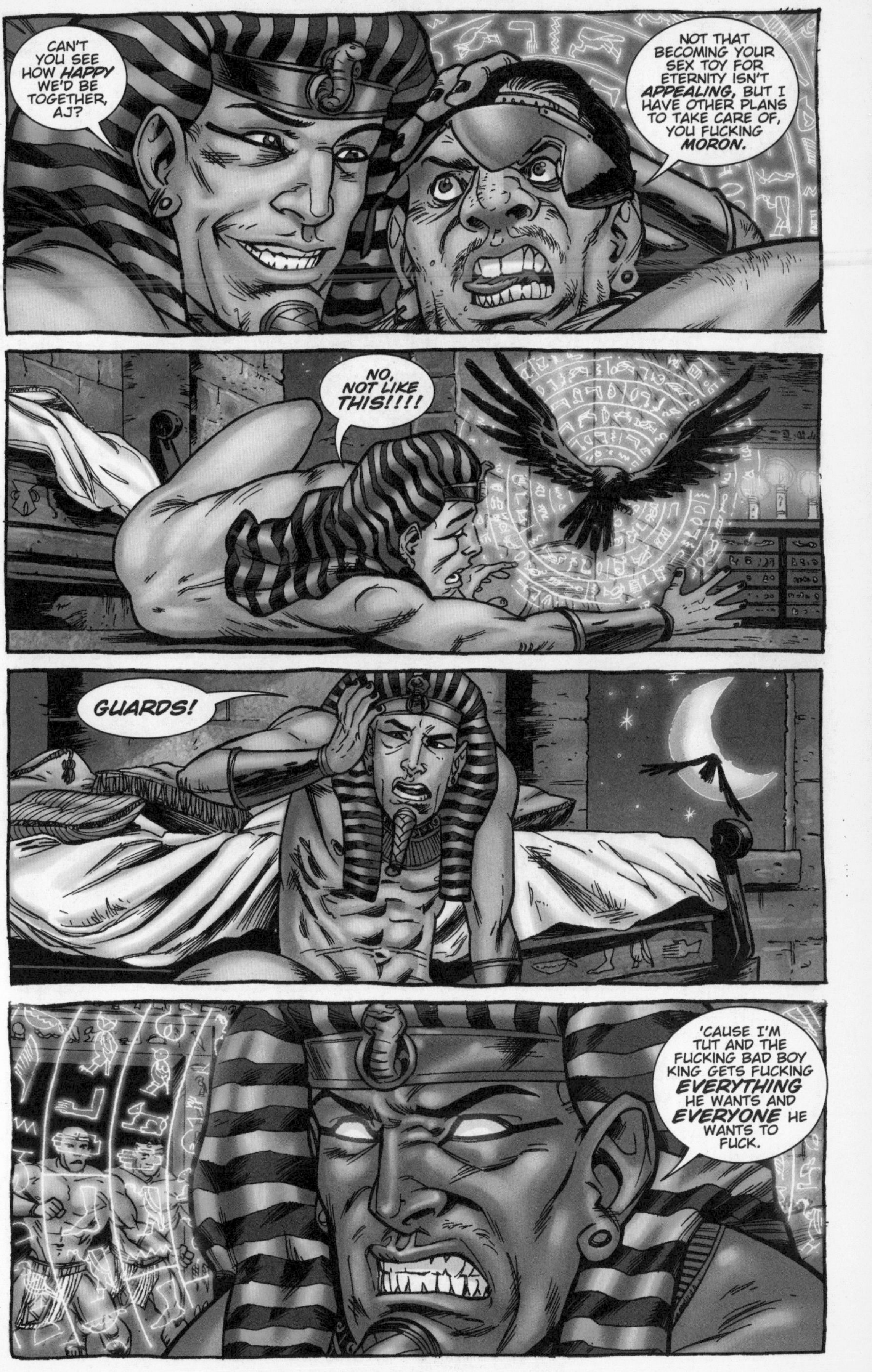
CAN'T YOU SEE HOW HAPPY WE'D BE TOGETHER, AJ?
NOT THAT BECOMING YOUR SEX TOY FOR ETERNITY ISN'T APPEALING, BUT I HAVE OTHER PLANS TO TAKE CARE OF, YOU FUCKING MORON.
NO, NOT LIKE THIS!!!!
GUARDS!
'CAUSE I'M TUT AND THE FUCKING BAD BOY KING GETS FUCKING EVERYTHING HE WANTS AND EVERYONE HE WANTS TO FUCK.

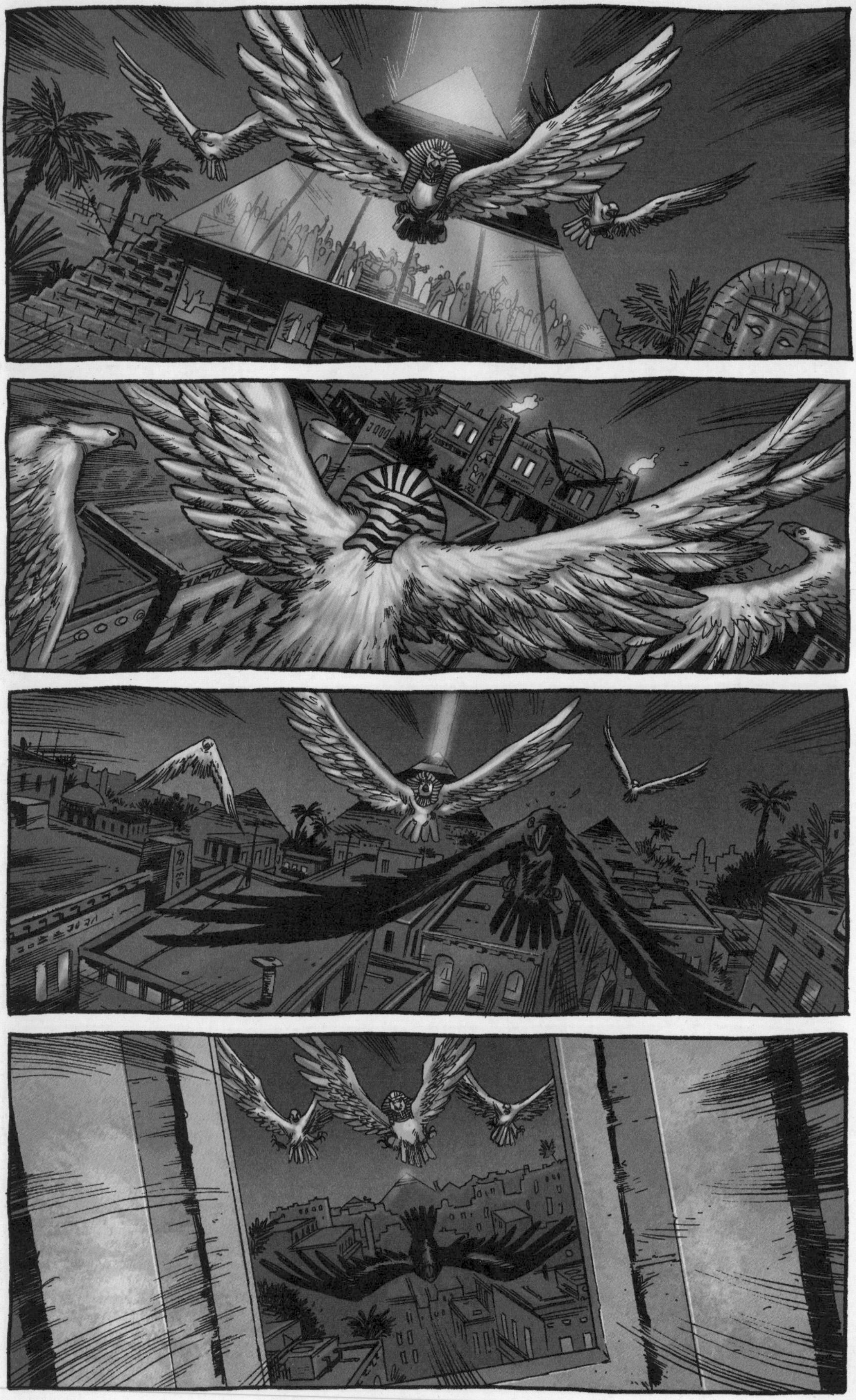

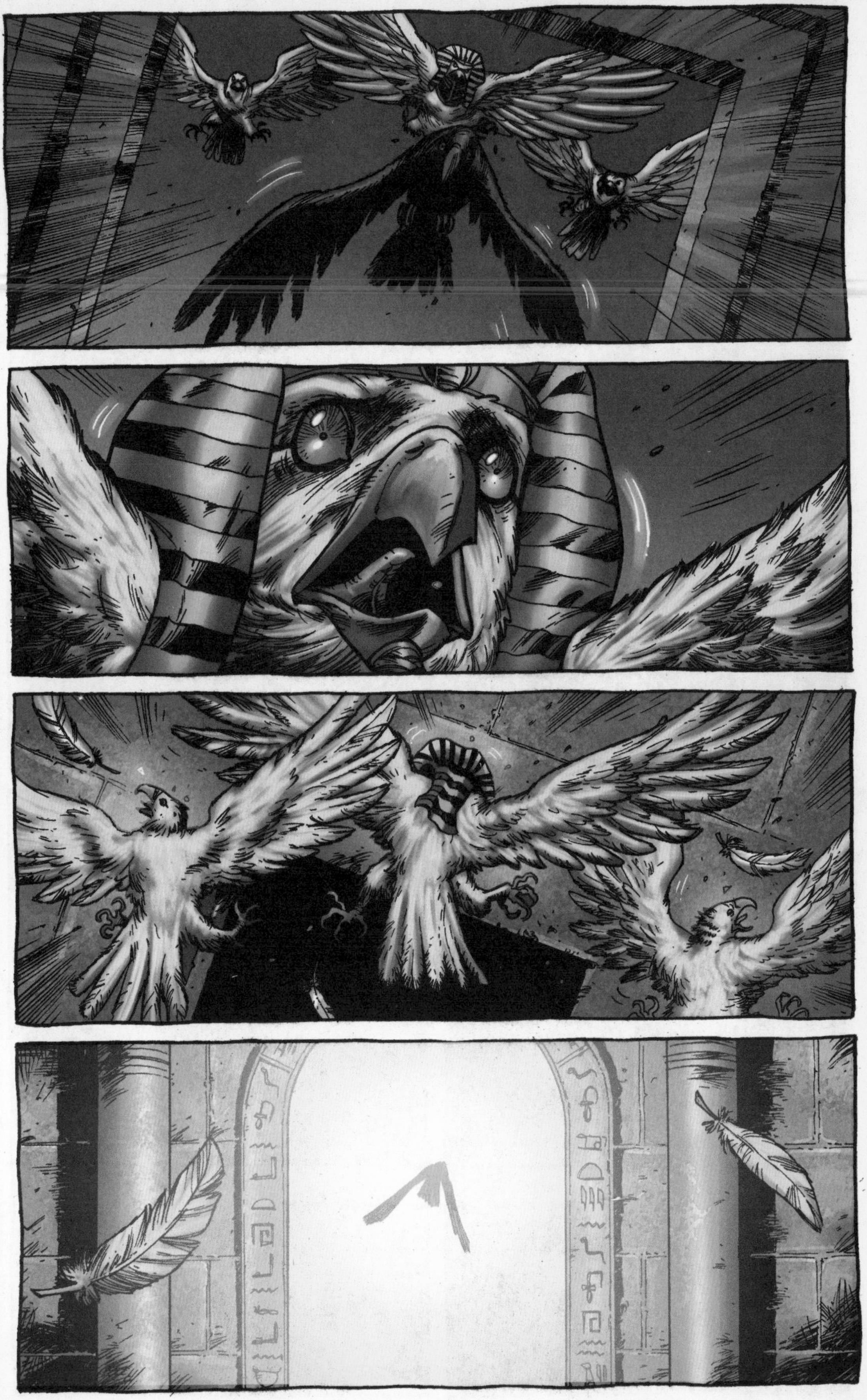

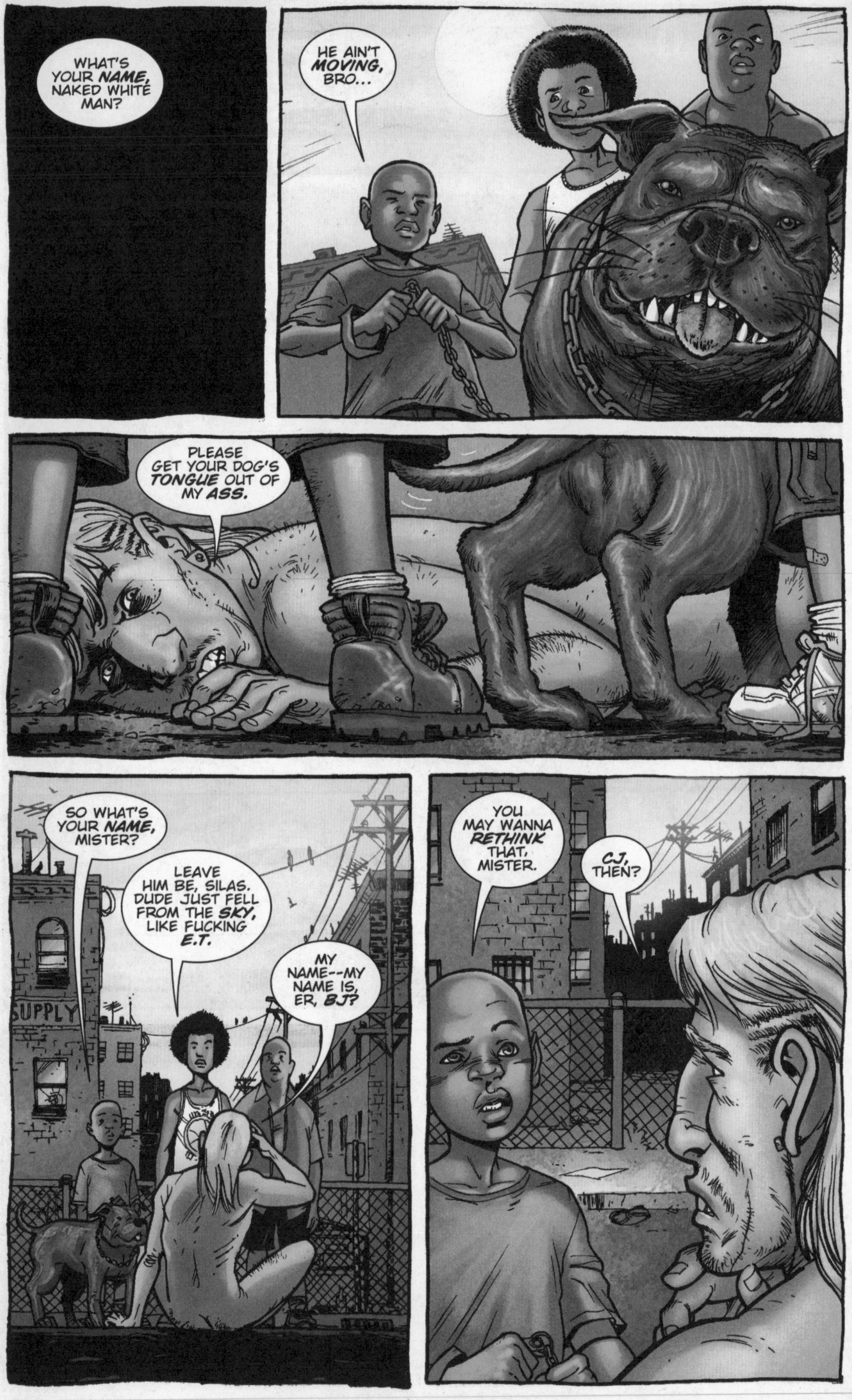
WHAT'S YOUR NAME, NAKED WHITE MAN?
HE AIN'T MOVING, BRO...
PLEASE GET YOUR DOG'S TONGUE OUT OF MY ASS.
SO WHAT'S YOUR NAME, MISTER?
LEAVE HIM BE, SILAS. DUDE JUST FELL FROM THE SKY, LIKE FUCKING E.T.
MY NAME--MY NAME IS, ER, BJ?
SUPPLY
YOU MAY WANNA RETHINK THAT, MISTER.
CJ, THEN?

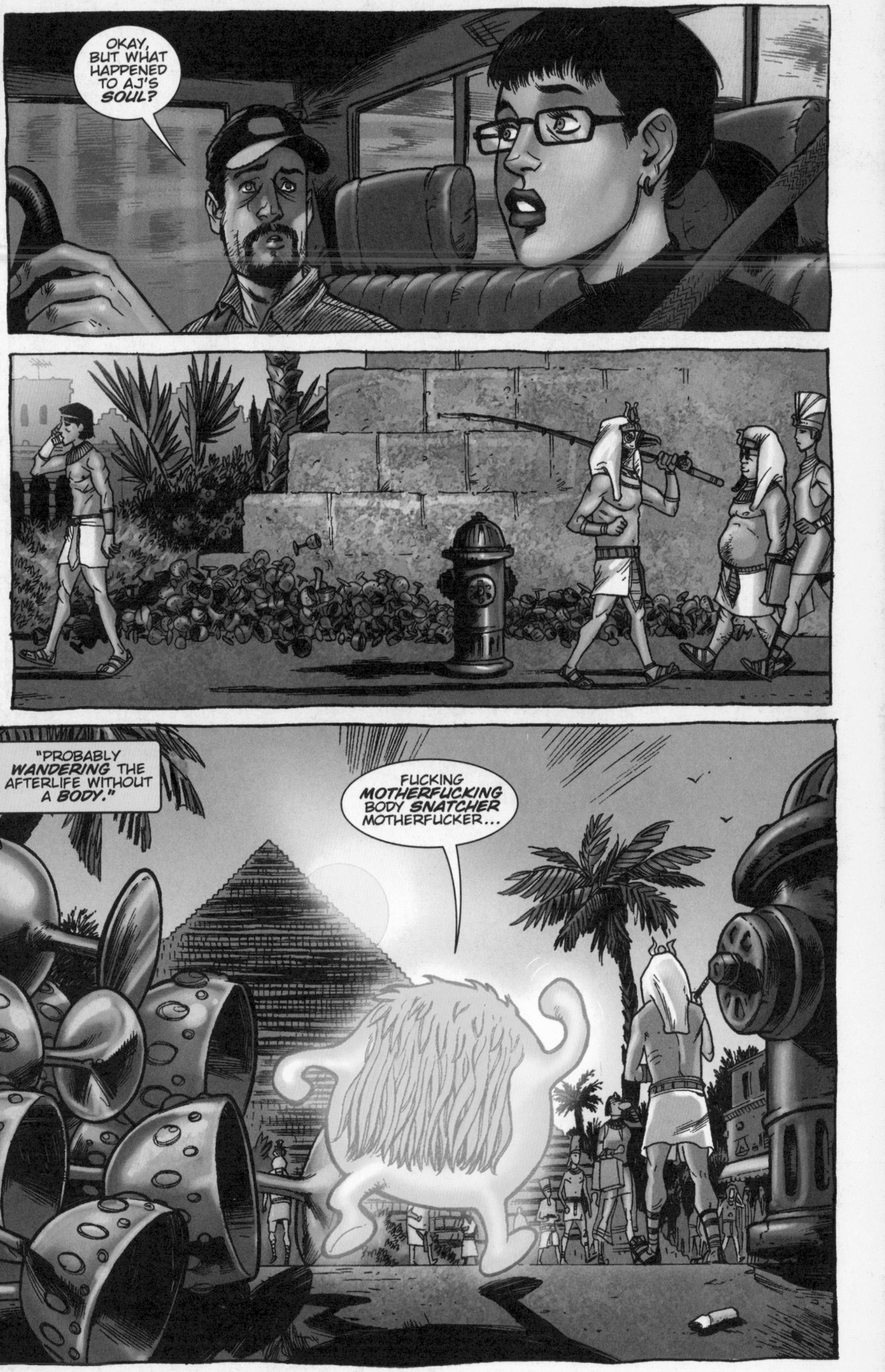

OKAY, BUT WHAT HAPPENED TO AJ'S SOUL?
"PROBABLY WANDERING THE AFTERLIFE WITHOUT A BODY."
FUCKING MOTHERFUCKING BODY SNATCHER MOTHERFUCKER...

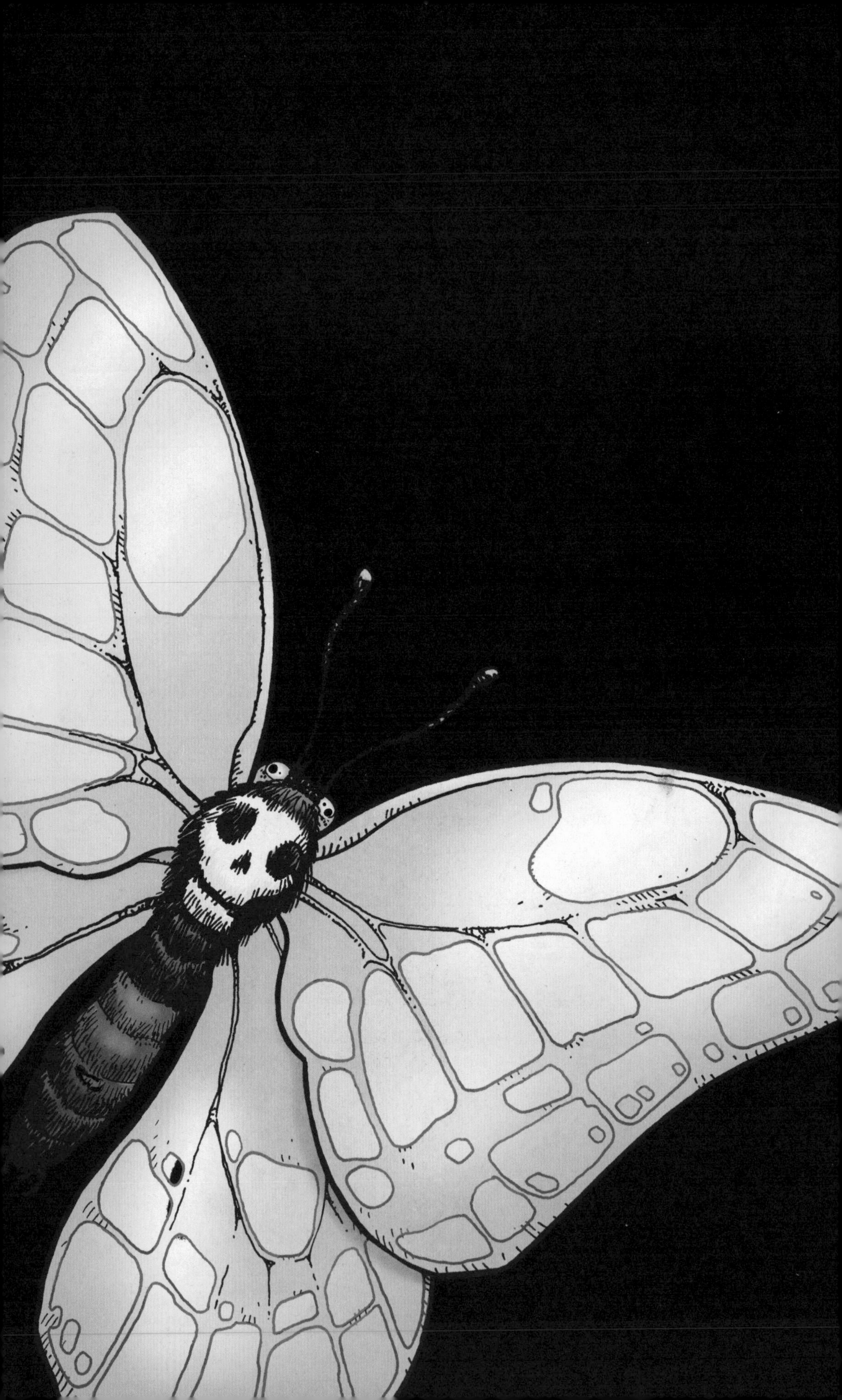

LAURA GOES DOWN

COVER ART BY PHILIP BOND AND DAVID HAHN

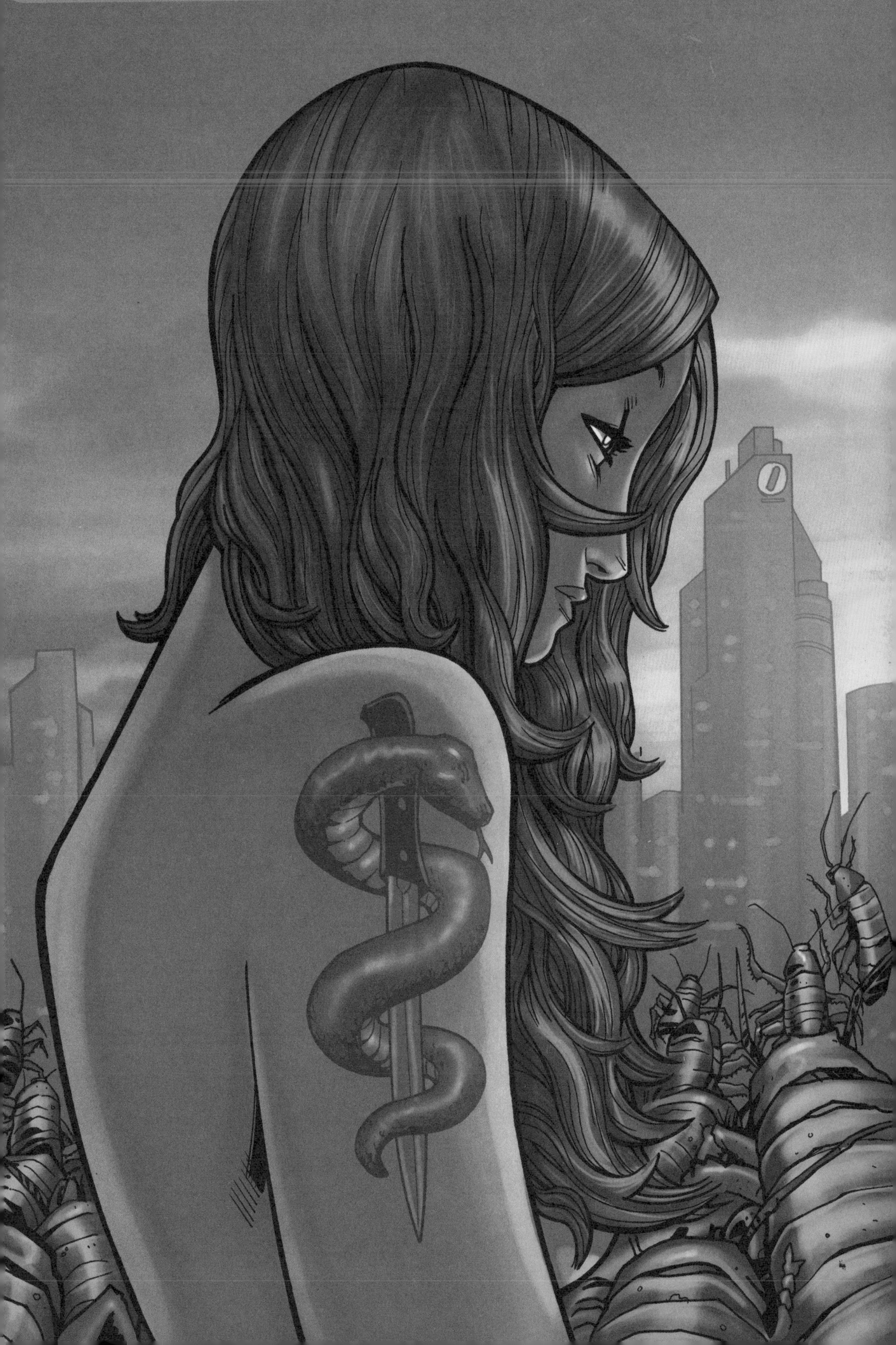

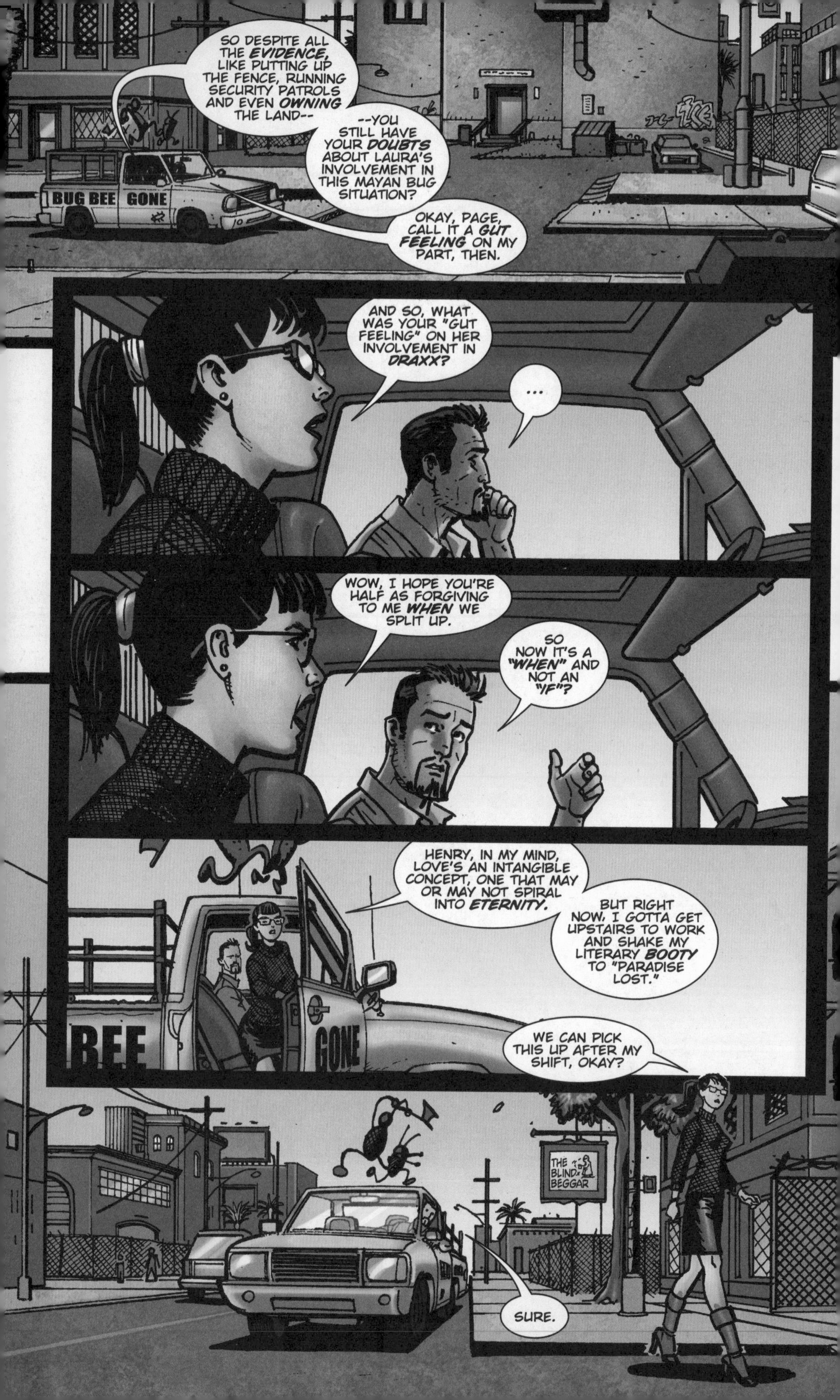
SO DESPITE ALL THE EVIDENCE, LIKE PUTTING UP THE FENCE, RUNNING SECURITY PATROLS AND EVEN OWNING THE LAND--
--YOU STILL HAVE YOUR DOUBTS ABOUT LAURA'S INVOLVEMENT IN THIS MAYAN BUG SITUATION?
OKAY, PAGE, CALL IT A GUT FEELING ON MY PART, THEN.
BUG BEE GONE
AND SO, WHAT WAS YOUR "GUT FEELING" ON HER INVOLVEMENT IN DRAXX?
...
WOW, I HOPE YOU'RE HALF AS FORGIVING TO ME WHEN WE SPLIT UP.
SO NOW IT'S A "WHEN" AND NOT AN "IF"?
HENRY, IN MY MIND, LOVE'S AN INTANGIBLE CONCEPT, ONE THAT MAY OR MAY NOT SPIRAL INTO ETERNITY.
BUT RIGHT NOW, I GOTTA GET UPSTAIRS TO WORK AND SHAKE MY LITERARY BOOTY TO "PARADISE LOST."
BEE
GONE
WE CAN PICK THIS UP AFTER MY SHIFT, OKAY?
THE BLIND BEGGAR
SURE.

WILL THAT BE ALL, MS. PHILLIPS?
OH, JUST ONE MORE THING, I WAS JUST WONDERING, YOUR NAME, "YNAS." WHAT DOES IT MEAN IN KORIBATIAN?
OCRAN INDUSTRIES
OCRAN INDUSTRIES
"WIFE OF THE MOON."
IT'S FROM A KORIBATIAN LEGEND ABOUT HOW THE MOON AND NIGHT STARS CAME TO BE.
I'D LIKE TO HEAR IT...

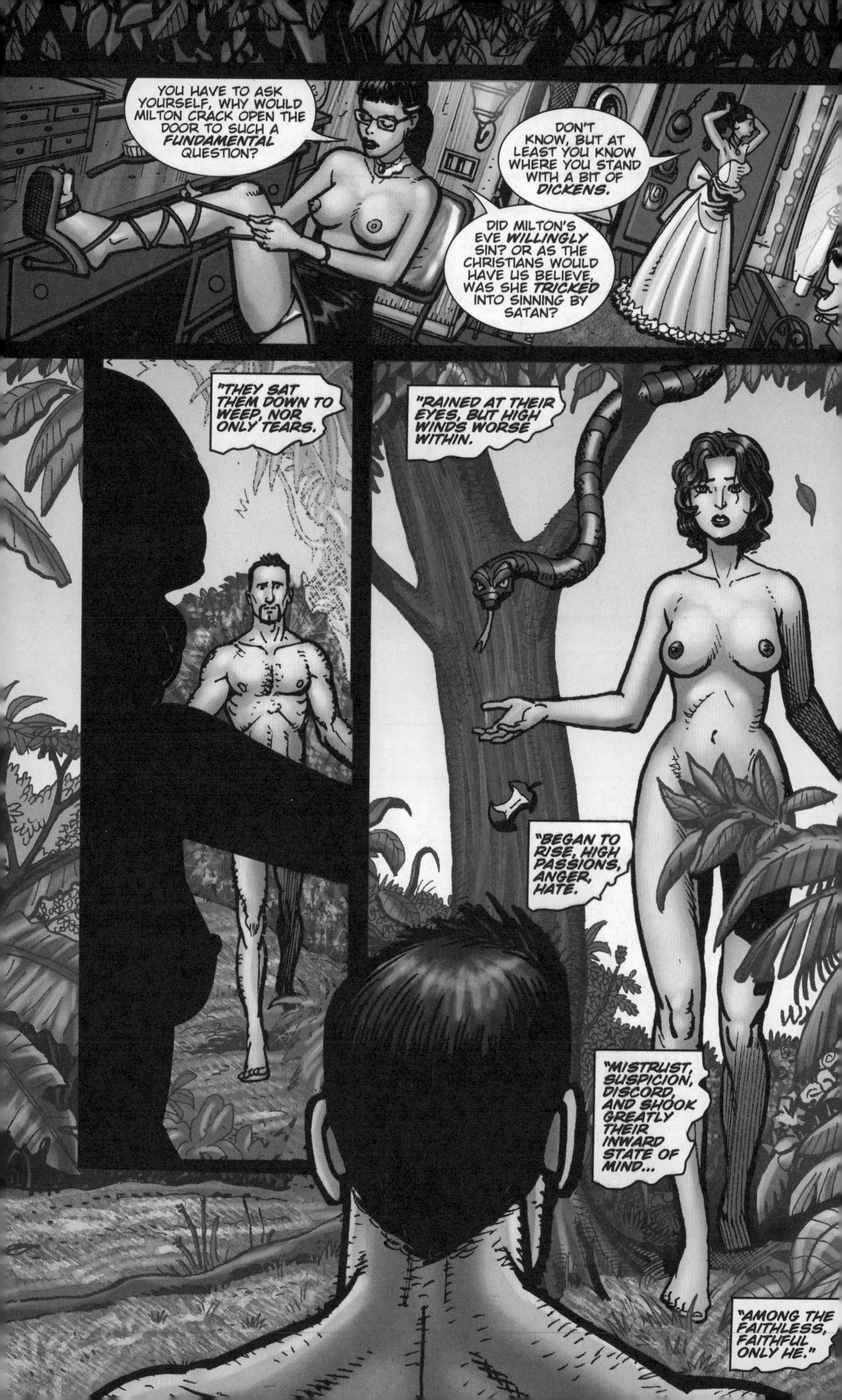

YOU HAVE TO ASK YOURSELF, WHY WOULD MILTON CRACK OPEN THE DOOR TO SUCH A FUNDAMENTAL QUESTION?
DON'T KNOW, BUT AT LEAST YOU KNOW WHERE YOU STAND WITH A BIT OF DICKENS.
DID MILTON'S EVE WILLINGLY SIN? OR AS THE CHRISTIANS WOULD HAVE US BELIEVE, WAS SHE TRICKED INTO SINNING BY SATAN?
"THEY SAT THEM DOWN TO WEEP, NOR ONLY TEARS.
"RAINED AT THEIR EYES, BUT HIGH WINDS WORSE WITHIN.
"BEGAN TO RISE, HIGH PASSIONS, ANGER, HATE.
"MISTRUST, SUSPICION, DISCORD, AND SHOOK GREATLY THEIR INWARD STATE OF MIND...
"AMONG THE FAITHLESS, FAITHFUL ONLY HE."

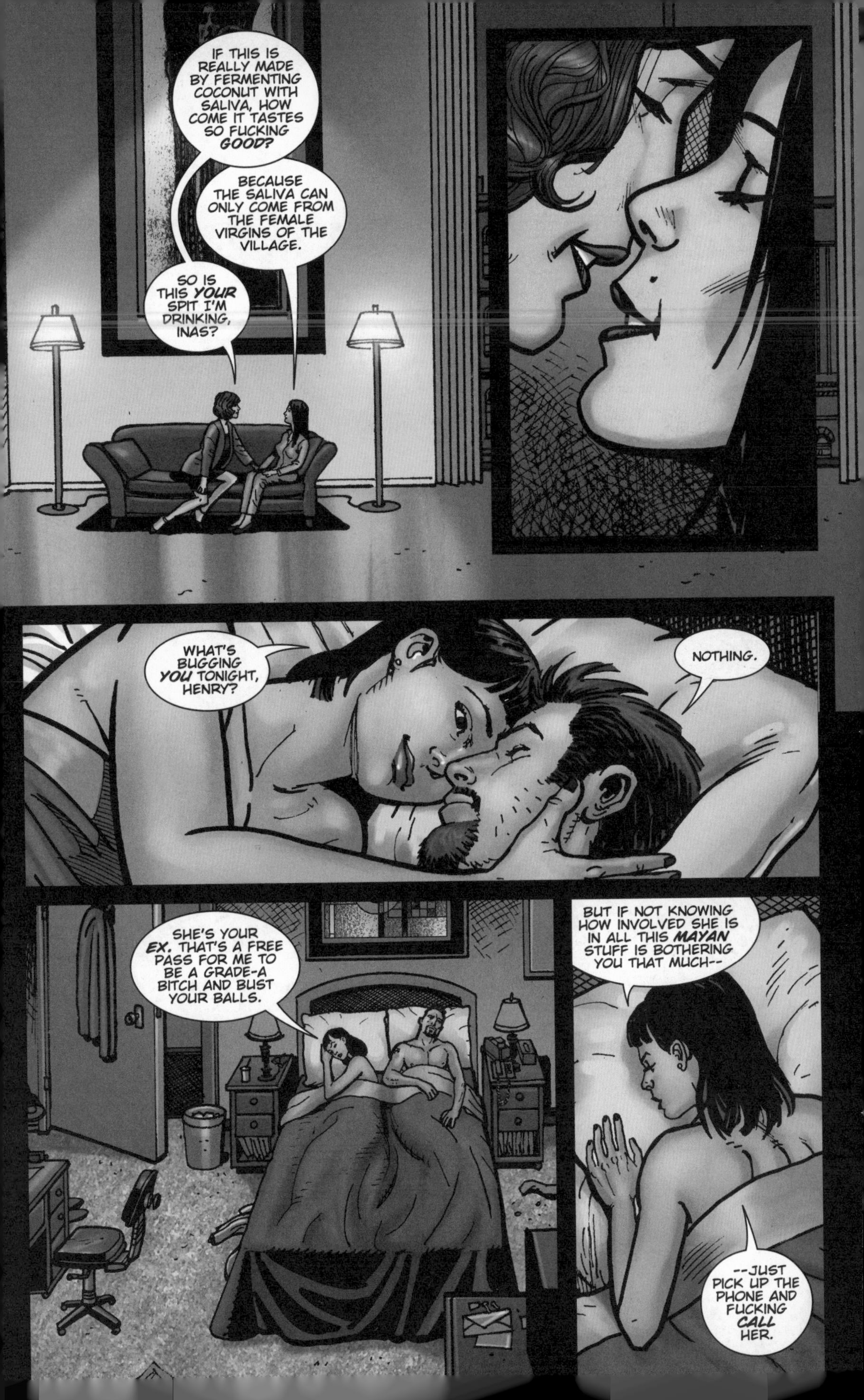
IF THIS IS REALLY MADE BY FERMENTING COCONUT WITH SALIVA, HOW COME IT TASTES SO FUCKING GOOD?
BECAUSE THE SALIVA CAN ONLY COME FROM THE FEMALE VIRGINS OF THE VILLAGE.
SO IS THIS YOUR SPIT I'M DRINKING, INAS?
WHAT'S BUGGING YOU TONIGHT, HENRY?
NOTHING.
SHE'S YOUR EX. THAT'S A FREE PASS FOR ME TO BE A GRADE-A BITCH AND BUST YOUR BALLS.
BUT IF NOT KNOWING HOW INVOLVED SHE IS IN ALL THIS MAYAN STUFF IS BOTHERING YOU THAT MUCH--
--JUST PICK UP THE PHONE AND FUCKING CALL HER.

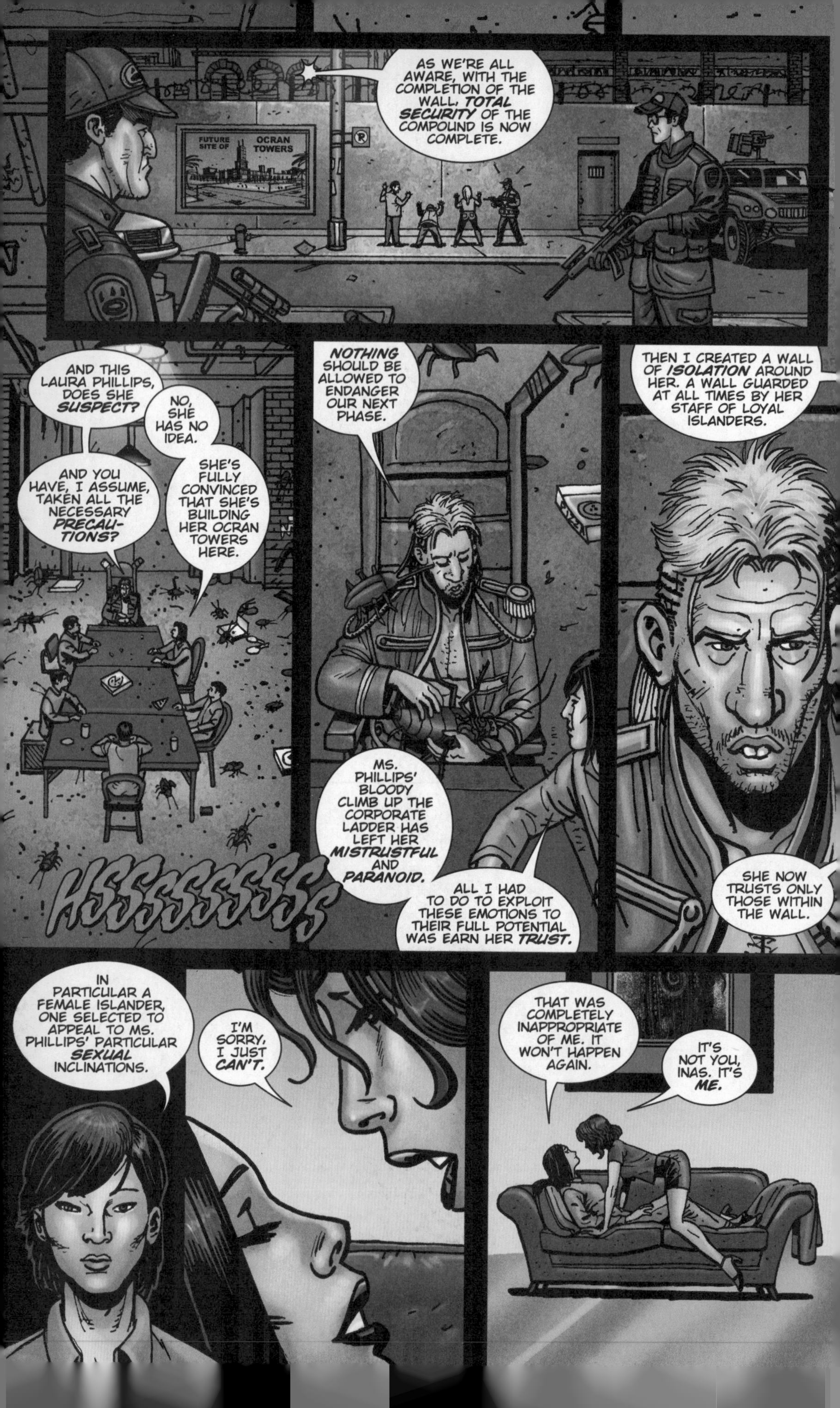
AS WE'RE ALL AWARE, WITH THE COMPLETION OF THE WALL, TOTAL SECURITY OF THE COMPOUND IS NOW COMPLETE.
FUTURE SITE OF OCRAN TOWERS
AND THIS LAURA PHILLIPS, DOES SHE SUSPECT?
NO, SHE HAS NO IDEA.
AND YOU HAVE, I ASSUME, TAKEN ALL THE NECESSARY PRECAUTIONS?
SHE'S FULLY CONVINCED THAT SHE'S BUILDING HER OCRAN TOWERS HERE.
HSSSSSSSSSS
NOTHING SHOULD BE ALLOWED TO ENDANGER OUR NEXT PHASE.
MS. PHILLIPS' BLOODY CLIMB UP THE CORPORATE LADDER HAS LEFT HER MISTRUSTFUL AND PARANOID.
ALL I HAD TO DO TO EXPLOIT THESE EMOTIONS TO THEIR FULL POTENTIAL WAS EARN HER TRUST.
THEN I CREATED A WALL OF ISOLATION AROUND HER. A WALL GUARDED AT ALL TIMES BY HER STAFF OF LOYAL ISLANDERS.
SHE NOW TRUSTS ONLY THOSE WITHIN THE WALL.
IN PARTICULAR A FEMALE ISLANDER, ONE SELECTED TO APPEAL TO MS. PHILLIPS' PARTICULAR SEXUAL INCLINATIONS.
I'M SORRY, I JUST CAN'T.
THAT WAS COMPLETELY INAPPROPRIATE OF ME. IT WON'T HAPPEN AGAIN.
IT'S NOT YOU, INAS. IT'S ME.

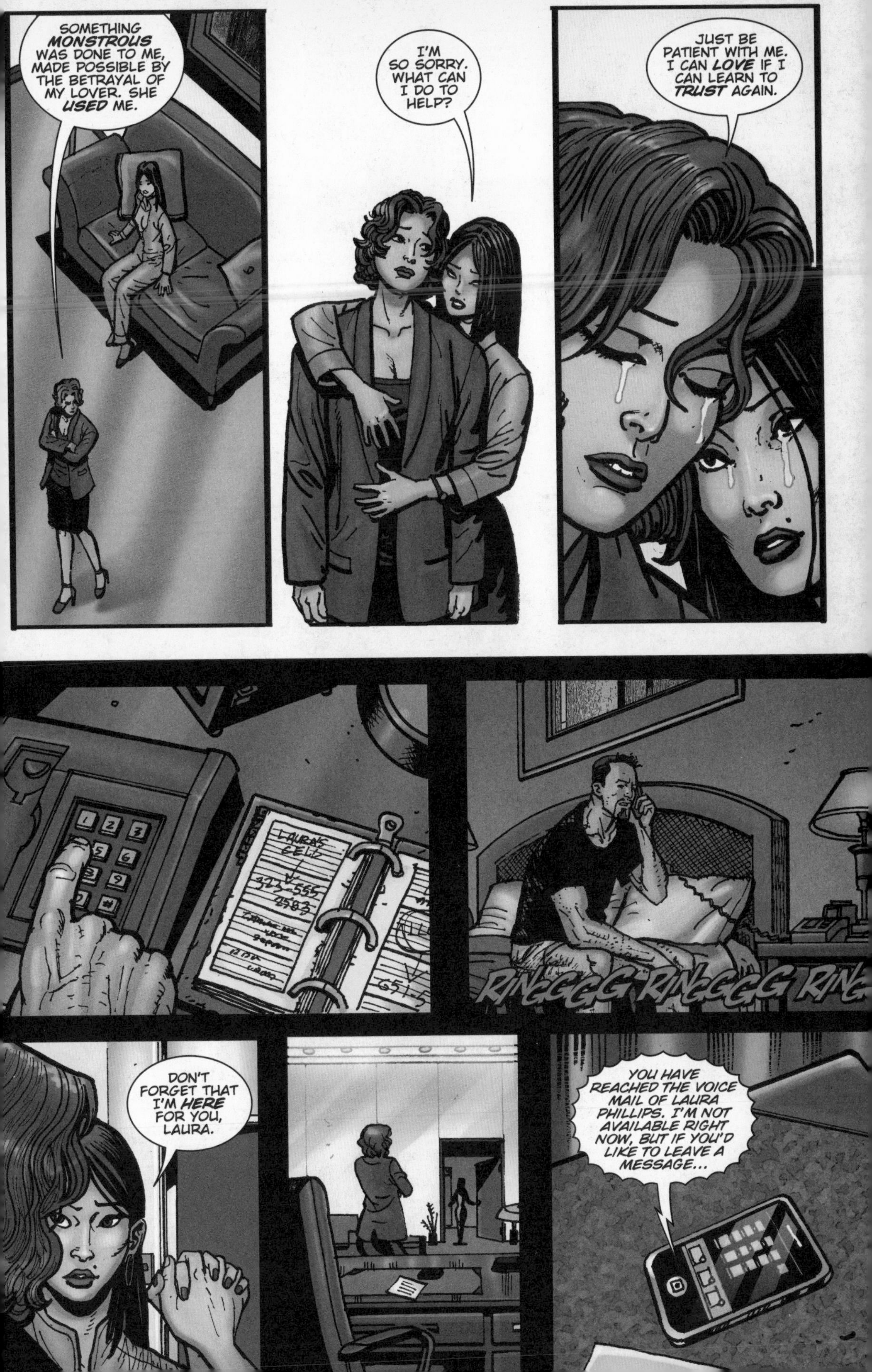
SOMETHING MONSTROUS WAS DONE TO ME, MADE POSSIBLE BY THE BETRAYAL OF MY LOVER. SHE USED ME.
I'M SO SORRY. WHAT CAN I DO TO HELP?
JUST BE PATIENT WITH ME. I CAN LOVE IF I CAN LEARN TO TRUST AGAIN.
LAURA'S CELL
RINGGGG RINGGGG RING
DON'T FORGET THAT I'M HERE FOR YOU, LAURA.
YOU HAVE REACHED THE VOICE MAIL OF LAURA PHILLIPS. I'M NOT AVAILABLE RIGHT NOW, BUT IF YOU'D LIKE TO LEAVE A MESSAGE...

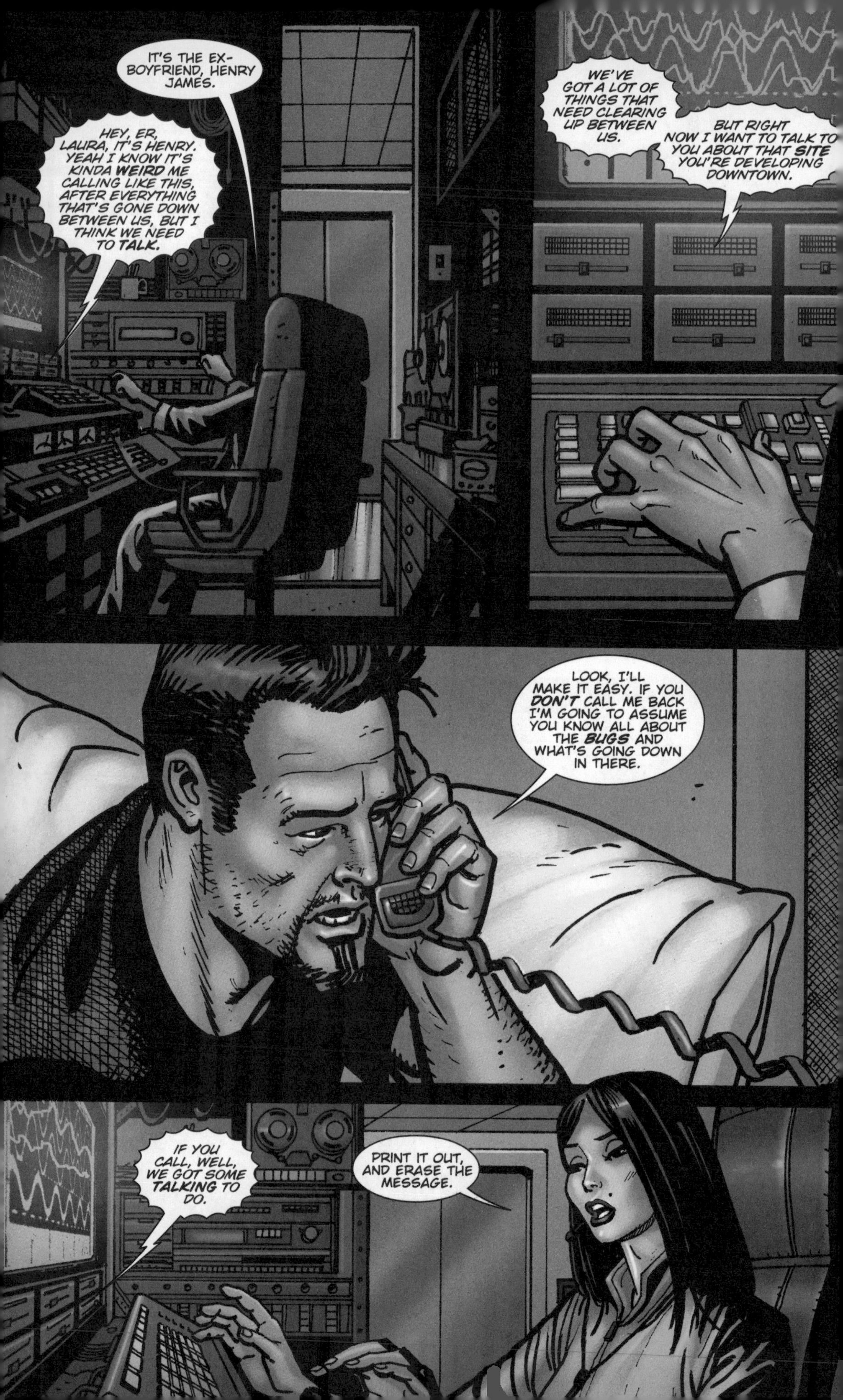
IT'S THE EX-BOYFRIEND, HENRY JAMES.
HEY, ER, LAURA, IT'S HENRY. YEAH I KNOW IT'S KINDA WEIRD ME CALLING LIKE THIS, AFTER EVERYTHING THAT'S GONE DOWN BETWEEN US, BUT I THINK WE NEED TO TALK.
WE'VE GOT A LOT OF THINGS THAT NEED CLEARING UP BETWEEN US.
BUT RIGHT NOW I WANT TO TALK TO YOU ABOUT THAT SITE YOU'RE DEVELOPING DOWNTOWN.
LOOK, I'LL MAKE IT EASY. IF YOU DON'T CALL ME BACK I'M GOING TO ASSUME YOU KNOW ALL ABOUT THE BUGS AND WHAT'S GOING DOWN IN THERE.
IF YOU CALL, WELL, WE GOT SOME TALKING TO DO.
PRINT IT OUT, AND ERASE THE MESSAGE.

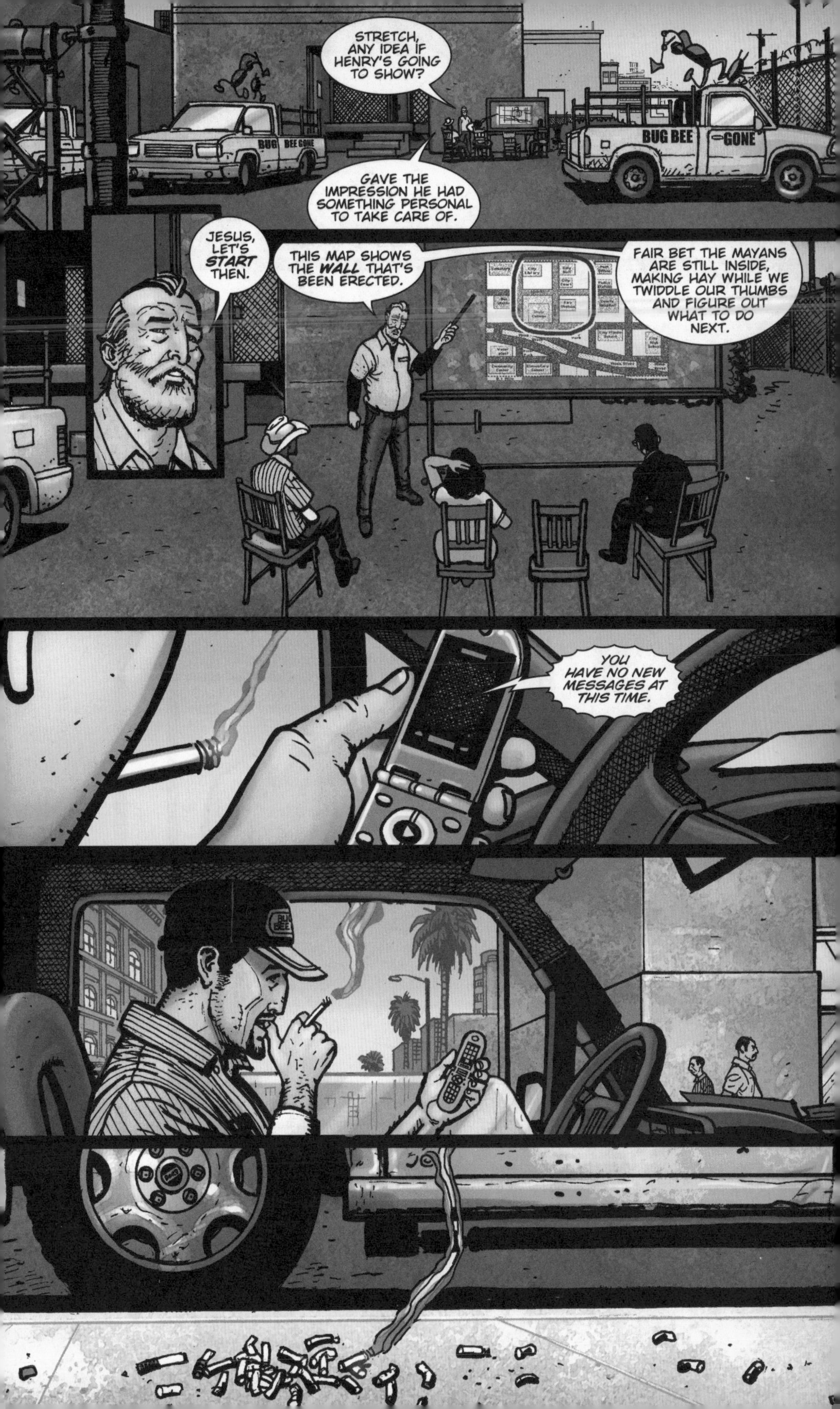

BUG BEE GONE
STRETCH, ANY IDEA IF HENRY'S GOING TO SHOW?
BUG BEE GONE
GAVE THE IMPRESSION HE HAD SOMETHING PERSONAL TO TAKE CARE OF.
JESUS, LET'S START THEN.
THIS MAP SHOWS THE WALL THAT'S BEEN ERECTED.
FAIR BET THE MAYANS ARE STILL INSIDE, MAKING HAY WHILE WE TWIDDLE OUR THUMBS AND FIGURE OUT WHAT TO DO NEXT.
YOU HAVE NO NEW MESSAGES AT THIS TIME.

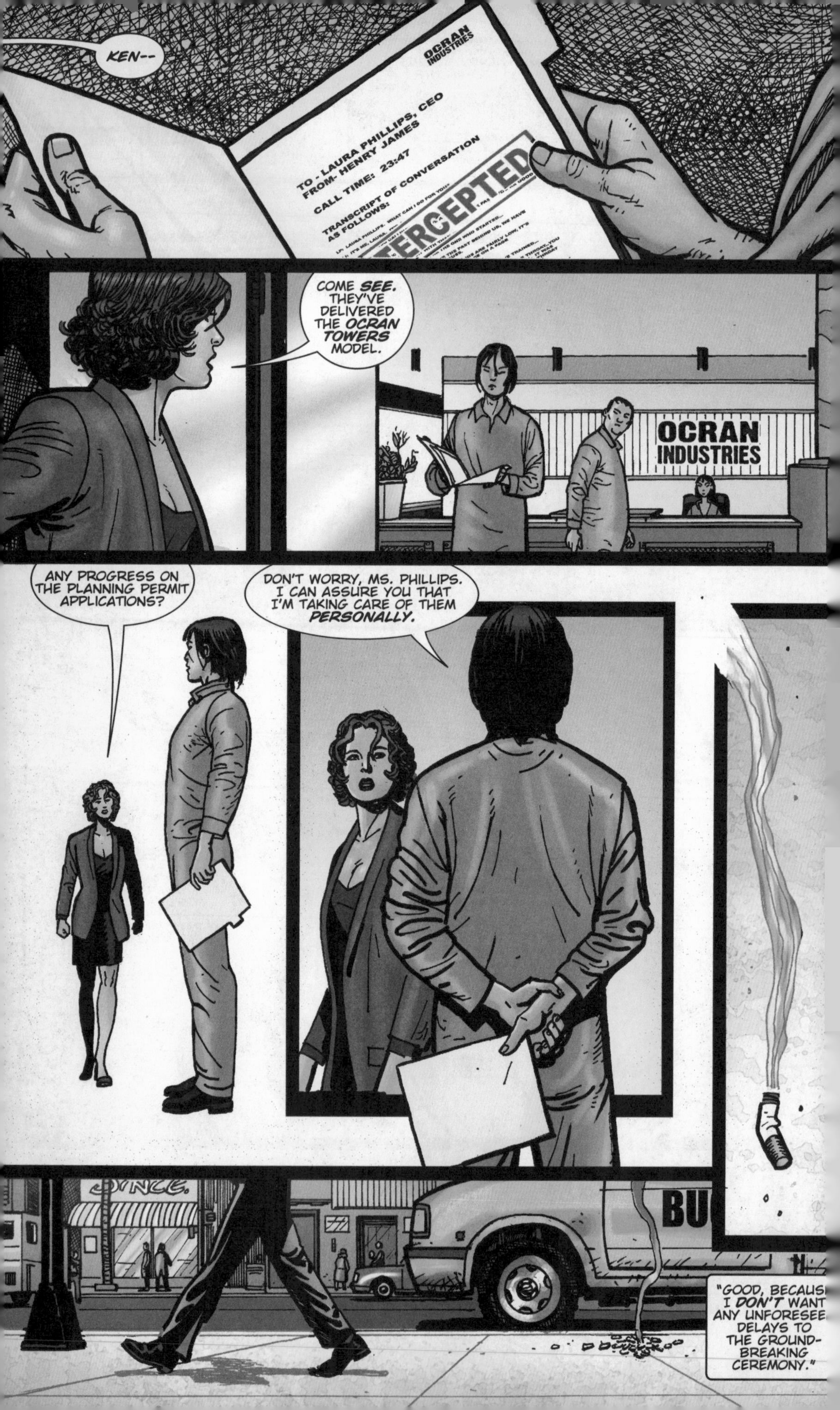
KEN--
OCRAN INDUSTRIES
TO - LAURA PHILLIPS, CEO
FROM- HENRY JAMES
CALL TIME: 23:47
TRANSCRIPT OF CONVERSATION AS FOLLOWS:
TERCEPTED
COME SEE. THEY'VE DELIVERED THE OCRAN TOWERS MODEL.
OCRAN INDUSTRIES
ANY PROGRESS ON THE PLANNING PERMIT APPLICATIONS?
DON'T WORRY, MS. PHILLIPS. I CAN ASSURE YOU THAT I'M TAKING CARE OF THEM PERSONALLY.
BU
"GOOD, BECAUS I DON'T WANT ANY UNFORESEE DELAYS TO THE GROUND-BREAKING CEREMONY."

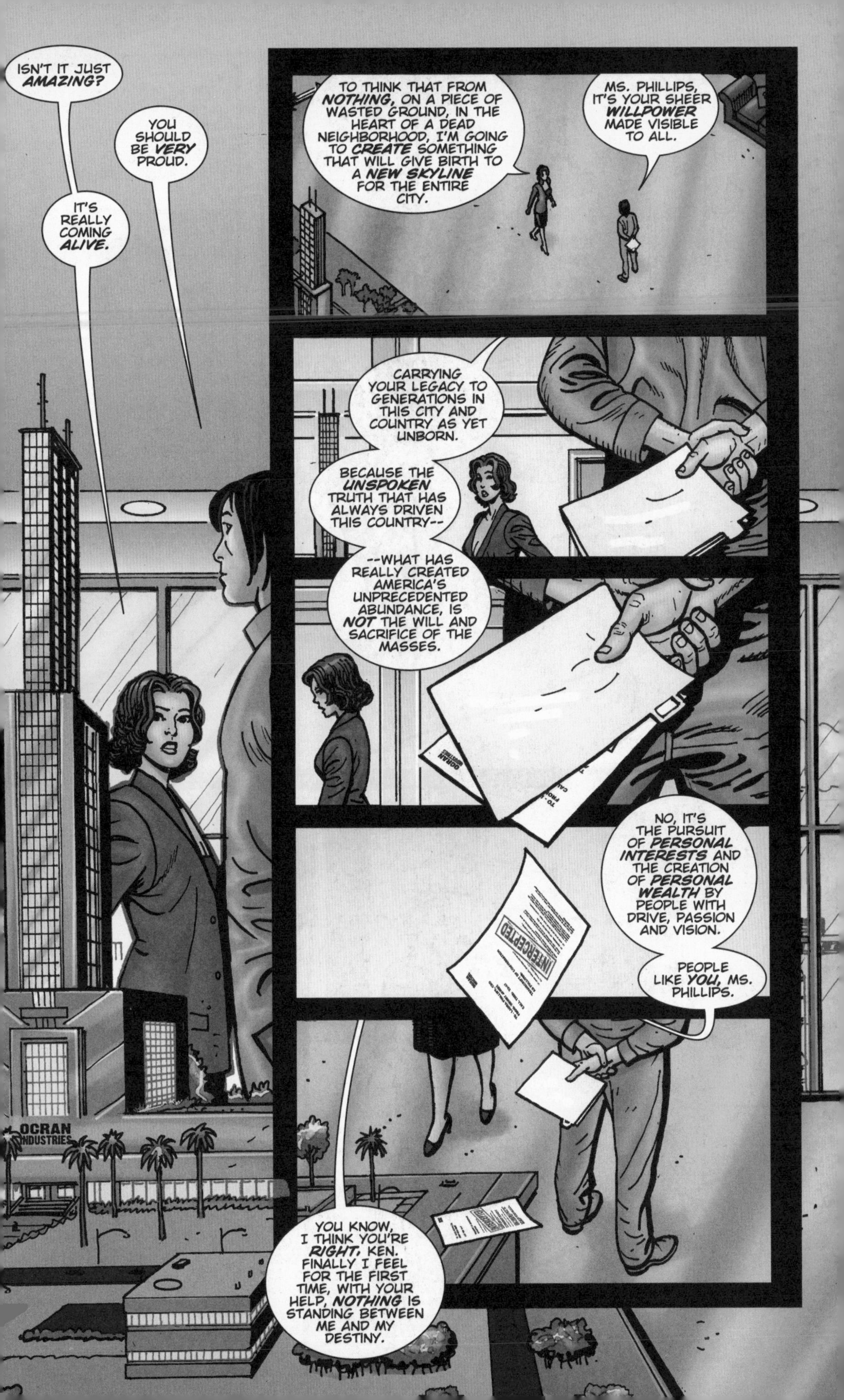
ISN'T IT JUST *AMAZING?*
YOU SHOULD BE *VERY* PROUD.
IT'S REALLY COMING *ALIVE.*
TO THINK THAT FROM *NOTHING,* ON A PIECE OF WASTED GROUND, IN THE HEART OF A DEAD NEIGHBORHOOD, I'M GOING TO *CREATE* SOMETHING THAT WILL GIVE BIRTH TO A *NEW SKYLINE* FOR THE ENTIRE CITY.
MS. PHILLIPS, IT'S YOUR SHEER *WILLPOWER* MADE VISIBLE TO ALL.
CARRYING YOUR LEGACY TO GENERATIONS IN THIS CITY AND COUNTRY AS YET UNBORN.
BECAUSE THE *UNSPOKEN* TRUTH THAT HAS ALWAYS DRIVEN THIS COUNTRY--
--WHAT HAS REALLY CREATED AMERICA'S UNPRECEDENTED ABUNDANCE, IS *NOT* THE WILL AND SACRIFICE OF THE MASSES.
NO, IT'S THE PURSUIT OF *PERSONAL INTERESTS* AND THE CREATION OF *PERSONAL WEALTH* BY PEOPLE WITH DRIVE, PASSION AND VISION.
PEOPLE LIKE *YOU,* MS. PHILLIPS.
YOU KNOW, I THINK YOU'RE *RIGHT,* KEN. FINALLY I FEEL FOR THE FIRST TIME, WITH YOUR HELP, *NOTHING* IS STANDING BETWEEN ME AND MY DESTINY.
OCRAN INDUSTRIES
INTERCEPTED

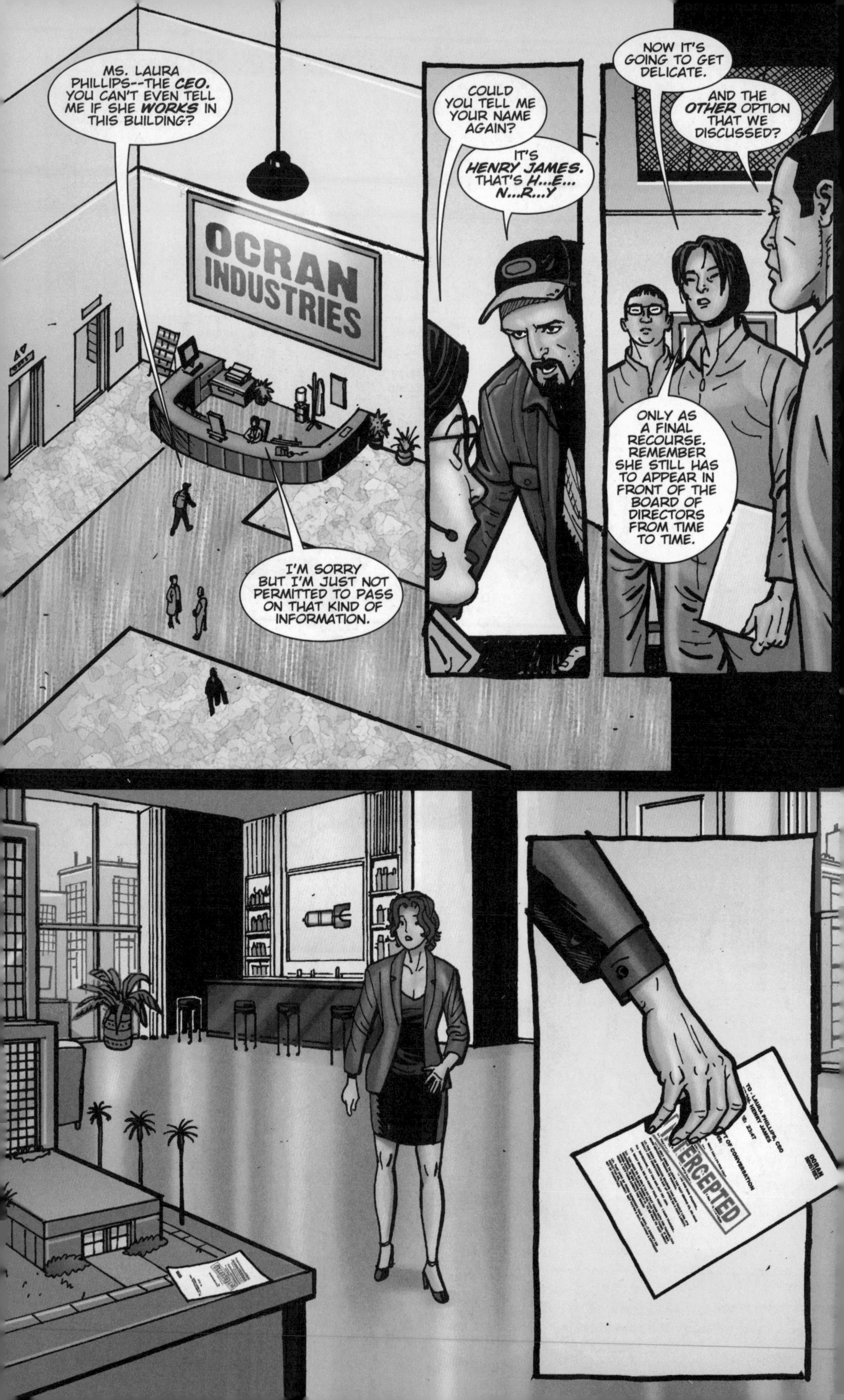
MS. LAURA PHILLIPS--THE CEO. YOU CAN'T EVEN TELL ME IF SHE WORKS IN THIS BUILDING?
OCRAN INDUSTRIES
I'M SORRY BUT I'M JUST NOT PERMITTED TO PASS ON THAT KIND OF INFORMATION.
COULD YOU TELL ME YOUR NAME AGAIN?
IT'S HENRY JAMES. THAT'S H...E... N...R...Y
NOW IT'S GOING TO GET DELICATE.
AND THE OTHER OPTION THAT WE DISCUSSED?
ONLY AS A FINAL RECOURSE. REMEMBER SHE STILL HAS TO APPEAR IN FRONT OF THE BOARD OF DIRECTORS FROM TIME TO TIME.

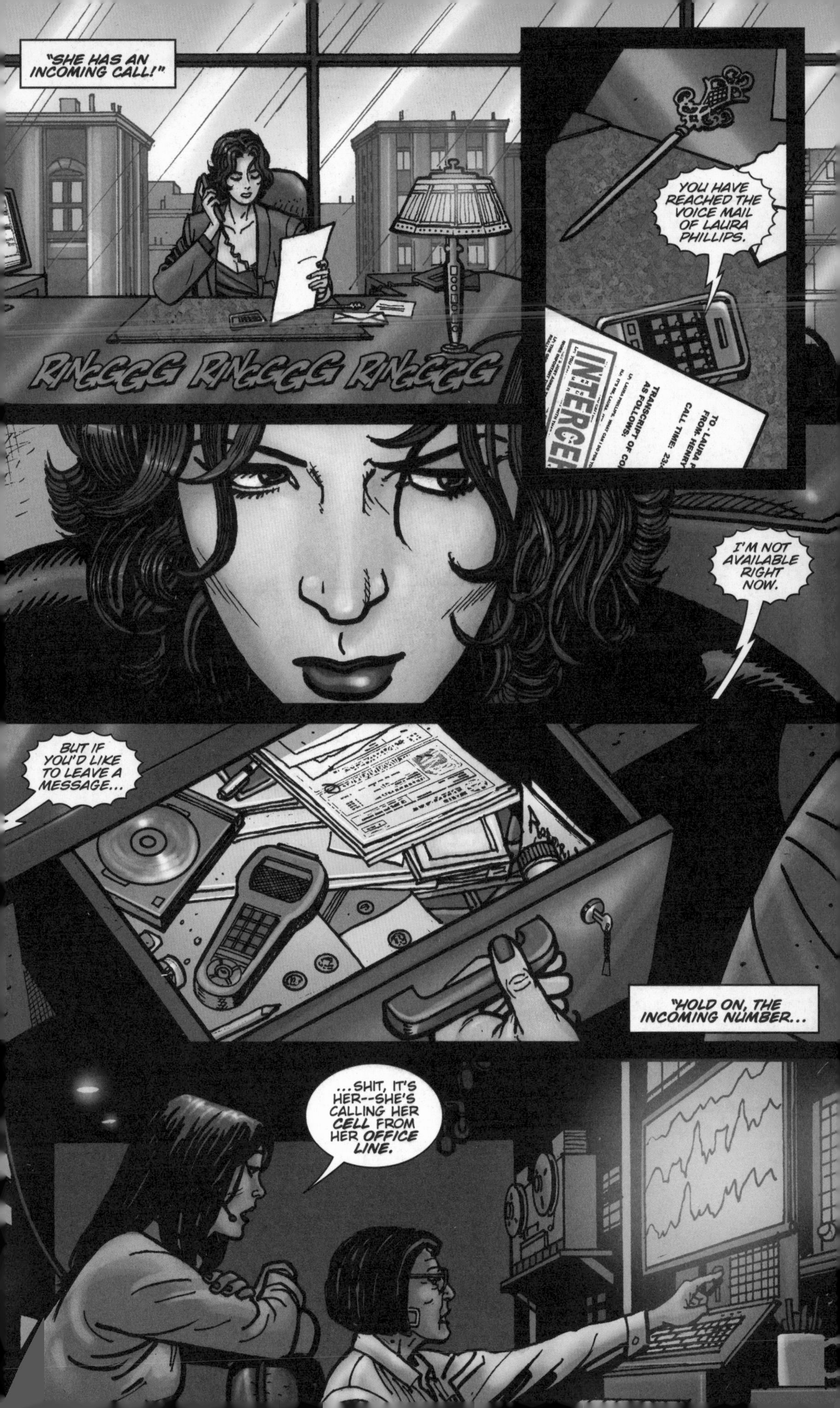
"SHE HAS AN INCOMING CALL!"
RINGGGG RINGGGG RINGGGG
YOU HAVE REACHED THE VOICE MAIL OF LAURA PHILLIPS.
INTERCEP
TO: LAURA
FROM: HENRY
CALL TIME: 23:
TRANSCRIPT OF CO
AS FOLLOWS:
I'M NOT AVAILABLE RIGHT NOW.
BUT IF YOU'D LIKE TO LEAVE A MESSAGE...
"HOLD ON, THE INCOMING NUMBER...
...SHIT, IT'S HER--SHE'S CALLING HER CELL FROM HER OFFICE LINE.

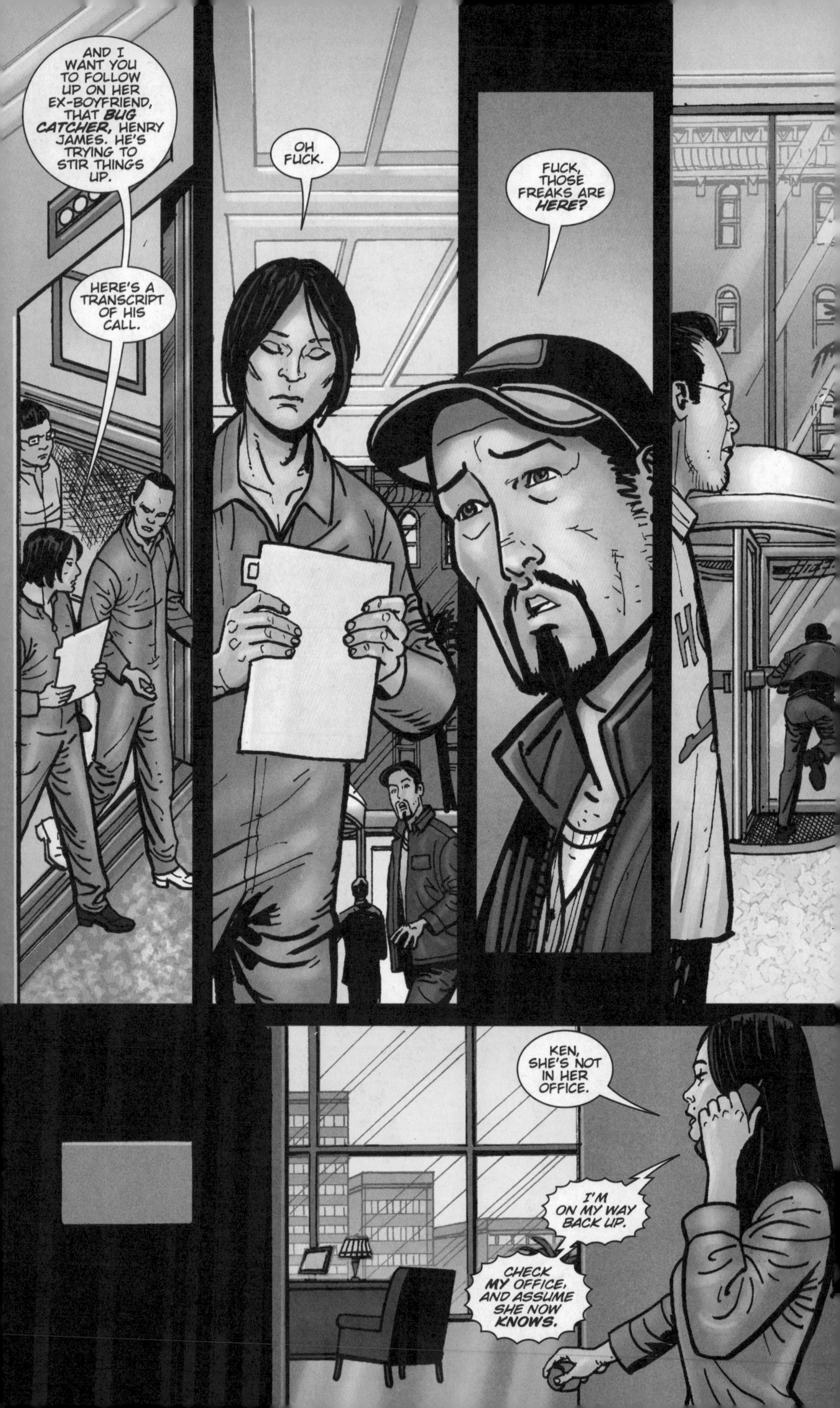
AND I WANT YOU TO FOLLOW UP ON HER EX-BOYFRIEND, THAT BUG CATCHER, HENRY JAMES. HE'S TRYING TO STIR THINGS UP.
HERE'S A TRANSCRIPT OF HIS CALL.
OH FUCK.
FUCK, THOSE FREAKS ARE HERE?
KEN, SHE'S NOT IN HER OFFICE.
I'M ON MY WAY BACK UP.
CHECK MY OFFICE, AND ASSUME SHE NOW KNOWS.

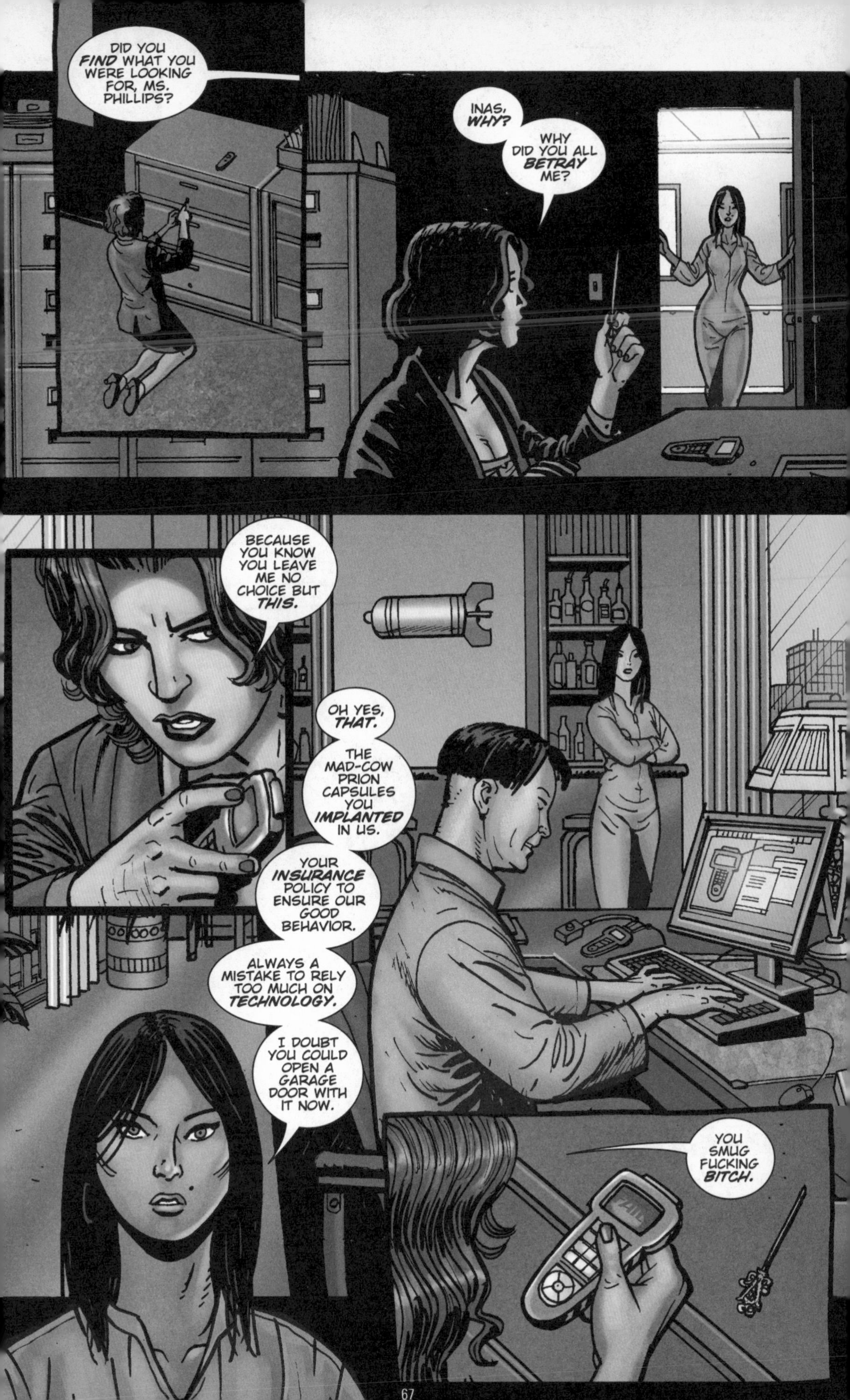

DID YOU FIND WHAT YOU WERE LOOKING FOR, MS. PHILLIPS?
INAS, WHY?
WHY DID YOU ALL BETRAY ME?
BECAUSE YOU KNOW YOU LEAVE ME NO CHOICE BUT THIS.
OH YES, THAT.
THE MAD-COW PRION CAPSULES YOU IMPLANTED IN US.
YOUR INSURANCE POLICY TO ENSURE OUR GOOD BEHAVIOR.
ALWAYS A MISTAKE TO RELY TOO MUCH ON TECHNOLOGY.
I DOUBT YOU COULD OPEN A GARAGE DOOR WITH IT NOW.
YOU SMUG FUCKING BITCH.

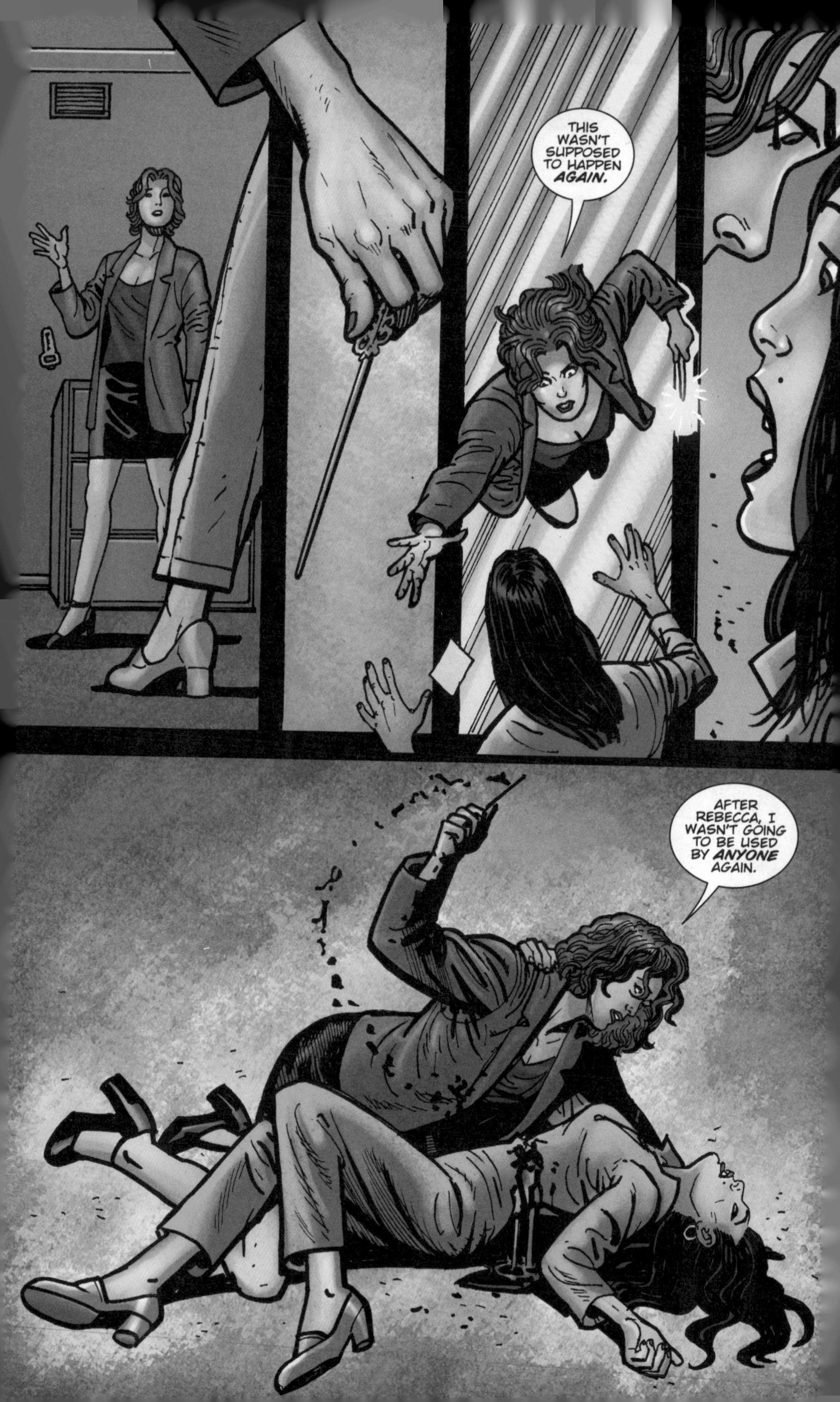
THIS WASN'T SUPPOSED TO HAPPEN *AGAIN.*
AFTER REBECCA, I WASN'T GOING TO BE USED BY *ANYONE* AGAIN.

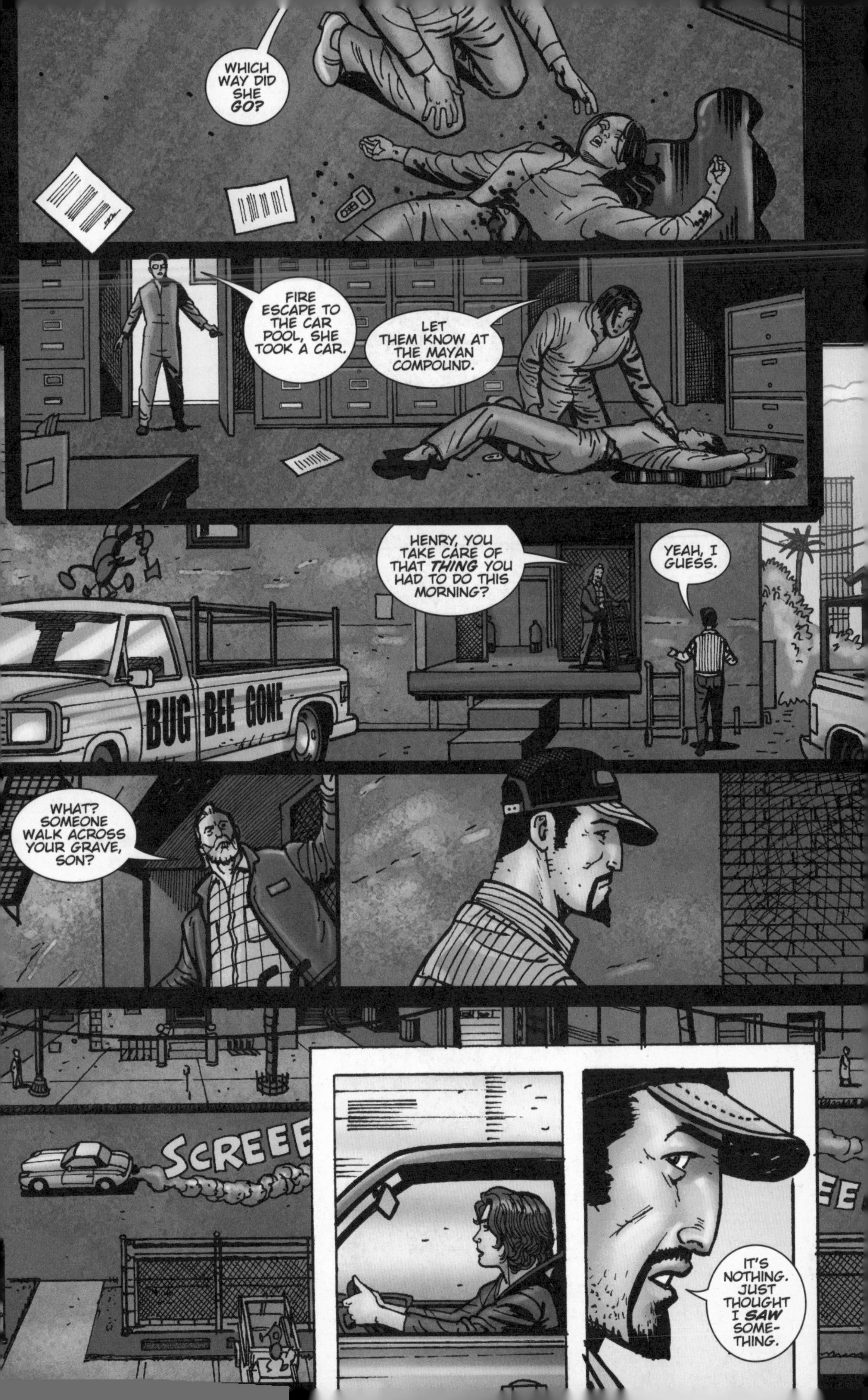
WHICH WAY DID SHE GO?
FIRE ESCAPE TO THE CAR POOL, SHE TOOK A CAR.
LET THEM KNOW AT THE MAYAN COMPOUND.
HENRY, YOU TAKE CARE OF THAT THING YOU HAD TO DO THIS MORNING?
YEAH, I GUESS.
BUG BEE GONE
WHAT? SOMEONE WALK ACROSS YOUR GRAVE, SON?
SCREEE
EE
IT'S NOTHING. JUST THOUGHT I SAW SOME-THING.

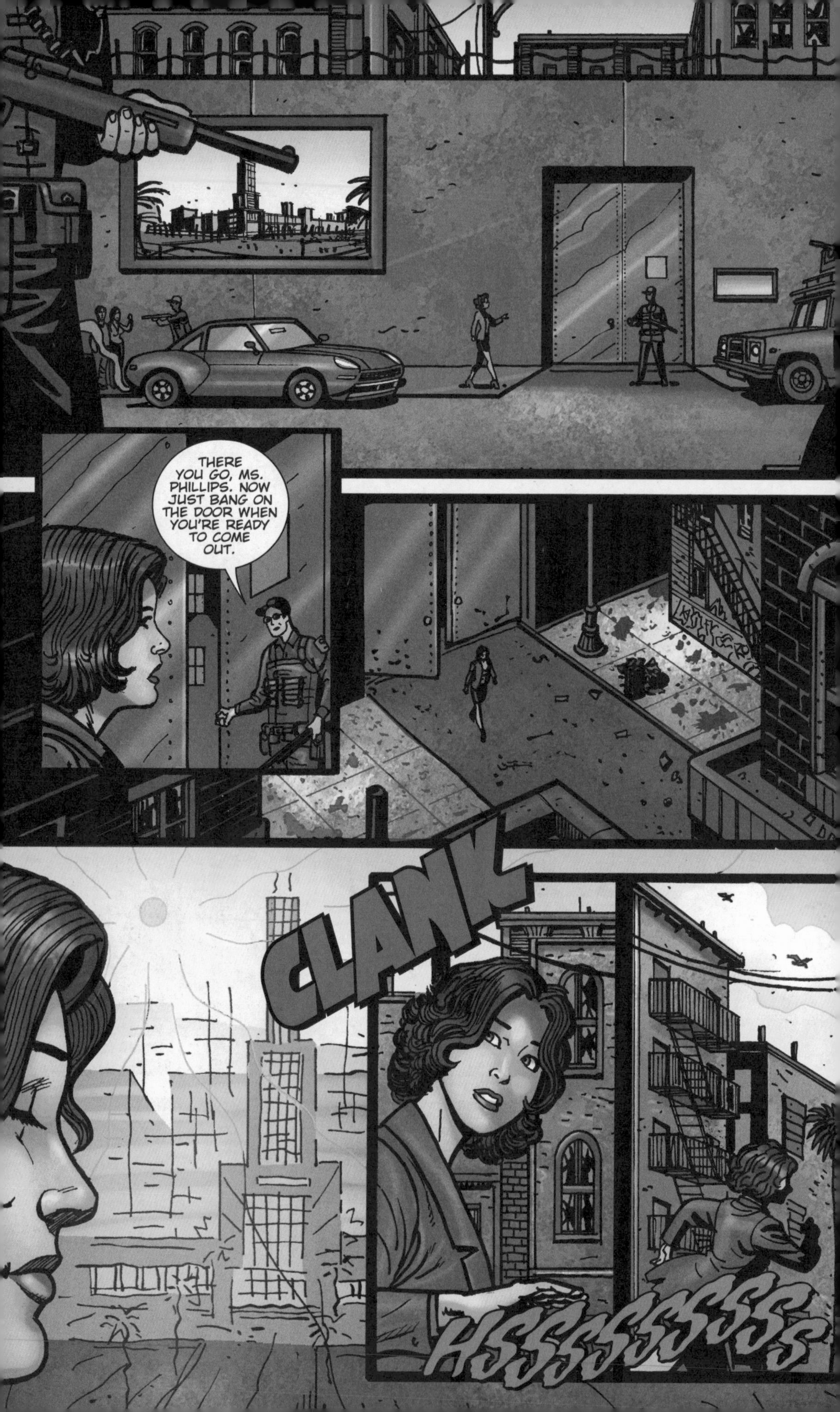
THERE YOU GO, MS. PHILLIPS. NOW JUST BANG ON THE DOOR WHEN YOU'RE READY TO COME OUT.
CLANK
HSSSSSSSSS

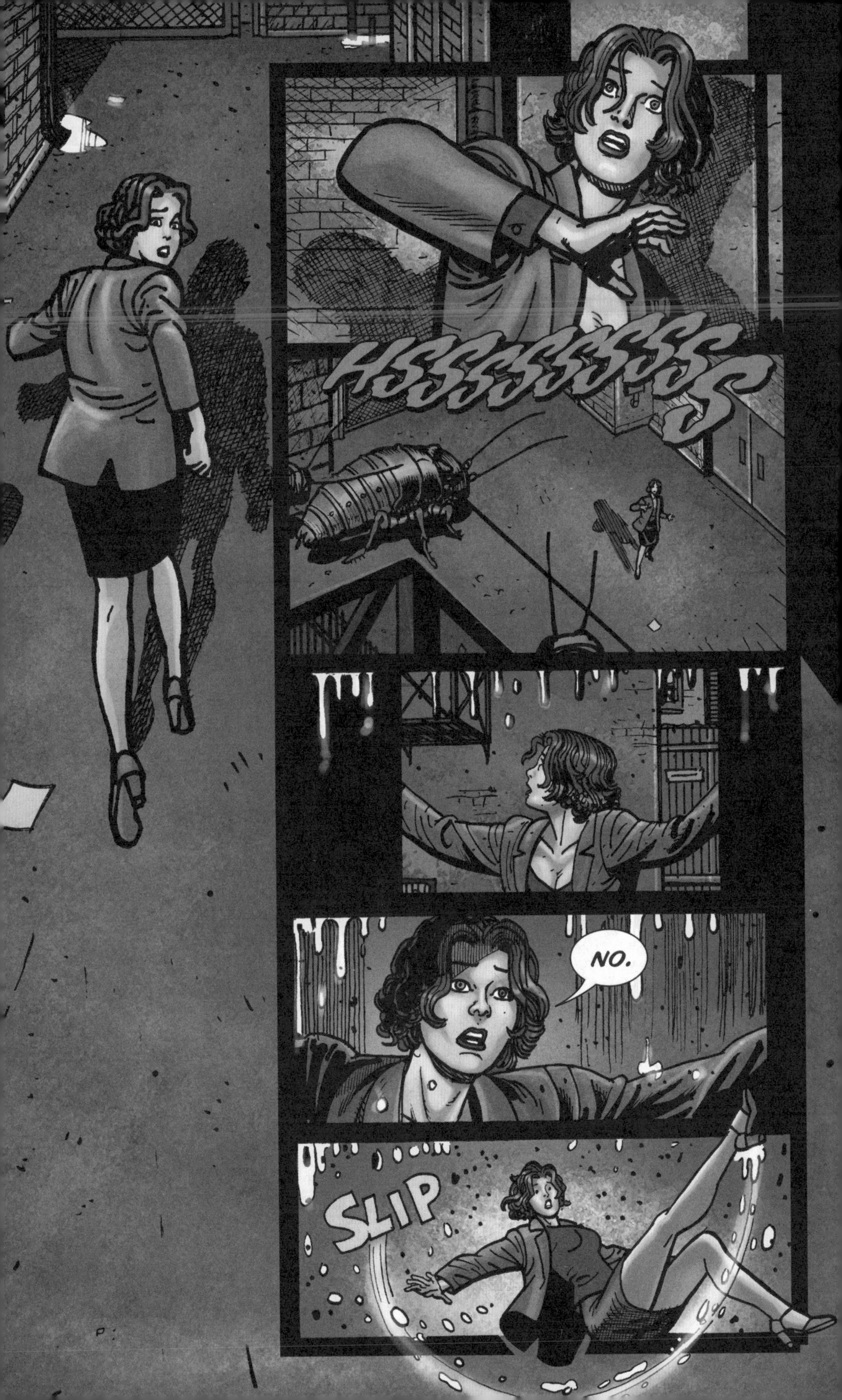
HSSSSSSSSSS
NO.
SLIP

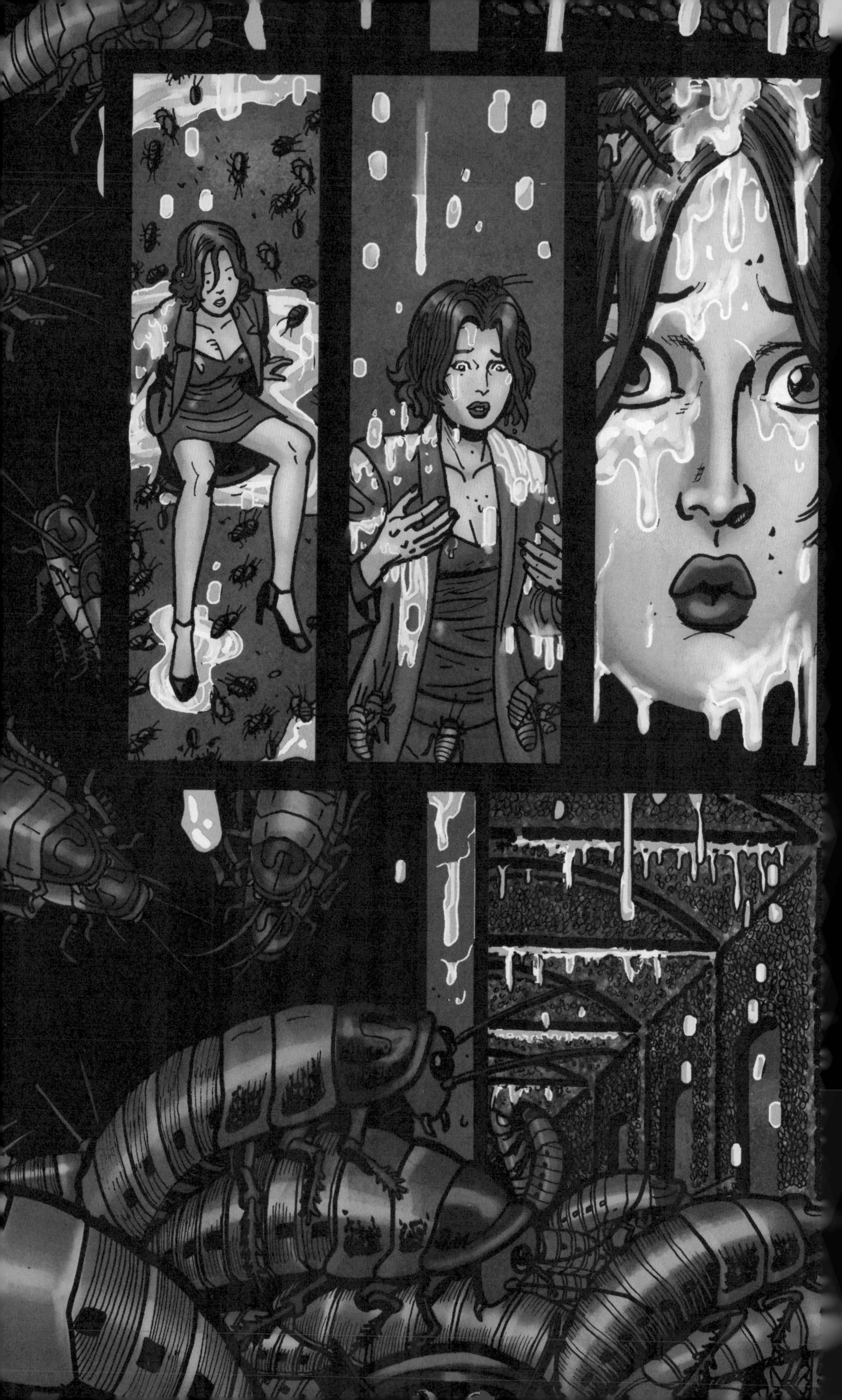

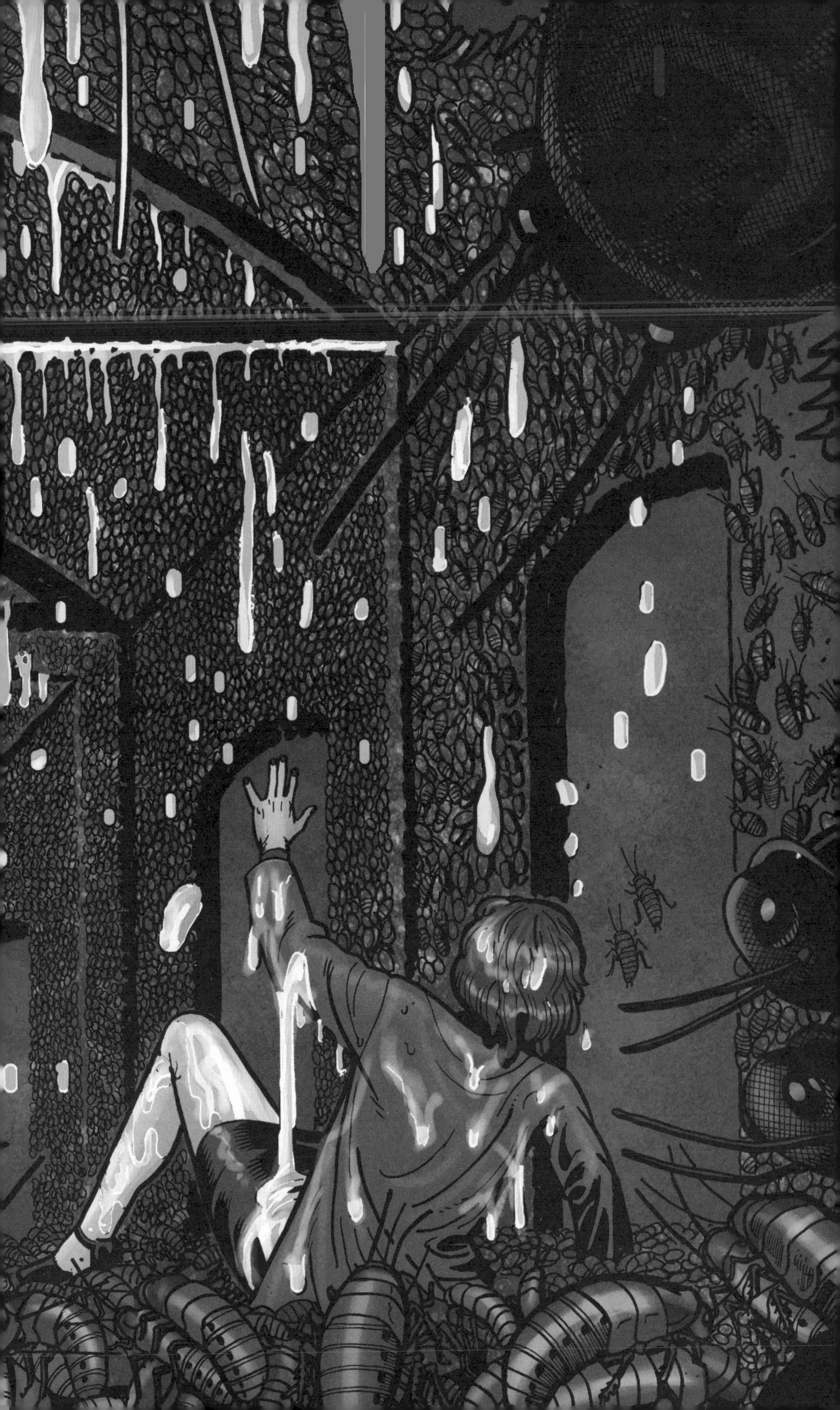

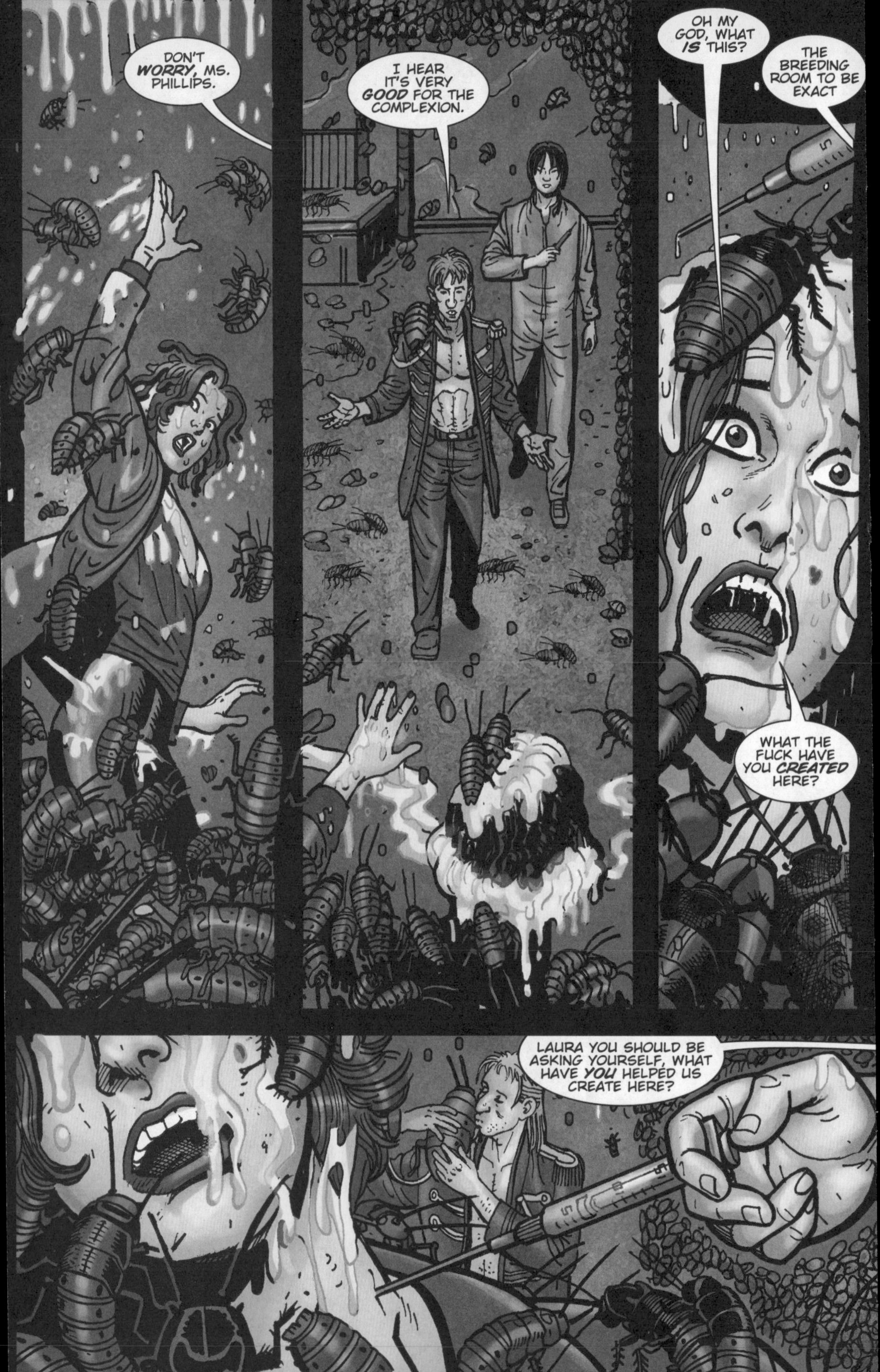
DON'T WORRY, MS. PHILLIPS.
I HEAR IT'S VERY GOOD FOR THE COMPLEXION.
OH MY GOD, WHAT IS THIS?
THE BREEDING ROOM TO BE EXACT
WHAT THE FUCK HAVE YOU CREATED HERE?
LAURA YOU SHOULD BE ASKING YOURSELF, WHAT HAVE YOU HELPED US CREATE HERE?

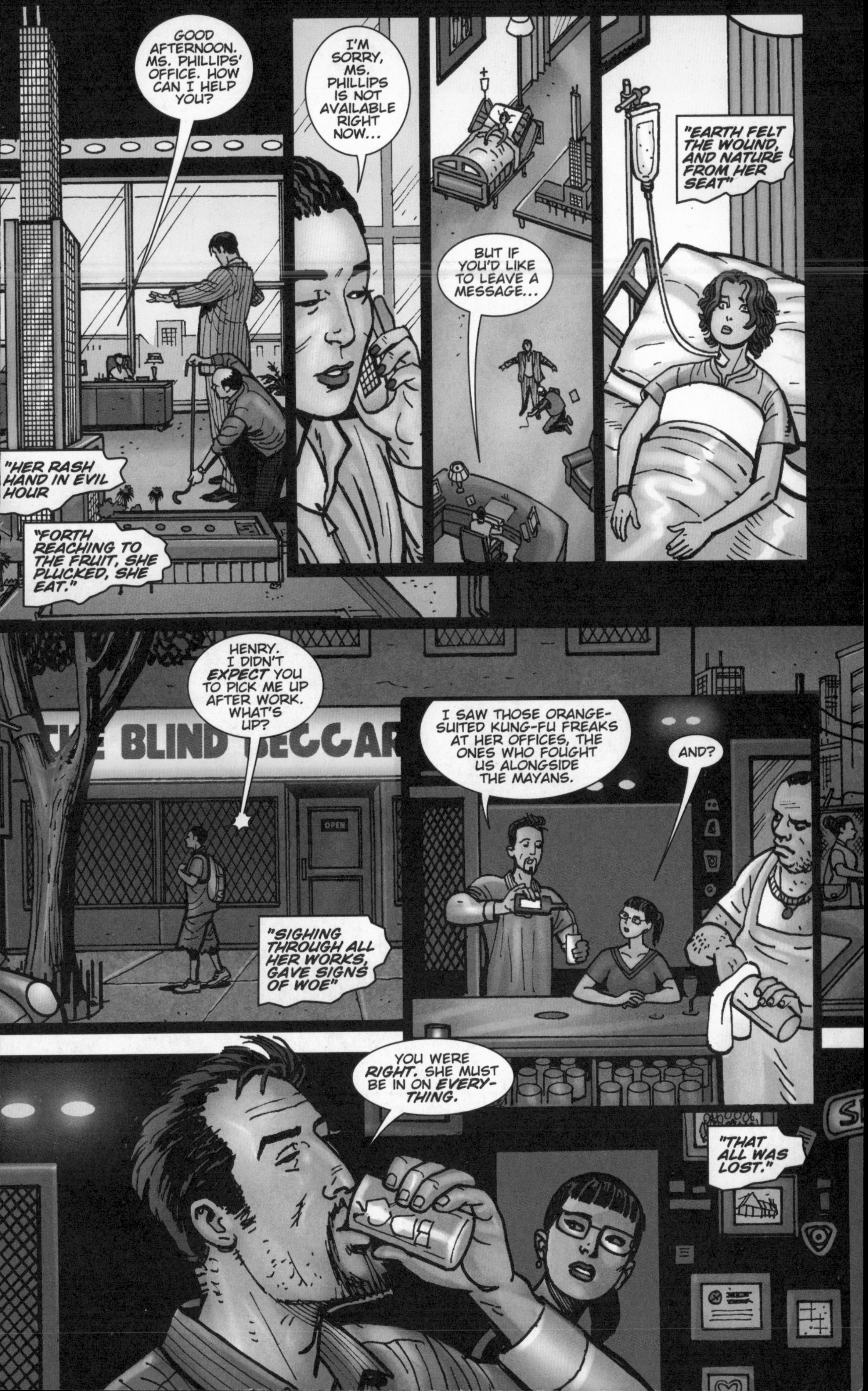
GOOD AFTERNOON. MS. PHILLIPS' OFFICE. HOW CAN I HELP YOU?
"HER RASH HAND IN EVIL HOUR
"FORTH REACHING TO THE FRUIT, SHE PLUCKED, SHE EAT."
I'M SORRY, MS. PHILLIPS IS NOT AVAILABLE RIGHT NOW...
BUT IF YOU'D LIKE TO LEAVE A MESSAGE...
"EARTH FELT THE WOUND, AND NATURE FROM HER SEAT"
THE BLIND BEGGAR
OPEN
HENRY. I DIDN'T EXPECT YOU TO PICK ME UP AFTER WORK. WHAT'S UP?
"SIGHING THROUGH ALL HER WORKS, GAVE SIGNS OF WOE"
I SAW THOSE ORANGE-SUITED KUNG-FU FREAKS AT HER OFFICES, THE ONES WHO FOUGHT US ALONGSIDE THE MAYANS.
AND?
YOU WERE RIGHT. SHE MUST BE IN ON EVERY-THING.
"THAT ALL WAS LOST."

RAISING CHÉ   cover art by TONY MOORE

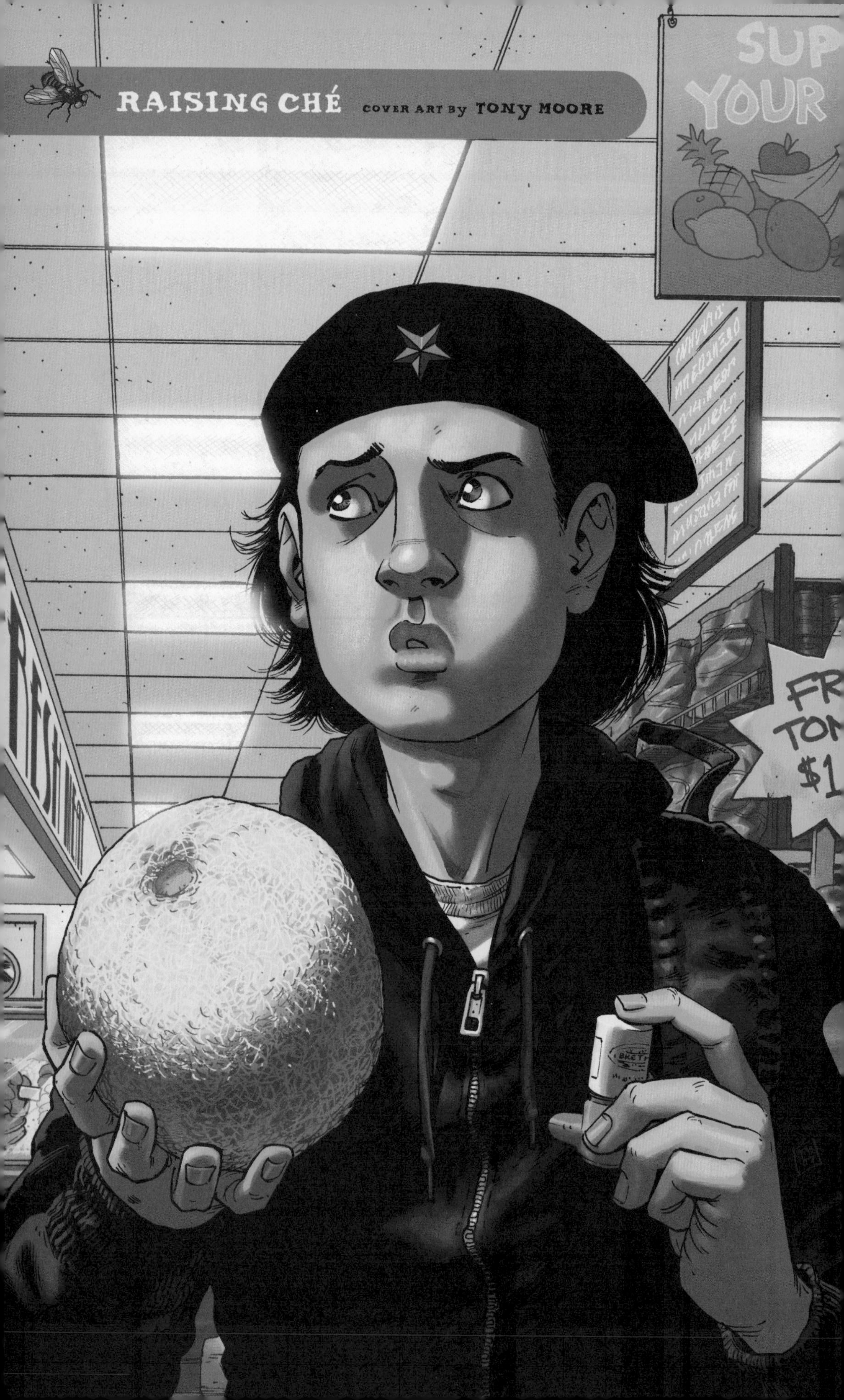
SUP
YOUR
FR
TON
$1

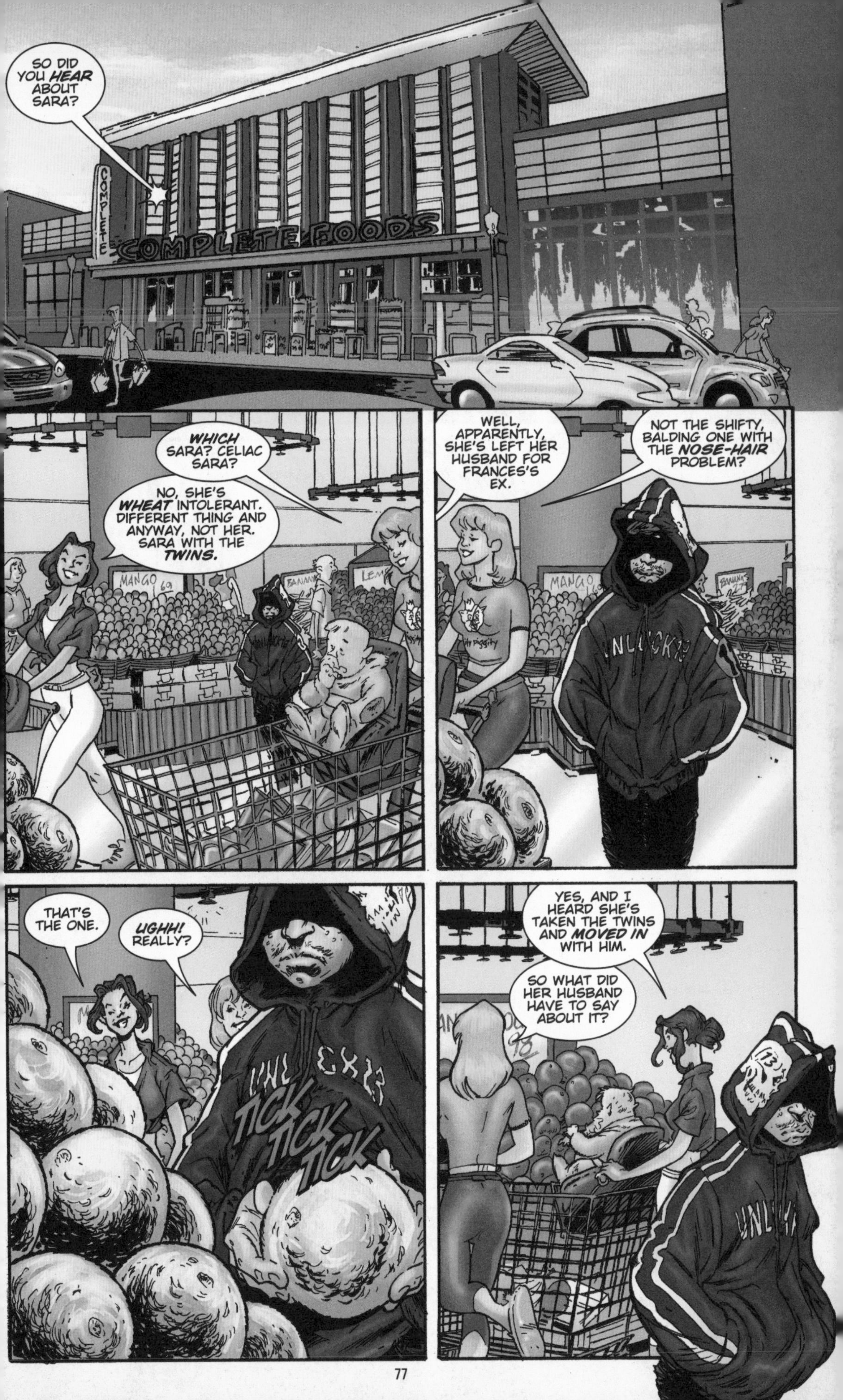
SO DID YOU HEAR ABOUT SARA?
COMPLETE
COMPLETE FOODS
WHICH SARA? CELIAC SARA?
NO, SHE'S WHEAT INTOLERANT. DIFFERENT THING AND ANYWAY, NOT HER. SARA WITH THE TWINS.
MANGO
WELL, APPARENTLY, SHE'S LEFT HER HUSBAND FOR FRANCES'S EX.
NOT THE SHIFTY, BALDING ONE WITH THE NOSE-HAIR PROBLEM?
THAT'S THE ONE.
UGHH! REALLY?
TICK TICK TICK
YES, AND I HEARD SHE'S TAKEN THE TWINS AND MOVED IN WITH HIM.
SO WHAT DID HER HUSBAND HAVE TO SAY ABOUT IT?

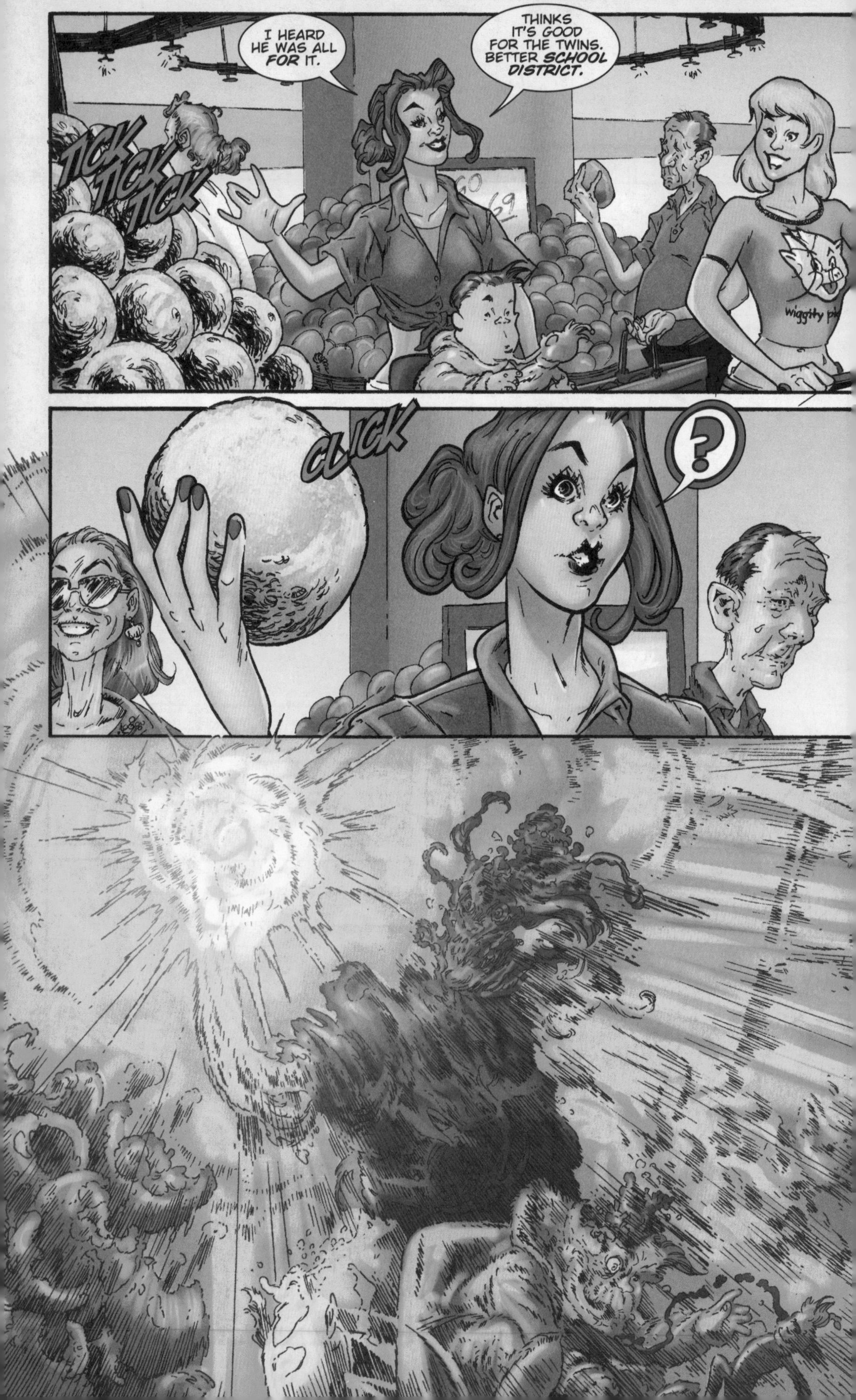
I HEARD HE WAS ALL FOR IT.
THINKS IT'S GOOD FOR THE TWINS. BETTER SCHOOL DISTRICT.
TICK TICK TICK
wiggity
CLICK
?

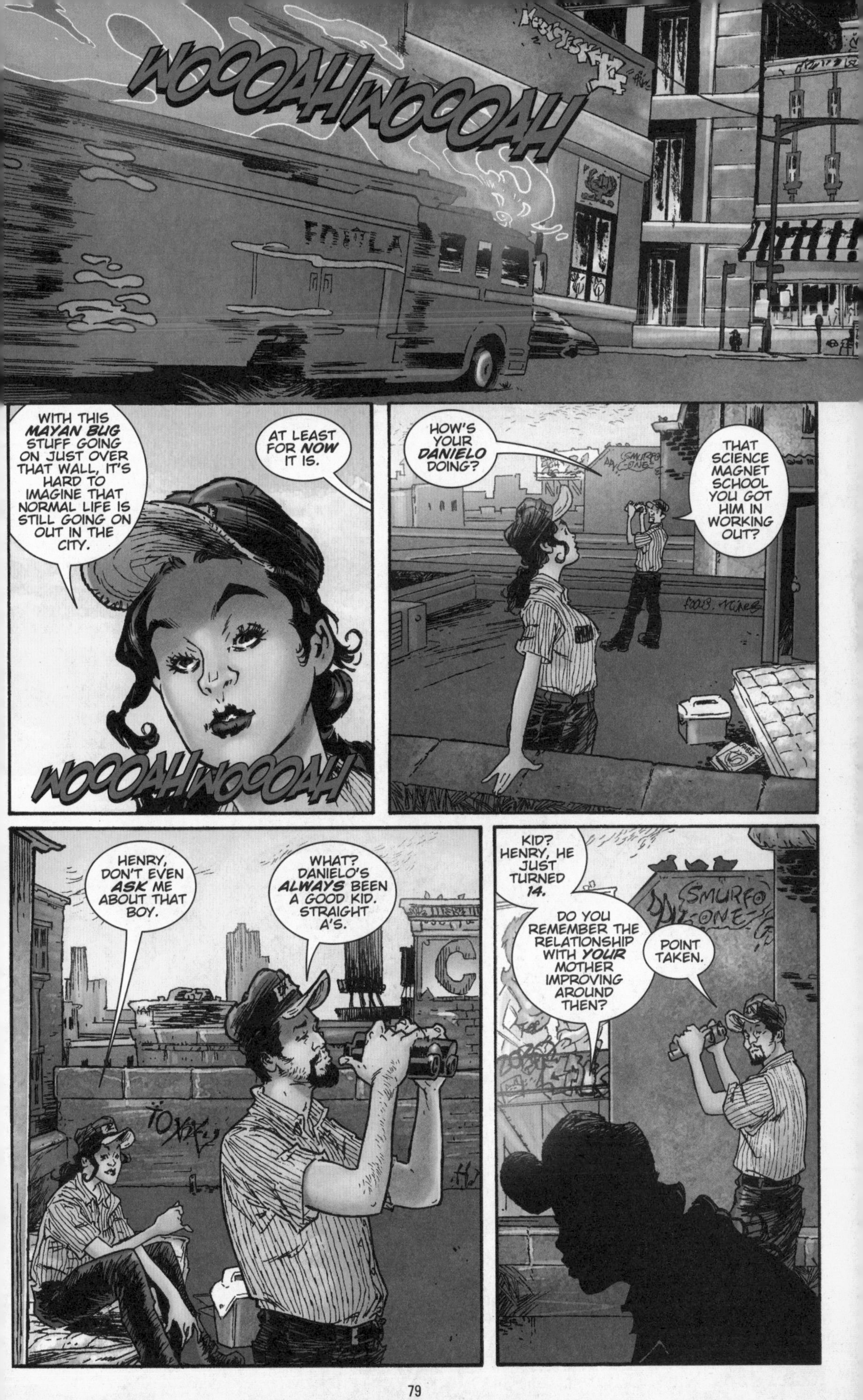
WOOOAHWOOOAH
WITH THIS MAYAN BUG STUFF GOING ON JUST OVER THAT WALL, IT'S HARD TO IMAGINE THAT NORMAL LIFE IS STILL GOING ON OUT IN THE CITY.
AT LEAST FOR NOW IT IS.
WOOOAHWOOOAH
HOW'S YOUR DANIELO DOING?
THAT SCIENCE MAGNET SCHOOL YOU GOT HIM IN WORKING OUT?
HENRY, DON'T EVEN ASK ME ABOUT THAT BOY.
WHAT? DANIELO'S ALWAYS BEEN A GOOD KID. STRAIGHT A'S.
KID? HENRY, HE JUST TURNED 14.
DO YOU REMEMBER THE RELATIONSHIP WITH YOUR MOTHER IMPROVING AROUND THEN?
POINT TAKEN.

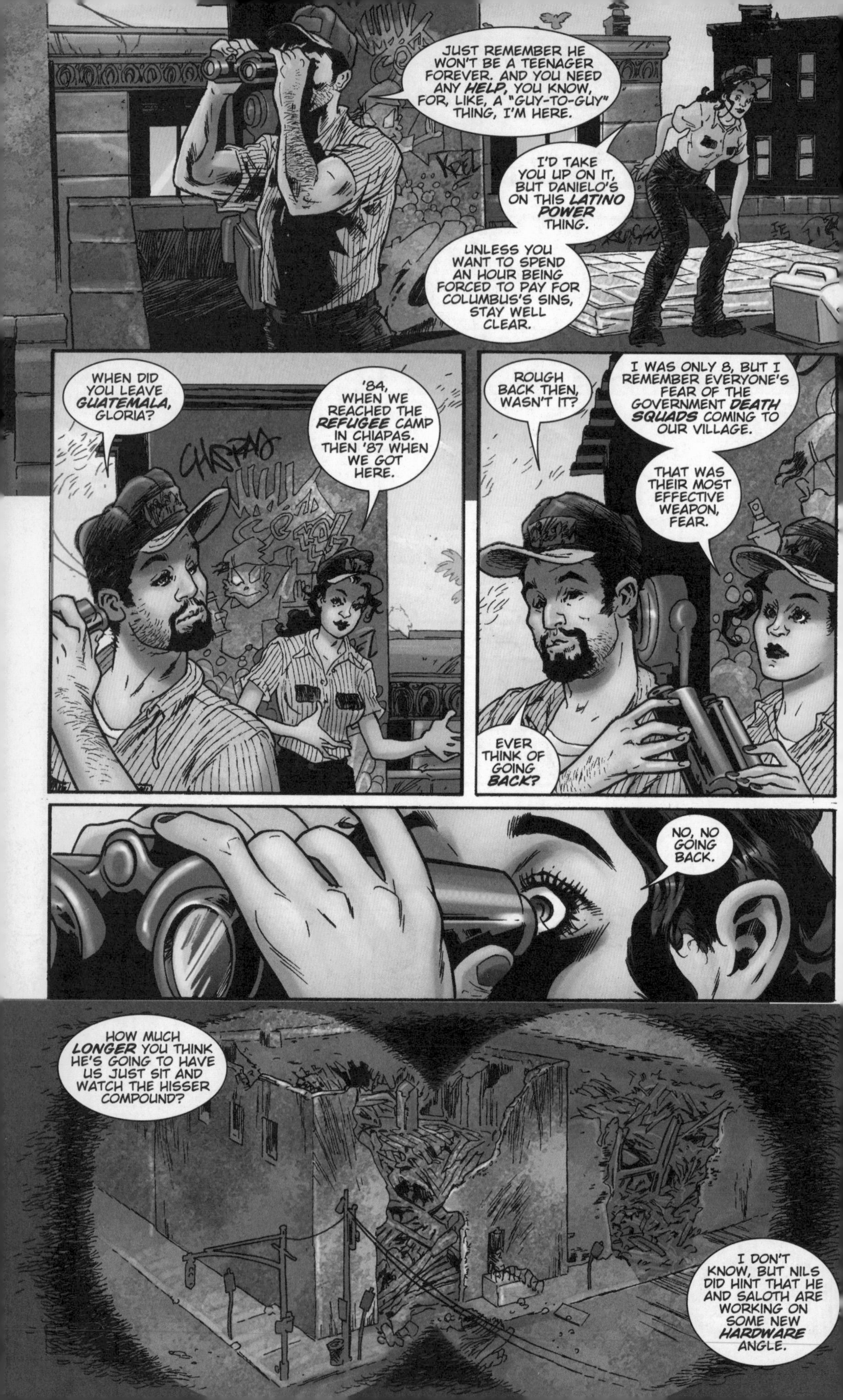
JUST REMEMBER HE WON'T BE A TEENAGER FOREVER. AND YOU NEED ANY HELP, YOU KNOW, FOR, LIKE, A "GUY-TO-GUY" THING, I'M HERE.
I'D TAKE YOU UP ON IT, BUT DANIELO'S ON THIS LATINO POWER THING.
UNLESS YOU WANT TO SPEND AN HOUR BEING FORCED TO PAY FOR COLUMBUS'S SINS, STAY WELL CLEAR.
WHEN DID YOU LEAVE GUATEMALA, GLORIA?
'84, WHEN WE REACHED THE REFUGEE CAMP IN CHIAPAS. THEN '87 WHEN WE GOT HERE.
ROUGH BACK THEN, WASN'T IT?
I WAS ONLY 8, BUT I REMEMBER EVERYONE'S FEAR OF THE GOVERNMENT DEATH SQUADS COMING TO OUR VILLAGE.
THAT WAS THEIR MOST EFFECTIVE WEAPON, FEAR.
EVER THINK OF GOING BACK?
NO, NO GOING BACK.
HOW MUCH LONGER YOU THINK HE'S GOING TO HAVE US JUST SIT AND WATCH THE HISSER COMPOUND?
I DON'T KNOW, BUT NILS DID HINT THAT HE AND SALOTH ARE WORKING ON SOME NEW HARDWARE ANGLE.

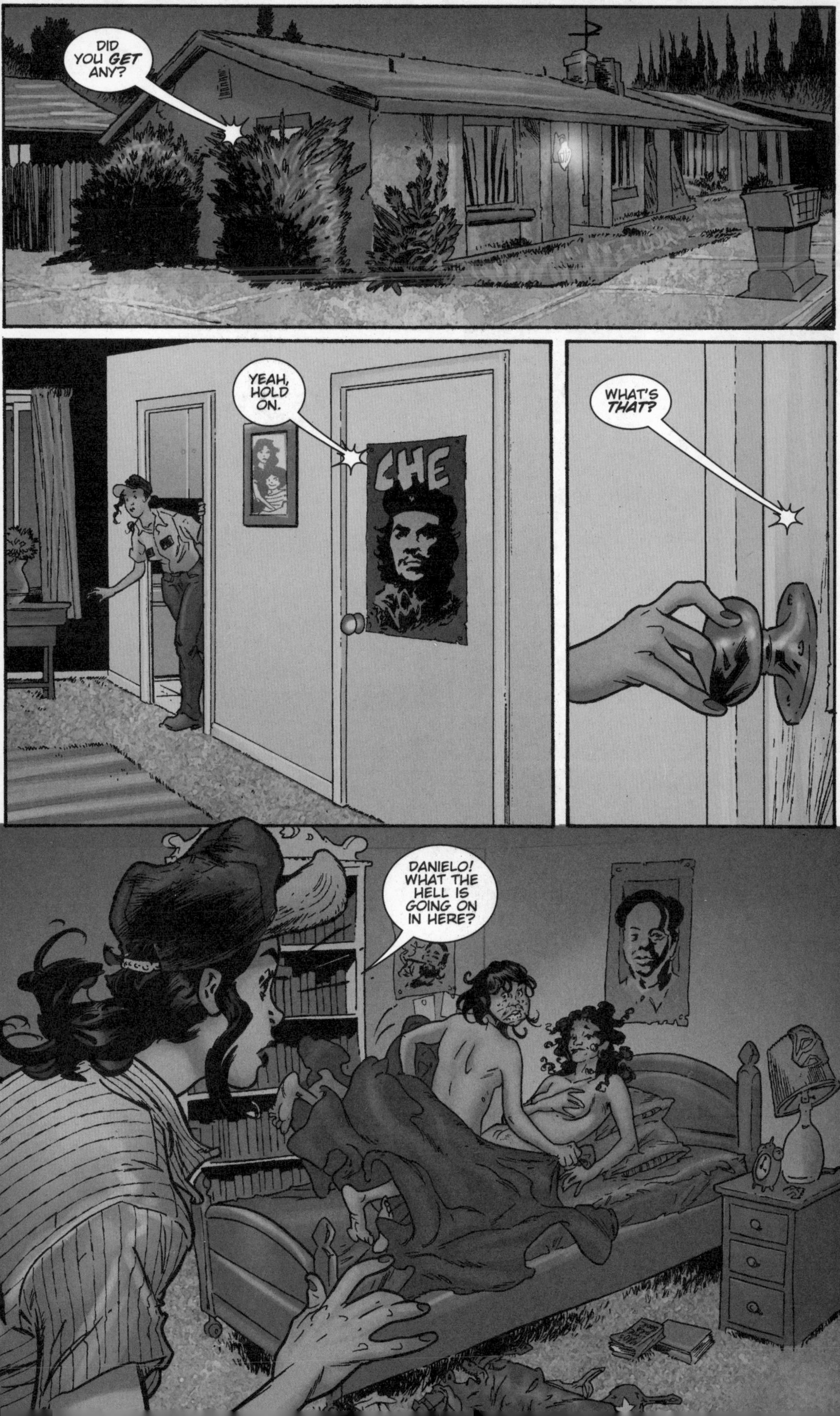
DID YOU GET ANY?
YEAH, HOLD ON.
CHE
WHAT'S THAT?
DANIELO! WHAT THE HELL IS GOING ON IN HERE?

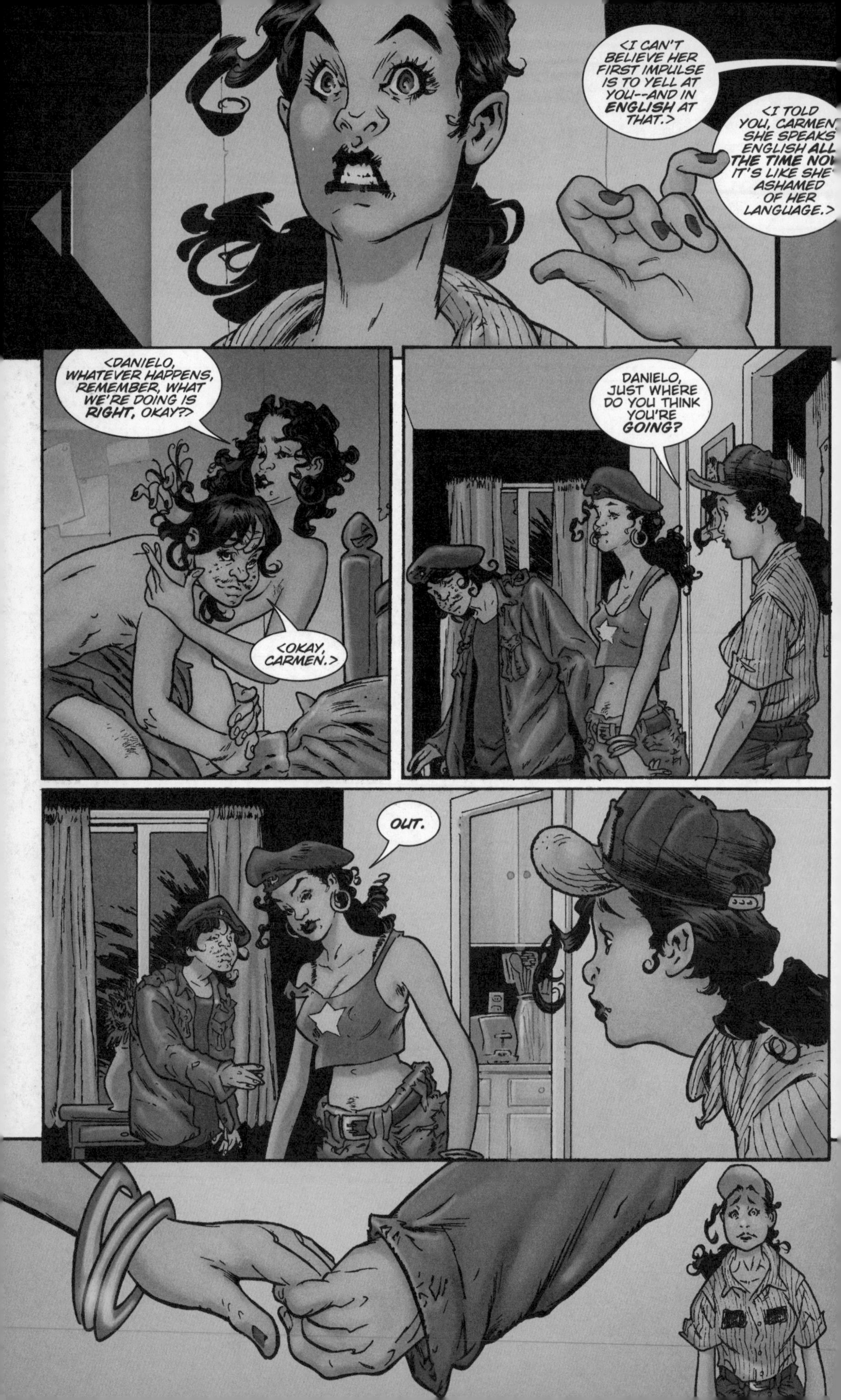

<I CAN'T BELIEVE HER FIRST IMPULSE IS TO YELL AT YOU--AND IN ENGLISH AT THAT.>
<I TOLD YOU, CARMEN SHE SPEAKS ENGLISH ALL THE TIME NO IT'S LIKE SHE ASHAMED OF HER LANGUAGE.>
<DANIELO, WHATEVER HAPPENS, REMEMBER, WHAT WE'RE DOING IS RIGHT, OKAY?>
<OKAY, CARMEN.>
DANIELO, JUST WHERE DO YOU THINK YOU'RE GOING?
OUT.

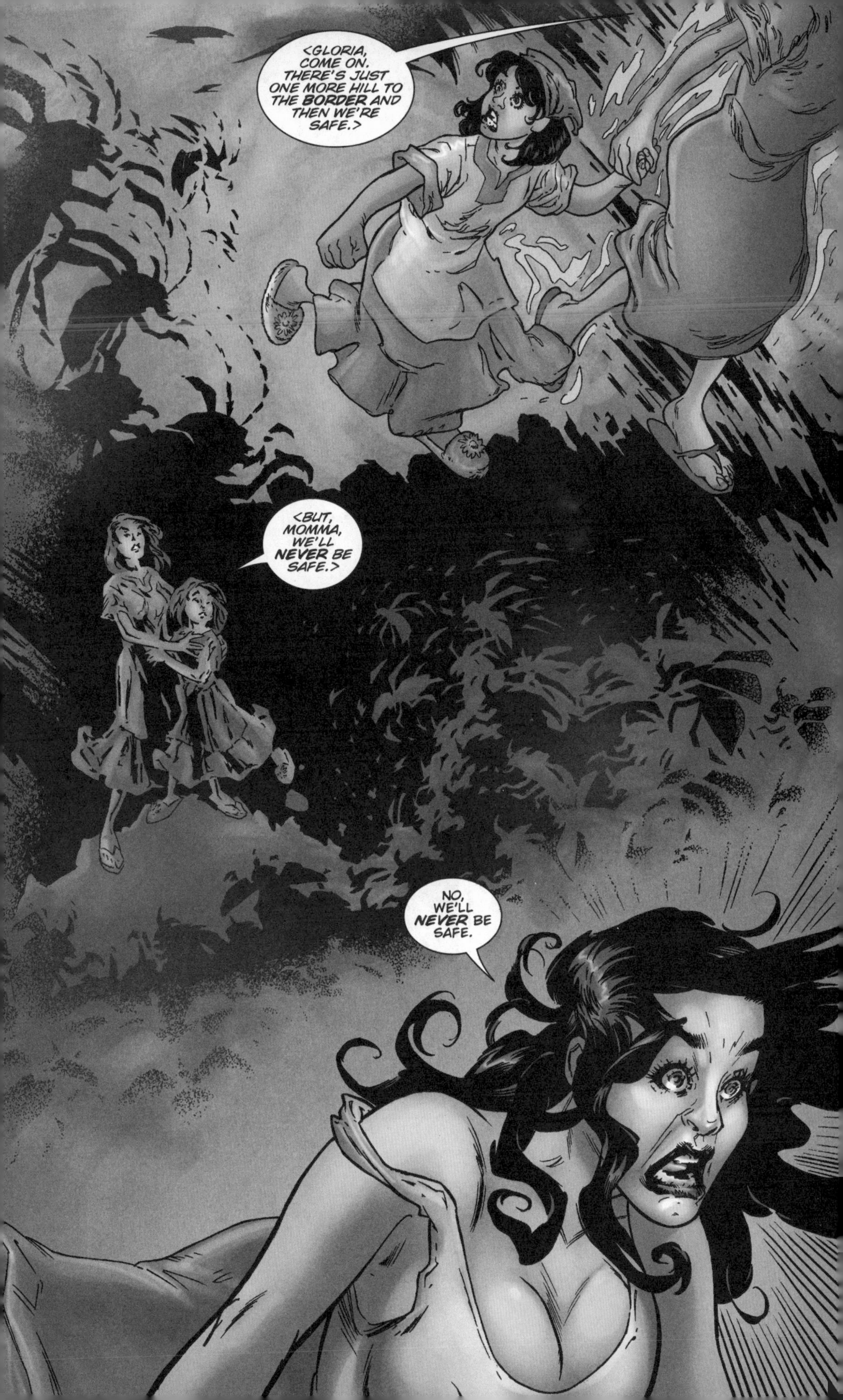
<GLORIA, COME ON. THERE'S JUST ONE MORE HILL TO THE BORDER AND THEN WE'RE SAFE.>
<BUT, MOMMA, WE'LL NEVER BE SAFE.>
NO, WE'LL NEVER BE SAFE.

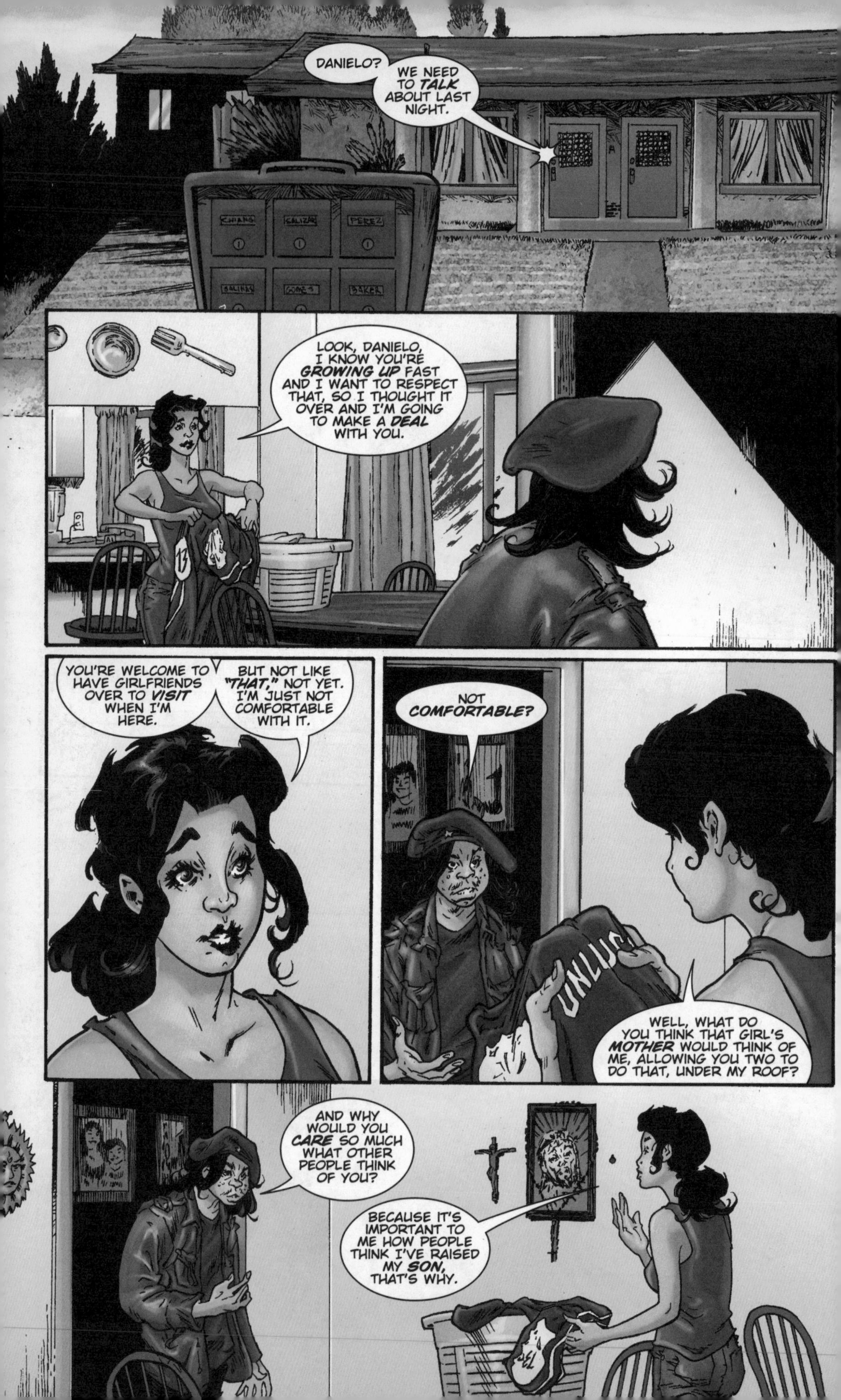

DANIELO?
WE NEED TO TALK ABOUT LAST NIGHT.
LOOK, DANIELO, I KNOW YOU'RE GROWING UP FAST AND I WANT TO RESPECT THAT, SO I THOUGHT IT OVER AND I'M GOING TO MAKE A DEAL WITH YOU.
YOU'RE WELCOME TO HAVE GIRLFRIENDS OVER TO VISIT WHEN I'M HERE.
BUT NOT LIKE "THAT," NOT YET. I'M JUST NOT COMFORTABLE WITH IT.
NOT COMFORTABLE?
WELL, WHAT DO YOU THINK THAT GIRL'S MOTHER WOULD THINK OF ME, ALLOWING YOU TWO TO DO THAT, UNDER MY ROOF?
AND WHY WOULD YOU CARE SO MUCH WHAT OTHER PEOPLE THINK OF YOU?
BECAUSE IT'S IMPORTANT TO ME HOW PEOPLE THINK I'VE RAISED MY SON, THAT'S WHY.

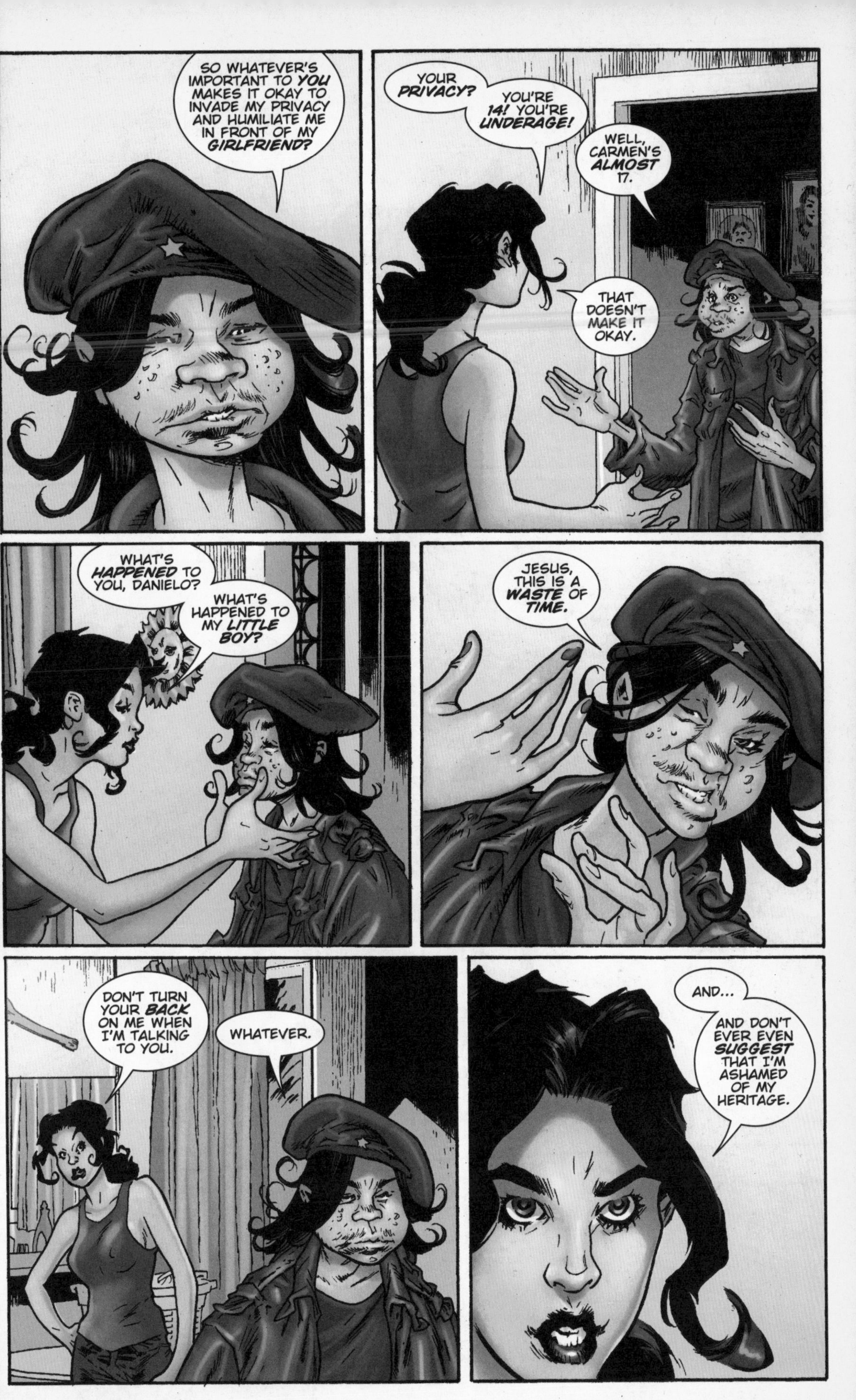
SO WHATEVER'S IMPORTANT TO YOU MAKES IT OKAY TO INVADE MY PRIVACY AND HUMILIATE ME IN FRONT OF MY GIRLFRIEND?
YOUR PRIVACY?
YOU'RE 14! YOU'RE UNDERAGE!
WELL, CARMEN'S ALMOST 17.
THAT DOESN'T MAKE IT OKAY.
WHAT'S HAPPENED TO YOU, DANIELO?
WHAT'S HAPPENED TO MY LITTLE BOY?
JESUS, THIS IS A WASTE OF TIME.
DON'T TURN YOUR BACK ON ME WHEN I'M TALKING TO YOU.
WHATEVER.
AND...
AND DON'T EVER EVEN SUGGEST THAT I'M ASHAMED OF MY HERITAGE.

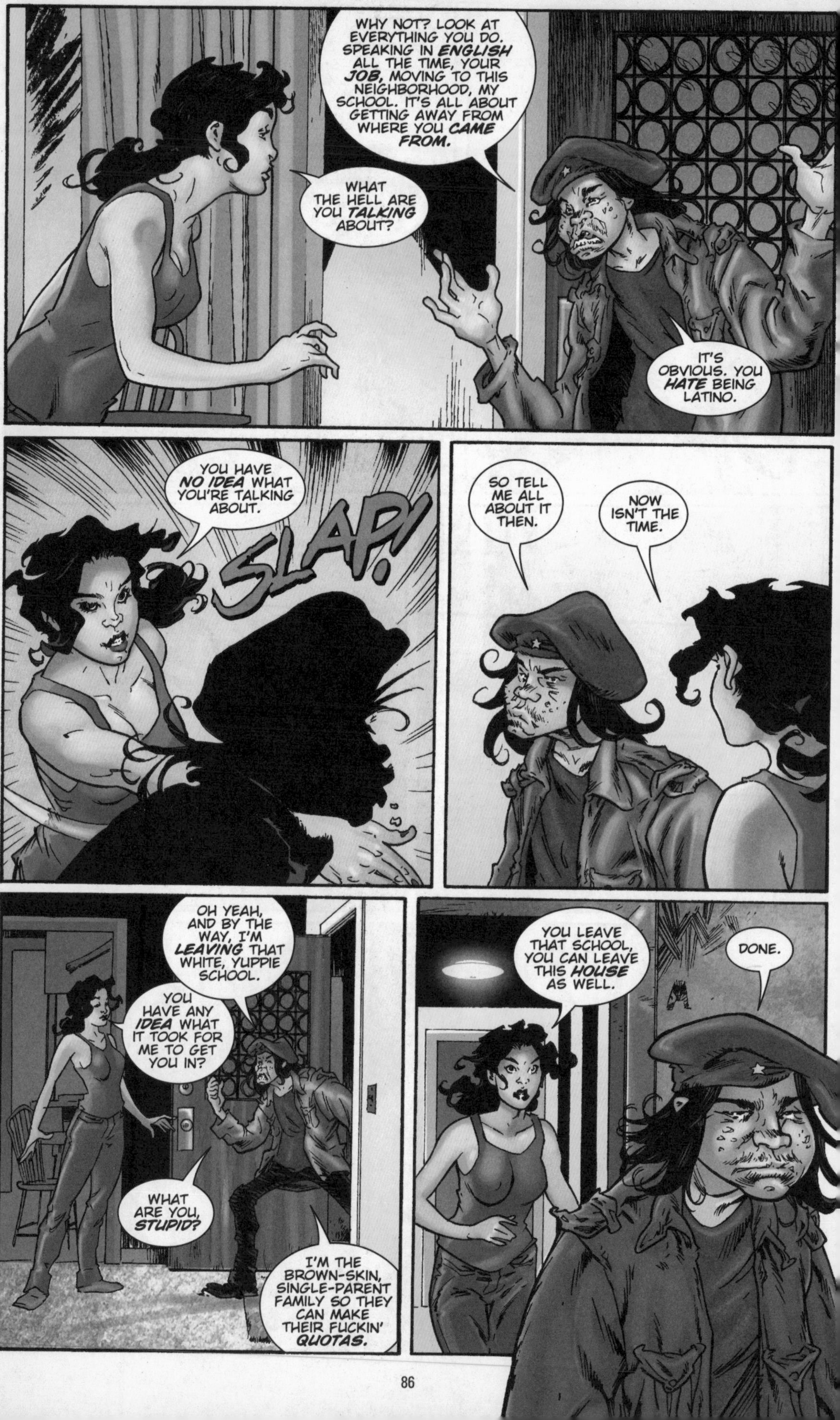
WHY NOT? LOOK AT EVERYTHING YOU DO. SPEAKING IN ENGLISH ALL THE TIME, YOUR JOB, MOVING TO THIS NEIGHBORHOOD, MY SCHOOL. IT'S ALL ABOUT GETTING AWAY FROM WHERE YOU CAME FROM.
WHAT THE HELL ARE YOU TALKING ABOUT?
IT'S OBVIOUS. YOU HATE BEING LATINO.
YOU HAVE NO IDEA WHAT YOU'RE TALKING ABOUT.
SLAP!
SO TELL ME ALL ABOUT IT THEN.
NOW ISN'T THE TIME.
OH YEAH, AND BY THE WAY, I'M LEAVING THAT WHITE, YUPPIE SCHOOL.
YOU HAVE ANY IDEA WHAT IT TOOK FOR ME TO GET YOU IN?
WHAT ARE YOU, STUPID?
I'M THE BROWN-SKIN, SINGLE-PARENT FAMILY SO THEY CAN MAKE THEIR FUCKIN' QUOTAS.
YOU LEAVE THAT SCHOOL, YOU CAN LEAVE THIS HOUSE AS WELL.
DONE.

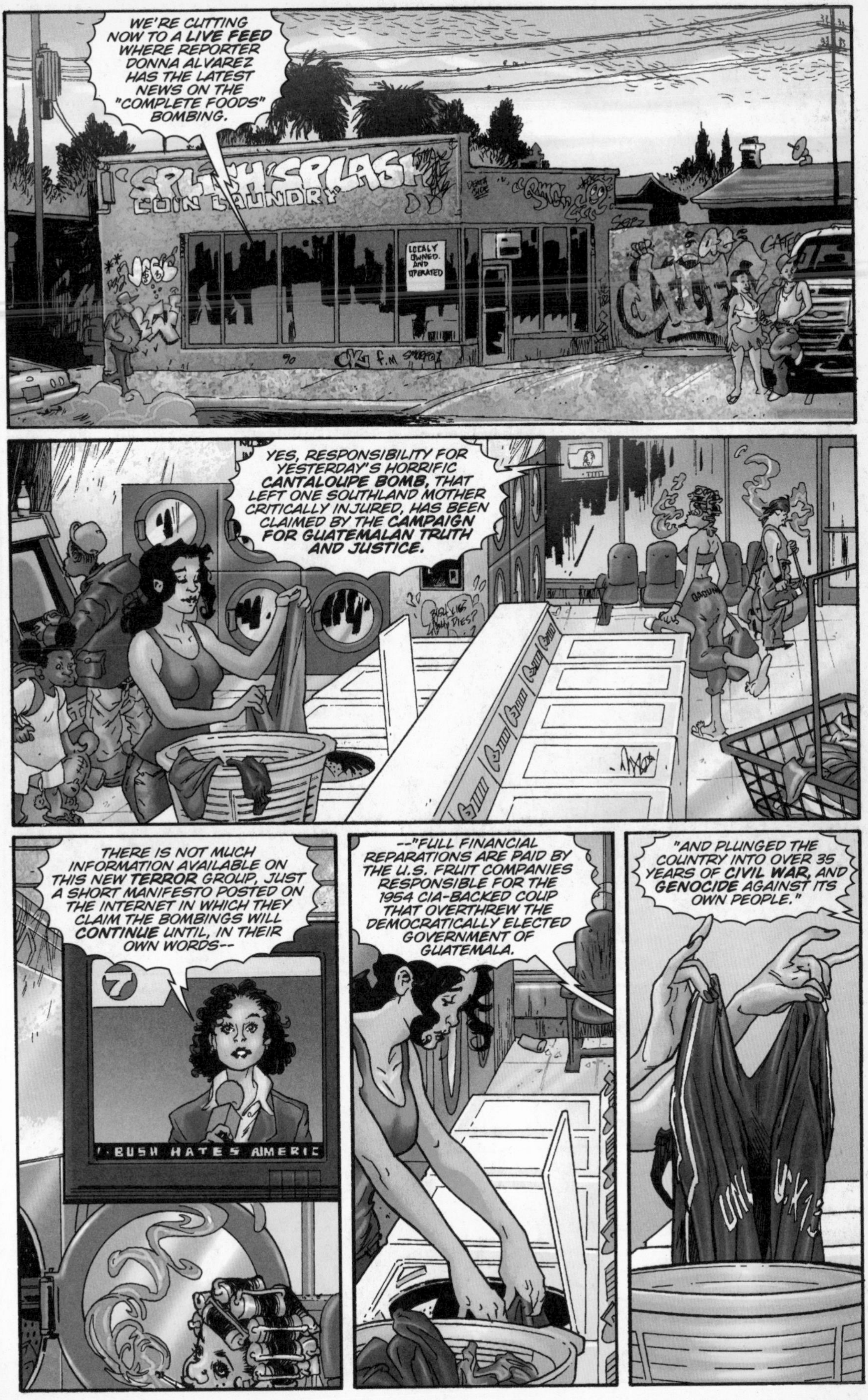
WE'RE CUTTING NOW TO A **LIVE FEED** WHERE REPORTER DONNA ALVAREZ HAS THE LATEST NEWS ON THE "COMPLETE FOODS" BOMBING.
SPLISH SPLASH
COIN LAUNDRY
LOCALY OWNED. AND OPERATED
YES, RESPONSIBILITY FOR YESTERDAY'S HORRIFIC **CANTALOUPE BOMB**, THAT LEFT ONE SOUTHLAND MOTHER CRITICALLY INJURED, HAS BEEN CLAIMED BY THE **CAMPAIGN FOR GUATEMALAN TRUTH AND JUSTICE.**
THERE IS NOT MUCH INFORMATION AVAILABLE ON THIS NEW **TERROR** GROUP, JUST A SHORT MANIFESTO POSTED ON THE INTERNET IN WHICH THEY CLAIM THE BOMBINGS WILL **CONTINUE** UNTIL, IN THEIR OWN WORDS--
7
BUSH HATES AMERIC
--"FULL FINANCIAL REPARATIONS ARE PAID BY THE U.S. FRUIT COMPANIES RESPONSIBLE FOR THE 1954 CIA-BACKED COUP THAT OVERTHREW THE DEMOCRATICALLY ELECTED GOVERNMENT OF GUATEMALA.
"AND PLUNGED THE COUNTRY INTO OVER 35 YEARS OF **CIVIL WAR**, AND **GENOCIDE** AGAINST ITS OWN PEOPLE."

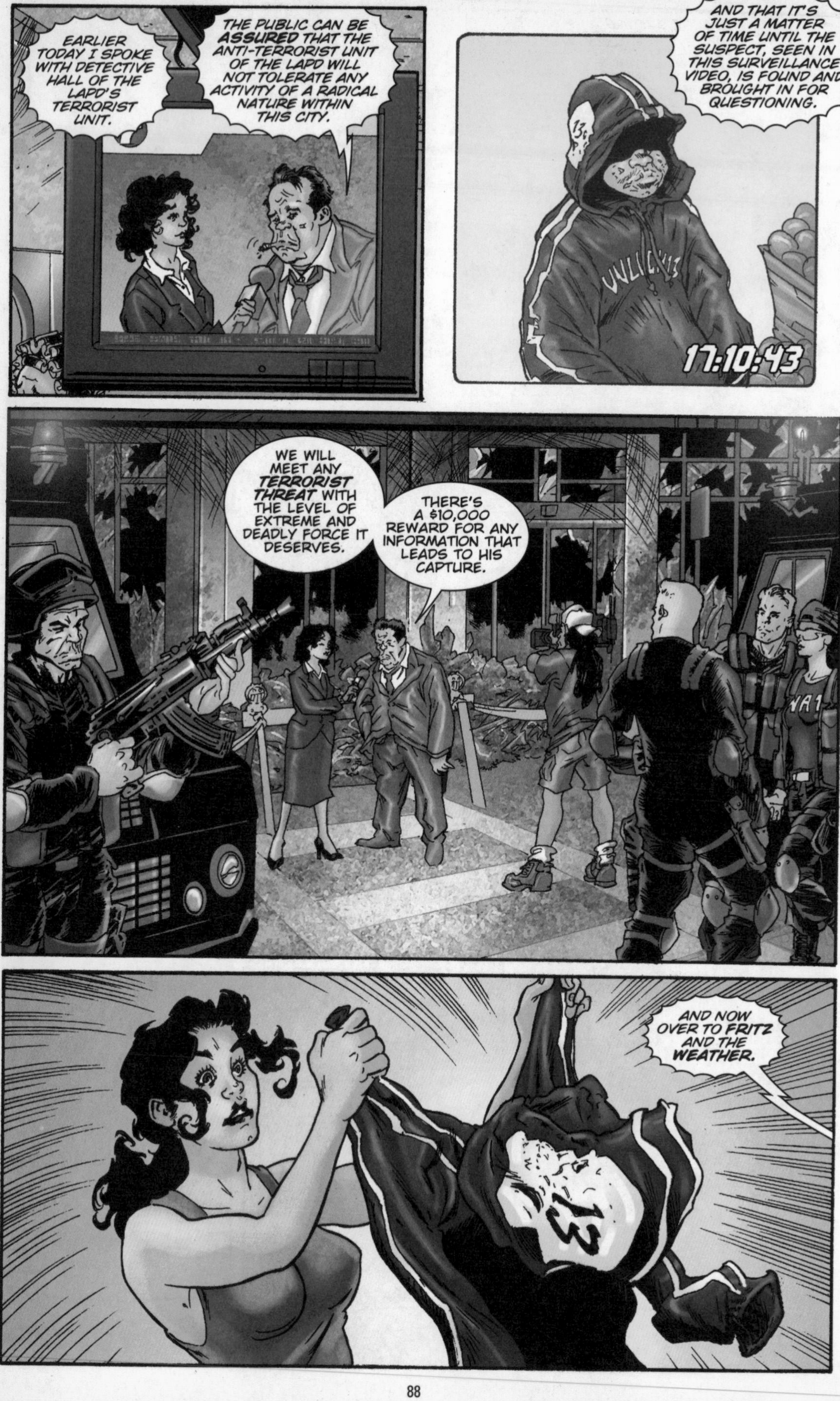
EARLIER TODAY I SPOKE WITH DETECTIVE HALL OF THE LAPD'S TERRORIST UNIT.
THE PUBLIC CAN BE ASSURED THAT THE ANTI-TERRORIST UNIT OF THE LAPD WILL NOT TOLERATE ANY ACTIVITY OF A RADICAL NATURE WITHIN THIS CITY.
AND THAT IT'S JUST A MATTER OF TIME UNTIL THE SUSPECT, SEEN IN THIS SURVEILLANCE VIDEO, IS FOUND AND BROUGHT IN FOR QUESTIONING.
17:10:43
WE WILL MEET ANY TERRORIST THREAT WITH THE LEVEL OF EXTREME AND DEADLY FORCE IT DESERVES.
THERE'S A $10,000 REWARD FOR ANY INFORMATION THAT LEADS TO HIS CAPTURE.
AND NOW OVER TO FRITZ AND THE WEATHER.
13

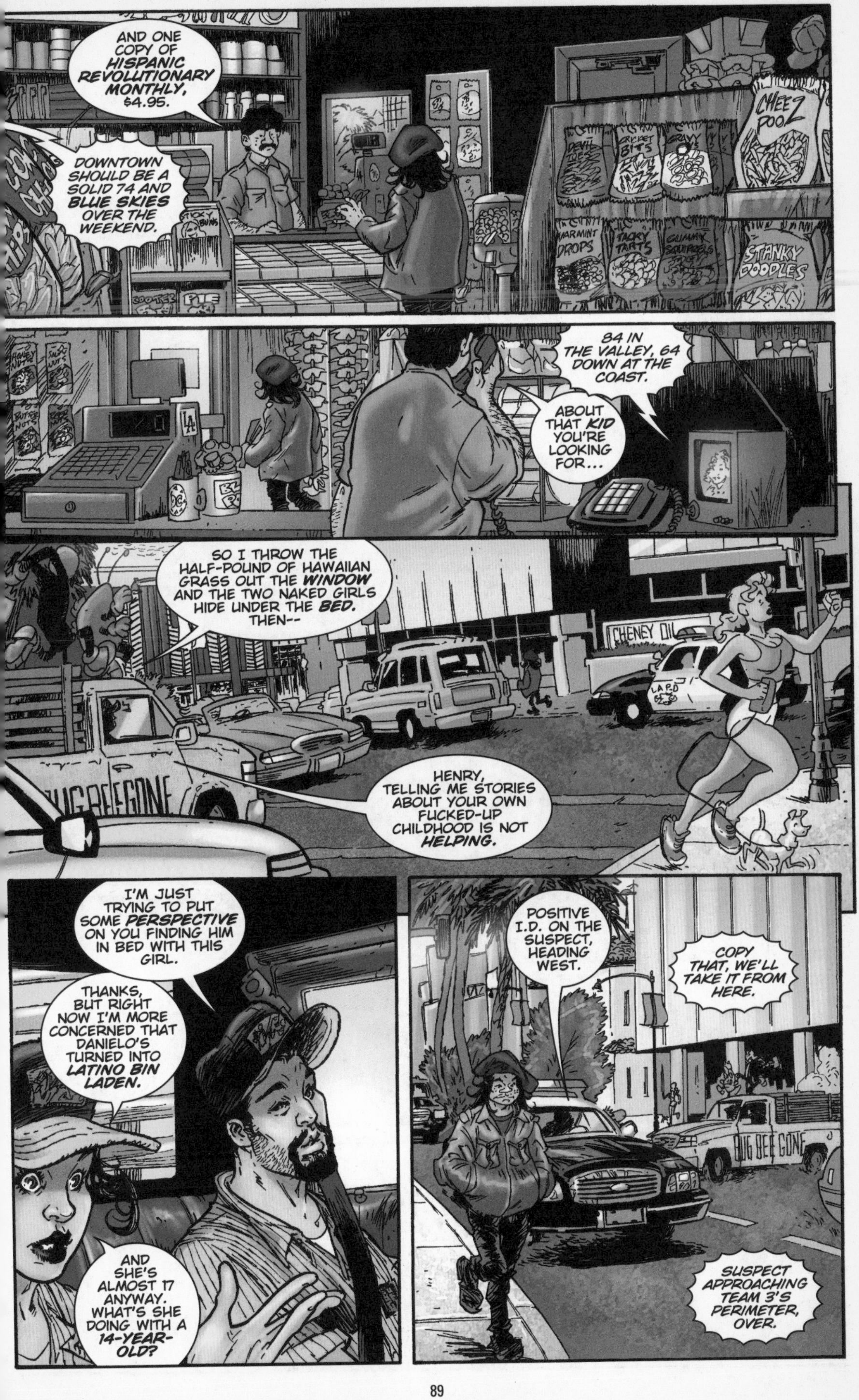
AND ONE COPY OF HISPANIC REVOLUTIONARY MONTHLY, $4.95.
DOWNTOWN SHOULD BE A SOLID 74 AND BLUE SKIES OVER THE WEEKEND.
CHEEZ POOZ
STANKY DOODLES
84 IN THE VALLEY, 64 DOWN AT THE COAST.
ABOUT THAT KID YOU'RE LOOKING FOR...
SO I THROW THE HALF-POUND OF HAWAIIAN GRASS OUT THE WINDOW AND THE TWO NAKED GIRLS HIDE UNDER THE BED. THEN--
HENRY, TELLING ME STORIES ABOUT YOUR OWN FUCKED-UP CHILDHOOD IS NOT HELPING.
I'M JUST TRYING TO PUT SOME PERSPECTIVE ON YOU FINDING HIM IN BED WITH THIS GIRL.
THANKS, BUT RIGHT NOW I'M MORE CONCERNED THAT DANIELO'S TURNED INTO LATINO BIN LADEN.
AND SHE'S ALMOST 17 ANYWAY. WHAT'S SHE DOING WITH A 14-YEAR-OLD?
POSITIVE I.D. ON THE SUSPECT, HEADING WEST.
COPY THAT, WE'LL TAKE IT FROM HERE.
BUG BEE GONE
SUSPECT APPROACHING TEAM 3'S PERIMETER, OVER.

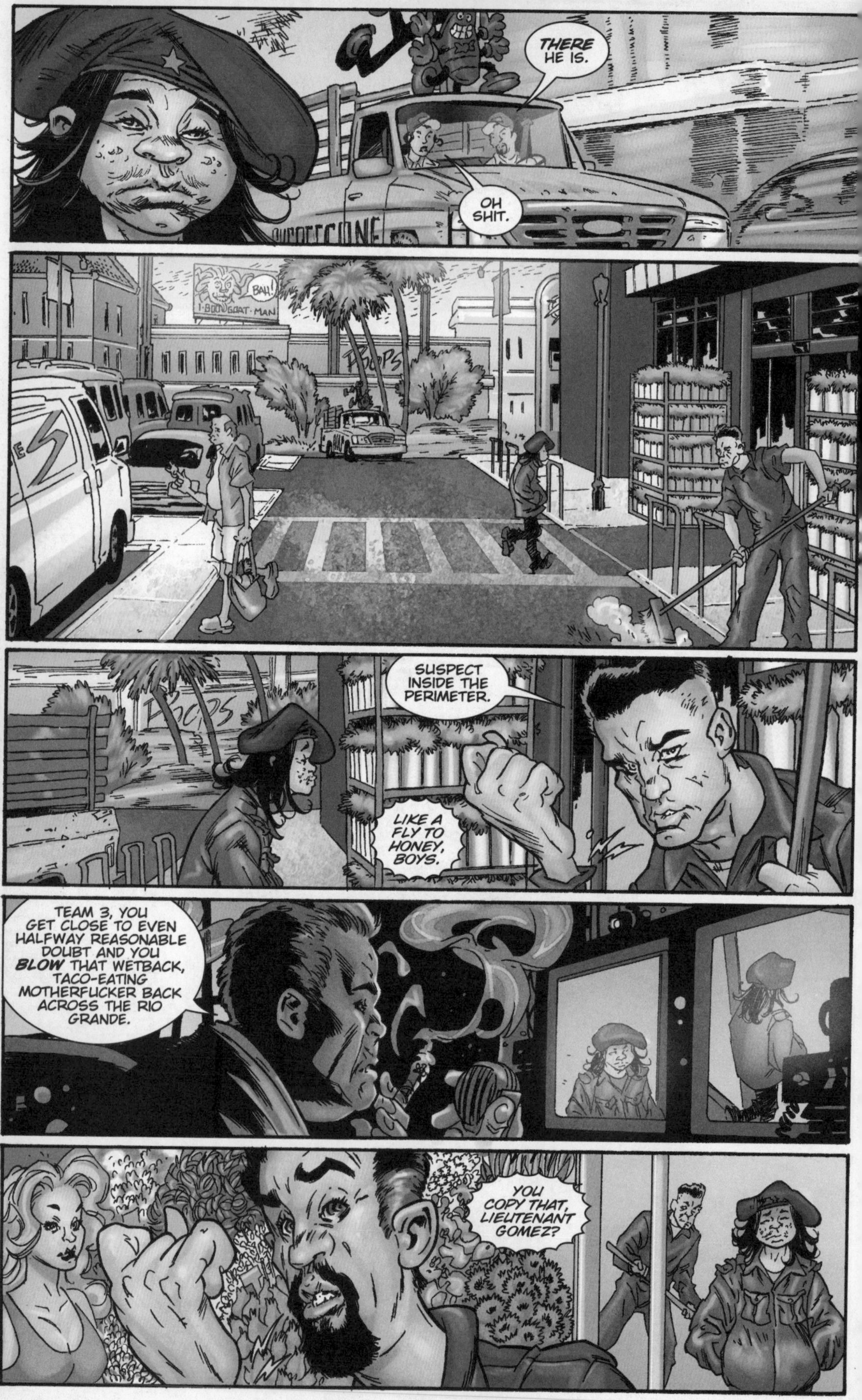
THERE HE IS.
OH SHIT.
BAH!
1·800·GOAT·MAN
SUSPECT INSIDE THE PERIMETER.
LIKE A FLY TO HONEY, BOYS.
TEAM 3, YOU GET CLOSE TO EVEN HALFWAY REASONABLE DOUBT AND YOU BLOW THAT WETBACK, TACO-EATING MOTHERFUCKER BACK ACROSS THE RIO GRANDE.
YOU COPY THAT, LIEUTENANT GOMEZ?

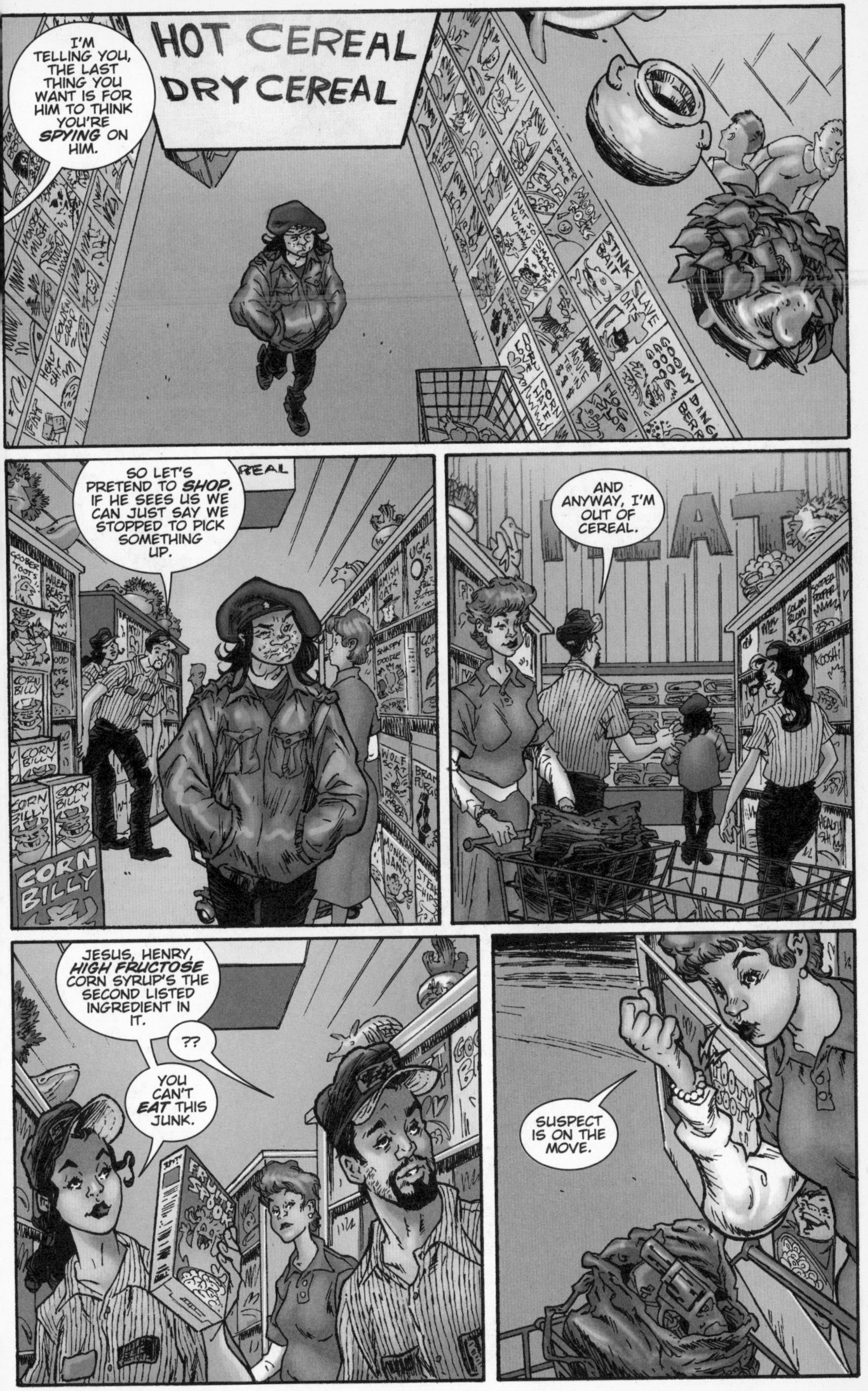
HOT CEREAL
DRY CEREAL
I'M TELLING YOU, THE LAST THING YOU WANT IS FOR HIM TO THINK YOU'RE SPYING ON HIM.
SO LET'S PRETEND TO SHOP. IF HE SEES US WE CAN JUST SAY WE STOPPED TO PICK SOMETHING UP.
AND ANYWAY, I'M OUT OF CEREAL.
JESUS, HENRY, HIGH FRUCTOSE CORN SYRUP'S THE SECOND LISTED INGREDIENT IN IT.
??
YOU CAN'T EAT THIS JUNK.
SUSPECT IS ON THE MOVE.

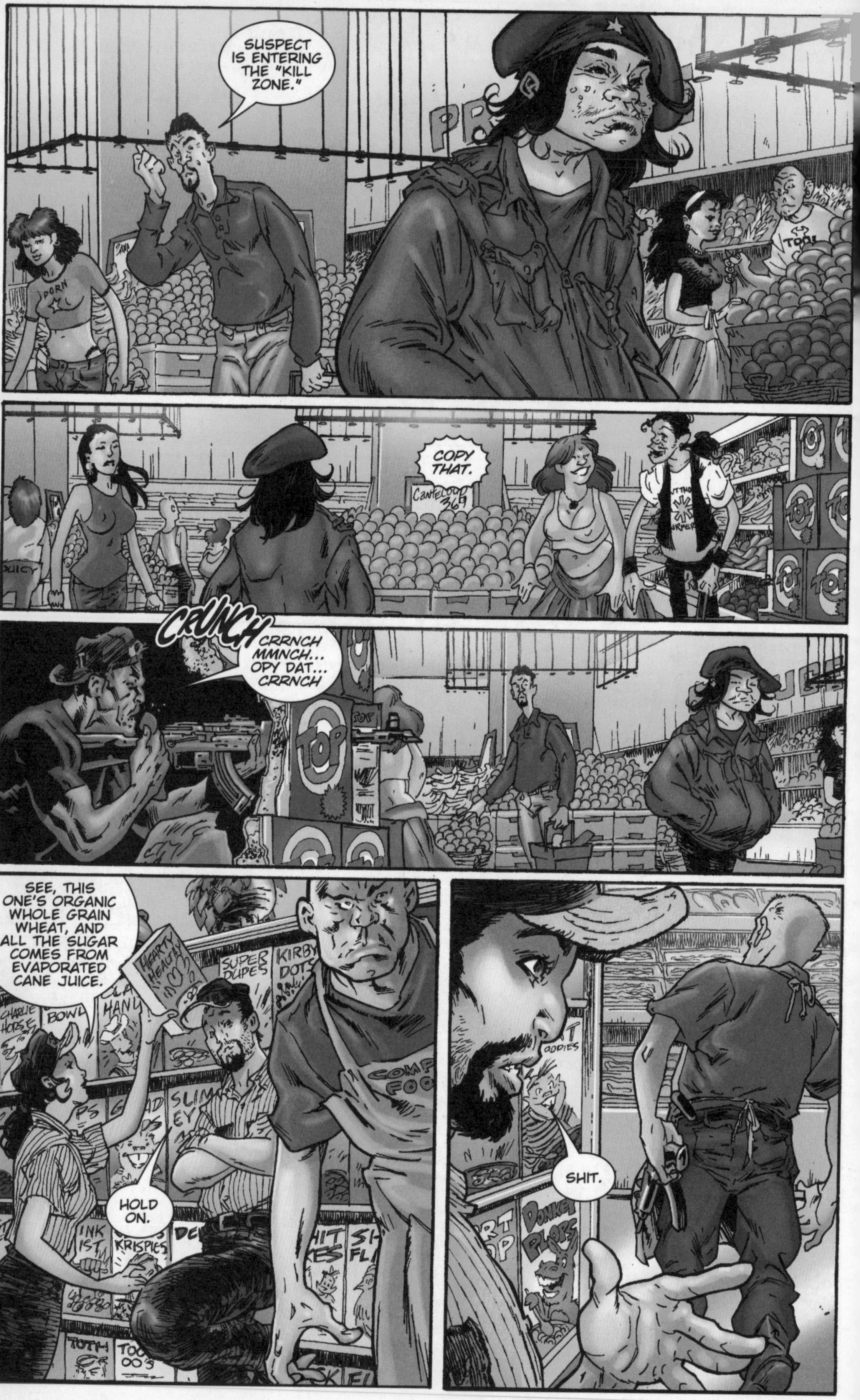
SUSPECT IS ENTERING THE "KILL ZONE."
COPY THAT.
CRUNCH
CRRNCH MMNCH... OPY DAT... CRRNCH
SEE, THIS ONE'S ORGANIC WHOLE GRAIN WHEAT, AND ALL THE SUGAR COMES FROM EVAPORATED CANE JUICE.
HOLD ON.
SHIT.

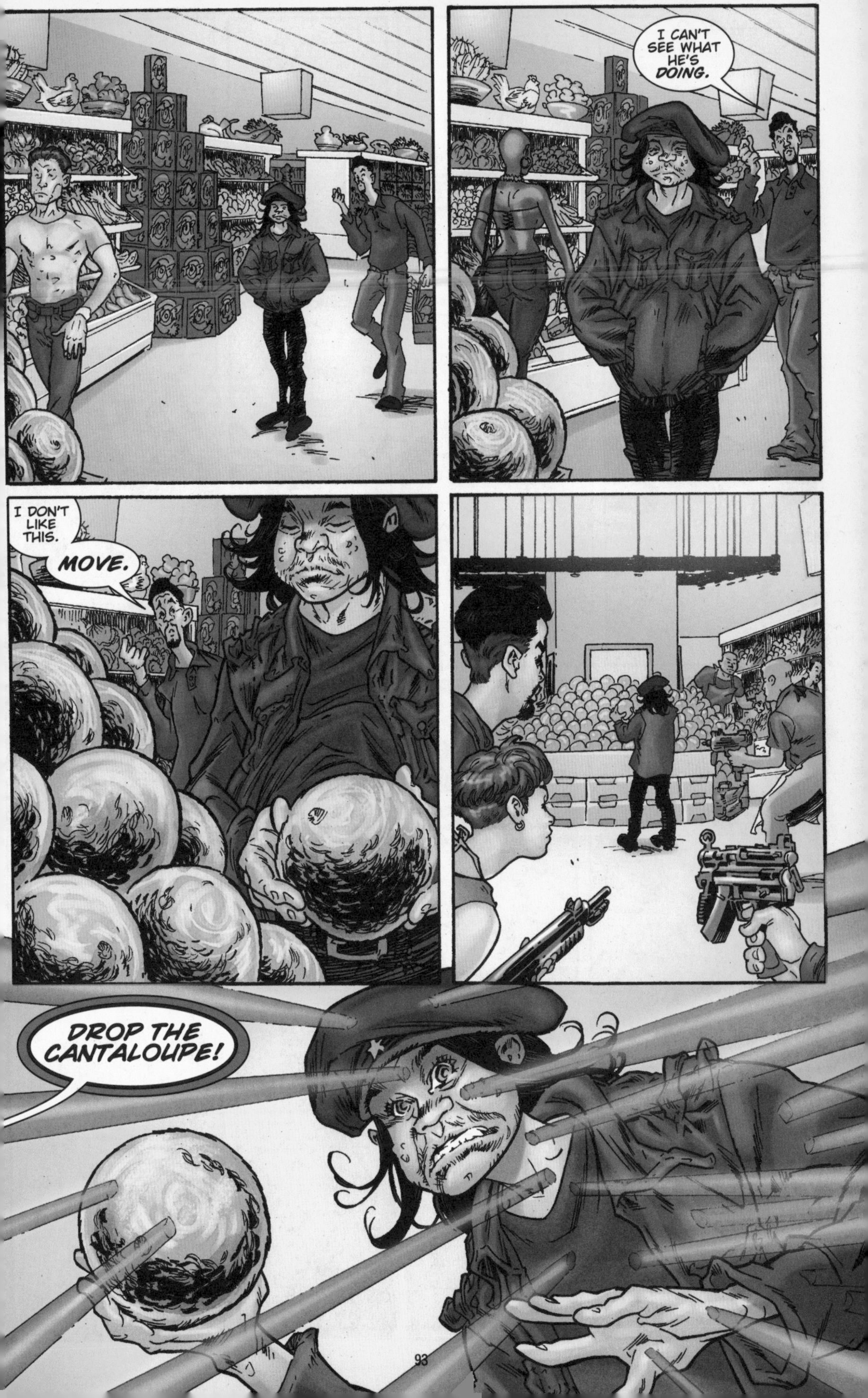
I CAN'T SEE WHAT HE'S DOING.
I DON'T LIKE THIS.
MOVE.
DROP THE CANTALOUPE!

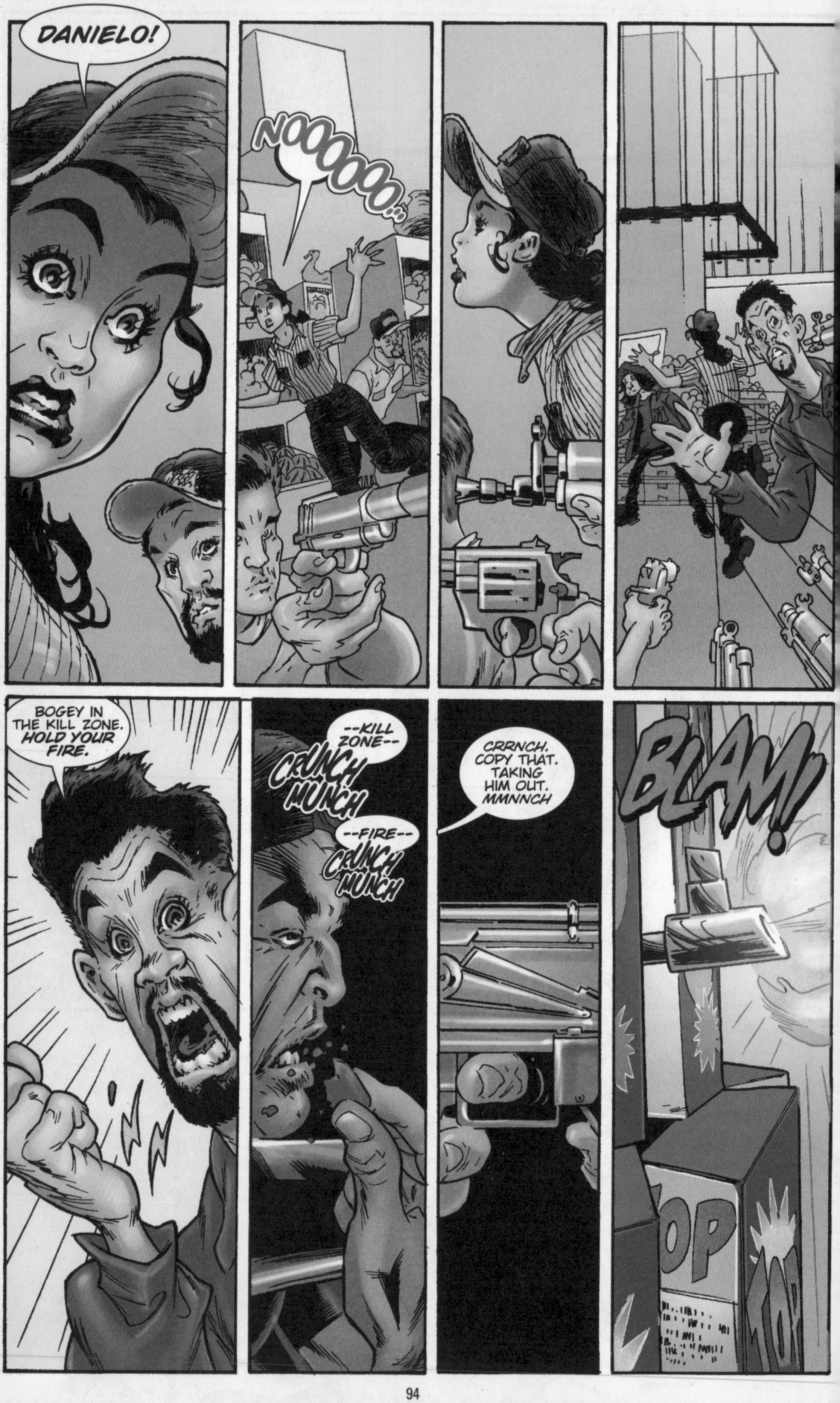
DANIELO!
NOOOOOO...
BOGEY IN THE KILL ZONE. HOLD YOUR FIRE.
--KILL ZONE--
CRUNCH MUNCH
--FIRE--
CRUNCH MUNCH
CRRNCH. COPY THAT. TAKING HIM OUT. MMNNCH
BLAM!

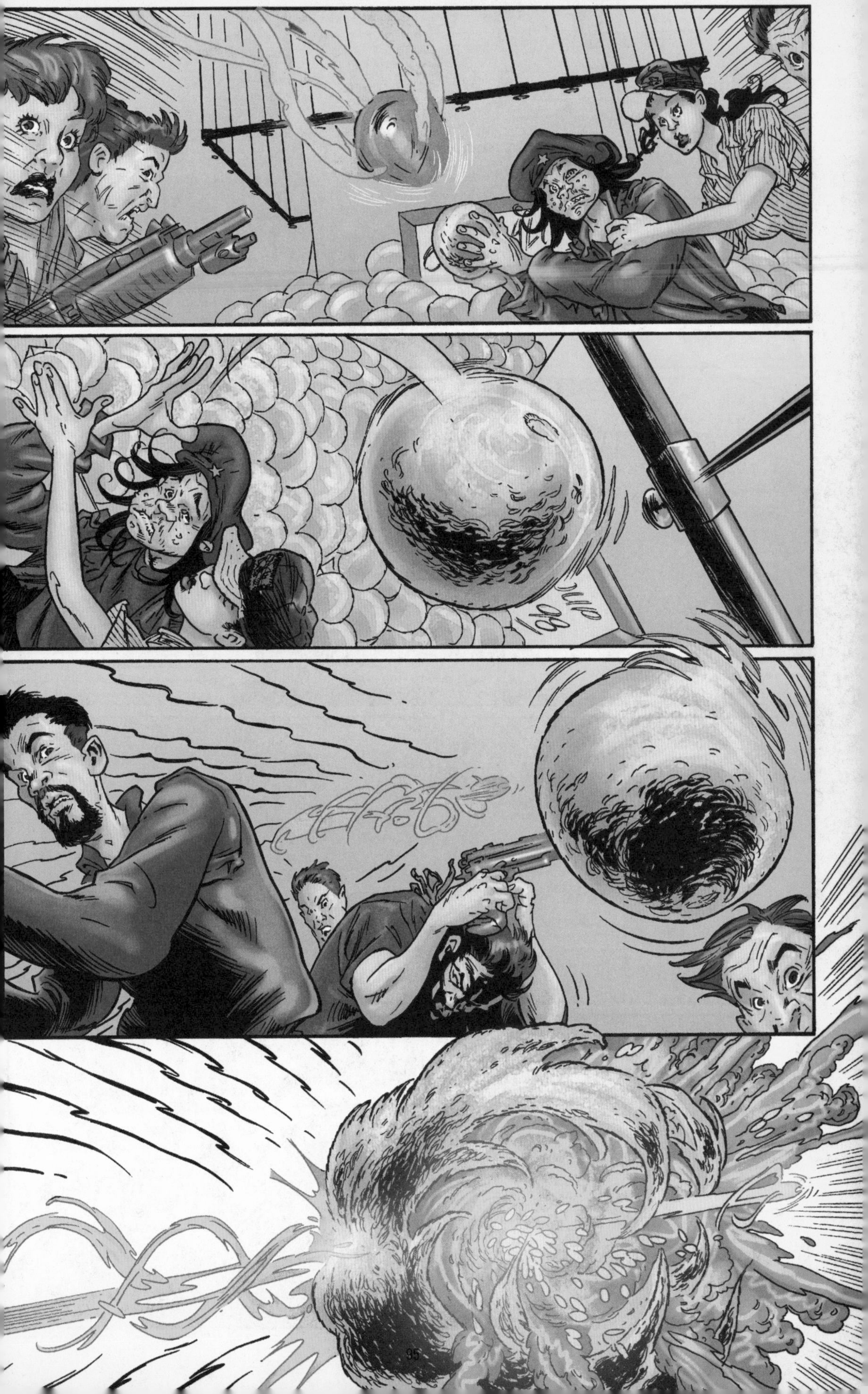

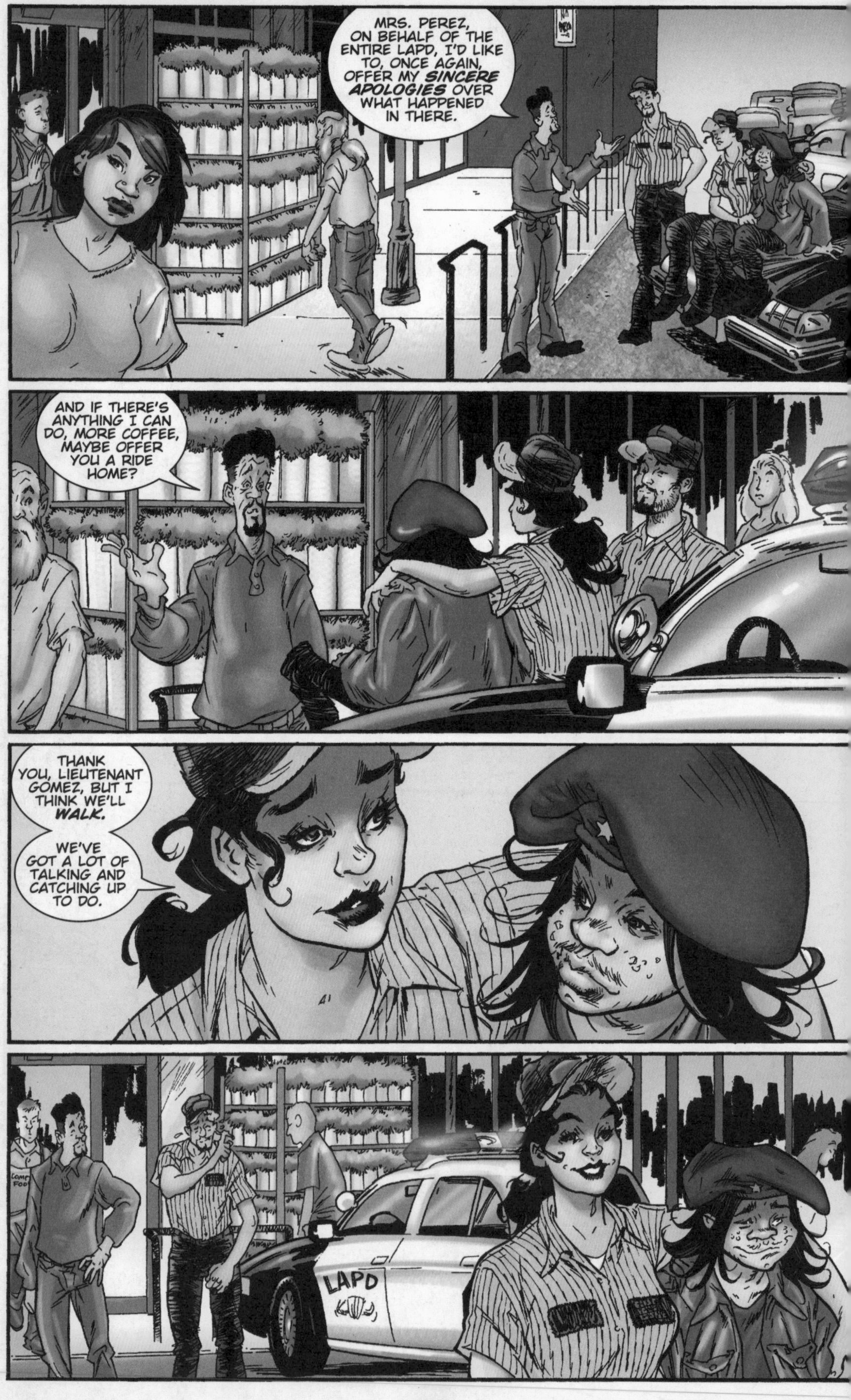
MRS. PEREZ, ON BEHALF OF THE ENTIRE LAPD, I'D LIKE TO, ONCE AGAIN, OFFER MY **SINCERE APOLOGIES** OVER WHAT HAPPENED IN THERE.
AND IF THERE'S ANYTHING I CAN DO, MORE COFFEE, MAYBE OFFER YOU A RIDE HOME?
THANK YOU, LIEUTENANT GOMEZ, BUT I THINK WE'LL **WALK.**
WE'VE GOT A LOT OF TALKING AND CATCHING UP TO DO.
LAPD

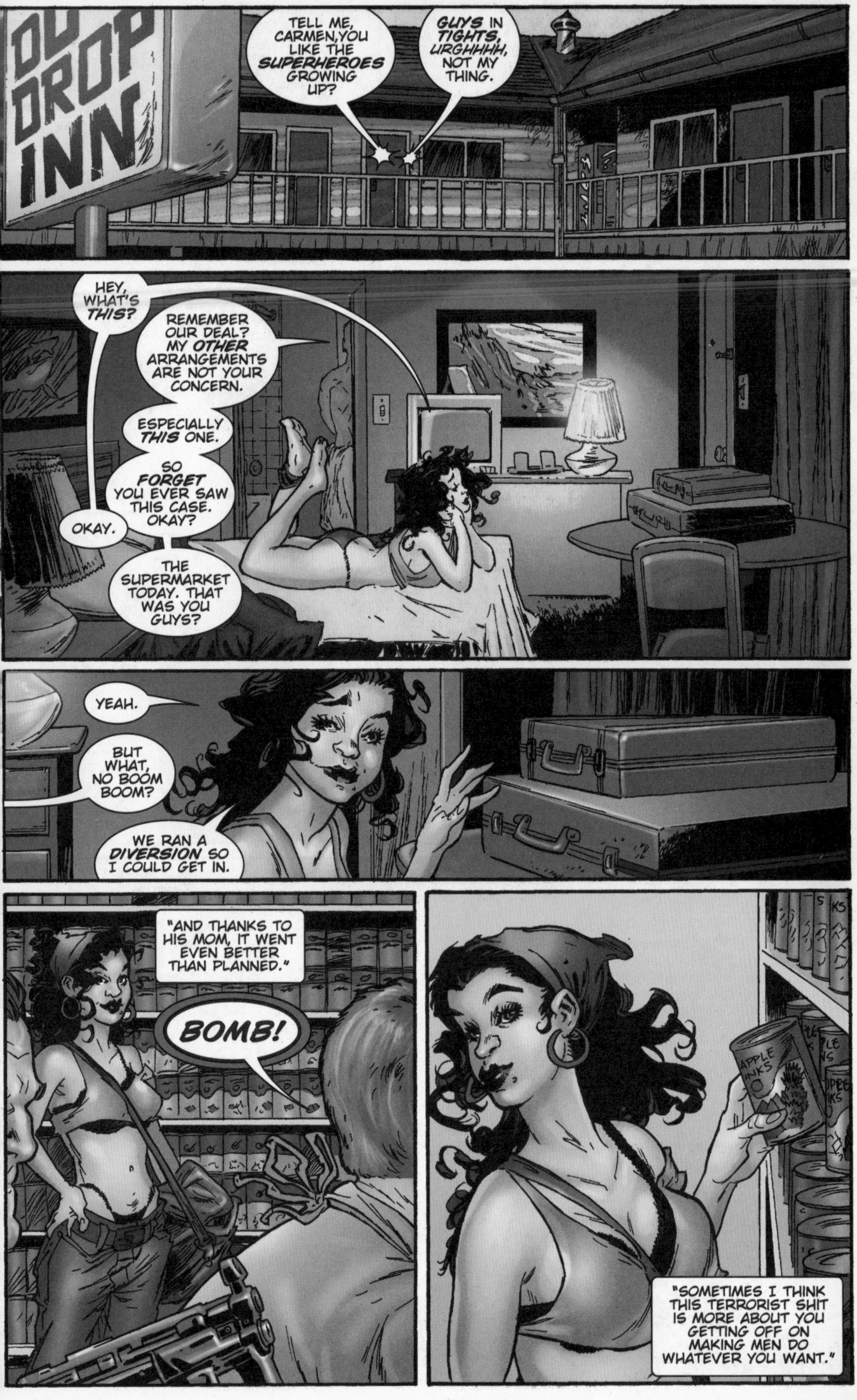
DU DROP INN
TELL ME, CARMEN, YOU LIKE THE SUPERHEROES GROWING UP?
GUYS IN TIGHTS, URGHHHH, NOT MY THING.
HEY, WHAT'S THIS?
REMEMBER OUR DEAL? MY OTHER ARRANGEMENTS ARE NOT YOUR CONCERN.
ESPECIALLY THIS ONE.
SO FORGET YOU EVER SAW THIS CASE. OKAY?
OKAY.
THE SUPERMARKET TODAY. THAT WAS YOU GUYS?
YEAH.
BUT WHAT, NO BOOM BOOM?
WE RAN A DIVERSION SO I COULD GET IN.
"AND THANKS TO HIS MOM, IT WENT EVEN BETTER THAN PLANNED."
BOMB!
"SOMETIMES I THINK THIS TERRORIST SHIT IS MORE ABOUT YOU GETTING OFF ON MAKING MEN DO WHATEVER YOU WANT."

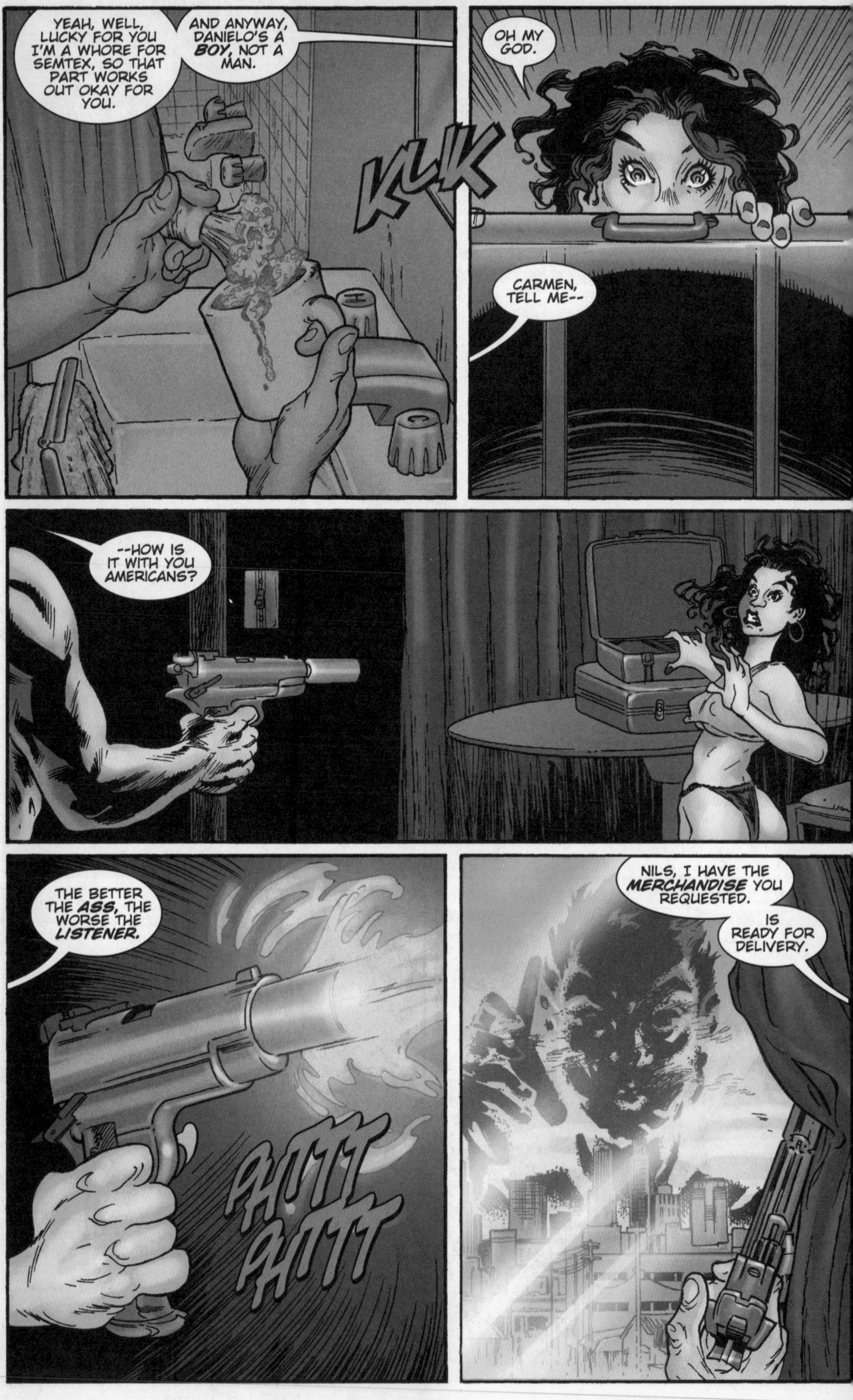
YEAH, WELL, LUCKY FOR YOU I'M A WHORE FOR SEMTEX, SO THAT PART WORKS OUT OKAY FOR YOU.
AND ANYWAY, DANIELO'S A BOY, NOT A MAN.
KLIK
OH MY GOD.
CARMEN, TELL ME--
--HOW IS IT WITH YOU AMERICANS?
THE BETTER THE ASS, THE WORSE THE LISTENER.
PHTTT PHTTT
NILS, I HAVE THE MERCHANDISE YOU REQUESTED.
IS READY FOR DELIVERY.

UG BROTHERS FOREVER CHAPTER ONE / COVER ART BY PHILIP BOND

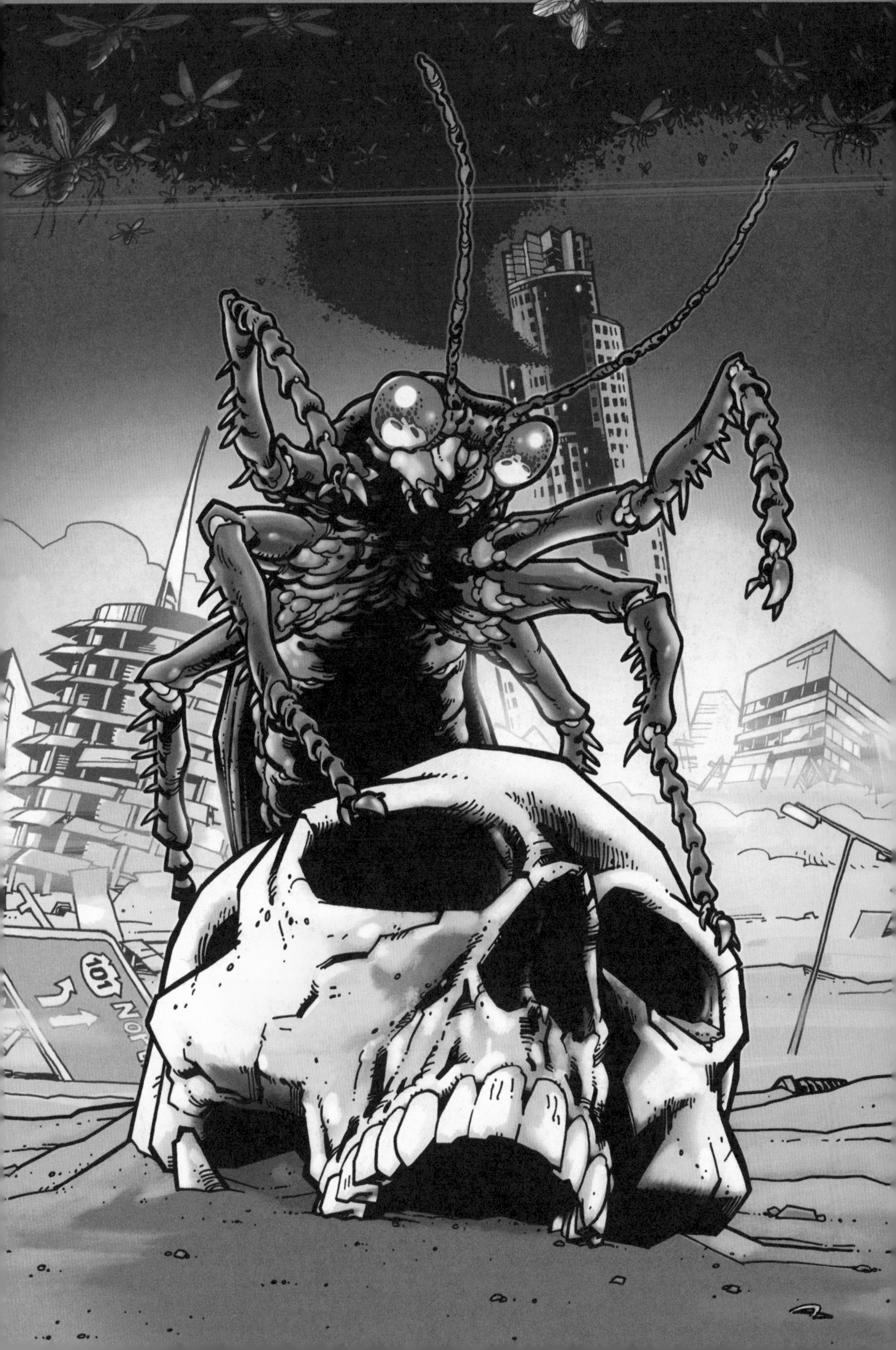

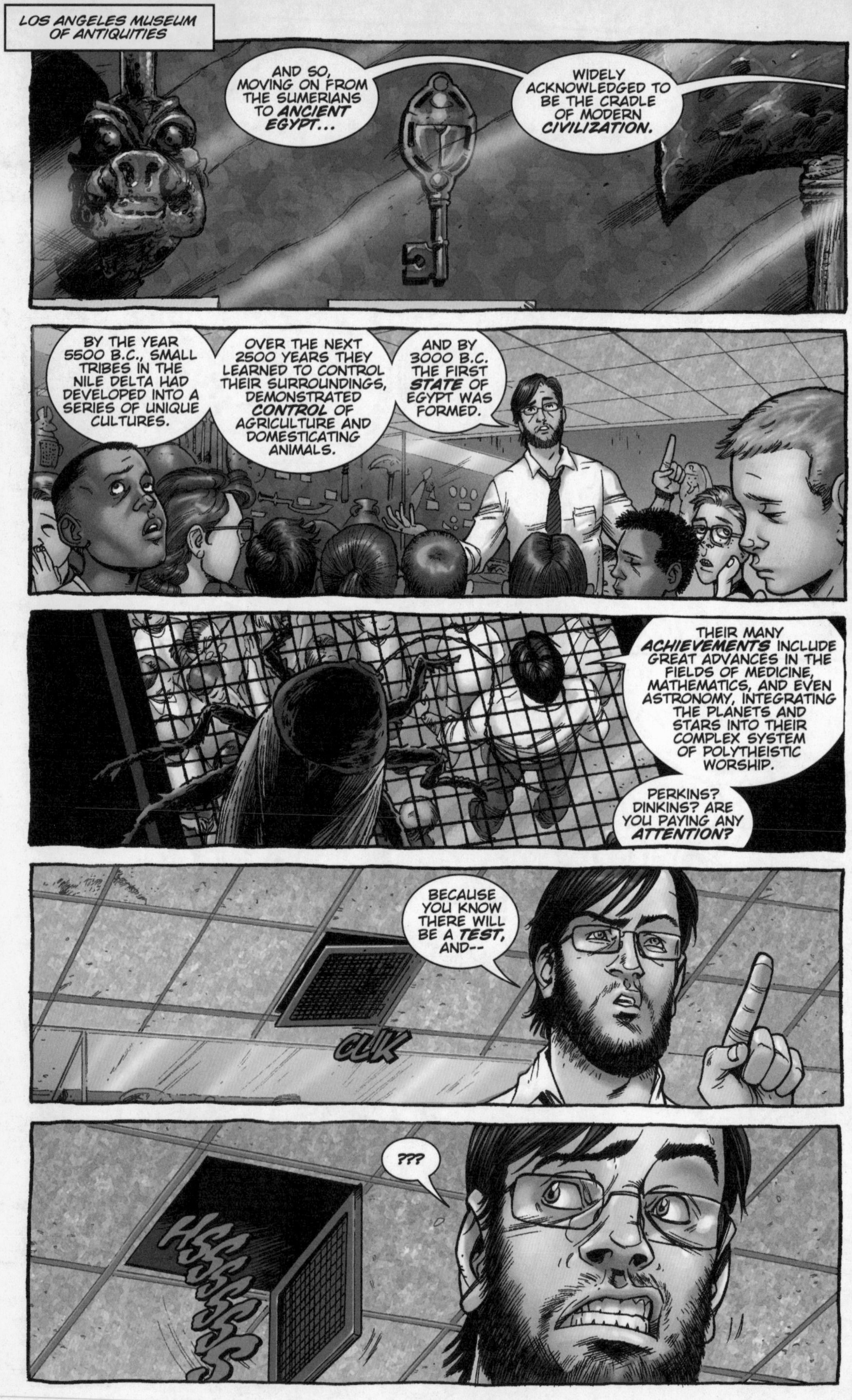
LOS ANGELES MUSEUM OF ANTIQUITIES
AND SO, MOVING ON FROM THE SUMERIANS TO ANCIENT EGYPT...
WIDELY ACKNOWLEDGED TO BE THE CRADLE OF MODERN CIVILIZATION.
BY THE YEAR 5500 B.C., SMALL TRIBES IN THE NILE DELTA HAD DEVELOPED INTO A SERIES OF UNIQUE CULTURES.
OVER THE NEXT 2500 YEARS THEY LEARNED TO CONTROL THEIR SURROUNDINGS, DEMONSTRATED CONTROL OF AGRICULTURE AND DOMESTICATING ANIMALS.
AND BY 3000 B.C. THE FIRST STATE OF EGYPT WAS FORMED.
THEIR MANY ACHIEVEMENTS INCLUDE GREAT ADVANCES IN THE FIELDS OF MEDICINE, MATHEMATICS, AND EVEN ASTRONOMY, INTEGRATING THE PLANETS AND STARS INTO THEIR COMPLEX SYSTEM OF POLYTHEISTIC WORSHIP.
PERKINS? DINKINS? ARE YOU PAYING ANY ATTENTION?
BECAUSE YOU KNOW THERE WILL BE A TEST, AND--
CLIK
???
HSSSSSSS

ER...

ARHHHHHHHHHH!!

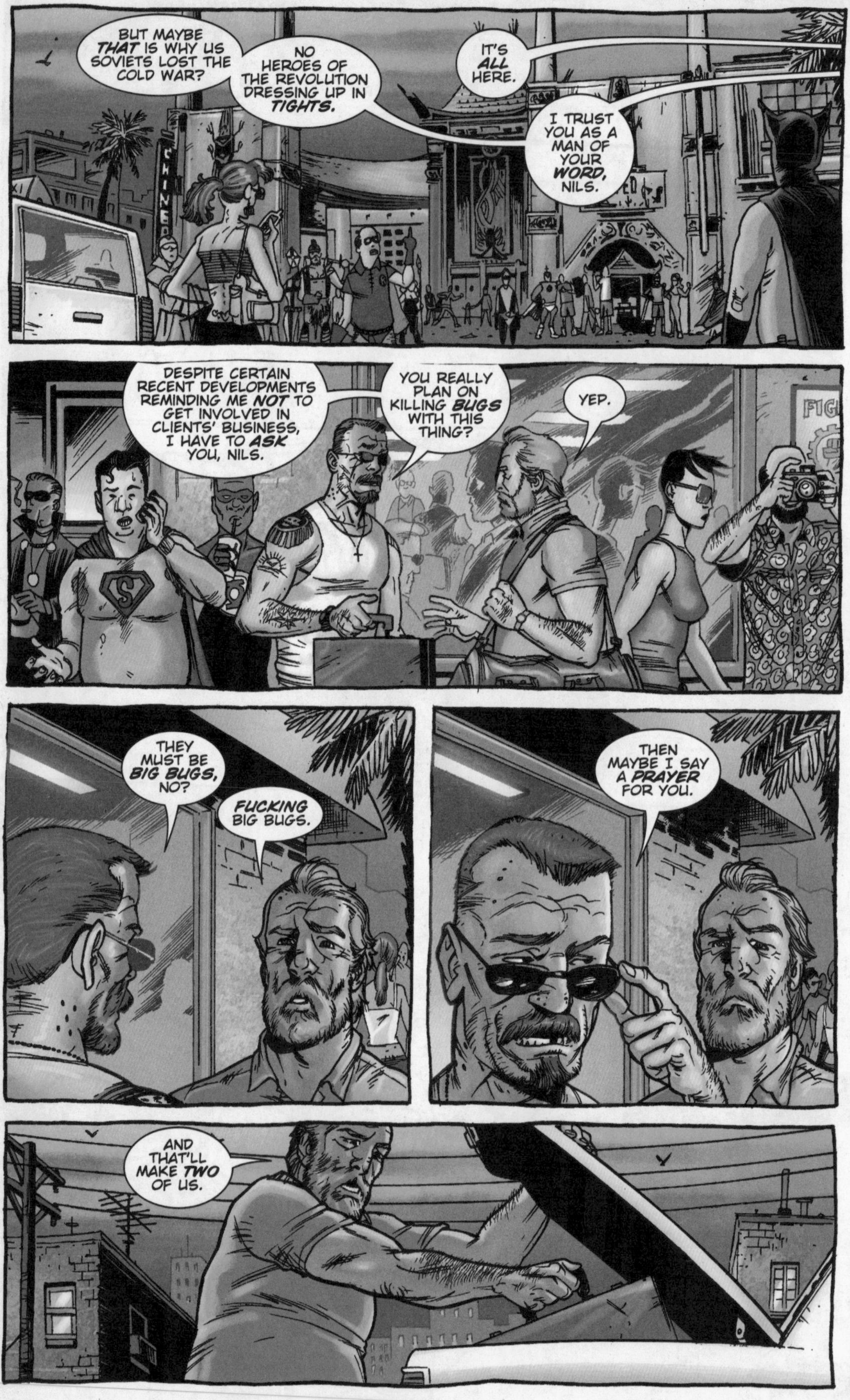

BUT MAYBE THAT IS WHY US SOVIETS LOST THE COLD WAR?
NO HEROES OF THE REVOLUTION DRESSING UP IN TIGHTS.
IT'S ALL HERE.
I TRUST YOU AS A MAN OF YOUR WORD, NILS.
CHINESE
DESPITE CERTAIN RECENT DEVELOPMENTS REMINDING ME NOT TO GET INVOLVED IN CLIENTS' BUSINESS, I HAVE TO ASK YOU, NILS.
YOU REALLY PLAN ON KILLING BUGS WITH THIS THING?
YEP.
THEY MUST BE BIG BUGS, NO?
FUCKING BIG BUGS.
THEN MAYBE I SAY A PRAYER FOR YOU.
AND THAT'LL MAKE TWO OF US.

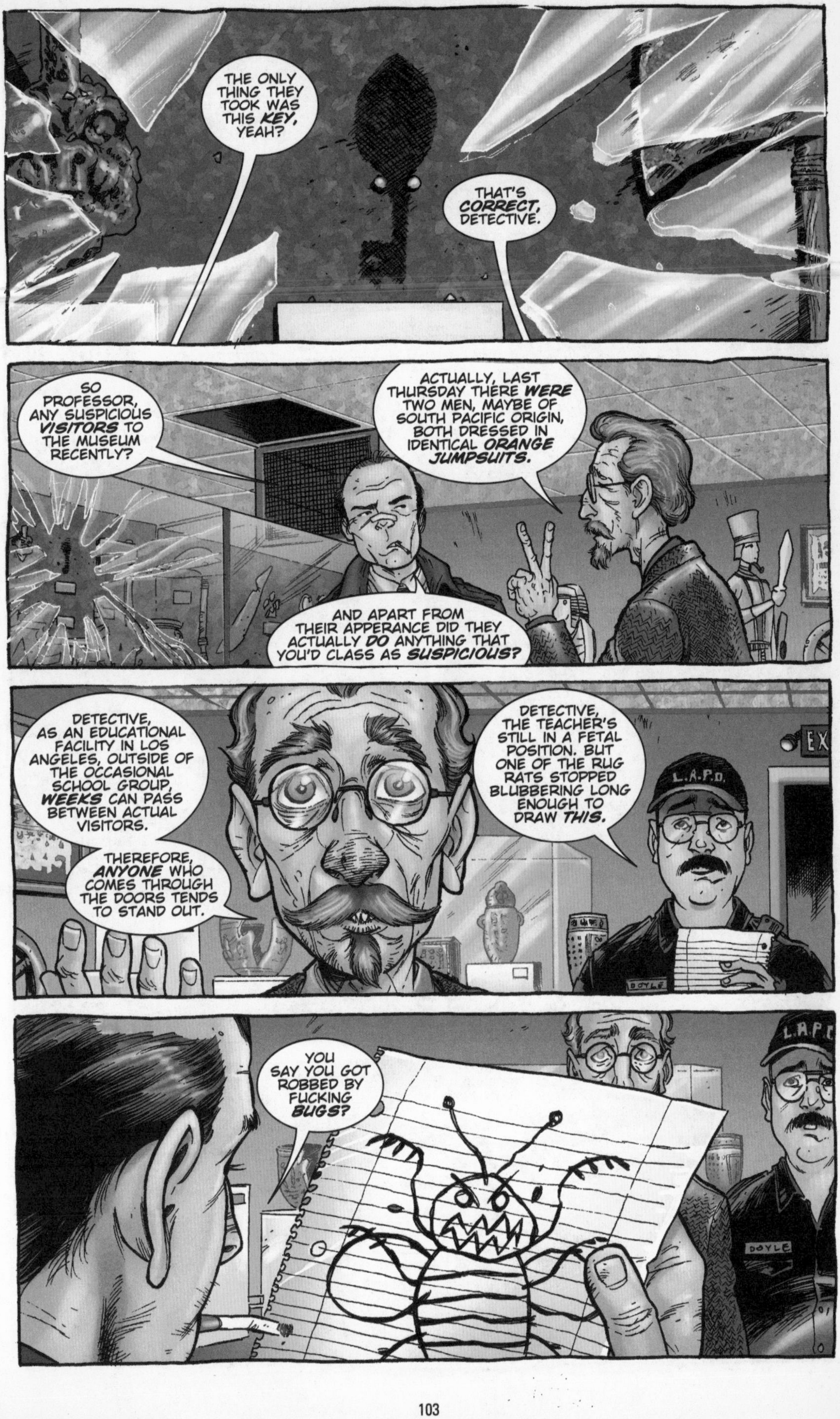
THE ONLY THING THEY TOOK WAS THIS KEY, YEAH?
THAT'S CORRECT, DETECTIVE.
SO PROFESSOR, ANY SUSPICIOUS VISITORS TO THE MUSEUM RECENTLY?
ACTUALLY, LAST THURSDAY THERE WERE TWO MEN, MAYBE OF SOUTH PACIFIC ORIGIN, BOTH DRESSED IN IDENTICAL ORANGE JUMPSUITS.
AND APART FROM THEIR APPERANCE DID THEY ACTUALLY DO ANYTHING THAT YOU'D CLASS AS SUSPICIOUS?
DETECTIVE, AS AN EDUCATIONAL FACILITY IN LOS ANGELES, OUTSIDE OF THE OCCASIONAL SCHOOL GROUP, WEEKS CAN PASS BETWEEN ACTUAL VISITORS.
THEREFORE, ANYONE WHO COMES THROUGH THE DOORS TENDS TO STAND OUT.
DETECTIVE, THE TEACHER'S STILL IN A FETAL POSITION. BUT ONE OF THE RUG RATS STOPPED BLUBBERING LONG ENOUGH TO DRAW THIS.
L.A.P.D.
DOYLE
YOU SAY YOU GOT ROBBED BY FUCKING BUGS?
L.A.P.D.
DOYLE

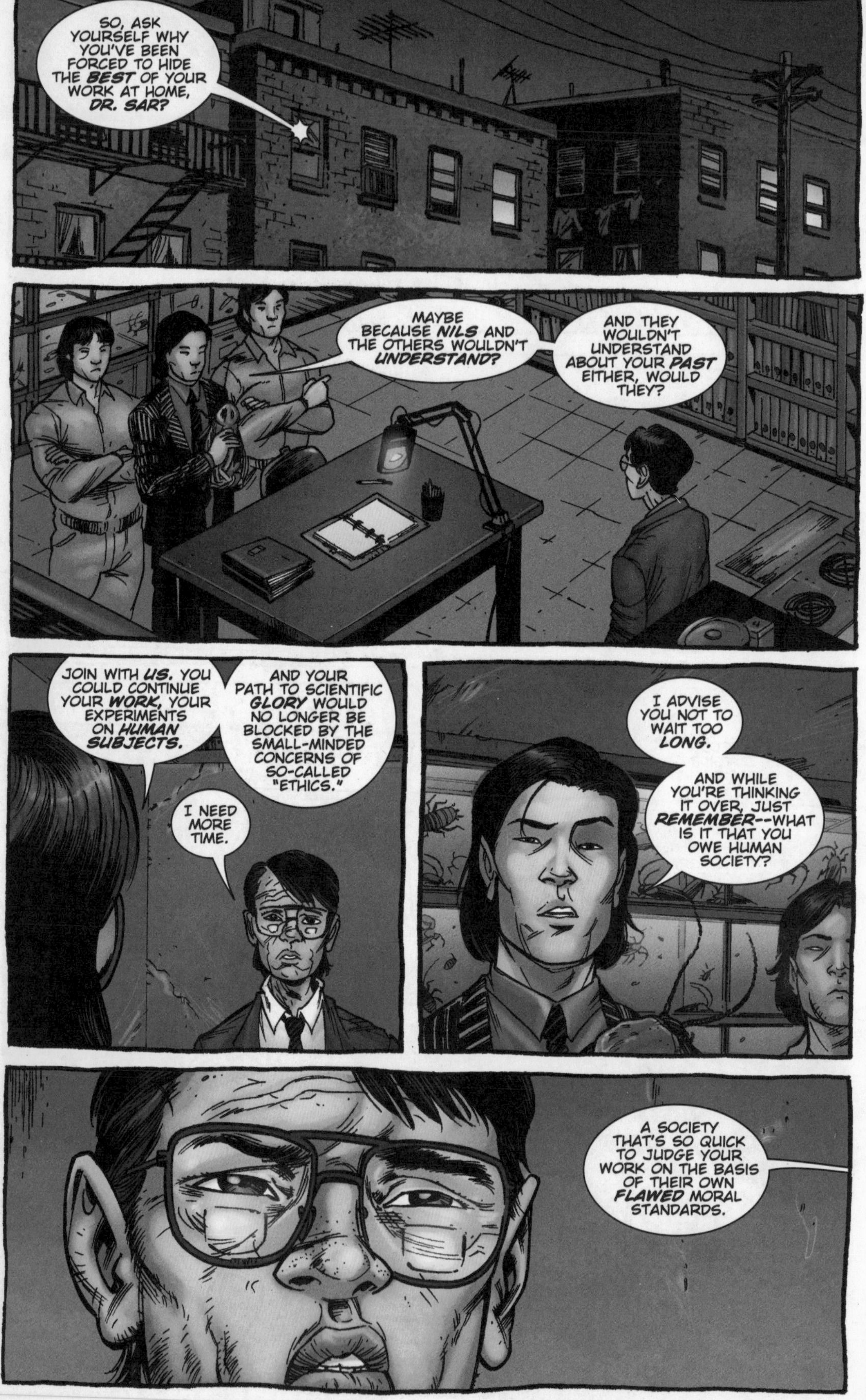

SO, ASK YOURSELF WHY YOU'VE BEEN FORCED TO HIDE THE BEST OF YOUR WORK AT HOME, DR. SAR?
MAYBE BECAUSE NILS AND THE OTHERS WOULDN'T UNDERSTAND?
AND THEY WOULDN'T UNDERSTAND ABOUT YOUR PAST EITHER, WOULD THEY?
JOIN WITH US. YOU COULD CONTINUE YOUR WORK, YOUR EXPERIMENTS ON HUMAN SUBJECTS.
AND YOUR PATH TO SCIENTIFIC GLORY WOULD NO LONGER BE BLOCKED BY THE SMALL-MINDED CONCERNS OF SO-CALLED "ETHICS."
I NEED MORE TIME.
I ADVISE YOU NOT TO WAIT TOO LONG.
AND WHILE YOU'RE THINKING IT OVER, JUST REMEMBER--WHAT IS IT THAT YOU OWE HUMAN SOCIETY?
A SOCIETY THAT'S SO QUICK TO JUDGE YOUR WORK ON THE BASIS OF THEIR OWN FLAWED MORAL STANDARDS.

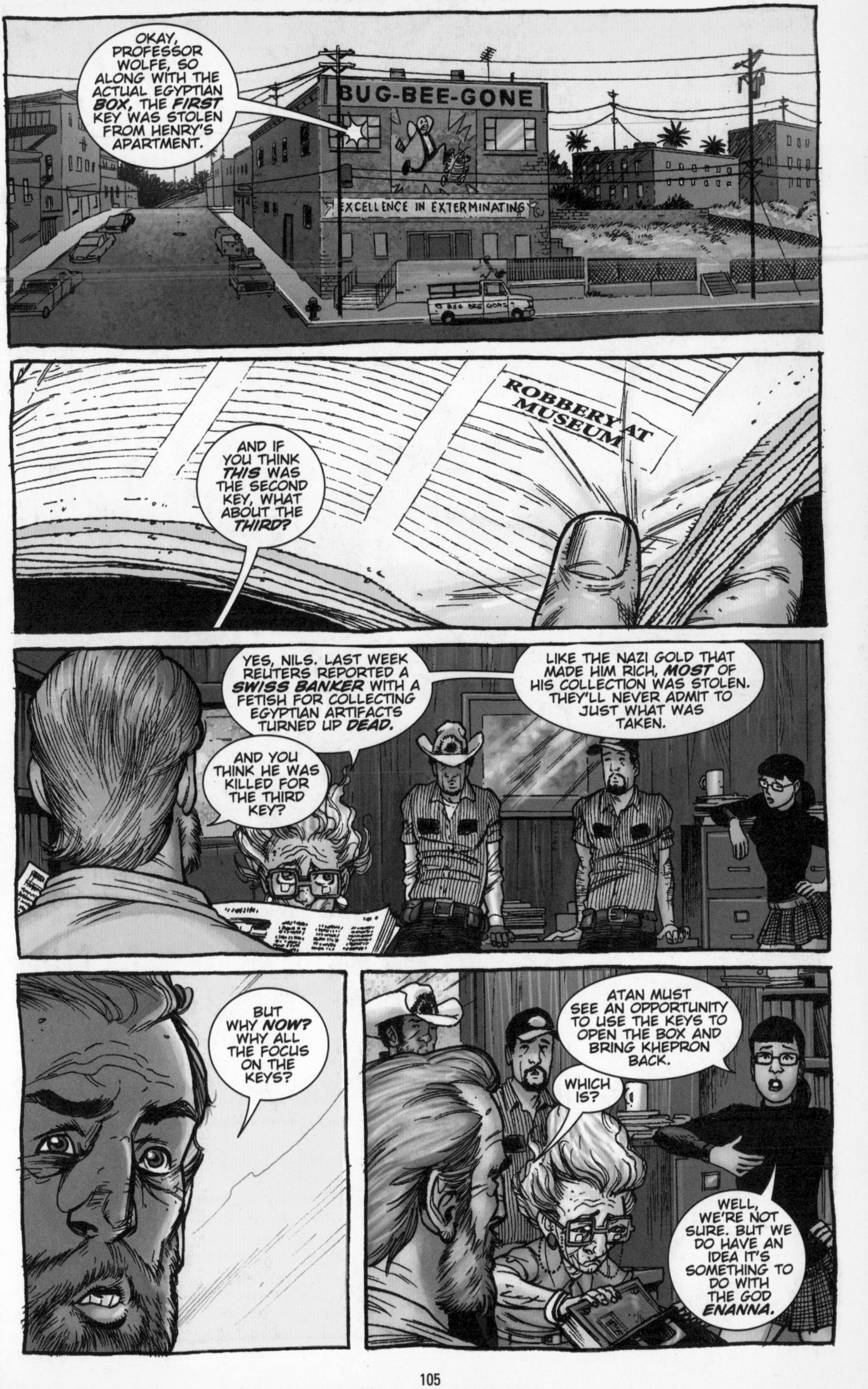
OKAY, PROFESSOR WOLFE, SO ALONG WITH THE ACTUAL EGYPTIAN BOX, THE FIRST KEY WAS STOLEN FROM HENRY'S APARTMENT.
BUG-BEE-GONE
EXCELLENCE IN EXTERMINATING
ROBBERY AT MUSEUM
AND IF YOU THINK THIS WAS THE SECOND KEY, WHAT ABOUT THE THIRD?
YES, NILS. LAST WEEK REUTERS REPORTED A SWISS BANKER WITH A FETISH FOR COLLECTING EGYPTIAN ARTIFACTS TURNED UP DEAD.
AND YOU THINK HE WAS KILLED FOR THE THIRD KEY?
LIKE THE NAZI GOLD THAT MADE HIM RICH, MOST OF HIS COLLECTION WAS STOLEN. THEY'LL NEVER ADMIT TO JUST WHAT WAS TAKEN.
BUT WHY NOW? WHY ALL THE FOCUS ON THE KEYS?
ATAN MUST SEE AN OPPORTUNITY TO USE THE KEYS TO OPEN THE BOX AND BRING KHEPRON BACK.
WHICH IS?
WELL, WE'RE NOT SURE. BUT WE DO HAVE AN IDEA IT'S SOMETHING TO DO WITH THE GOD ENANNA.

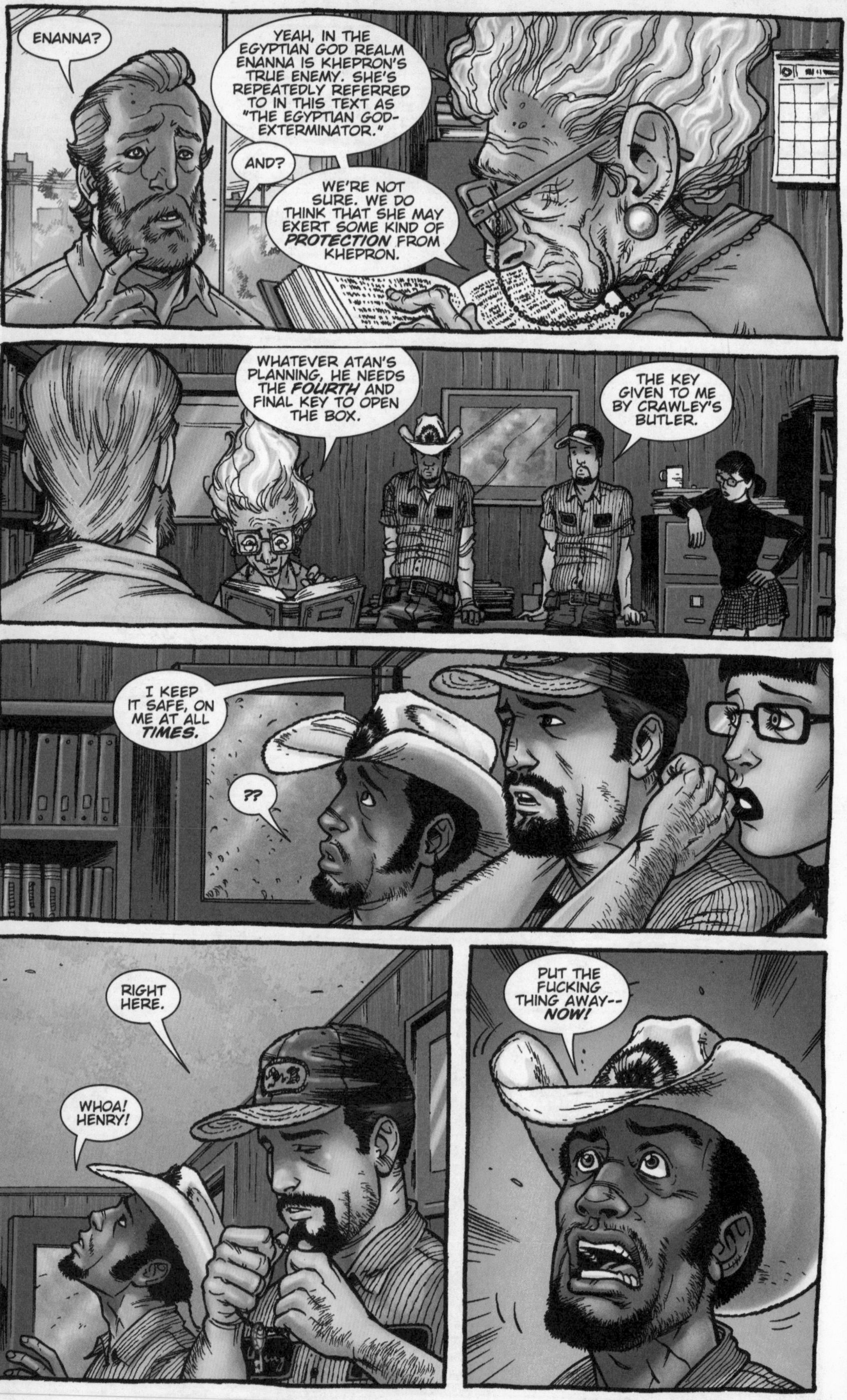
ENANNA?
YEAH, IN THE EGYPTIAN GOD REALM ENANNA IS KHEPRON'S TRUE ENEMY. SHE'S REPEATEDLY REFERRED TO IN THIS TEXT AS "THE EGYPTIAN GOD-EXTERMINATOR."
AND?
WE'RE NOT SURE. WE DO THINK THAT SHE MAY EXERT SOME KIND OF *PROTECTION* FROM KHEPRON.
WHATEVER ATAN'S PLANNING, HE NEEDS THE *FOURTH* AND FINAL KEY TO OPEN THE BOX.
THE KEY GIVEN TO ME BY CRAWLEY'S BUTLER.
I KEEP IT SAFE, ON ME AT ALL *TIMES.*
??
RIGHT HERE.
WHOA! HENRY!
PUT THE FUCKING THING AWAY-- *NOW!*

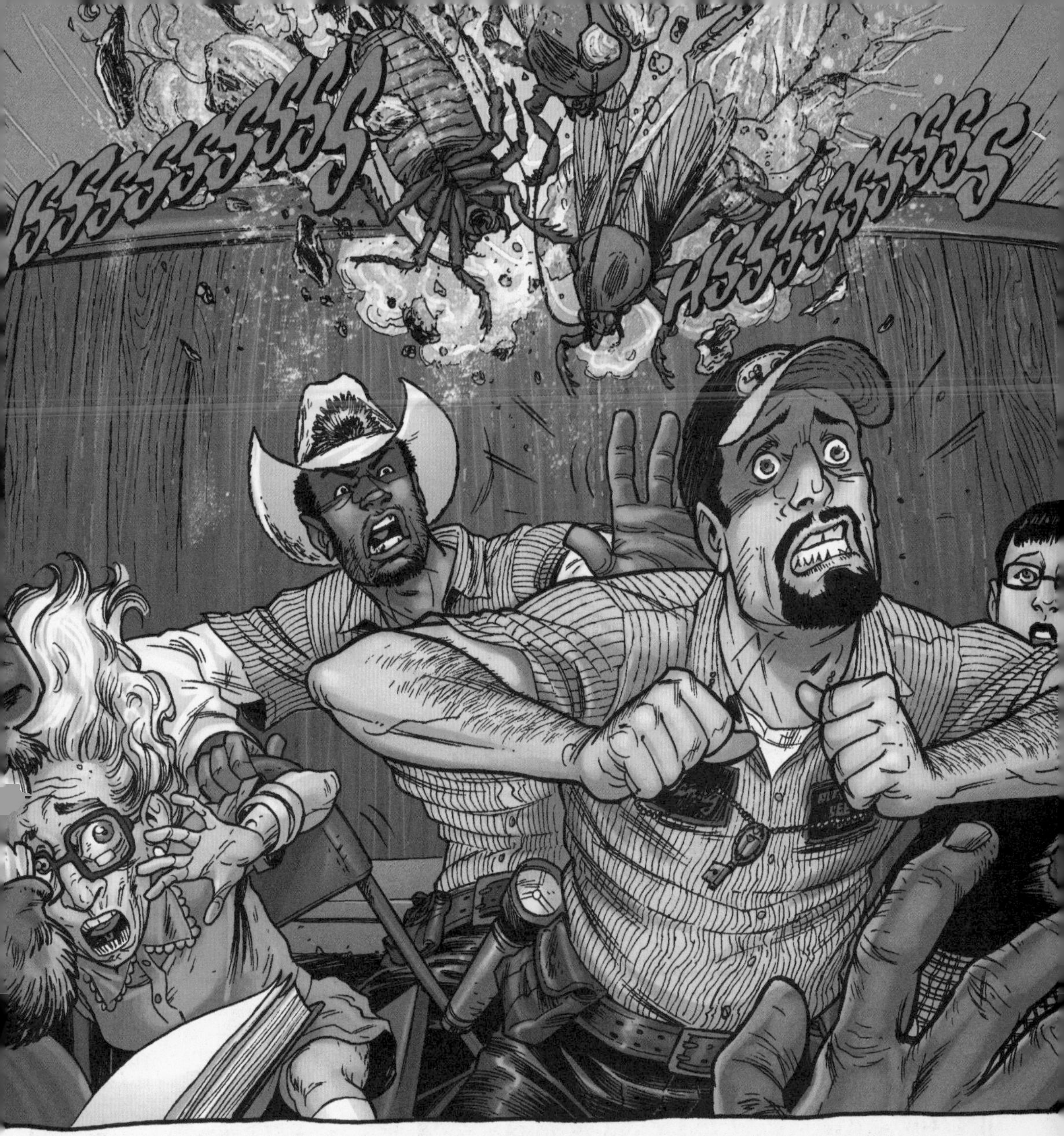
HSSSSSSSSS
HSSSSSSSSSS

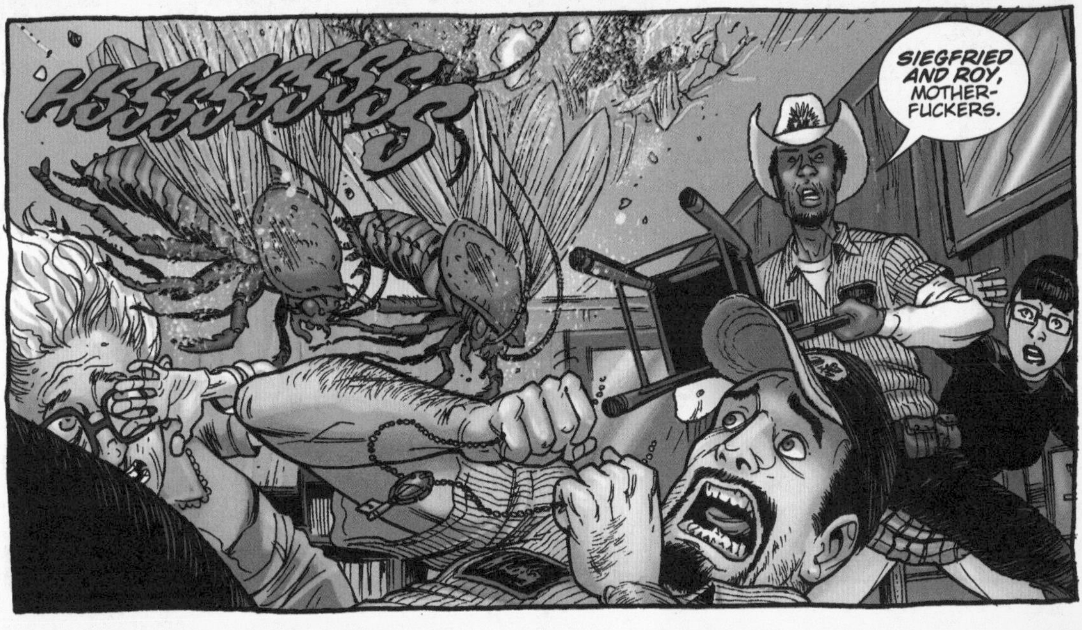
HSSSSSSSSS
SIEGFRIED AND ROY, MOTHER-FUCKERS.

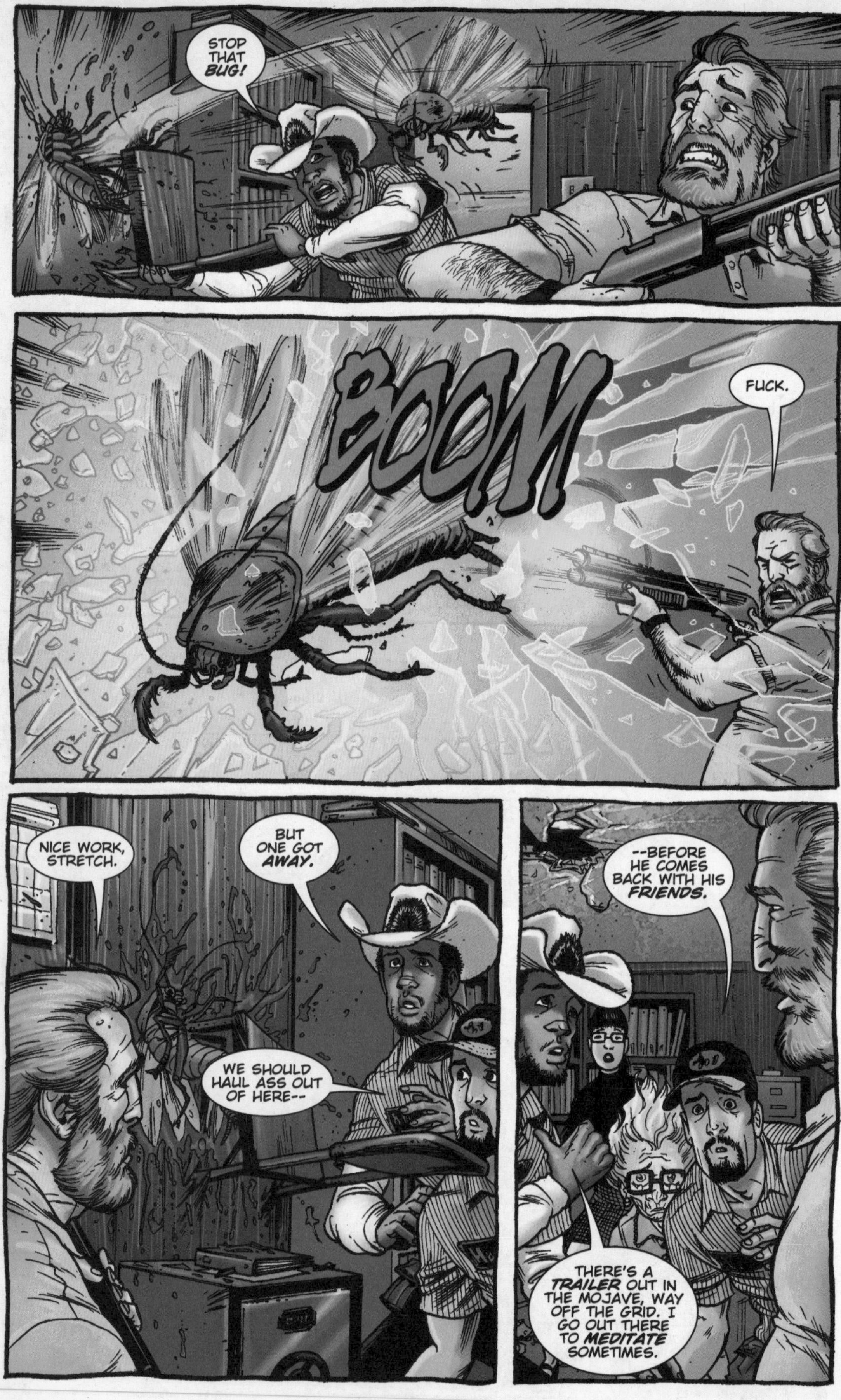
STOP THAT BUG!
BOOM
FUCK.
NICE WORK, STRETCH.
BUT ONE GOT AWAY.
WE SHOULD HAUL ASS OUT OF HERE--
--BEFORE HE COMES BACK WITH HIS FRIENDS.
THERE'S A TRAILER OUT IN THE MOJAVE, WAY OFF THE GRID. I GO OUT THERE TO MEDITATE SOMETIMES.

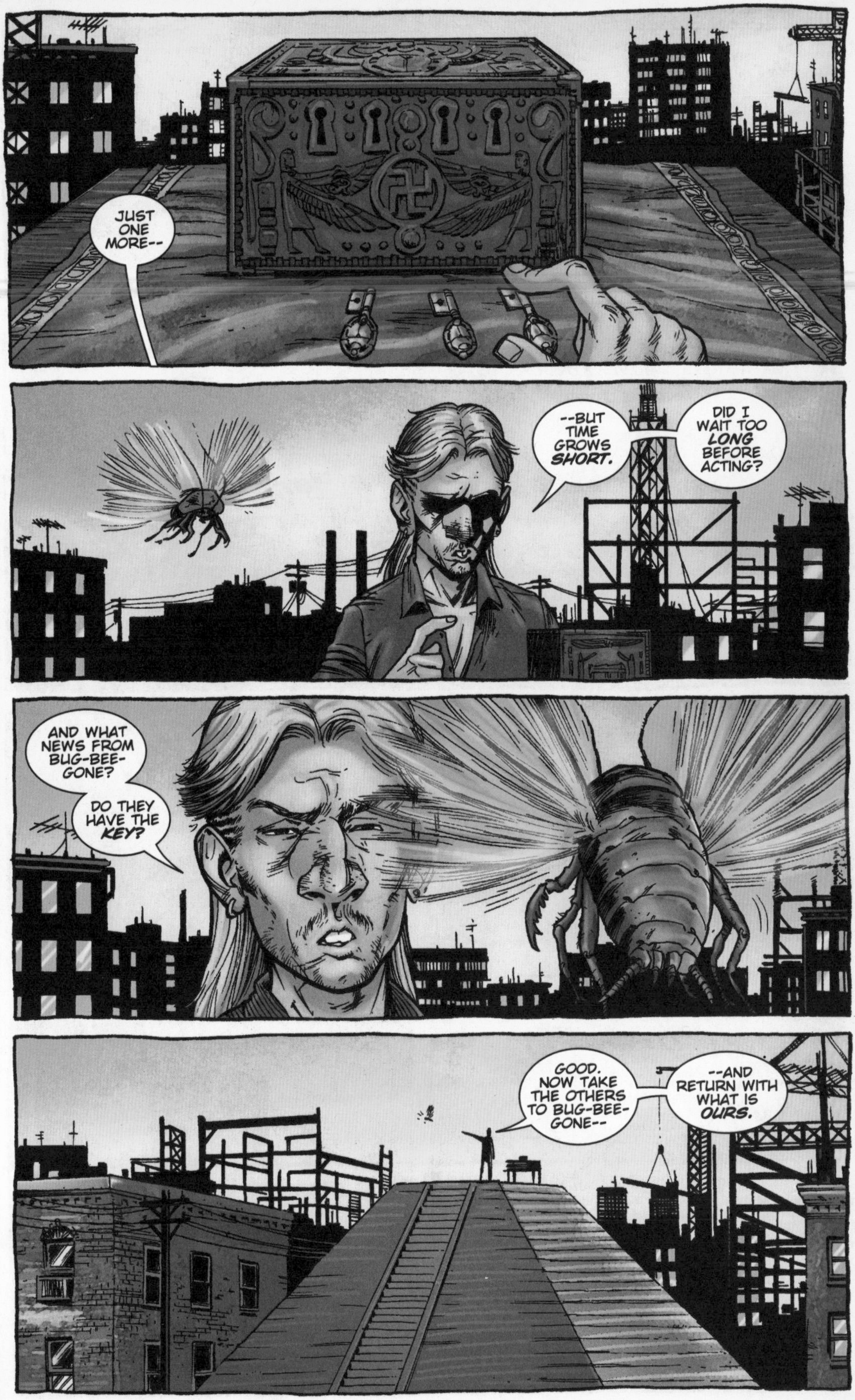
JUST ONE MORE--
--BUT TIME GROWS SHORT.
DID I WAIT TOO LONG BEFORE ACTING?
AND WHAT NEWS FROM BUG-BEE-GONE?
DO THEY HAVE THE KEY?
GOOD. NOW TAKE THE OTHERS TO BUG-BEE-GONE--
--AND RETURN WITH WHAT IS OURS.

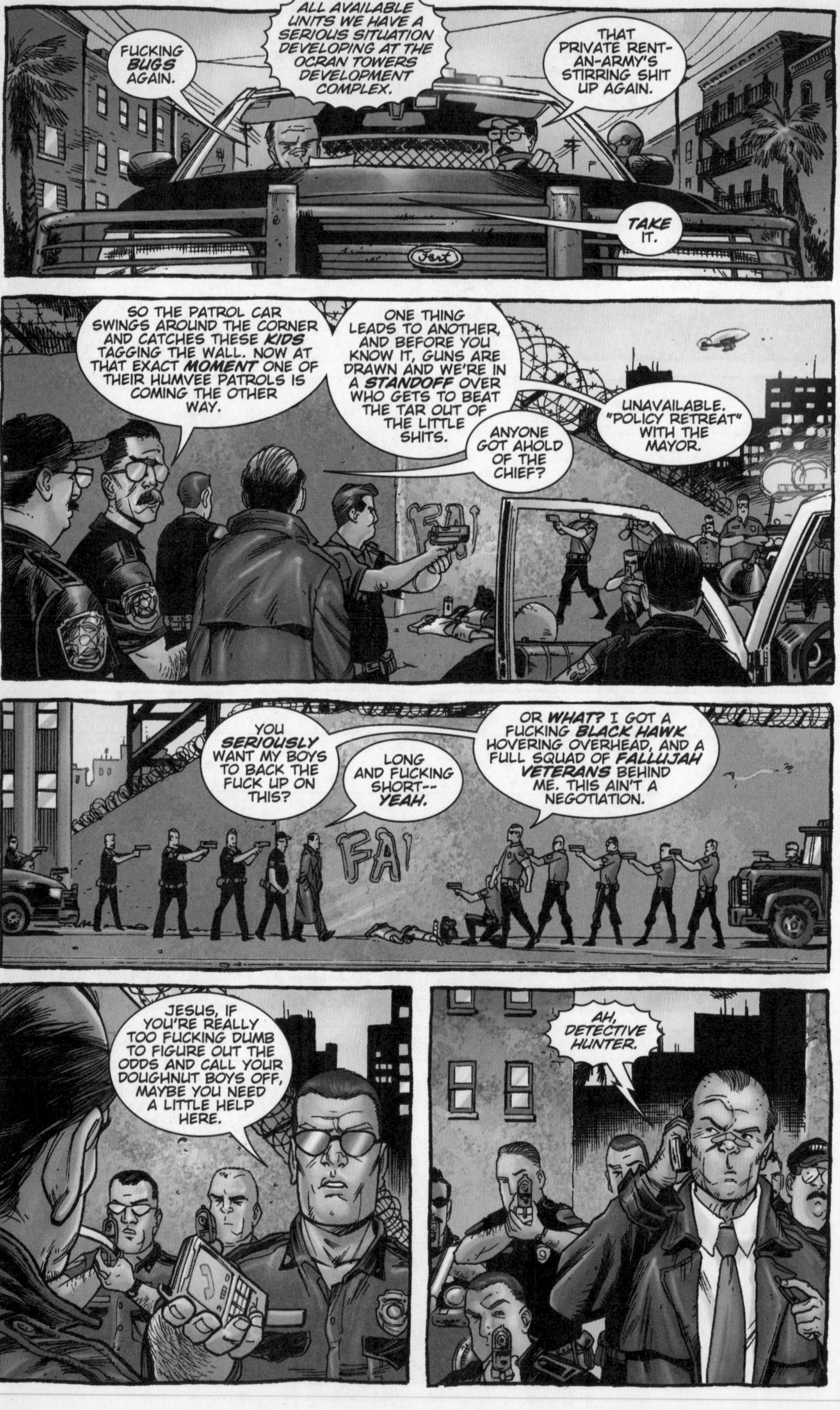
FUCKING BUGS AGAIN.
ALL AVAILABLE UNITS WE HAVE A SERIOUS SITUATION DEVELOPING AT THE OCRAN TOWERS DEVELOPMENT COMPLEX.
THAT PRIVATE RENT-AN-ARMY'S STIRRING SHIT UP AGAIN.
TAKE IT.
SO THE PATROL CAR SWINGS AROUND THE CORNER AND CATCHES THESE KIDS TAGGING THE WALL. NOW AT THAT EXACT MOMENT ONE OF THEIR HUMVEE PATROLS IS COMING THE OTHER WAY.
ONE THING LEADS TO ANOTHER, AND BEFORE YOU KNOW IT, GUNS ARE DRAWN AND WE'RE IN A STANDOFF OVER WHO GETS TO BEAT THE TAR OUT OF THE LITTLE SHITS.
ANYONE GOT AHOLD OF THE CHIEF?
UNAVAILABLE. "POLICY RETREAT" WITH THE MAYOR.
YOU SERIOUSLY WANT MY BOYS TO BACK THE FUCK UP ON THIS?
LONG AND FUCKING SHORT-- YEAH.
OR WHAT? I GOT A FUCKING BLACK HAWK HOVERING OVERHEAD, AND A FULL SQUAD OF FALLUJAH VETERANS BEHIND ME. THIS AIN'T A NEGOTIATION.
JESUS, IF YOU'RE REALLY TOO FUCKING DUMB TO FIGURE OUT THE ODDS AND CALL YOUR DOUGHNUT BOYS OFF, MAYBE YOU NEED A LITTLE HELP HERE.
AH, DETECTIVE HUNTER.

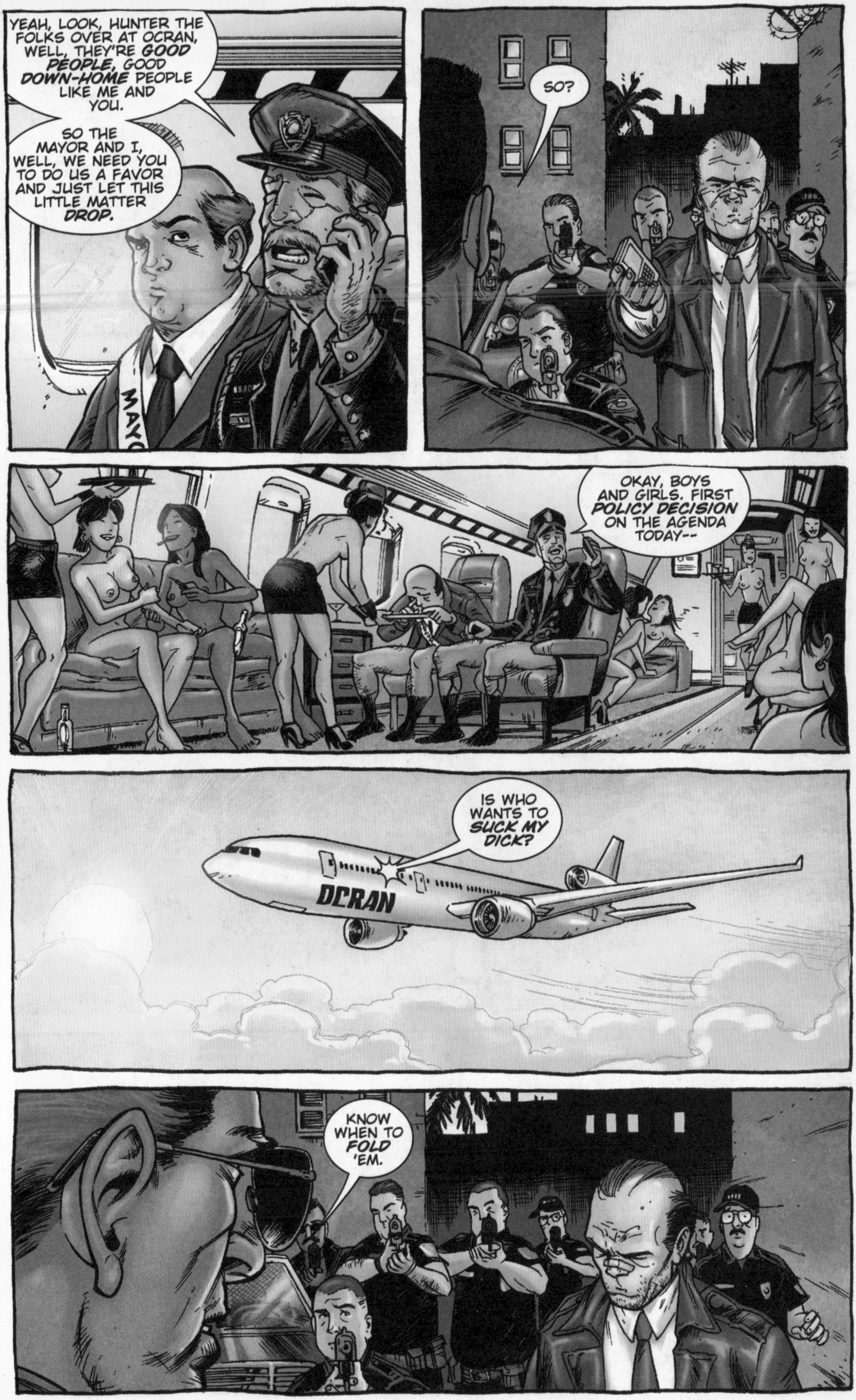
YEAH, LOOK, HUNTER THE FOLKS OVER AT OCRAN, WELL, THEY'RE GOOD PEOPLE, GOOD DOWN-HOME PEOPLE LIKE ME AND YOU.
SO THE MAYOR AND I, WELL, WE NEED YOU TO DO US A FAVOR AND JUST LET THIS LITTLE MATTER DROP.
SO?
OKAY, BOYS AND GIRLS. FIRST POLICY DECISION ON THE AGENDA TODAY--
IS WHO WANTS TO SUCK MY DICK?
OCRAN
KNOW WHEN TO FOLD 'EM.

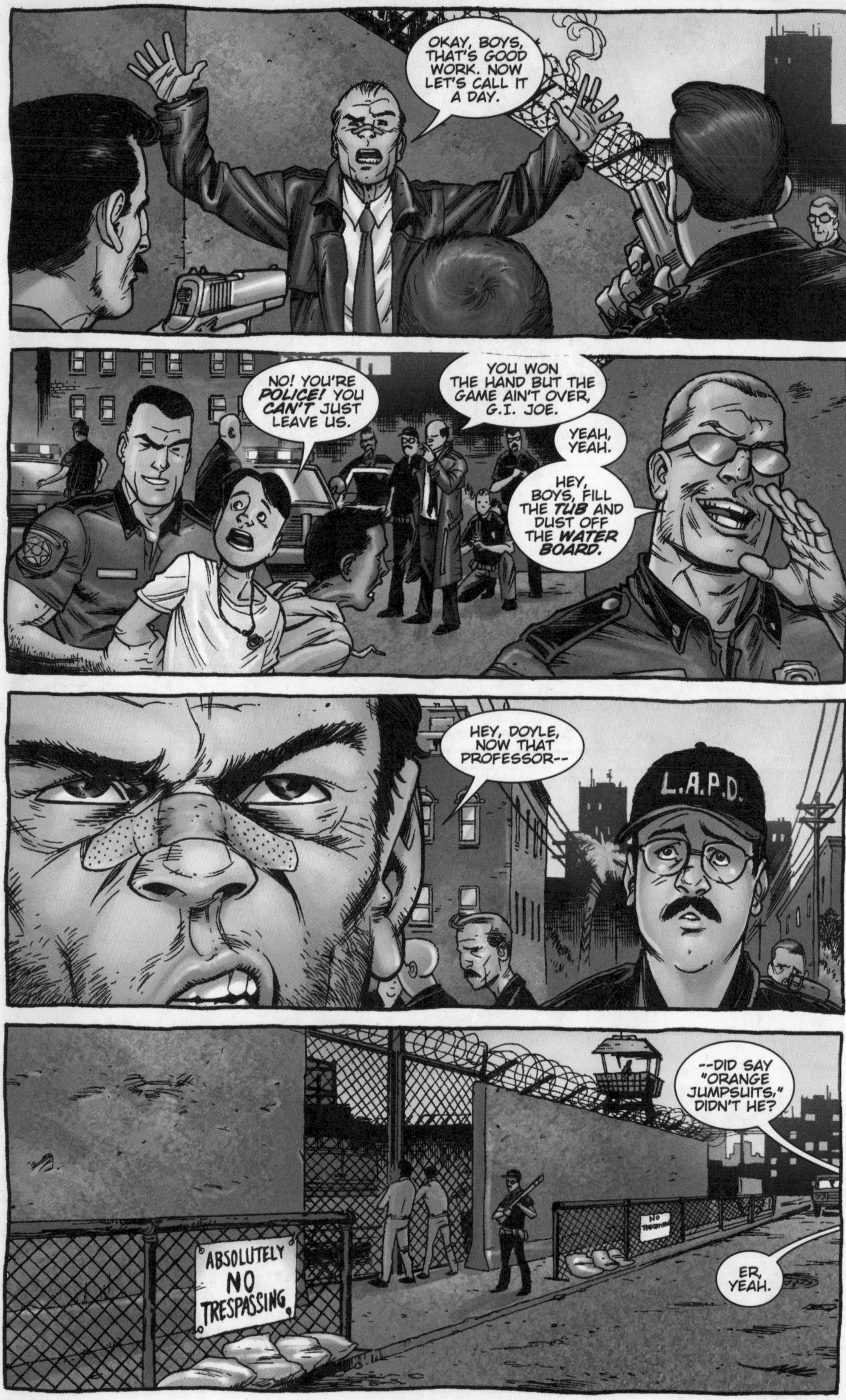

OKAY, BOYS, THAT'S GOOD WORK. NOW LET'S CALL IT A DAY.
NO! YOU'RE POLICE! YOU CAN'T JUST LEAVE US.
YOU WON THE HAND BUT THE GAME AIN'T OVER, G.I. JOE.
YEAH, YEAH.
HEY, BOYS, FILL THE TUB AND DUST OFF THE WATER BOARD.
HEY, DOYLE, NOW THAT PROFESSOR--
L.A.P.D.
--DID SAY "ORANGE JUMPSUITS," DIDN'T HE?
ER, YEAH.
ABSOLUTELY NO TRESPASSING

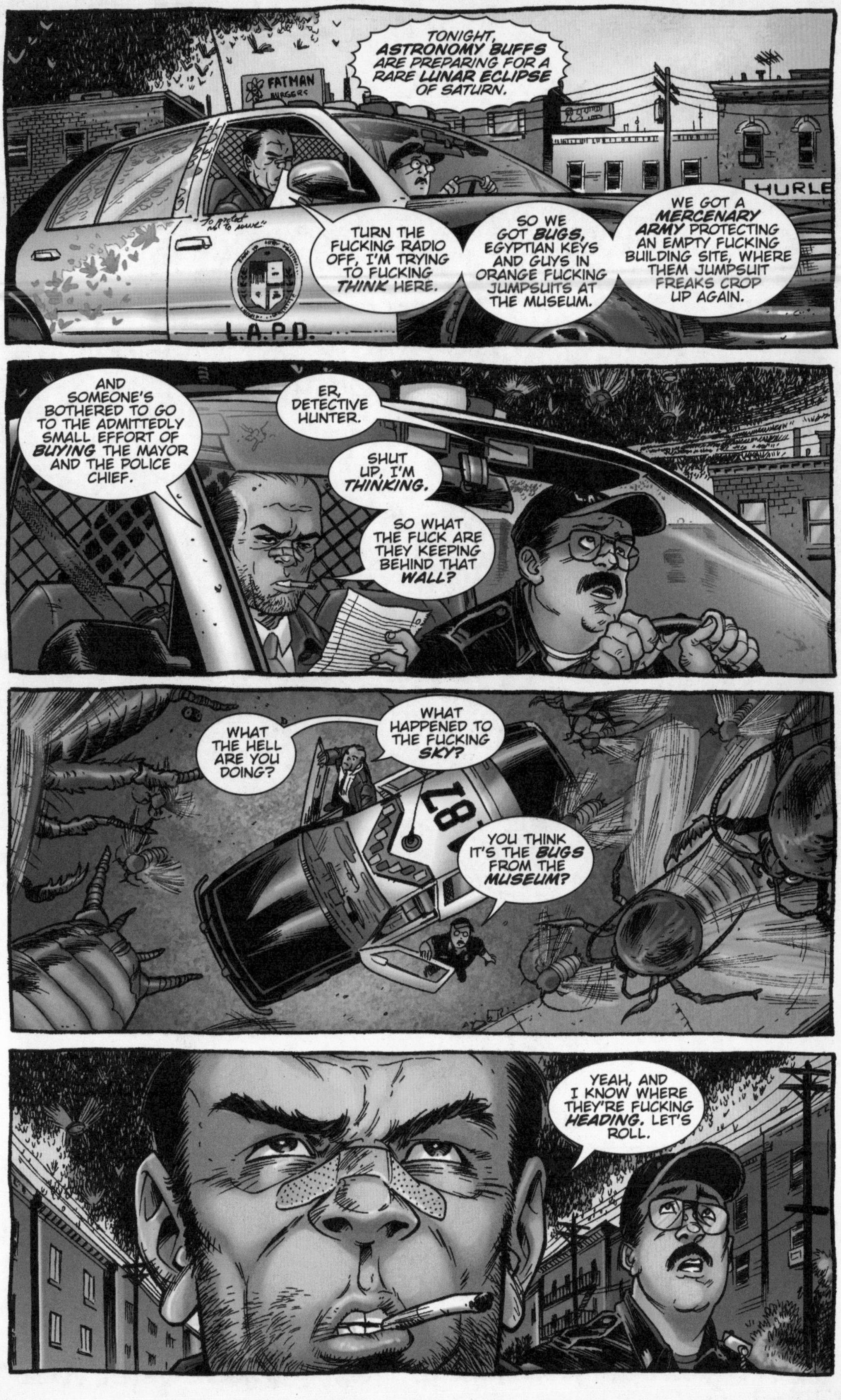

TONIGHT, ASTRONOMY BUFFS ARE PREPARING FOR A RARE LUNAR ECLIPSE OF SATURN.
FATMAN BURGERS
HURLE
TURN THE FUCKING RADIO OFF, I'M TRYING TO FUCKING THINK HERE.
SO WE GOT BUGS, EGYPTIAN KEYS AND GUYS IN ORANGE FUCKING JUMPSUITS AT THE MUSEUM.
WE GOT A MERCENARY ARMY PROTECTING AN EMPTY FUCKING BUILDING SITE, WHERE THEM JUMPSUIT FREAKS CROP UP AGAIN.
L.A.P.D.
AND SOMEONE'S BOTHERED TO GO TO THE ADMITTEDLY SMALL EFFORT OF BUYING THE MAYOR AND THE POLICE CHIEF.
ER, DETECTIVE HUNTER.
SHUT UP, I'M THINKING.
SO WHAT THE FUCK ARE THEY KEEPING BEHIND THAT WALL?
WHAT THE HELL ARE YOU DOING?
WHAT HAPPENED TO THE FUCKING SKY?
YOU THINK IT'S THE BUGS FROM THE MUSEUM?
YEAH, AND I KNOW WHERE THEY'RE FUCKING HEADING. LET'S ROLL.

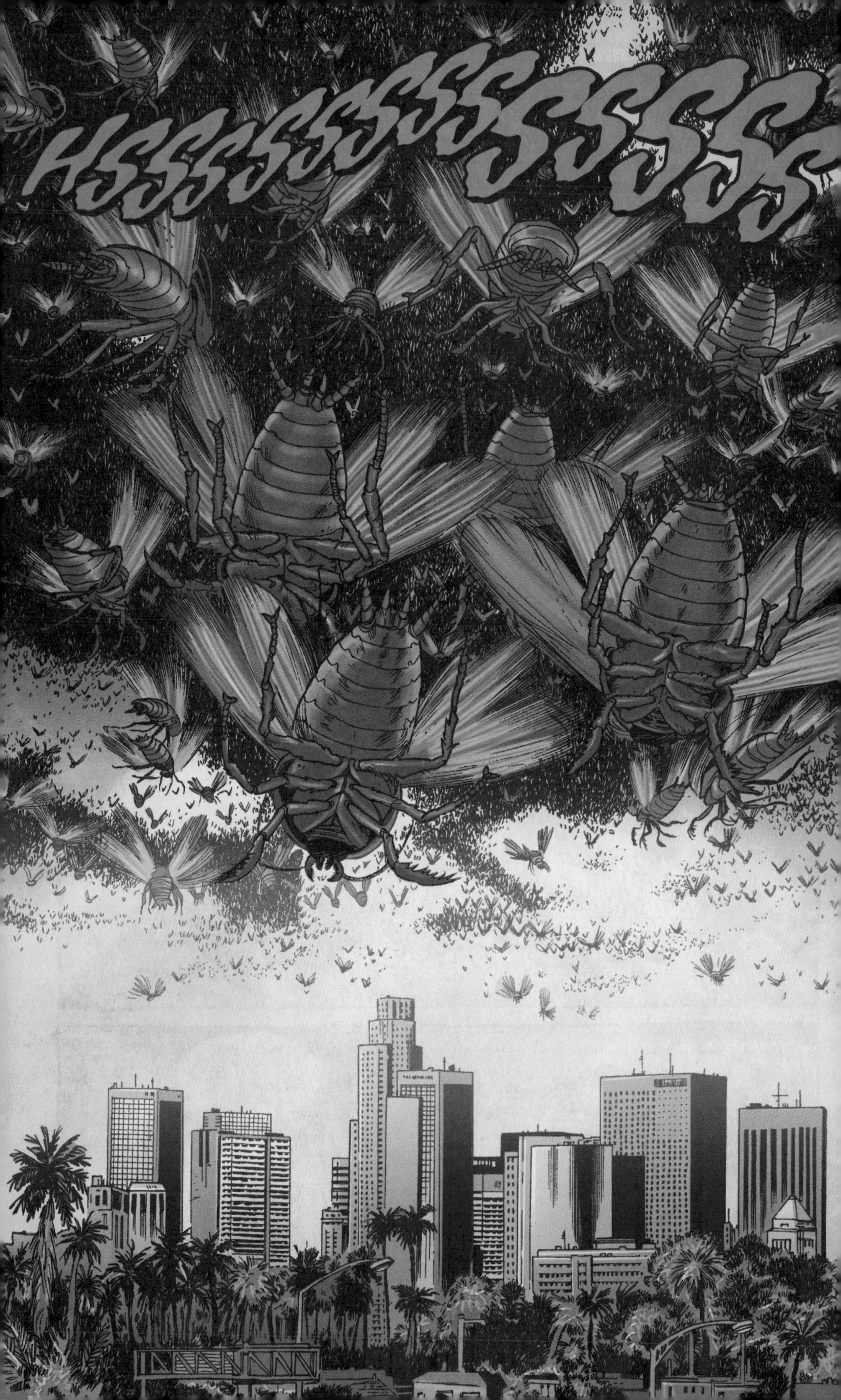
HSSSSSSSSSSSSSS

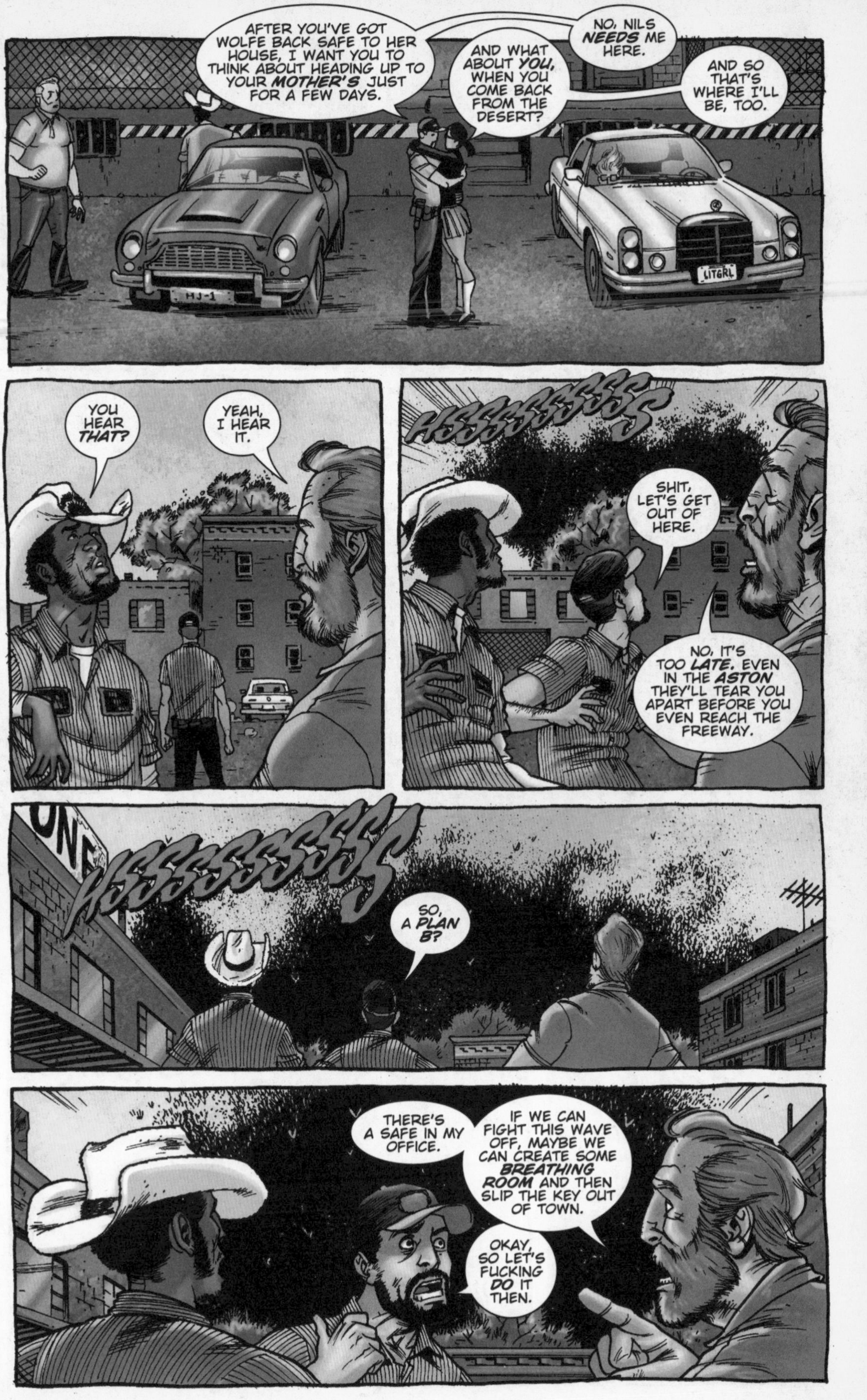
AFTER YOU'VE GOT WOLFE BACK SAFE TO HER HOUSE, I WANT YOU TO THINK ABOUT HEADING UP TO YOUR MOTHER'S JUST FOR A FEW DAYS.
NO, NILS NEEDS ME HERE.
AND WHAT ABOUT YOU, WHEN YOU COME BACK FROM THE DESERT?
AND SO THAT'S WHERE I'LL BE, TOO.
HJ-1
LITGRL
YOU HEAR THAT?
YEAH, I HEAR IT.
HSSSSSSSSS
SHIT, LET'S GET OUT OF HERE.
NO, IT'S TOO LATE. EVEN IN THE ASTON THEY'LL TEAR YOU APART BEFORE YOU EVEN REACH THE FREEWAY.
HSSSSSSSSSS
SO, A PLAN B?
THERE'S A SAFE IN MY OFFICE.
IF WE CAN FIGHT THIS WAVE OFF, MAYBE WE CAN CREATE SOME BREATHING ROOM AND THEN SLIP THE KEY OUT OF TOWN.
OKAY, SO LET'S FUCKING DO IT THEN.

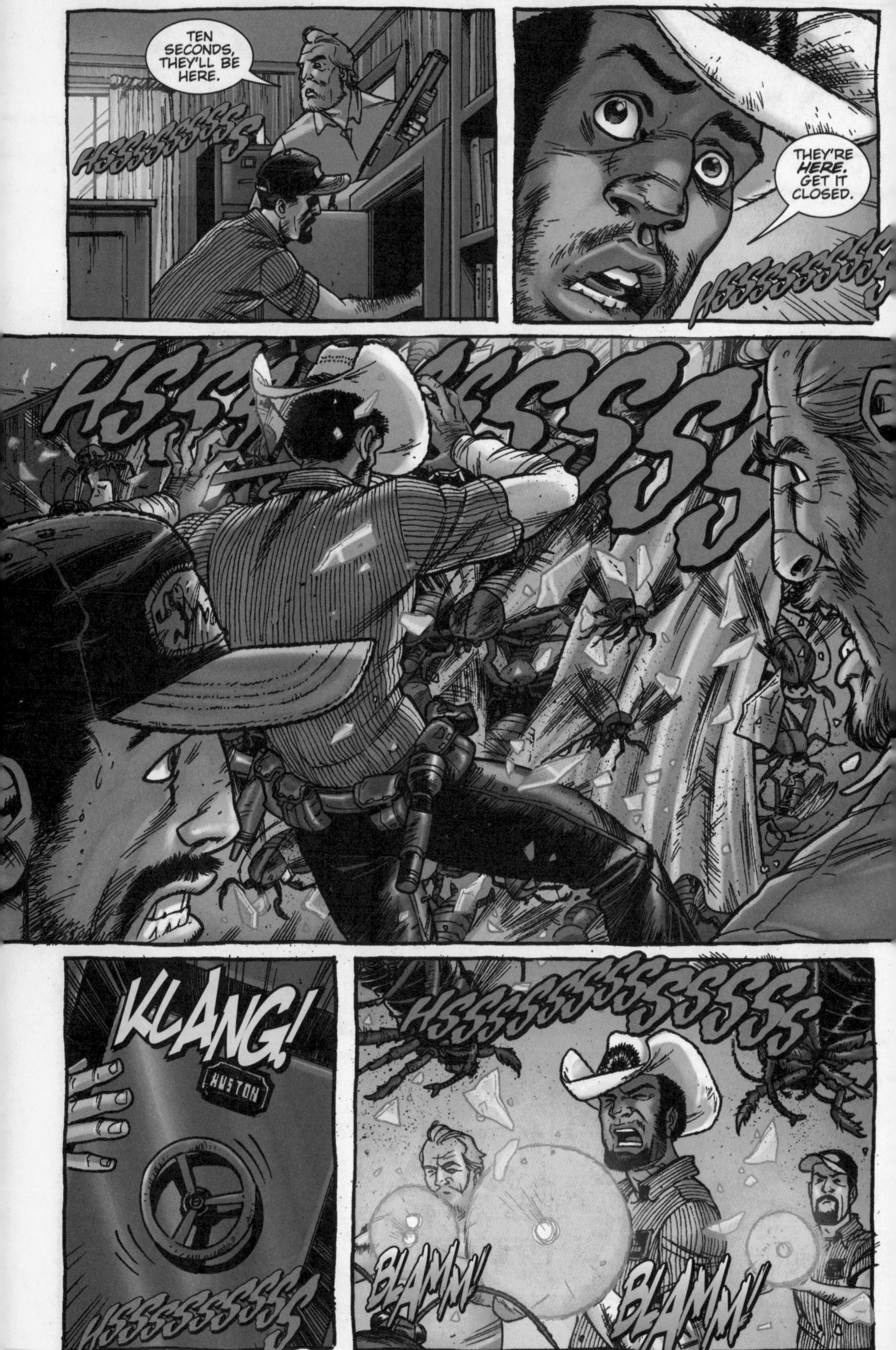
TEN SECONDS, THEY'LL BE HERE.
HSSSSSSSSS
THEY'RE HERE. GET IT CLOSED.
HSSSSSSSSSS
HSSSSSSSSS
KLANG!
HUSTON
HSSSSSSSSSS
HSSSSSSSSSSSSSS
BLAMM!
BLAMM!

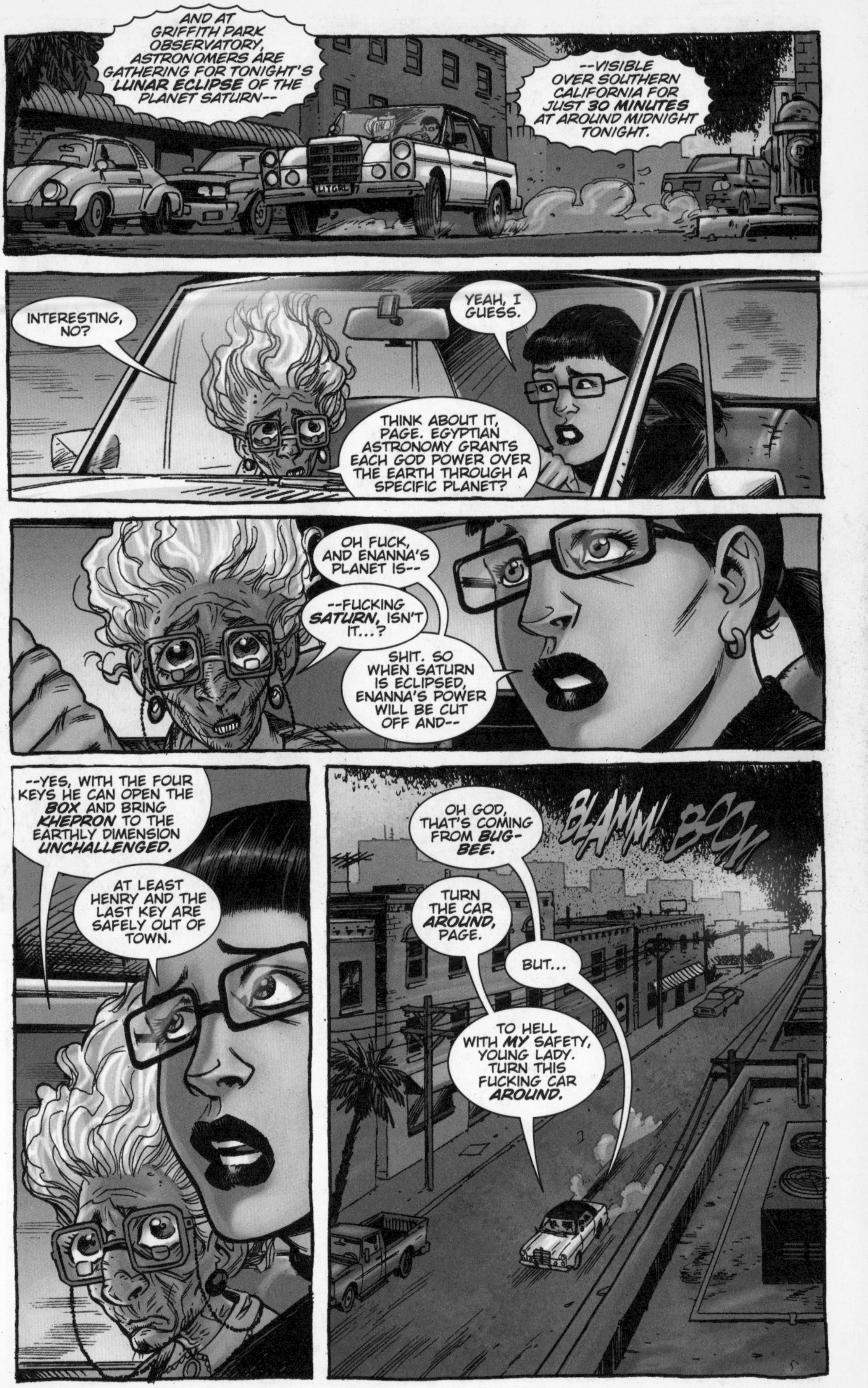
AND AT GRIFFITH PARK OBSERVATORY, ASTRONOMERS ARE GATHERING FOR TONIGHT'S LUNAR ECLIPSE OF THE PLANET SATURN--
--VISIBLE OVER SOUTHERN CALIFORNIA FOR JUST 30 MINUTES AT AROUND MIDNIGHT TONIGHT.
INTERESTING, NO?
YEAH, I GUESS.
THINK ABOUT IT, PAGE. EGYPTIAN ASTRONOMY GRANTS EACH GOD POWER OVER THE EARTH THROUGH A SPECIFIC PLANET?
OH FUCK, AND ENANNA'S PLANET IS--
--FUCKING SATURN, ISN'T IT...?
SHIT. SO WHEN SATURN IS ECLIPSED, ENANNA'S POWER WILL BE CUT OFF AND--
--YES, WITH THE FOUR KEYS HE CAN OPEN THE BOX AND BRING KHEPRON TO THE EARTHLY DIMENSION UNCHALLENGED.
AT LEAST HENRY AND THE LAST KEY ARE SAFELY OUT OF TOWN.
BLAMM! BOOM
OH GOD, THAT'S COMING FROM BUGBEE.
TURN THE CAR AROUND, PAGE.
BUT...
TO HELL WITH MY SAFETY, YOUNG LADY. TURN THIS FUCKING CAR AROUND.

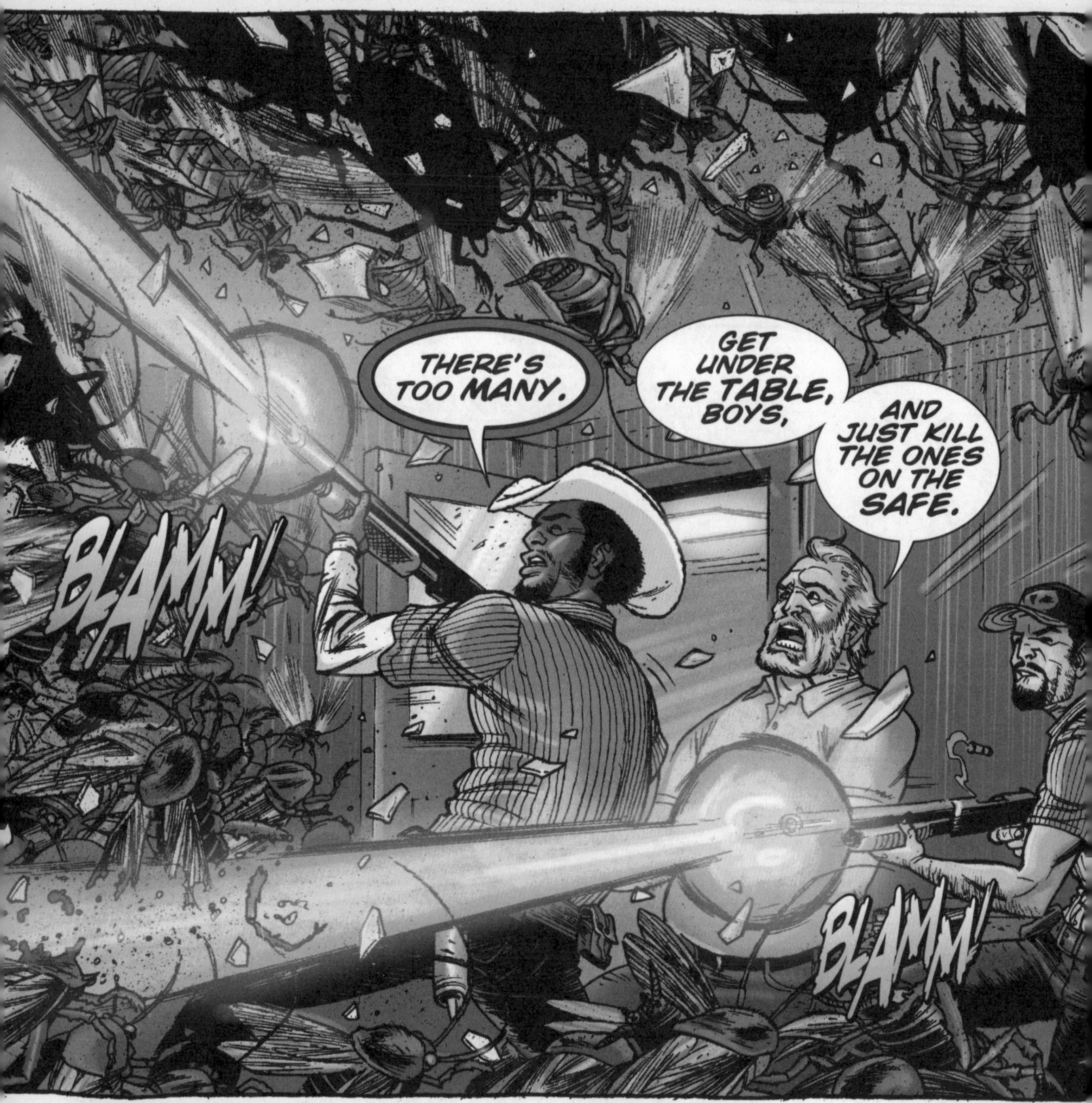
THERE'S TOO MANY.
GET UNDER THE TABLE, BOYS,
AND JUST KILL THE ONES ON THE SAFE.
BLAMM!
BLAMM!

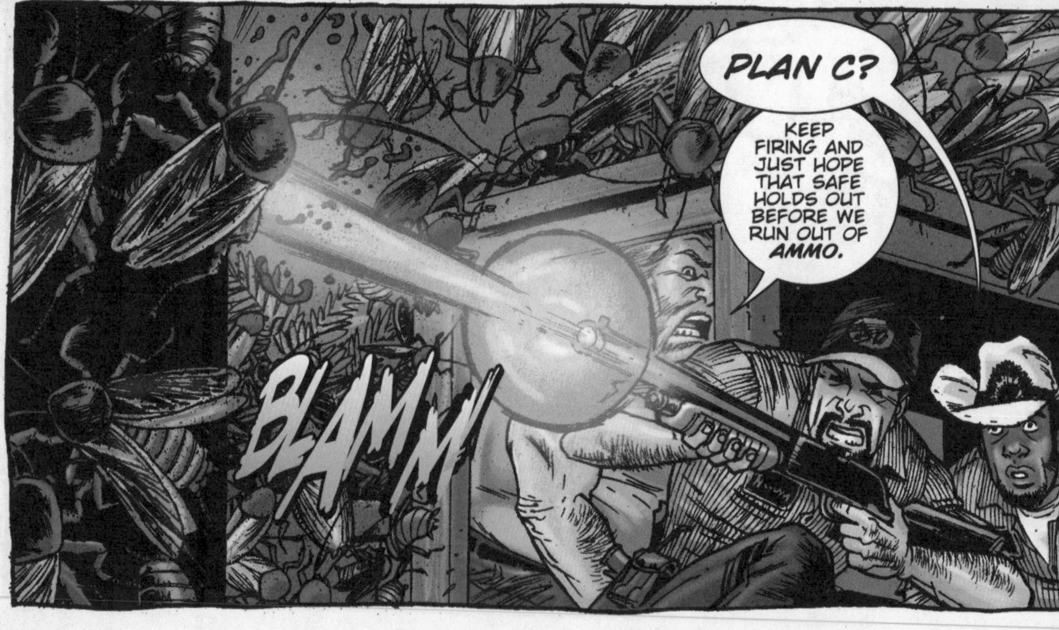
PLAN C?
KEEP FIRING AND JUST HOPE THAT SAFE HOLDS OUT BEFORE WE RUN OUT OF AMMO.
BLAMM!

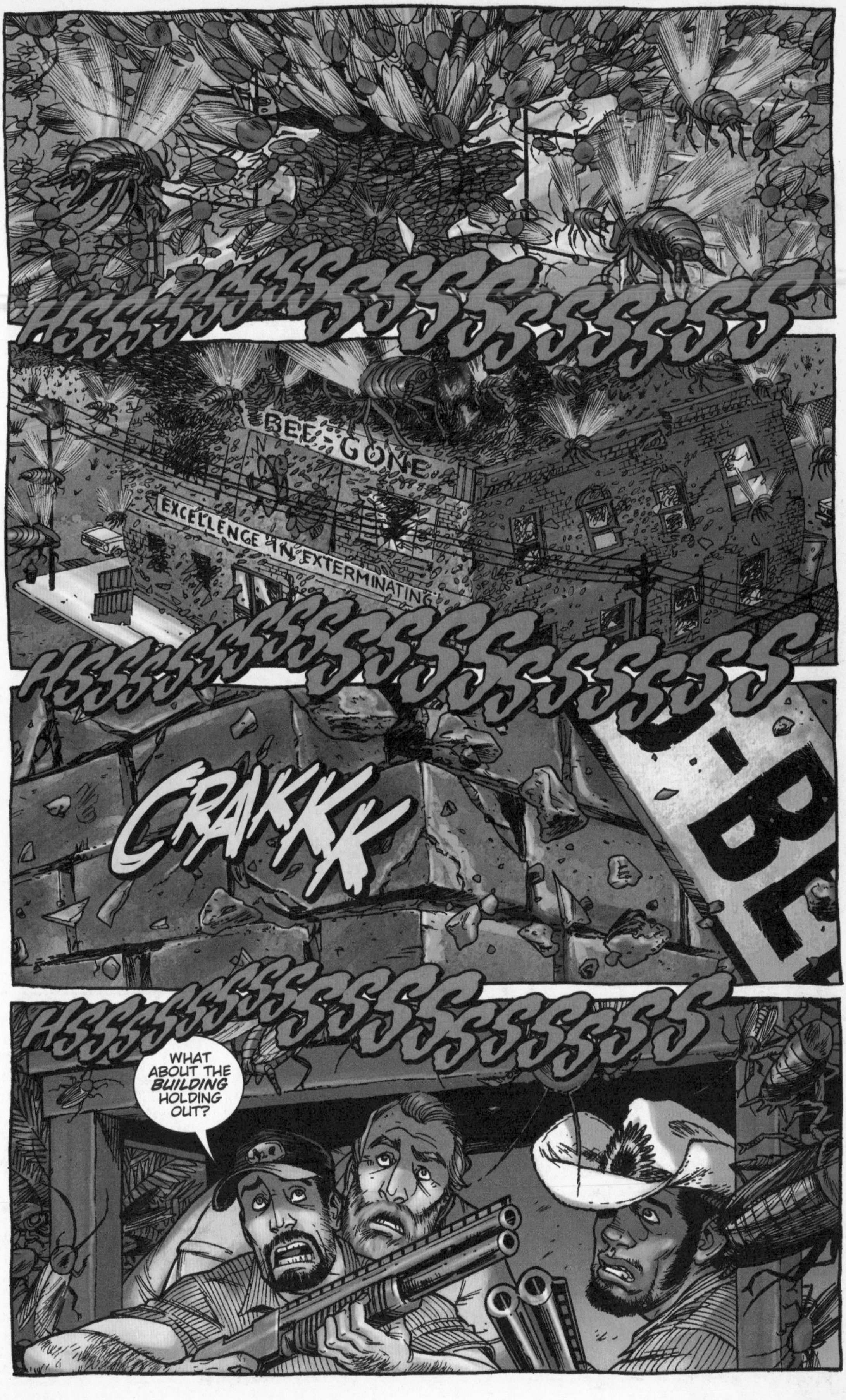
HSSSSSSSSSSSSSSSSSSSS
BEE-GONE
EXCELLENCE IN EXTERMINATING
HSSSSSSSSSSSSSSSSSSSS
CRAKKK
HSSSSSSSSSSSSSSSSSSSS
WHAT ABOUT THE BUILDING HOLDING OUT?

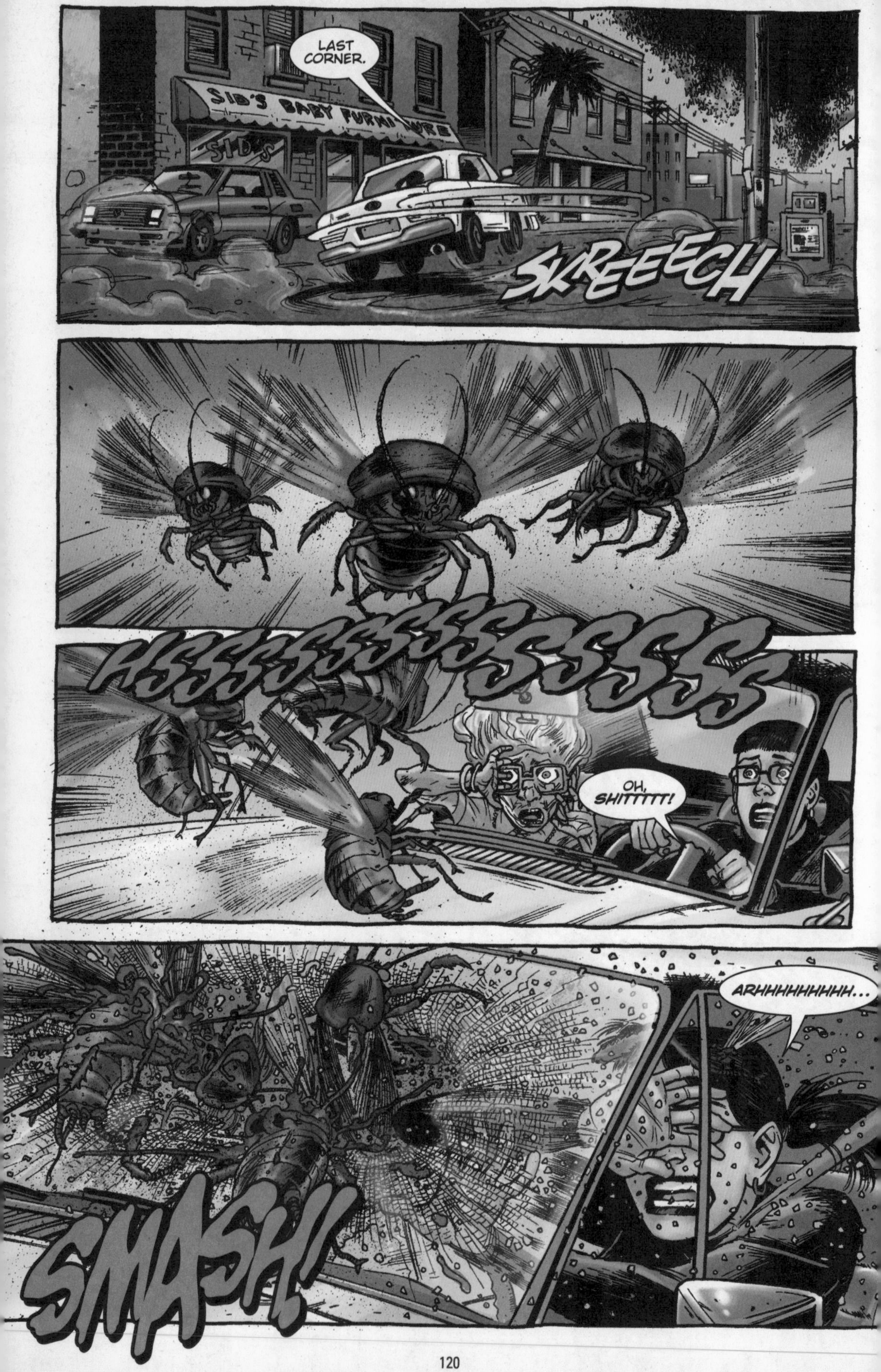
LAST CORNER.
SID'S BABY FURNITURE
SID'S
SKREEECH
HSSSSSSSSSSSSSSS
OH, SHITTTTTT!
ARHHHHHHHHH...
SMASH!

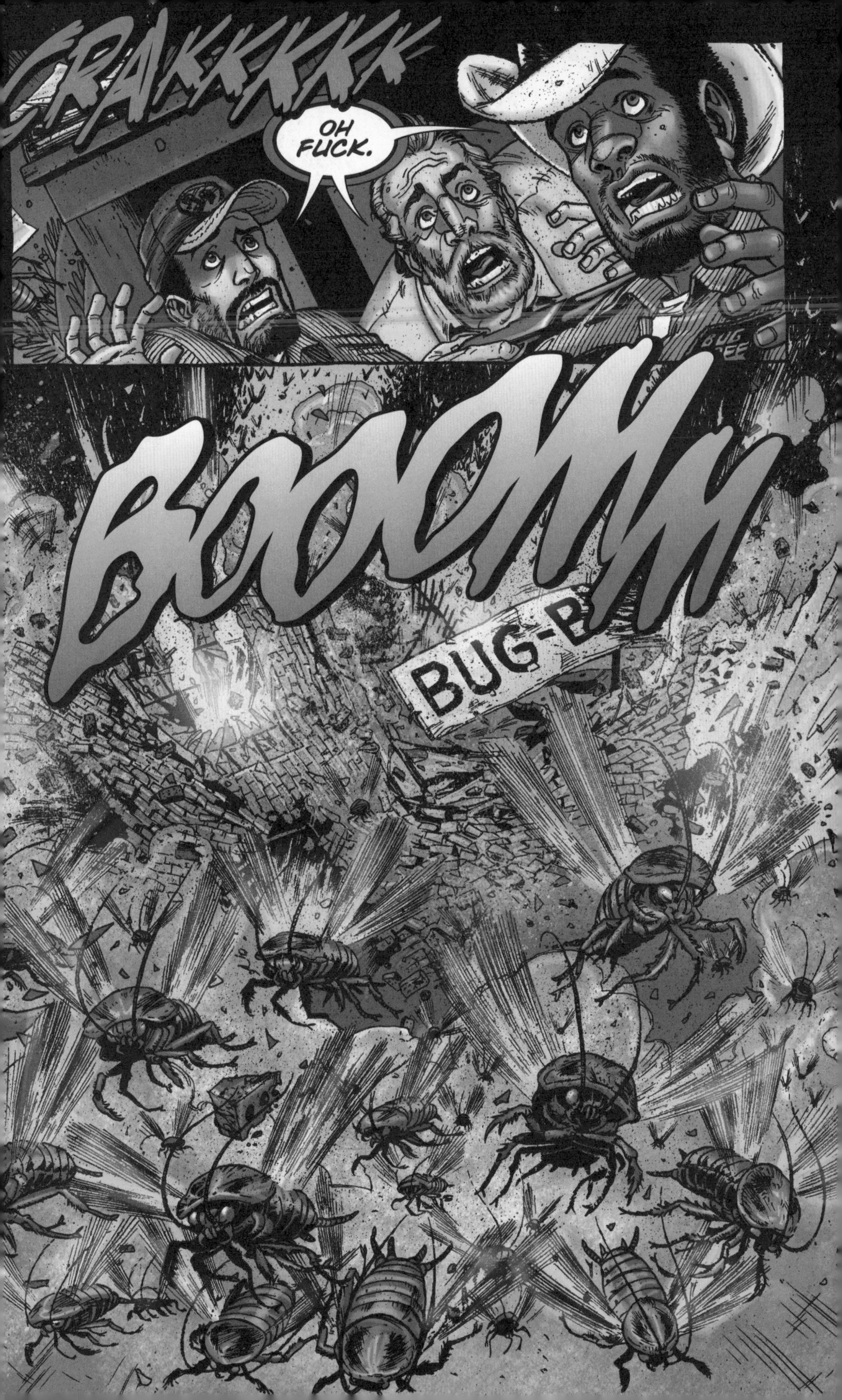
CRAKKKKK
OH FUCK.
BOOOMM
BUG-B

BUG BROTHERS FOREVER CHAPTER TWO COVER ART BY PHILIP BO

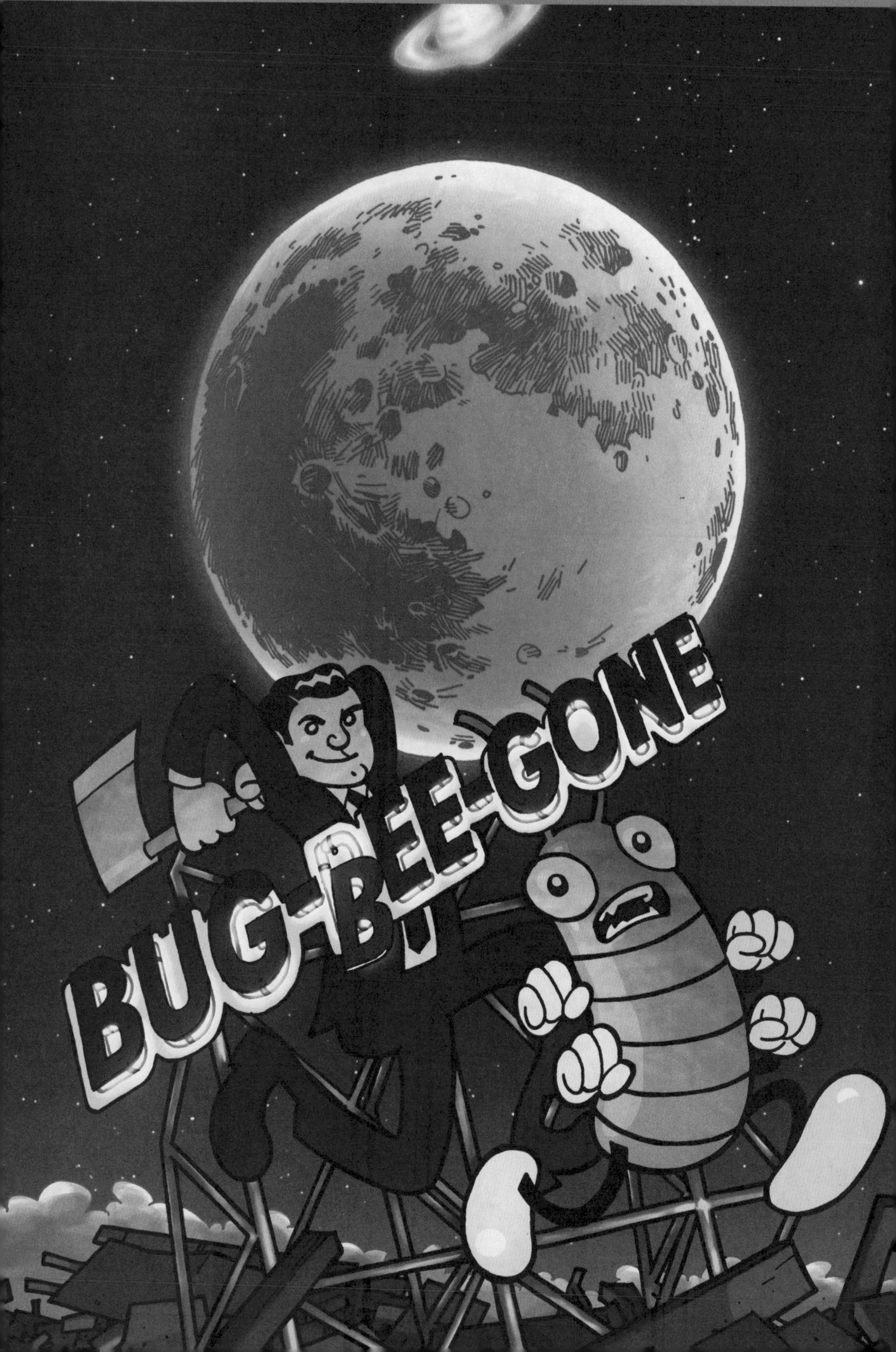
BUG-BEE-GONE

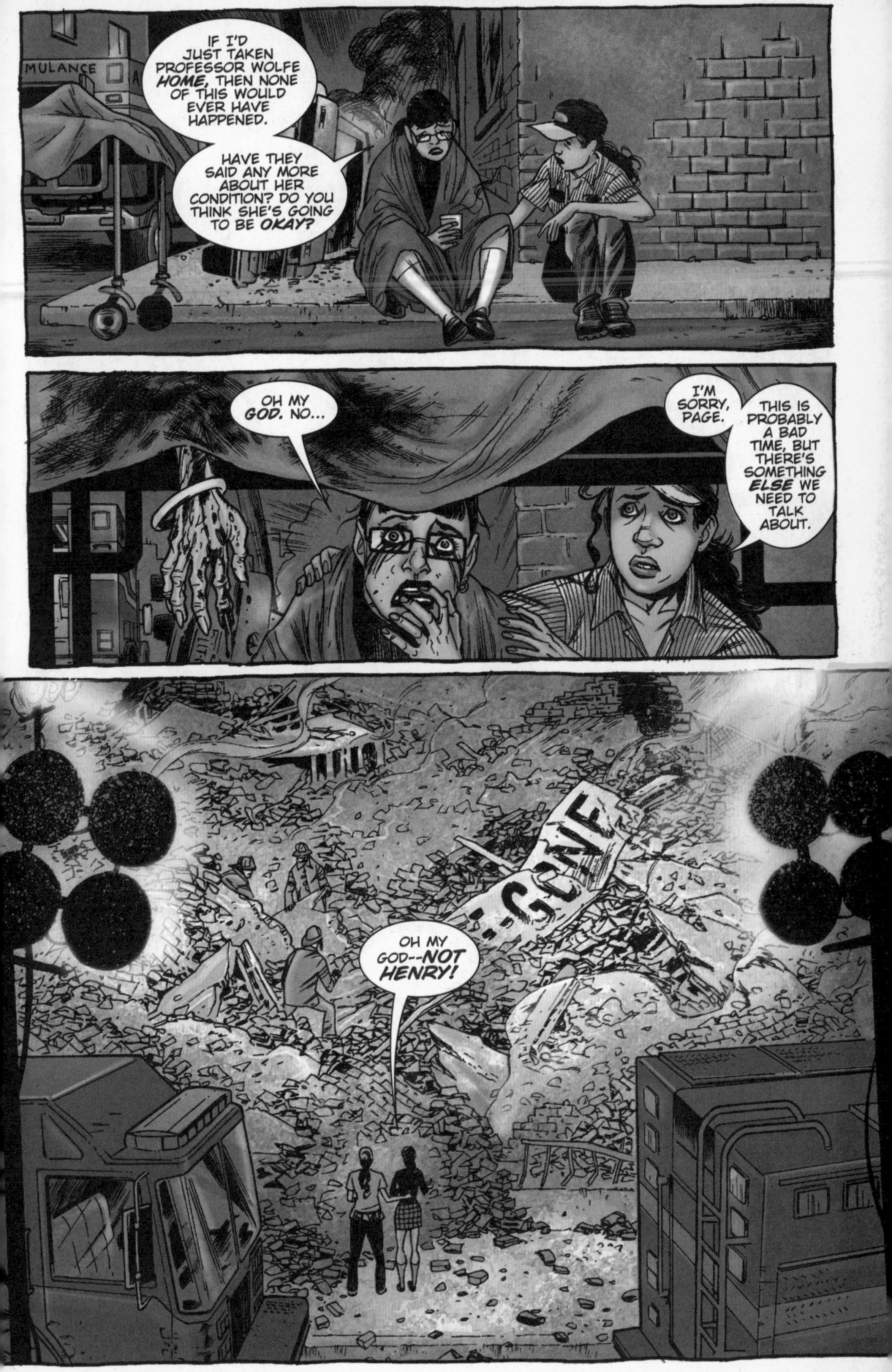

MULANCE
IF I'D JUST TAKEN PROFESSOR WOLFE HOME, THEN NONE OF THIS WOULD EVER HAVE HAPPENED.
HAVE THEY SAID ANY MORE ABOUT HER CONDITION? DO YOU THINK SHE'S GOING TO BE OKAY?
OH MY GOD. NO...
I'M SORRY, PAGE.
THIS IS PROBABLY A BAD TIME, BUT THERE'S SOMETHING ELSE WE NEED TO TALK ABOUT.
GONE
OH MY GOD--NOT HENRY!

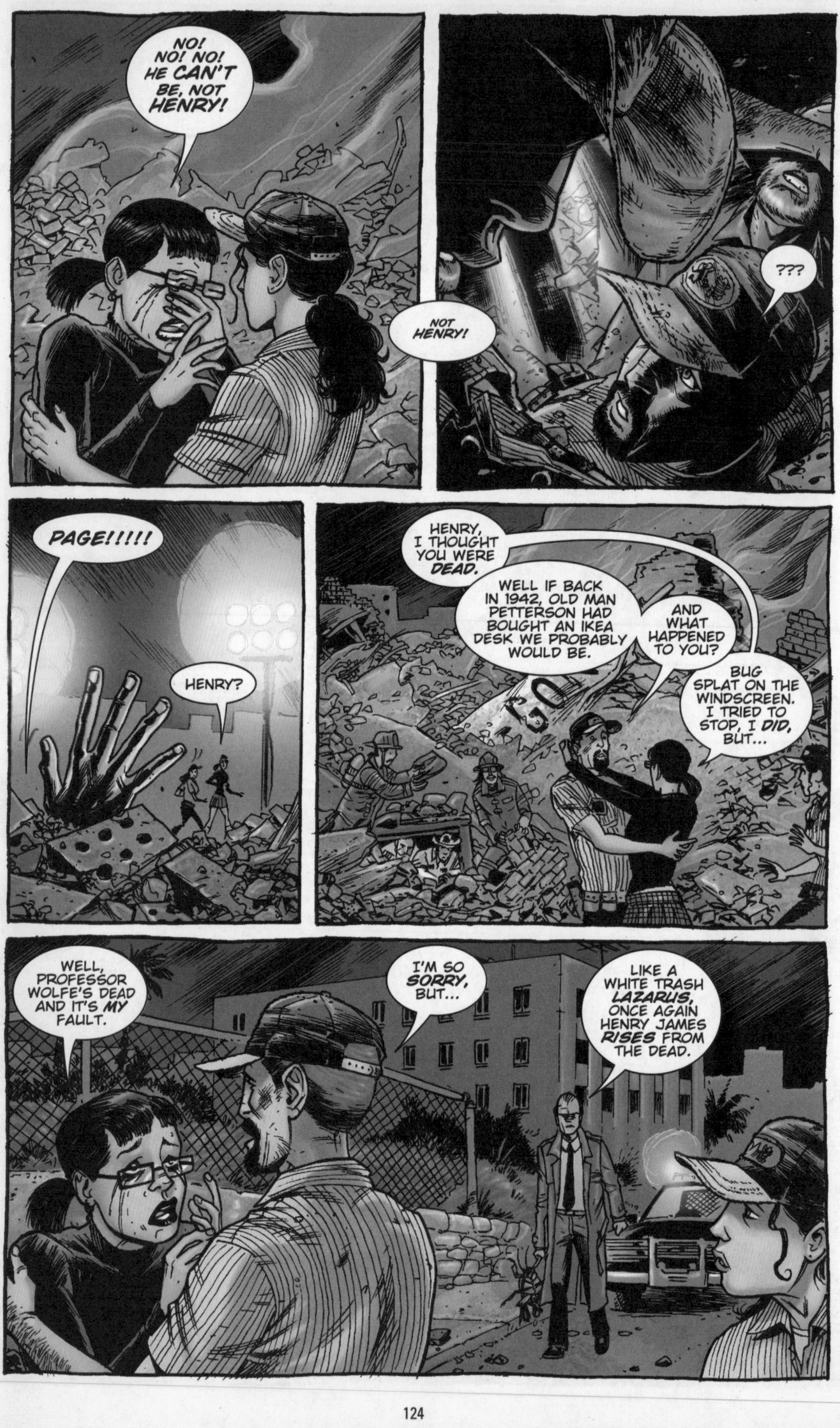
NO! NO! NO! HE CAN'T BE, NOT HENRY!
NOT HENRY!
???
PAGE!!!!!
HENRY?
HENRY, I THOUGHT YOU WERE DEAD.
WELL IF BACK IN 1942, OLD MAN PETTERSON HAD BOUGHT AN IKEA DESK WE PROBABLY WOULD BE.
AND WHAT HAPPENED TO YOU?
BUG SPLAT ON THE WINDSCREEN. I TRIED TO STOP, I DID, BUT...
WELL, PROFESSOR WOLFE'S DEAD AND IT'S MY FAULT.
I'M SO SORRY, BUT...
LIKE A WHITE TRASH LAZARUS, ONCE AGAIN HENRY JAMES RISES FROM THE DEAD.

A COUPLE OF QUICK QUESTIONS IF YOU DON'T MIND.

WELL, I DO MIND. WE'RE KIND OF IN THE MIDDLE OF SOMETHING. MY GIRLFRIEND HERE--

YEAH, SURE, I HEARD. THE OLD BROAD TOOK IT HEAD FIRST THROUGH THE *WINDSHIELD*.

NOW DON'T GO BLAMING YOURSELF, SWEETHEART. BUT NEXT TIME, YOU MIGHT WANNA DITCH THE CLASSY RIDE FOR SOMETHING WITH *AIRBAGS* AND CRUMPLE ZONES.

OKAY, SO THESE INSECT FUCKERS DEMOLISHED BUG-BEE-GONE?

YEAH, I GUESS SO.

AND THESE BUGS, THAT'S THEM THE *SECURITY GOONS* ARE PROTECTING, BEHIND THE WALL, INSIDE THE OCRAN TOWERS DEVELOPMENT?

YEAH.

SO WHAT'S THIS *ABOUT*?

THAT'LL BE ALL FOR NOW.

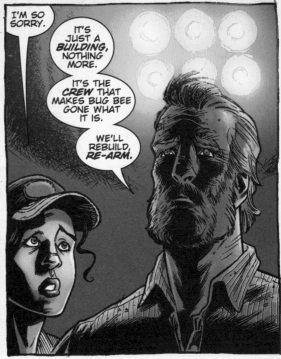

I'M SO SORRY.

IT'S JUST A *BUILDING*, NOTHING MORE.

IT'S THE *CREW* THAT MAKES BUG BEE GONE WHAT IT IS.

WE'LL REBUILD, *RE-ARM*.

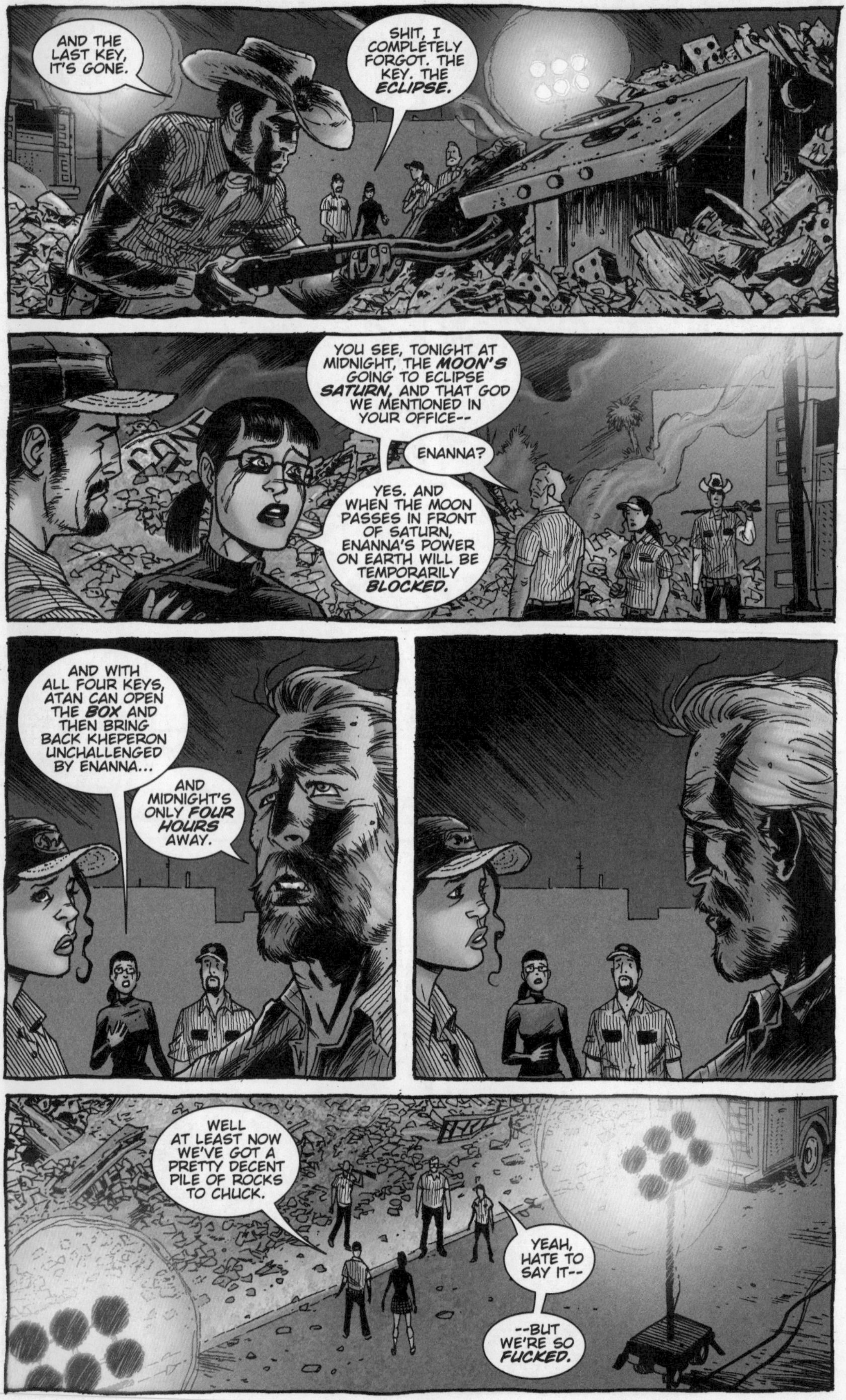
AND THE LAST KEY, IT'S GONE.
SHIT, I COMPLETELY FORGOT. THE KEY. THE ECLIPSE.
YOU SEE, TONIGHT AT MIDNIGHT, THE MOON'S GOING TO ECLIPSE SATURN, AND THAT GOD WE MENTIONED IN YOUR OFFICE--
ENANNA?
YES. AND WHEN THE MOON PASSES IN FRONT OF SATURN, ENANNA'S POWER ON EARTH WILL BE TEMPORARILY BLOCKED.
AND WITH ALL FOUR KEYS, ATAN CAN OPEN THE BOX AND THEN BRING BACK KHEPERON UNCHALLENGED BY ENANNA...
AND MIDNIGHT'S ONLY FOUR HOURS AWAY.
WELL AT LEAST NOW WE'VE GOT A PRETTY DECENT PILE OF ROCKS TO CHUCK.
YEAH, HATE TO SAY IT--
--BUT WE'RE SO FUCKED.

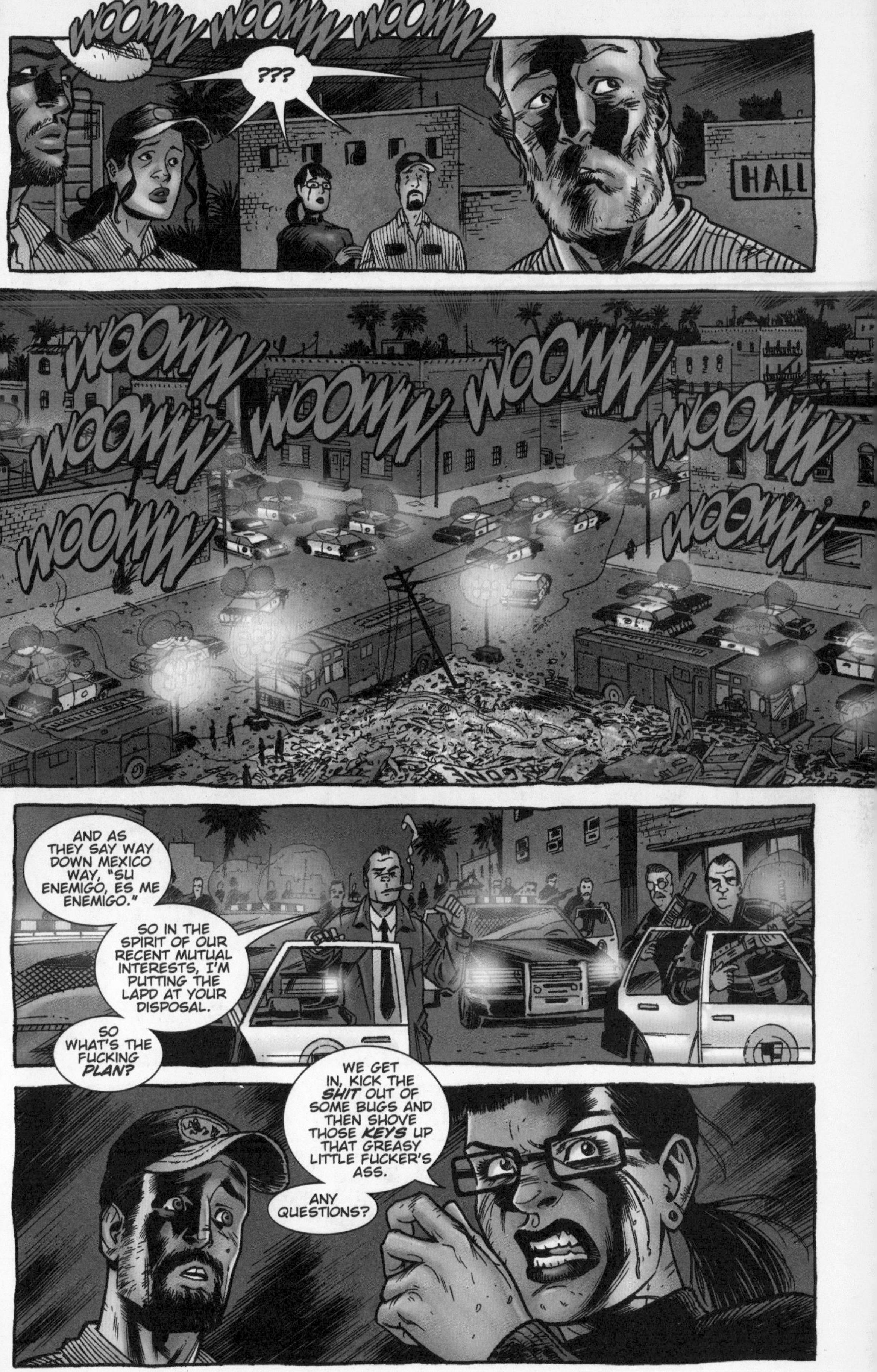
WOOWW WOOWW WOOWW
???
HALL
WOOWW WOOWW WOOWW WOOWW WOOWW WOOWW WOOWW
AND AS THEY SAY WAY DOWN MEXICO WAY, "SU ENEMIGO, ES ME ENEMIGO."
SO IN THE SPIRIT OF OUR RECENT MUTUAL INTERESTS, I'M PUTTING THE LAPD AT YOUR DISPOSAL.
SO WHAT'S THE FUCKING PLAN?
WE GET IN, KICK THE SHIT OUT OF SOME BUGS AND THEN SHOVE THOSE KEYS UP THAT GREASY LITTLE FUCKER'S ASS.
ANY QUESTIONS?

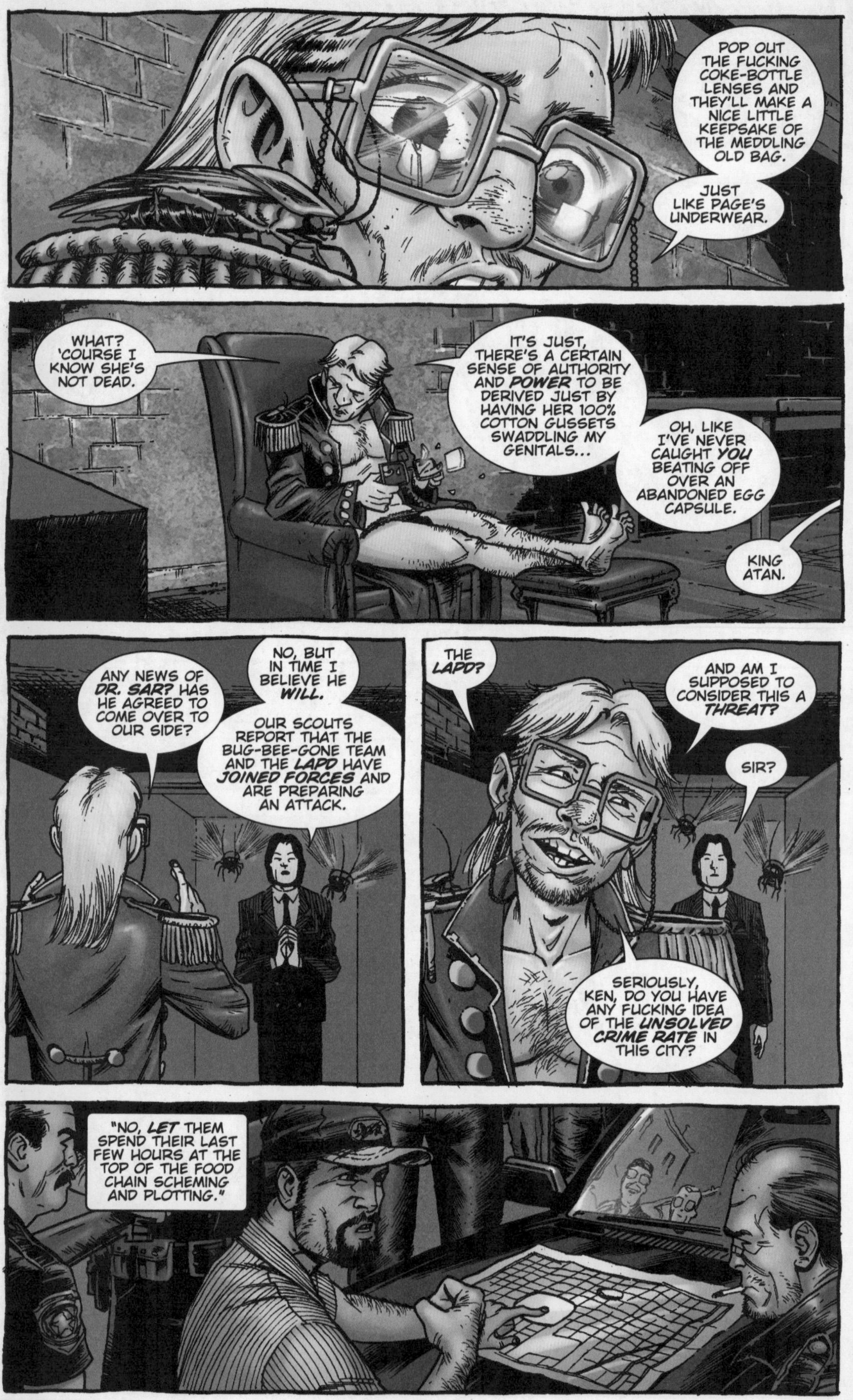
POP OUT THE FUCKING COKE-BOTTLE LENSES AND THEY'LL MAKE A NICE LITTLE KEEPSAKE OF THE MEDDLING OLD BAG.
JUST LIKE PAGE'S UNDERWEAR.
WHAT? 'COURSE I KNOW SHE'S NOT DEAD.
IT'S JUST, THERE'S A CERTAIN SENSE OF AUTHORITY AND POWER TO BE DERIVED JUST BY HAVING HER 100% COTTON GUSSETS SWADDLING MY GENITALS...
OH, LIKE I'VE NEVER CAUGHT YOU BEATING OFF OVER AN ABANDONED EGG CAPSULE.
KING ATAN.
ANY NEWS OF DR. SAR? HAS HE AGREED TO COME OVER TO OUR SIDE?
NO, BUT IN TIME I BELIEVE HE WILL.
OUR SCOUTS REPORT THAT THE BUG-BEE-GONE TEAM AND THE LAPD HAVE JOINED FORCES AND ARE PREPARING AN ATTACK.
THE LAPD?
AND AM I SUPPOSED TO CONSIDER THIS A THREAT?
SIR?
SERIOUSLY, KEN, DO YOU HAVE ANY FUCKING IDEA OF THE UNSOLVED CRIME RATE IN THIS CITY?
"NO, LET THEM SPEND THEIR LAST FEW HOURS AT THE TOP OF THE FOOD CHAIN SCHEMING AND PLOTTING."

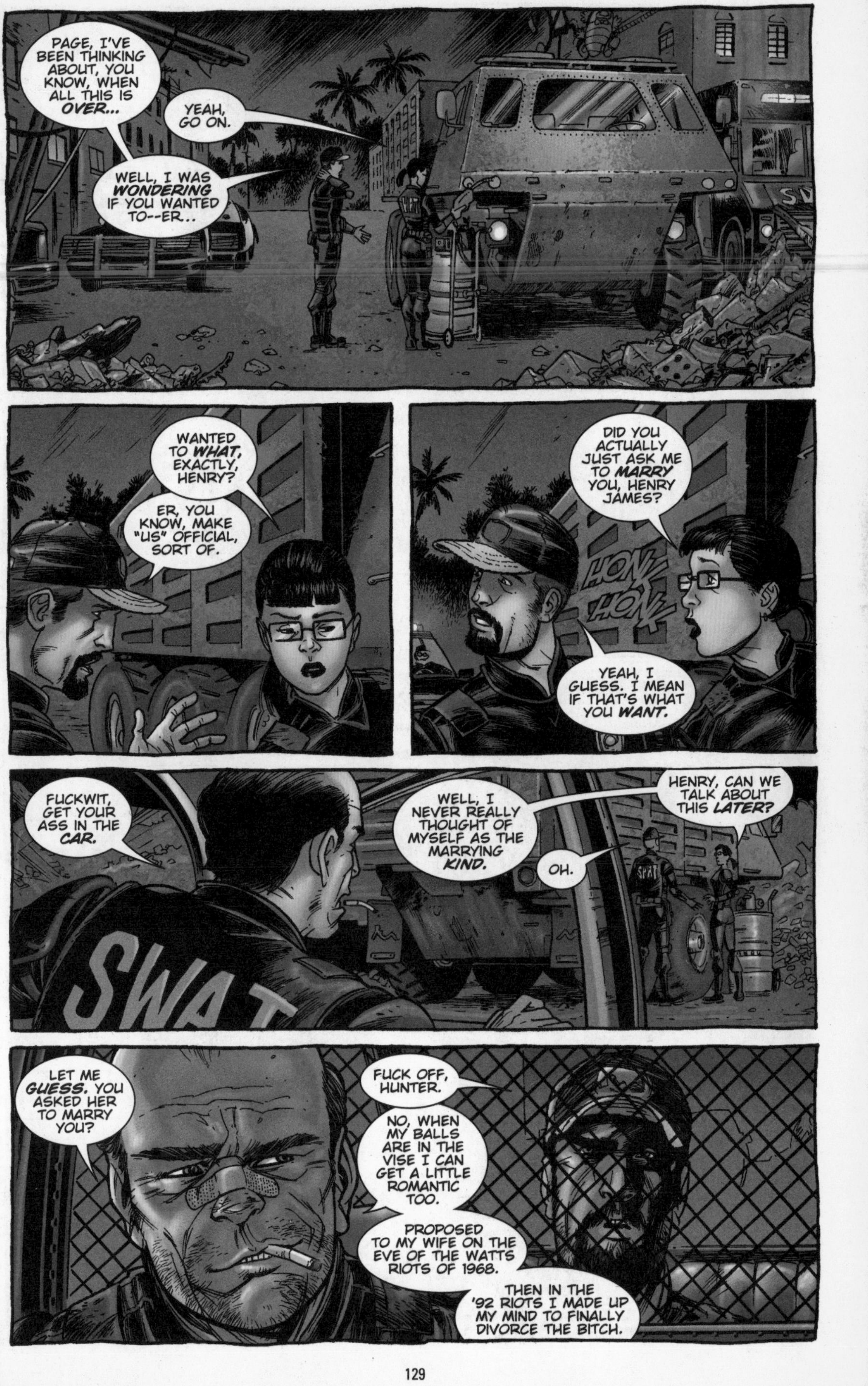

PAGE, I'VE BEEN THINKING ABOUT, YOU KNOW, WHEN ALL THIS IS OVER...
YEAH, GO ON.
WELL, I WAS WONDERING IF YOU WANTED TO--ER...
SW
WANTED TO WHAT, EXACTLY, HENRY?
ER, YOU KNOW, MAKE "US" OFFICIAL, SORT OF.
DID YOU ACTUALLY JUST ASK ME TO MARRY YOU, HENRY JAMES?
HONK HONK
YEAH, I GUESS. I MEAN IF THAT'S WHAT YOU WANT.
FUCKWIT, GET YOUR ASS IN THE CAR.
WELL, I NEVER REALLY THOUGHT OF MYSELF AS THE MARRYING KIND.
OH.
HENRY, CAN WE TALK ABOUT THIS LATER?
SWAT
LET ME GUESS. YOU ASKED HER TO MARRY YOU?
FUCK OFF, HUNTER.
NO, WHEN MY BALLS ARE IN THE VISE I CAN GET A LITTLE ROMANTIC TOO.
PROPOSED TO MY WIFE ON THE EVE OF THE WATTS RIOTS OF 1968.
THEN IN THE '92 RIOTS I MADE UP MY MIND TO FINALLY DIVORCE THE BITCH.

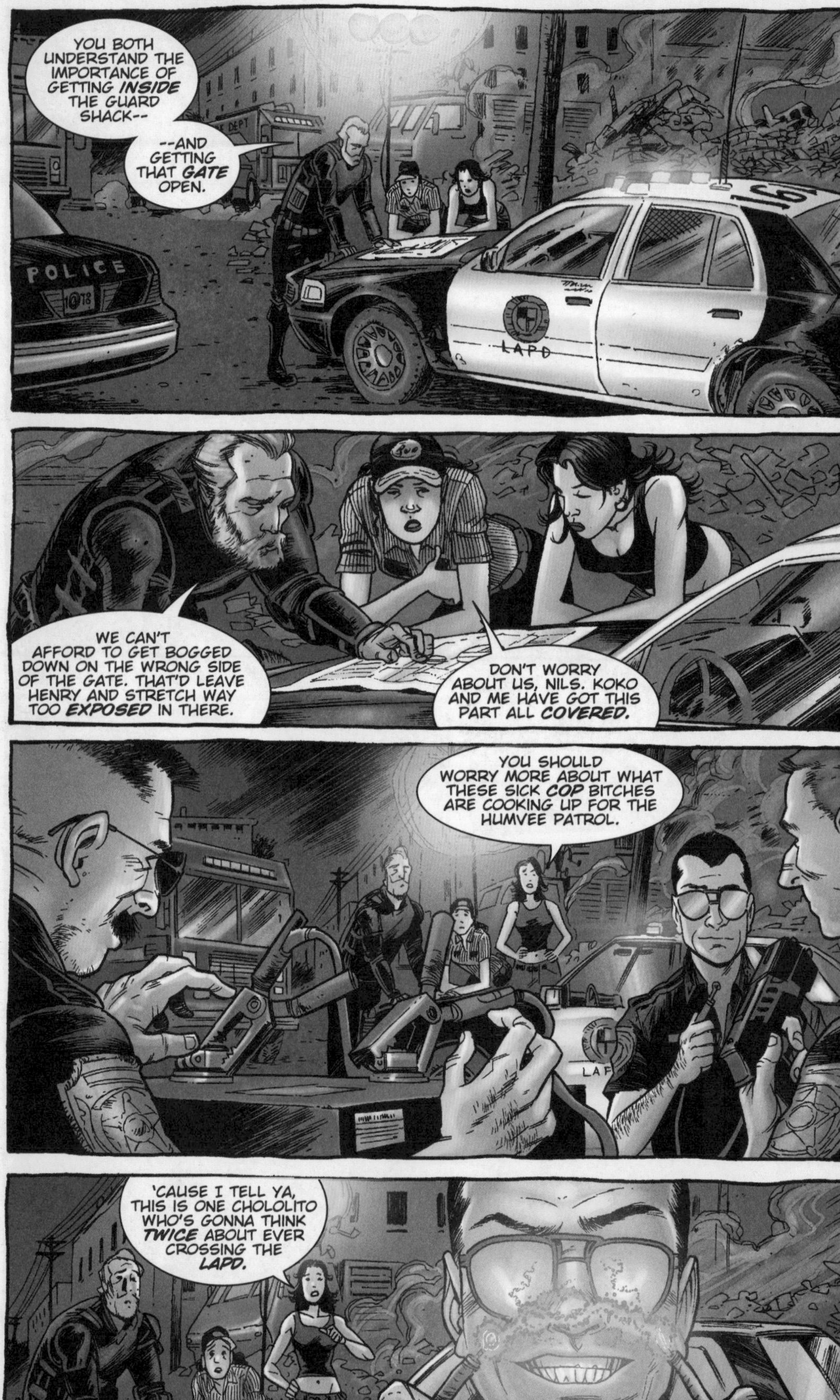
YOU BOTH UNDERSTAND THE IMPORTANCE OF GETTING INSIDE THE GUARD SHACK--
--AND GETTING THAT GATE OPEN.
POLICE
LAPD
WE CAN'T AFFORD TO GET BOGGED DOWN ON THE WRONG SIDE OF THE GATE. THAT'D LEAVE HENRY AND STRETCH WAY TOO EXPOSED IN THERE.
DON'T WORRY ABOUT US, NILS. KOKO AND ME HAVE GOT THIS PART ALL COVERED.
YOU SHOULD WORRY MORE ABOUT WHAT THESE SICK COP BITCHES ARE COOKING UP FOR THE HUMVEE PATROL.
'CAUSE I TELL YA, THIS IS ONE CHOLOLITO WHO'S GONNA THINK TWICE ABOUT EVER CROSSING THE LAPD.

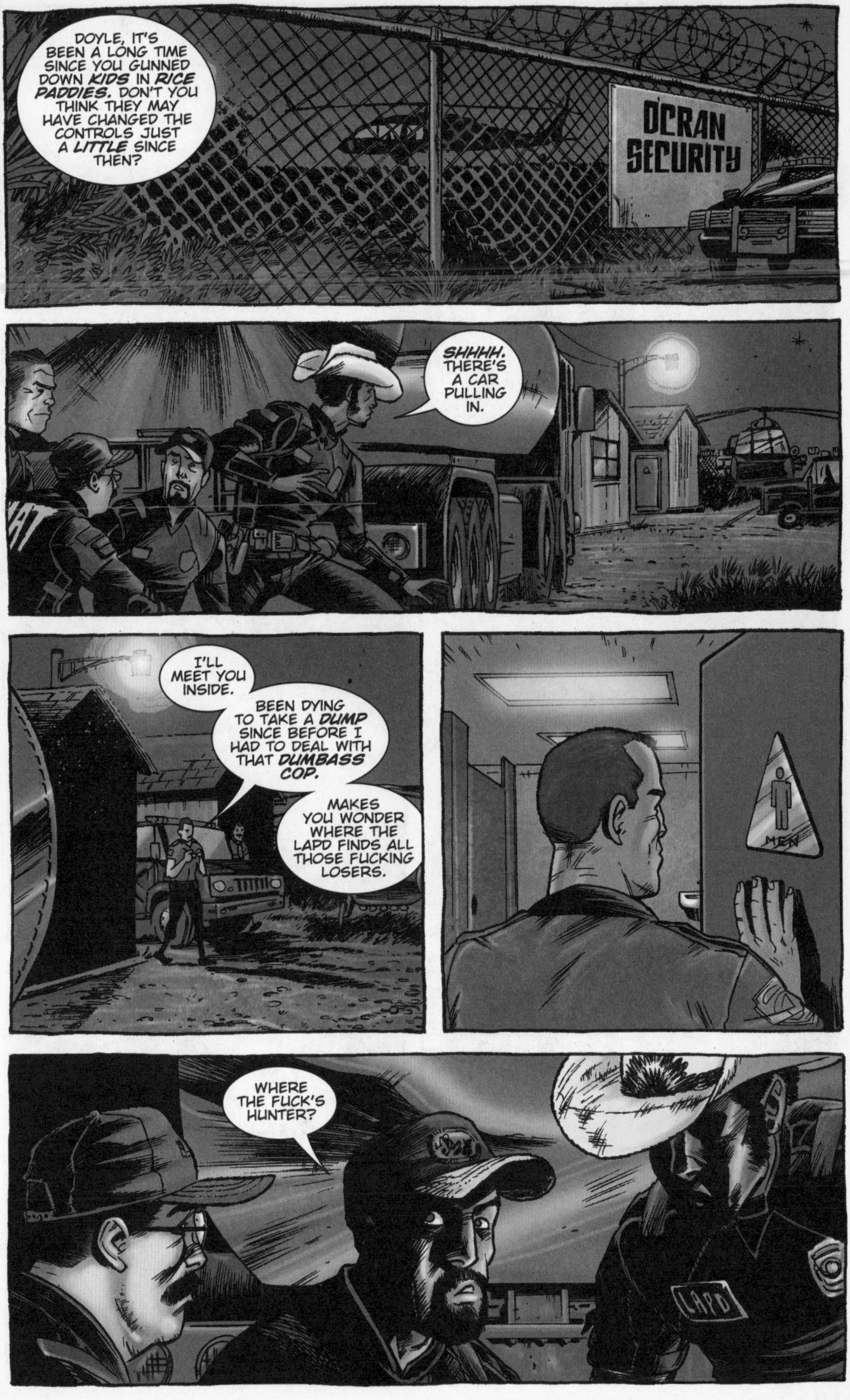
DOYLE, IT'S BEEN A LONG TIME SINCE YOU GUNNED DOWN KIDS IN RICE PADDIES. DON'T YOU THINK THEY MAY HAVE CHANGED THE CONTROLS JUST A LITTLE SINCE THEN?
OCRAN SECURITY
SHHHH. THERE'S A CAR PULLING IN.
I'LL MEET YOU INSIDE.
BEEN DYING TO TAKE A DUMP SINCE BEFORE I HAD TO DEAL WITH THAT DUMBASS COP.
MAKES YOU WONDER WHERE THE LAPD FINDS ALL THOSE FUCKING LOSERS.
MEN
WHERE THE FUCK'S HUNTER?
LAPD

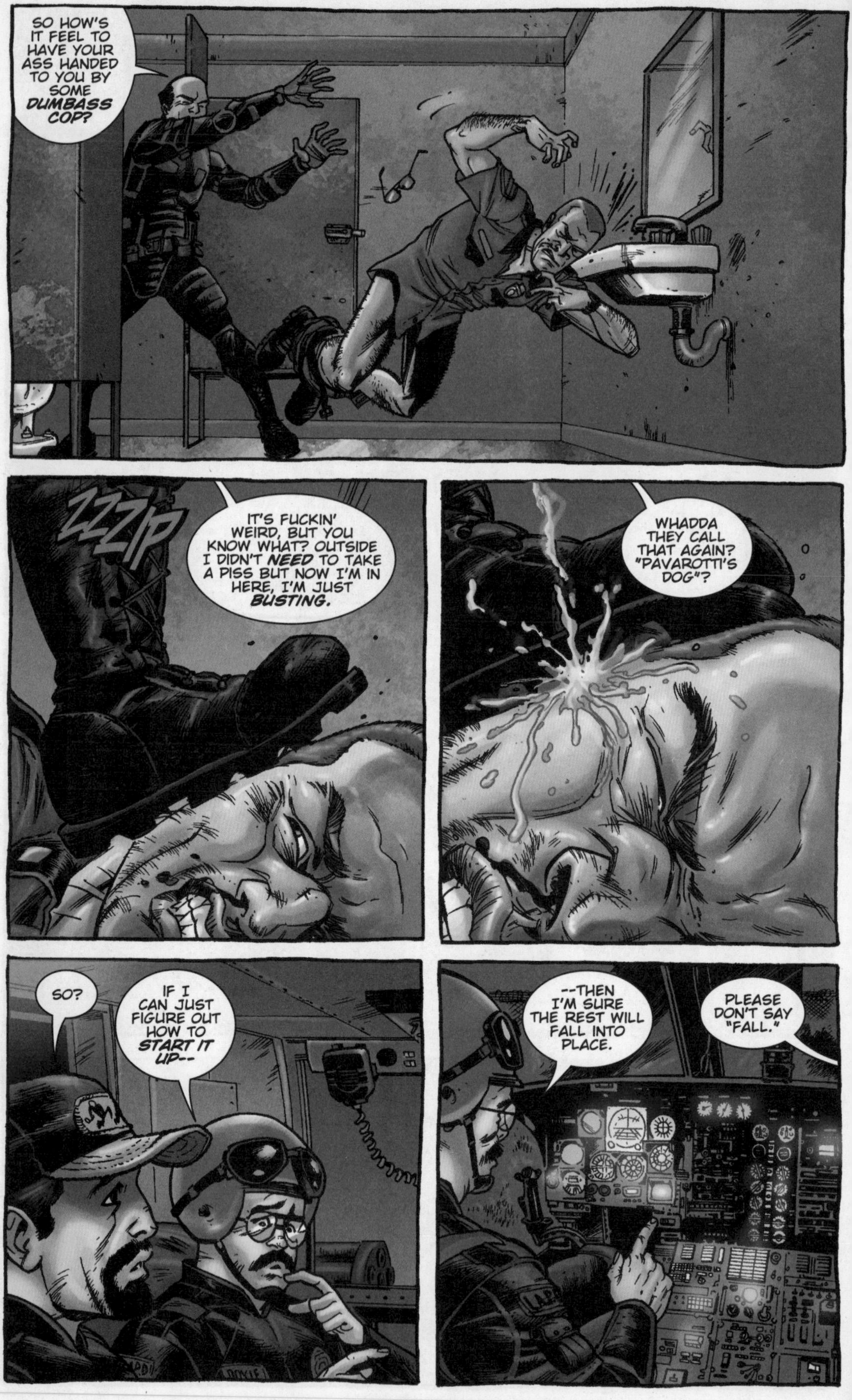
SO HOW'S IT FEEL TO HAVE YOUR ASS HANDED TO YOU BY SOME DUMBASS COP?
ZZZIP
IT'S FUCKIN' WEIRD, BUT YOU KNOW WHAT? OUTSIDE I DIDN'T NEED TO TAKE A PISS BUT NOW I'M IN HERE, I'M JUST BUSTING.
WHADDA THEY CALL THAT AGAIN? "PAVAROTTI'S DOG"?
SO?
IF I CAN JUST FIGURE OUT HOW TO START IT UP--
--THEN I'M SURE THE REST WILL FALL INTO PLACE.
PLEASE DON'T SAY "FALL."

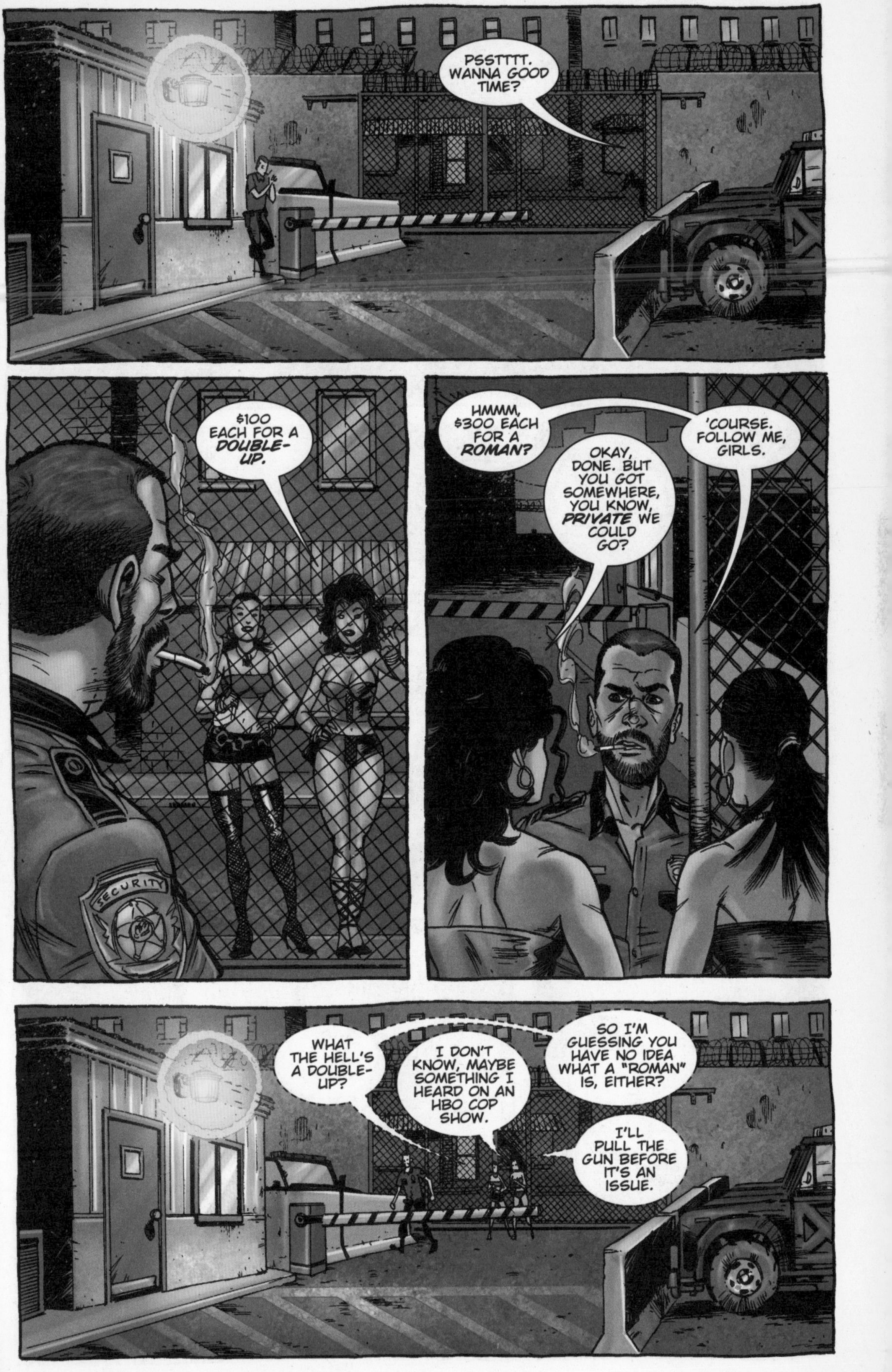
PSSTTTT. WANNA GOOD TIME?
$100 EACH FOR A DOUBLE-UP.
HMMM, $300 EACH FOR A ROMAN?
'COURSE. FOLLOW ME, GIRLS.
OKAY, DONE. BUT YOU GOT SOMEWHERE, YOU KNOW, PRIVATE WE COULD GO?
SECURITY
WHAT THE HELL'S A DOUBLE-UP?
I DON'T KNOW, MAYBE SOMETHING I HEARD ON AN HBO COP SHOW.
SO I'M GUESSING YOU HAVE NO IDEA WHAT A "ROMAN" IS, EITHER?
I'LL PULL THE GUN BEFORE IT'S AN ISSUE.

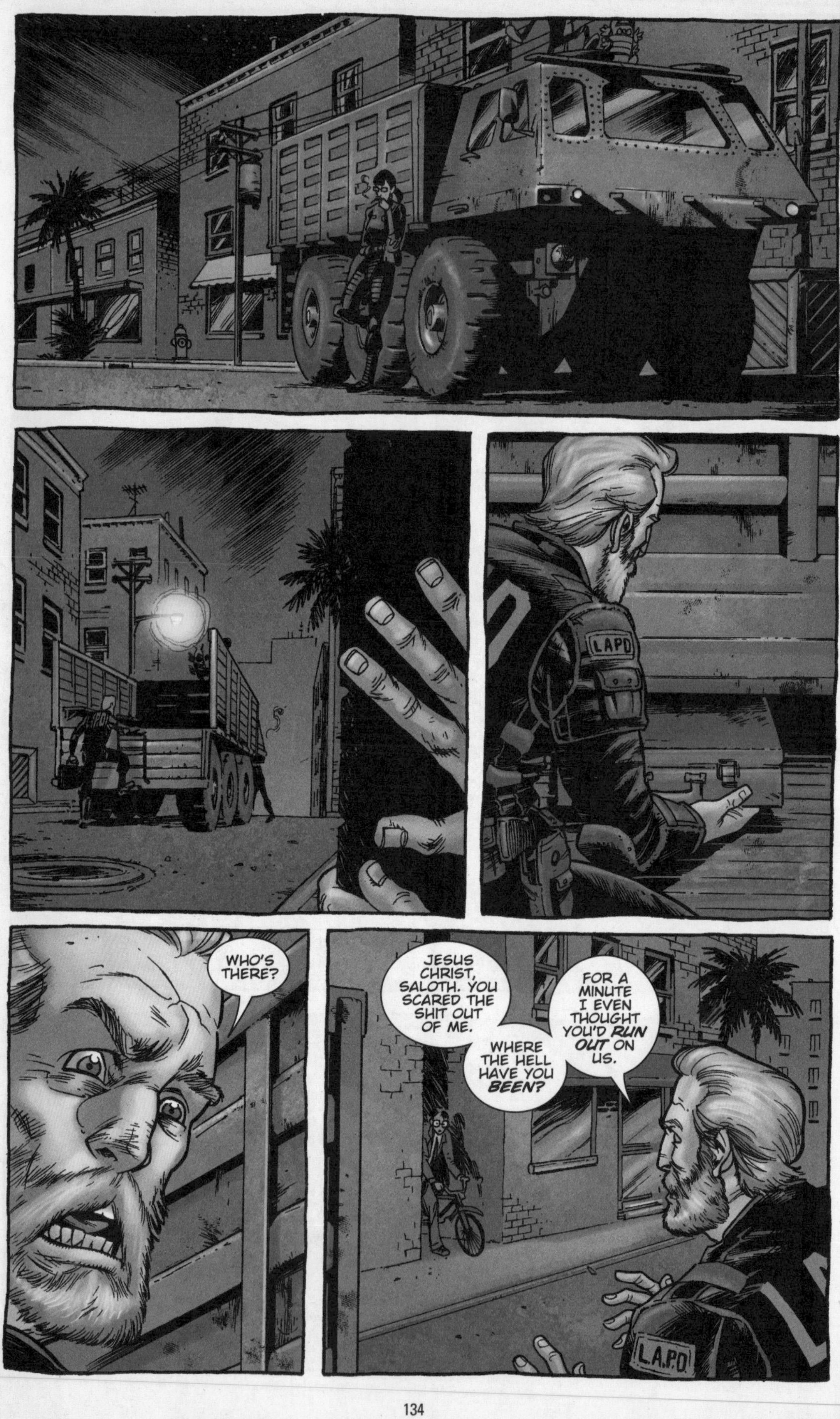
L.A.P.D
WHO'S THERE?
JESUS CHRIST, SALOTH. YOU SCARED THE SHIT OUT OF ME.
WHERE THE HELL HAVE YOU *BEEN?*
FOR A MINUTE I EVEN THOUGHT YOU'D *RUN OUT* ON US.
L.A.P.D

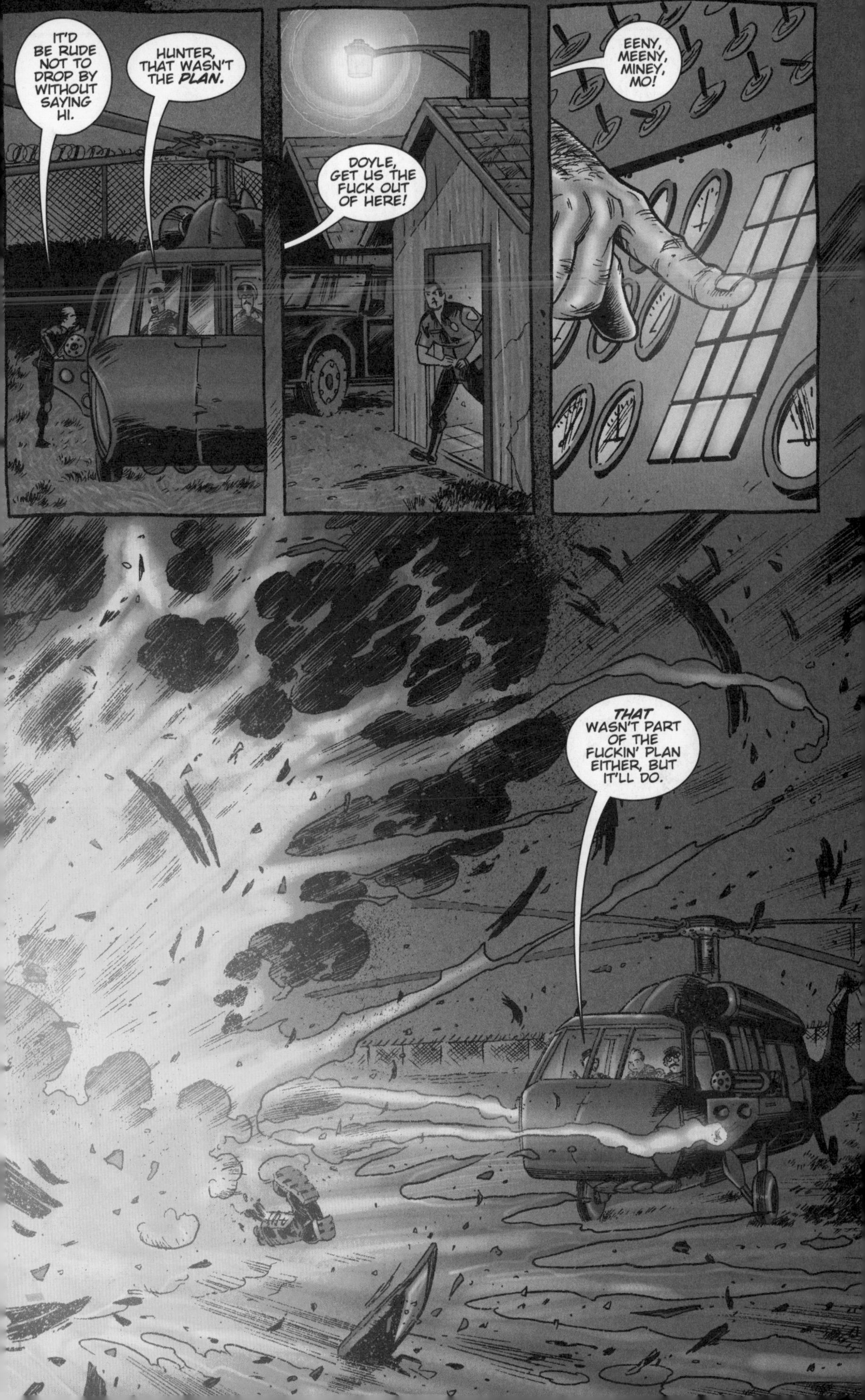
IT'D BE RUDE NOT TO DROP BY WITHOUT SAYING HI.
HUNTER, THAT WASN'T THE *PLAN.*
DOYLE, GET US THE FUCK OUT OF HERE!
EENY, MEENY, MINEY, MO!
THAT WASN'T PART OF THE FUCKIN' PLAN EITHER, BUT IT'LL DO.

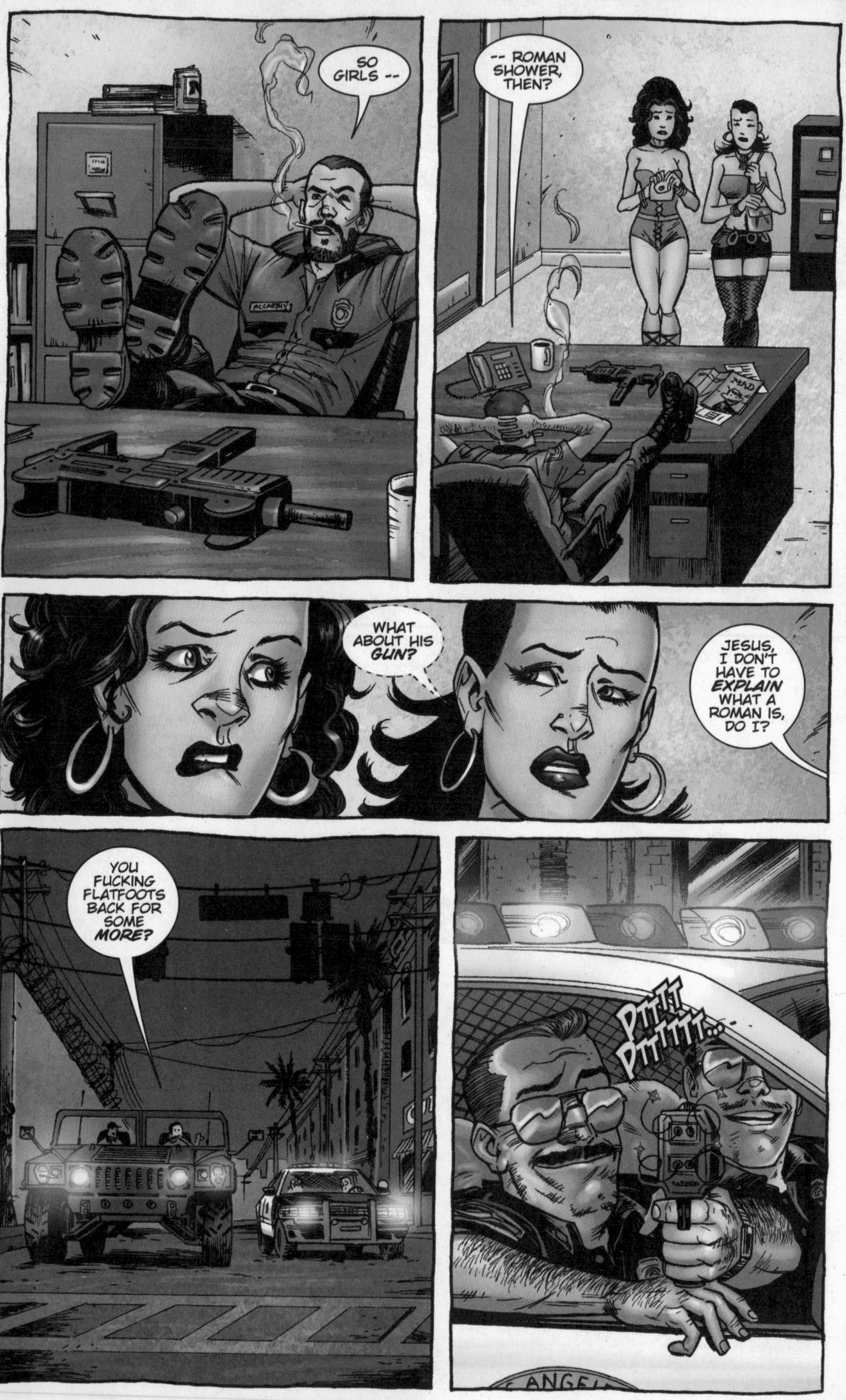
SO GIRLS --
-- ROMAN SHOWER, THEN?
WHAT ABOUT HIS GUN?
JESUS, I DON'T HAVE TO EXPLAIN WHAT A ROMAN IS, DO I?
YOU FUCKING FLATFOOTS BACK FOR SOME MORE?
PTTTT PTTTTTT...

???

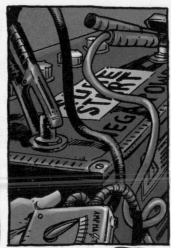

AMPMASTER

ARGHHHHHHHH

ZZZZZZZZZZ

OKAY, A GREEK MUD SAUSAGE? OR A GUATEMALAN MUDSLIDE? YOU *GOTTA* KNOW THOSE!

ARGHHHH

WHAT THE FUCK WAS *THAT?*

OKAY, *DO* IT.

YOU GIRLS AREN'T REALLY *HOOKERS,* ARE YOU?

SORRY, NO. WE'RE *PEST EXTERMINATORS,* ACTUALLY.

UNDERCOVER.

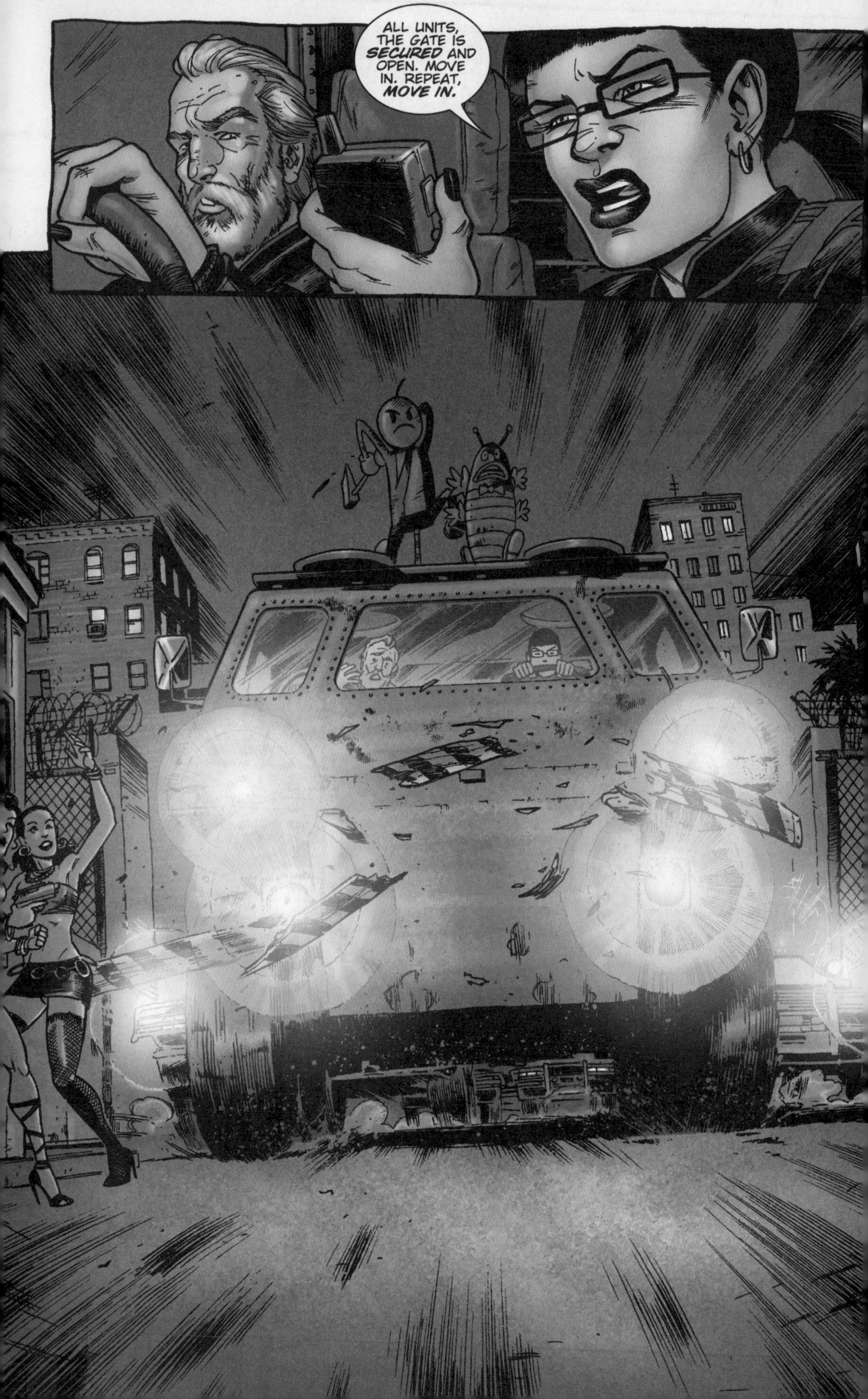
ALL UNITS, THE GATE IS SECURED AND OPEN. MOVE IN. REPEAT, MOVE IN.

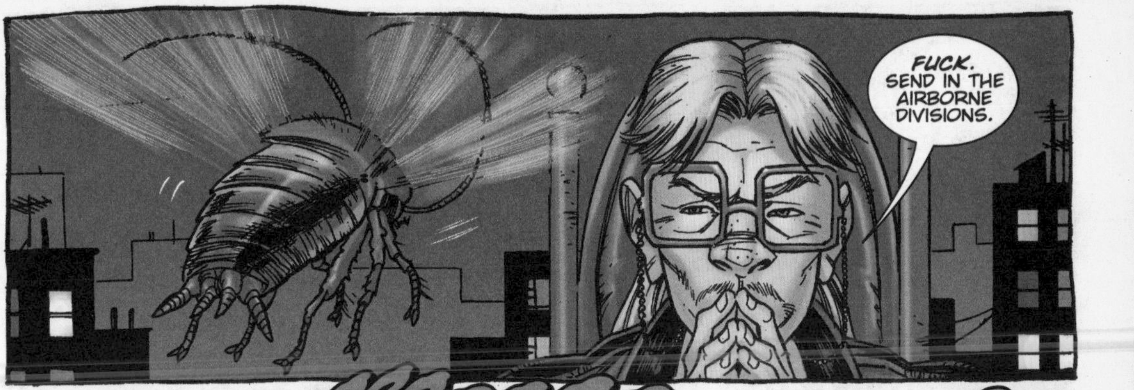
FUCK. SEND IN THE AIRBORNE DIVISIONS.

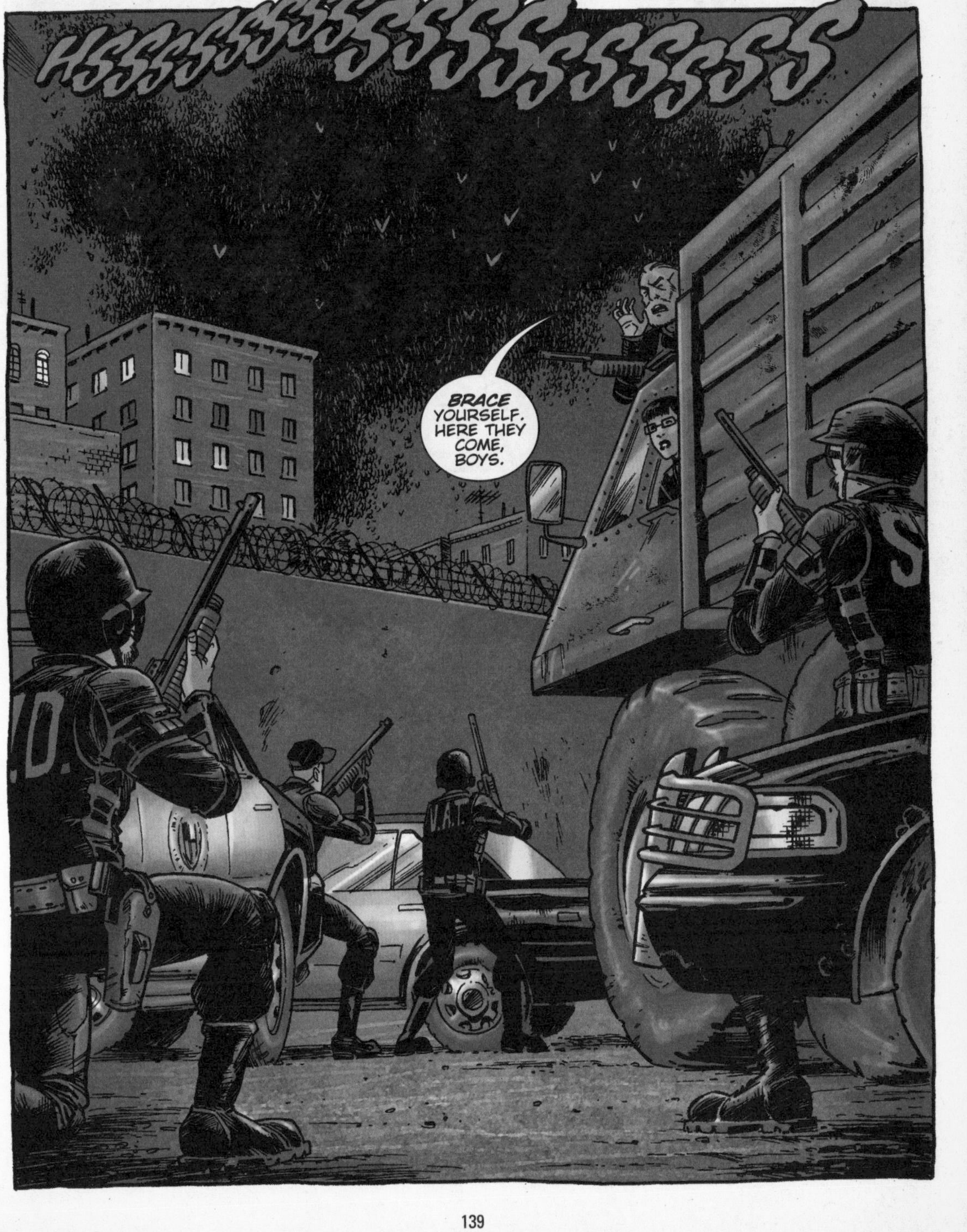
HSSSSSSSSSSSSSSSSSSSSS
BRACE YOURSELF. HERE THEY COME, BOYS.

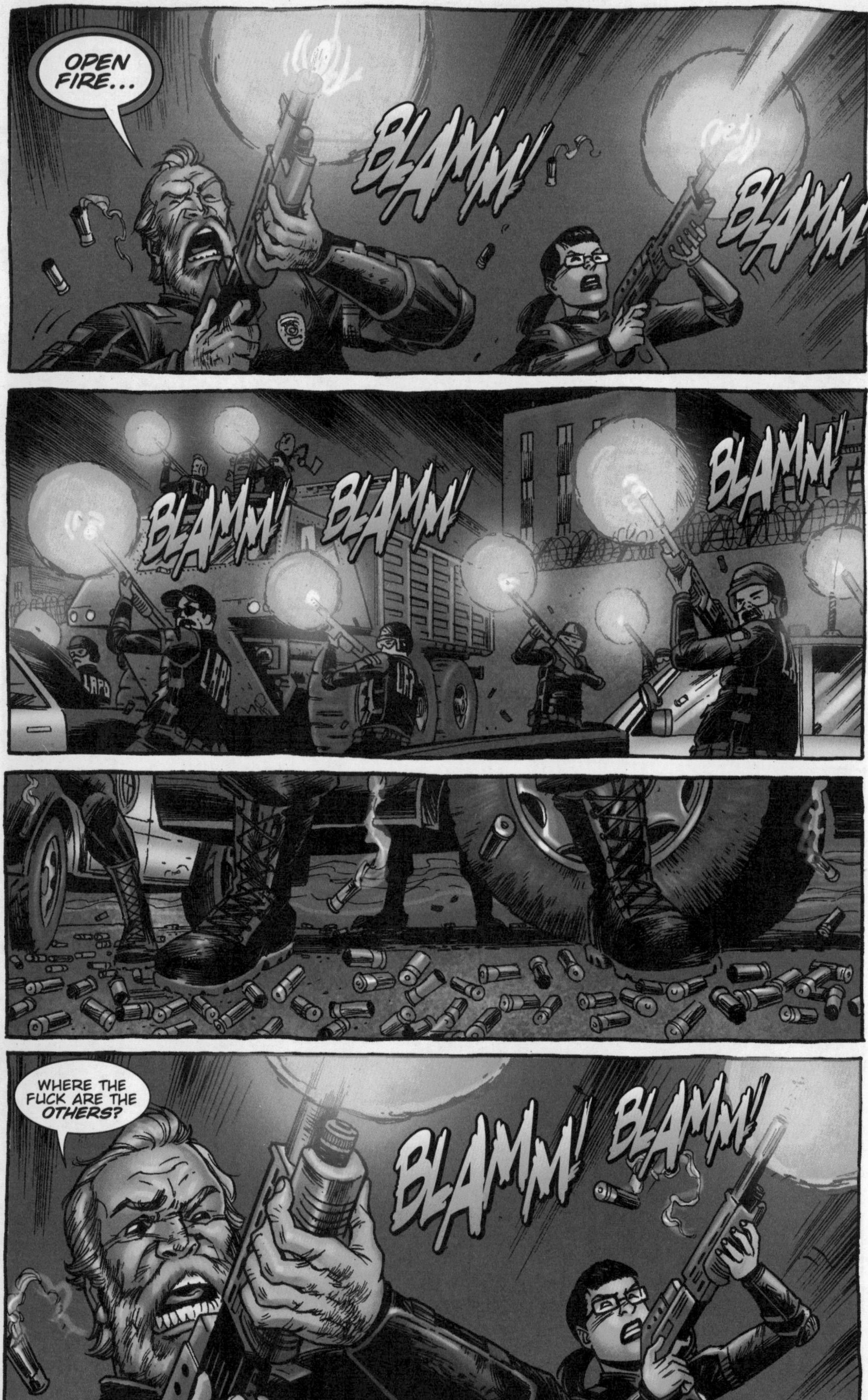
OPEN FIRE...
BLAMM!
BLAMM!
BLAMM!
BLAMM!
BLAMM!
WHERE THE FUCK ARE THE OTHERS?
BLAMM!
BLAMM!

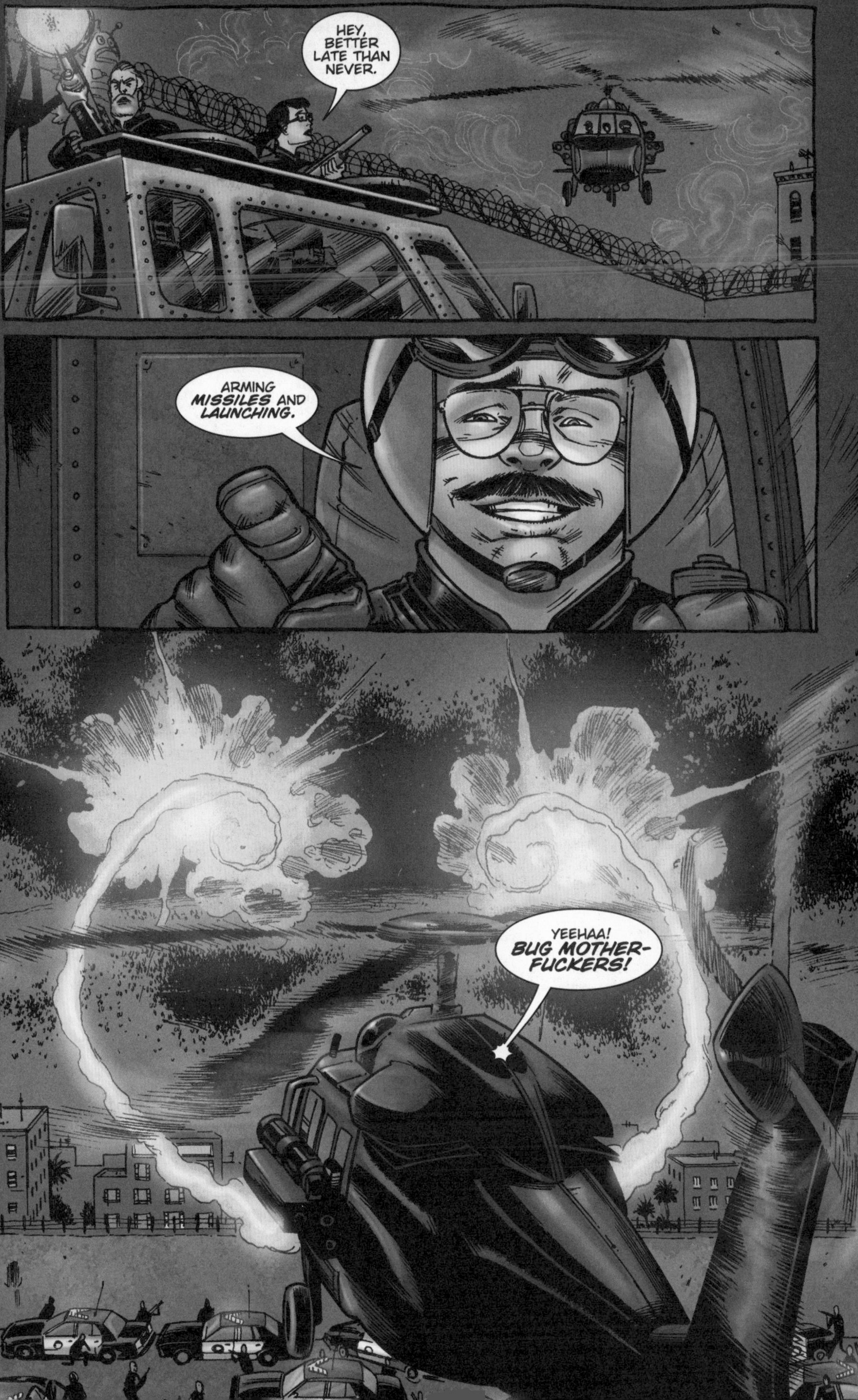
HEY, BETTER LATE THAN NEVER.
ARMING MISSILES AND LAUNCHING.
YEEHAA! BUG MOTHER-FUCKERS!

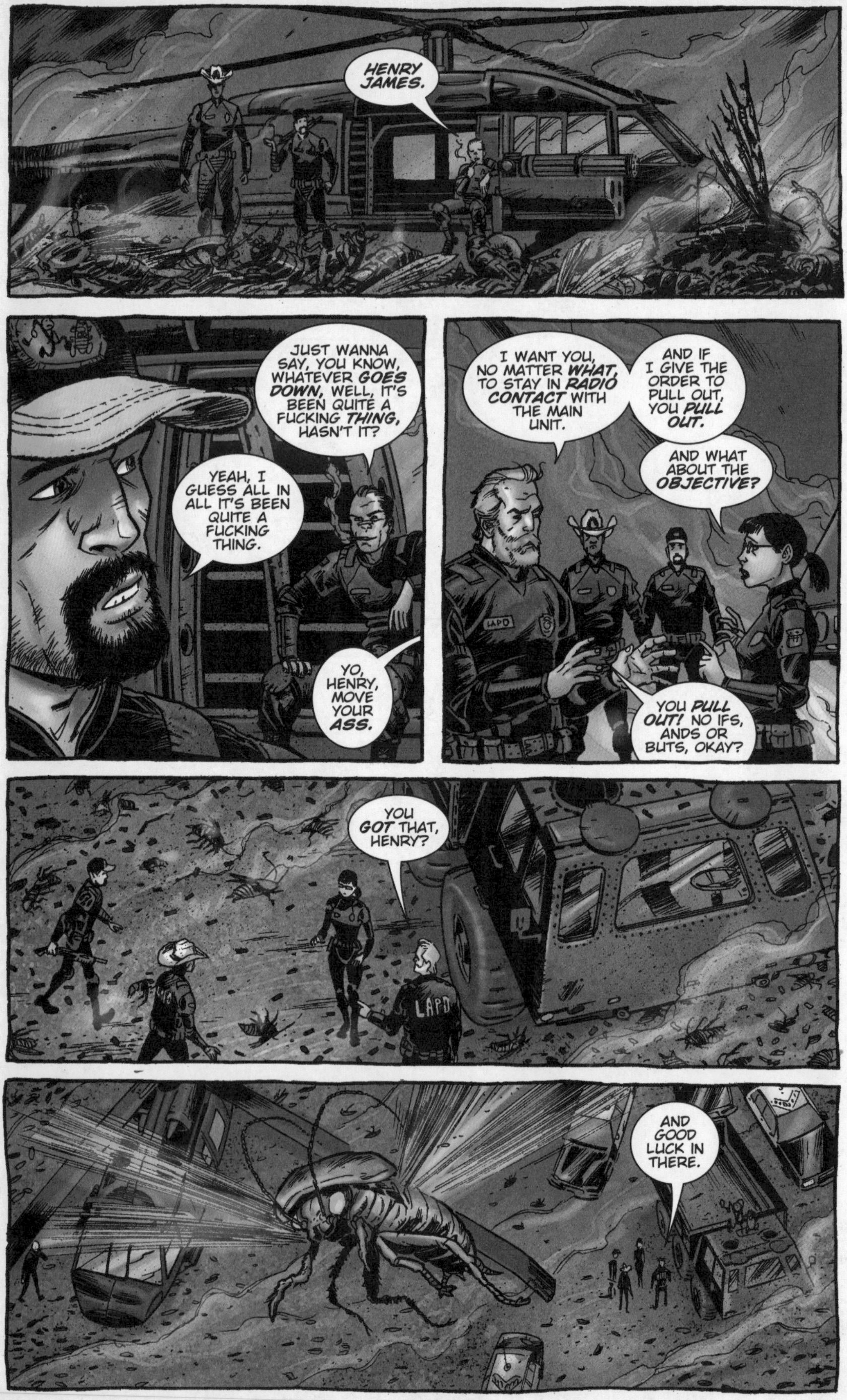
HENRY JAMES.
JUST WANNA SAY, YOU KNOW, WHATEVER GOES DOWN, WELL, IT'S BEEN QUITE A FUCKING THING, HASN'T IT?
YEAH, I GUESS ALL IN ALL IT'S BEEN QUITE A FUCKING THING.
YO, HENRY, MOVE YOUR ASS.
I WANT YOU, NO MATTER WHAT, TO STAY IN RADIO CONTACT WITH THE MAIN UNIT.
AND IF I GIVE THE ORDER TO PULL OUT, YOU PULL OUT.
AND WHAT ABOUT THE OBJECTIVE?
YOU PULL OUT! NO IFS, ANDS OR BUTS, OKAY?
LAPD
LAPD
YOU GOT THAT, HENRY?
AND GOOD LUCK IN THERE.

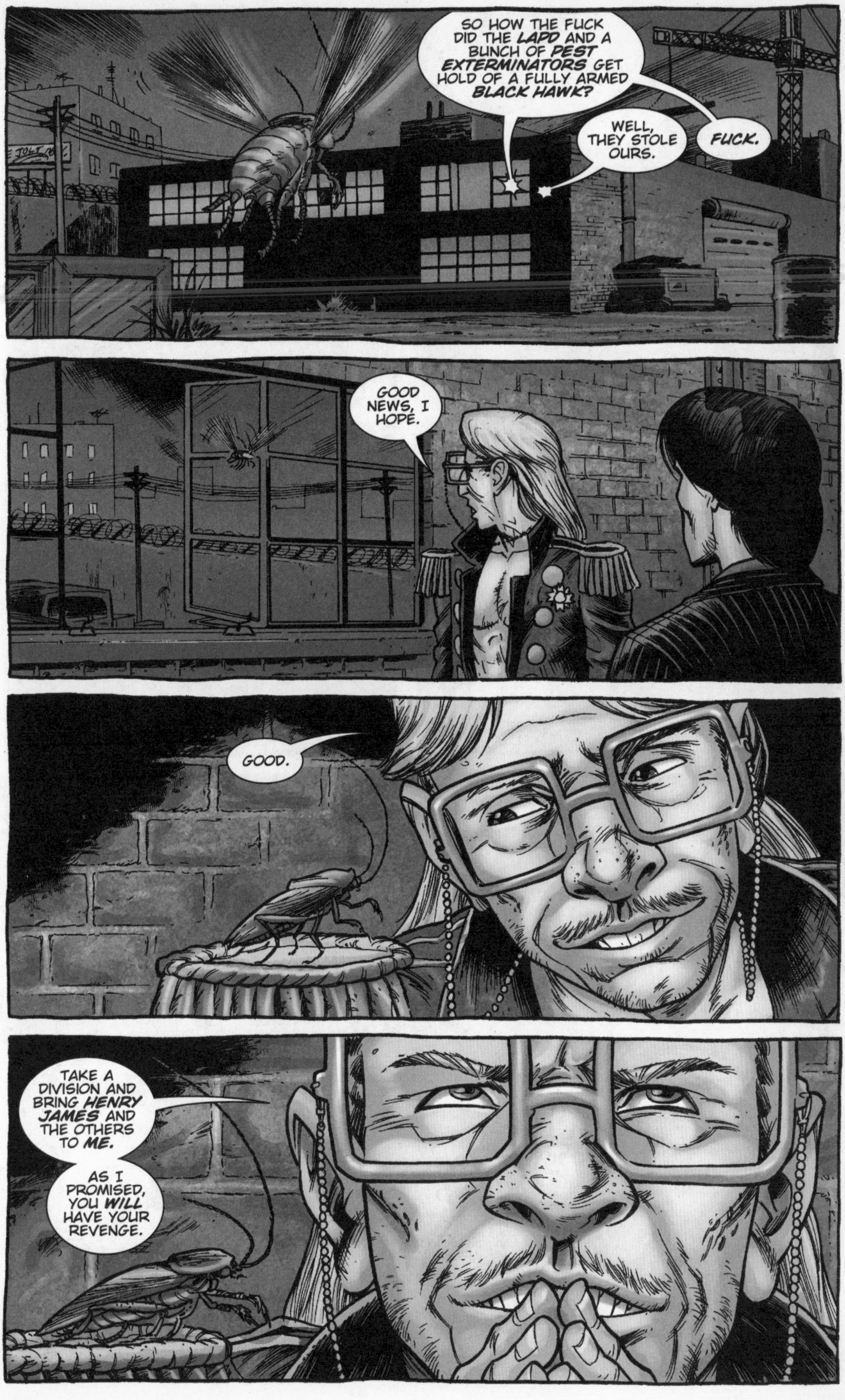
SO HOW THE FUCK DID THE LAPD AND A BUNCH OF PEST EXTERMINATORS GET HOLD OF A FULLY ARMED BLACK HAWK?
WELL, THEY STOLE OURS.
FUCK.
GOOD NEWS, I HOPE.
GOOD.
TAKE A DIVISION AND BRING HENRY JAMES AND THE OTHERS TO ME.
AS I PROMISED, YOU WILL HAVE YOUR REVENGE.

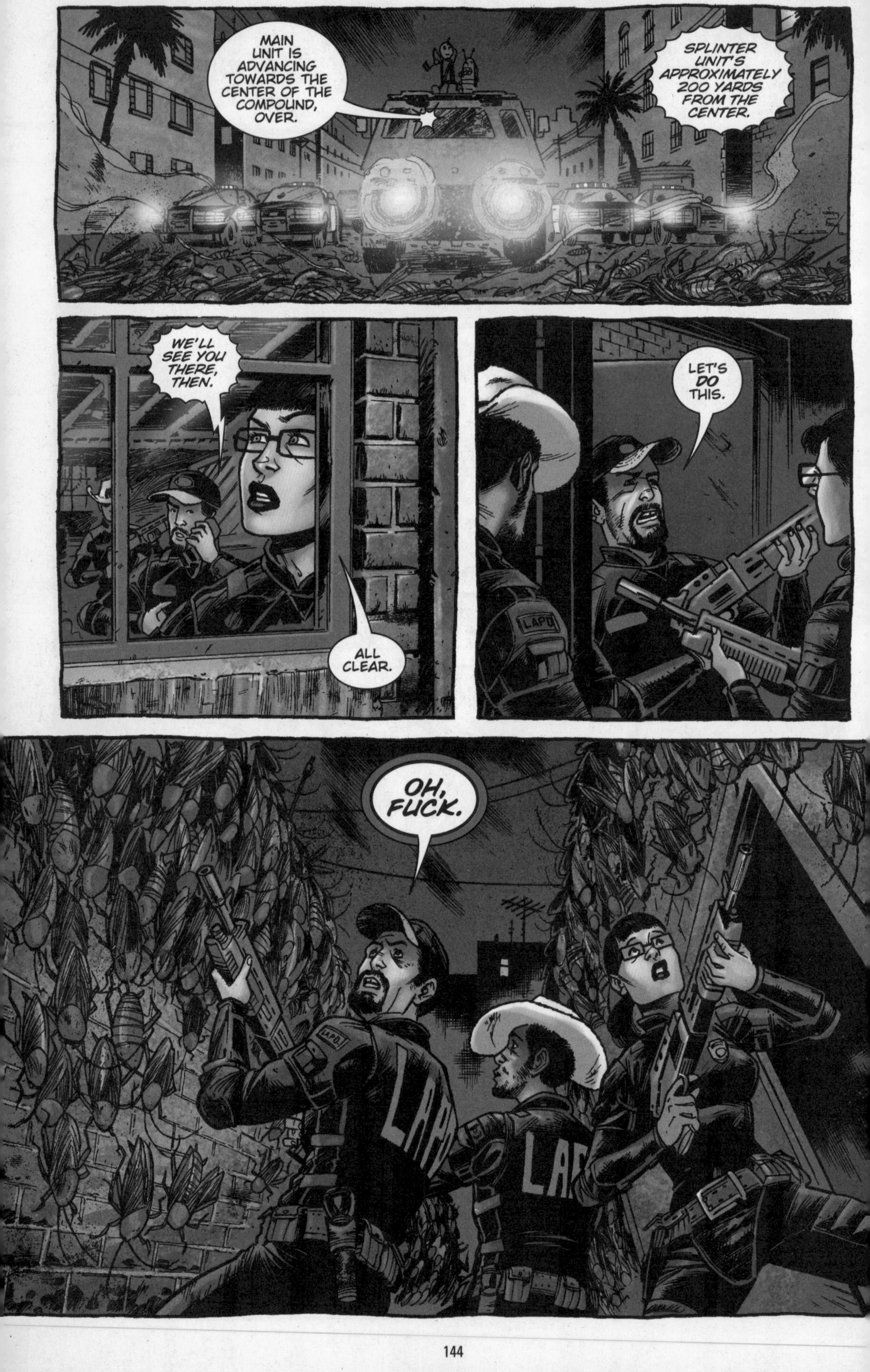
MAIN UNIT IS ADVANCING TOWARDS THE CENTER OF THE COMPOUND, OVER.
SPLINTER UNIT'S APPROXIMATELY 200 YARDS FROM THE CENTER.
WE'LL SEE YOU THERE, THEN.
ALL CLEAR.
LET'S DO THIS.
OH, FUCK.
LAPD

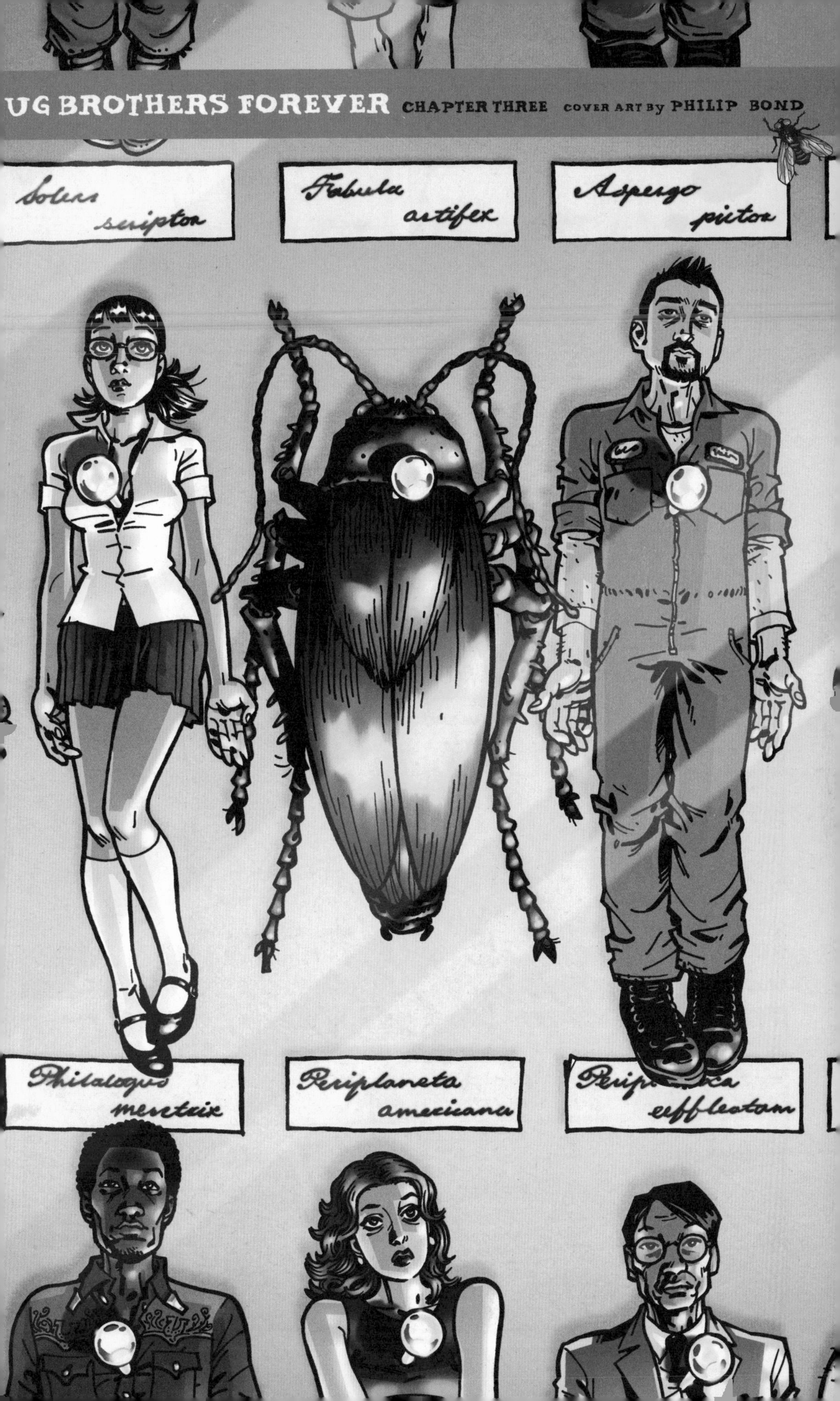
UG BROTHERS FOREVER CHAPTER THREE COVER ART BY PHILIP BOND
Fabula artifex
Aspergo pictor
Periplaneta americana

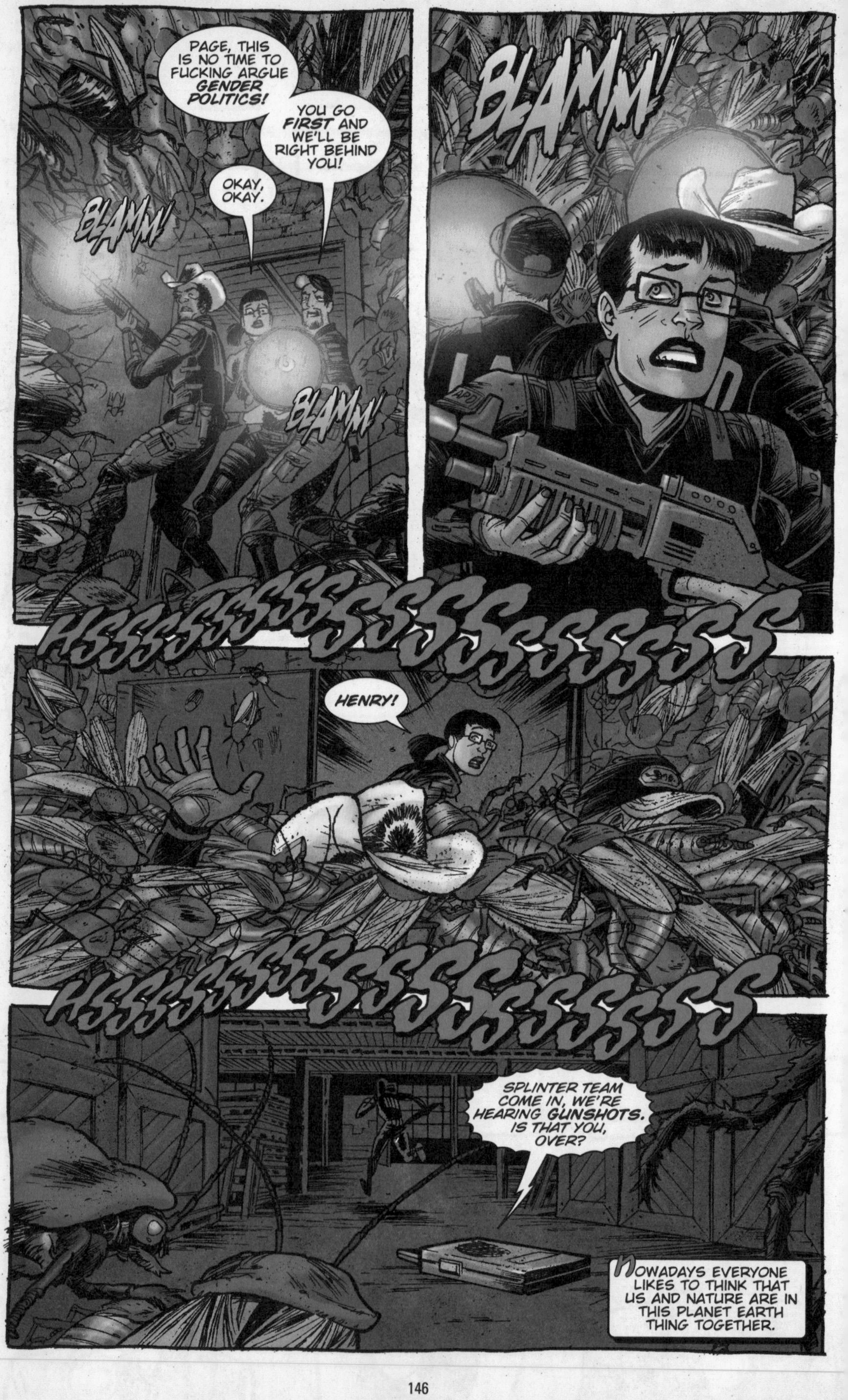
PAGE, THIS IS NO TIME TO FUCKING ARGUE GENDER POLITICS!
YOU GO FIRST AND WE'LL BE RIGHT BEHIND YOU!
OKAY, OKAY.
BLAMM!
BLAMM!
BLAMM!
HSSSSSSSSSSSSSSSSSSS
HENRY!
HSSSSSSSSSSSSSSSSSSS
SPLINTER TEAM COME IN, WE'RE HEARING GUNSHOTS. IS THAT YOU, OVER?
NOWADAYS EVERYONE LIKES TO THINK THAT US AND NATURE ARE IN THIS PLANET EARTH THING TOGETHER.

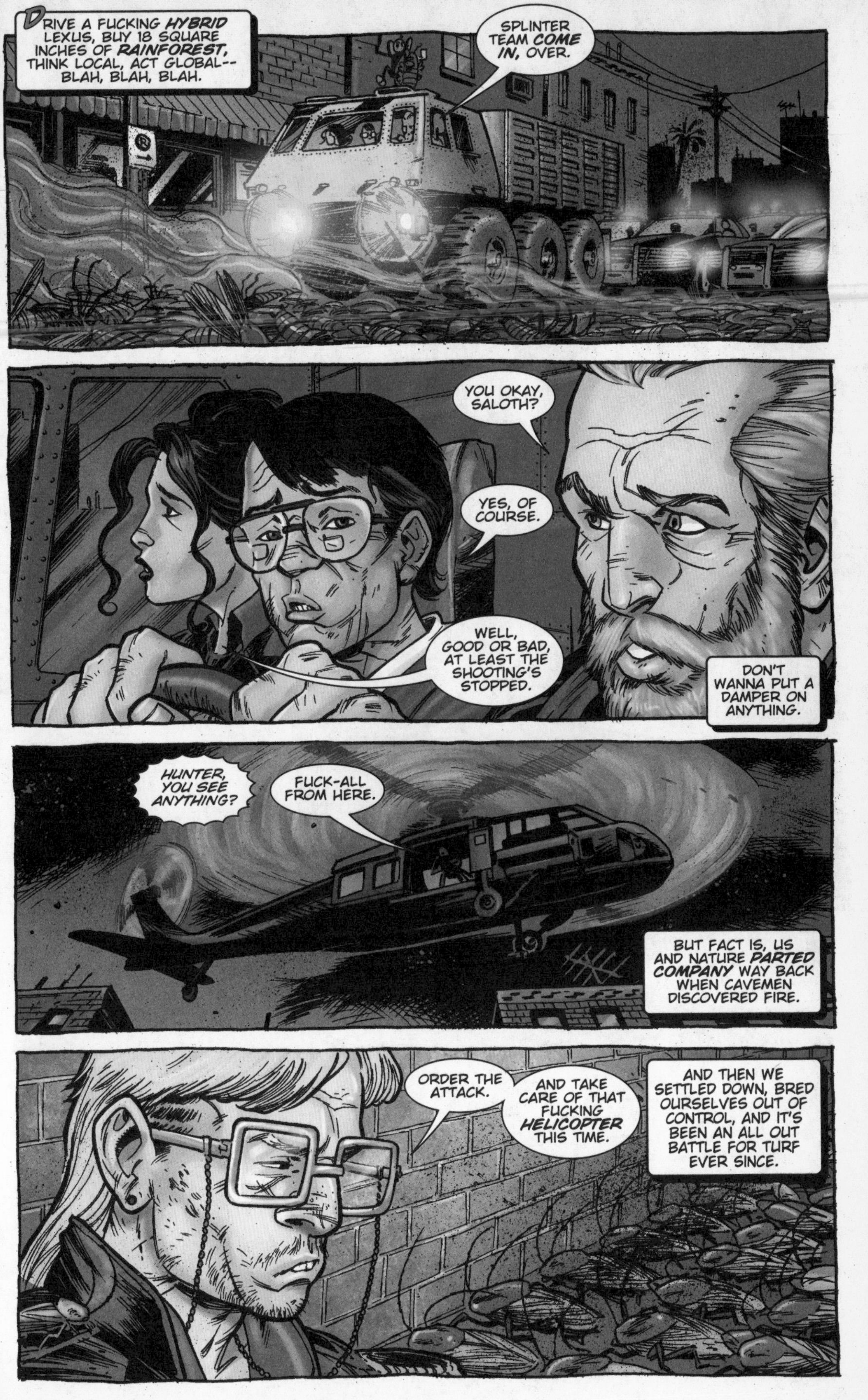

DRIVE A FUCKING HYBRID LEXUS, BUY 18 SQUARE INCHES OF RAINFOREST, THINK LOCAL, ACT GLOBAL--BLAH, BLAH, BLAH.
SPLINTER TEAM COME IN, OVER.
YOU OKAY, SALOTH?
YES, OF COURSE.
WELL, GOOD OR BAD, AT LEAST THE SHOOTING'S STOPPED.
DON'T WANNA PUT A DAMPER ON ANYTHING.
HUNTER, YOU SEE ANYTHING?
FUCK-ALL FROM HERE.
BUT FACT IS, US AND NATURE PARTED COMPANY WAY BACK WHEN CAVEMEN DISCOVERED FIRE.
ORDER THE ATTACK.
AND TAKE CARE OF THAT FUCKING HELICOPTER THIS TIME.
AND THEN WE SETTLED DOWN, BRED OURSELVES OUT OF CONTROL, AND IT'S BEEN AN ALL OUT BATTLE FOR TURF EVER SINCE.

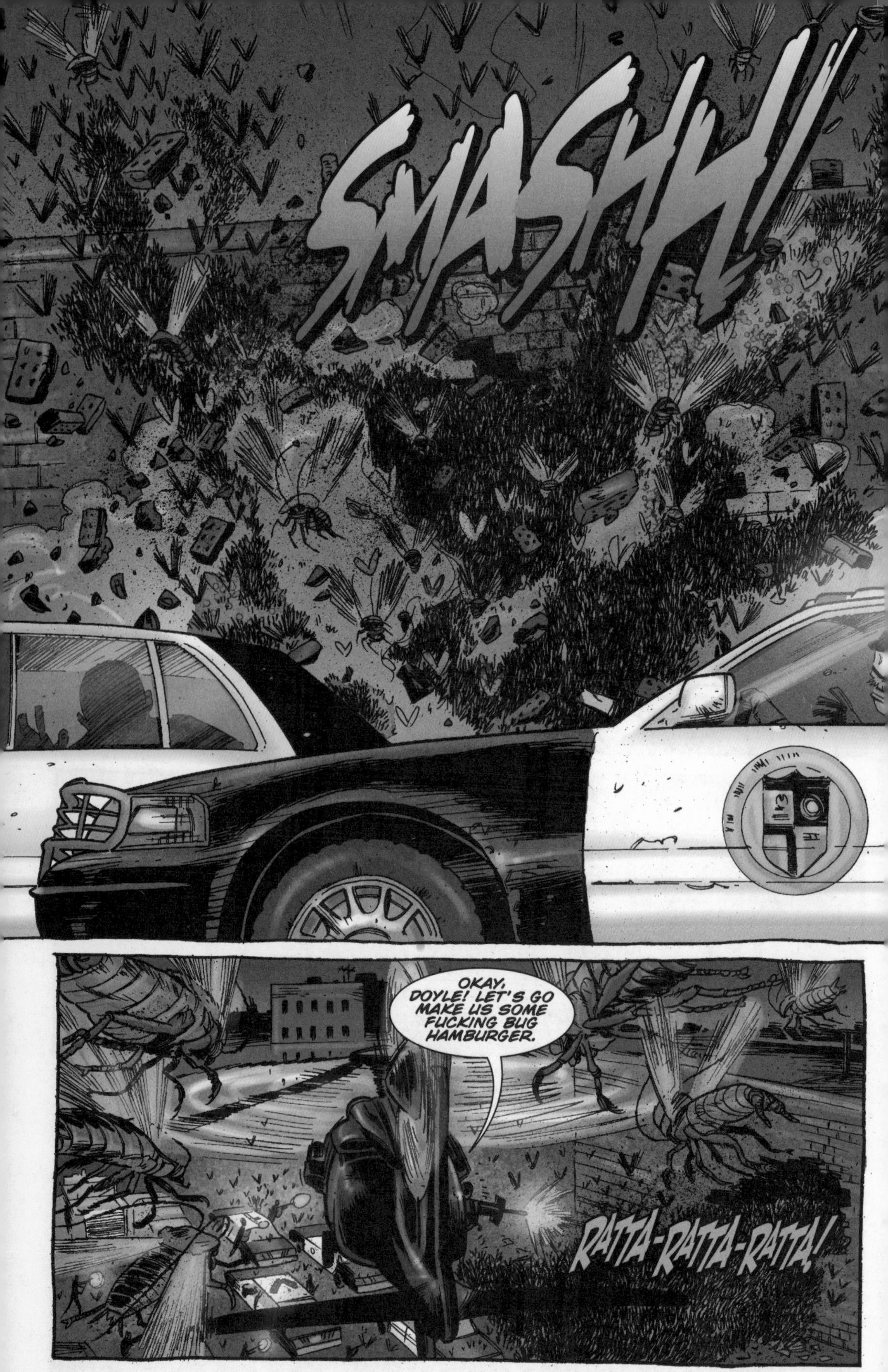
SMASH!
OKAY, DOYLE! LET'S GO MAKE US SOME FUCKING BUG HAMBURGER.
RATTA-RATTA-RATTA!

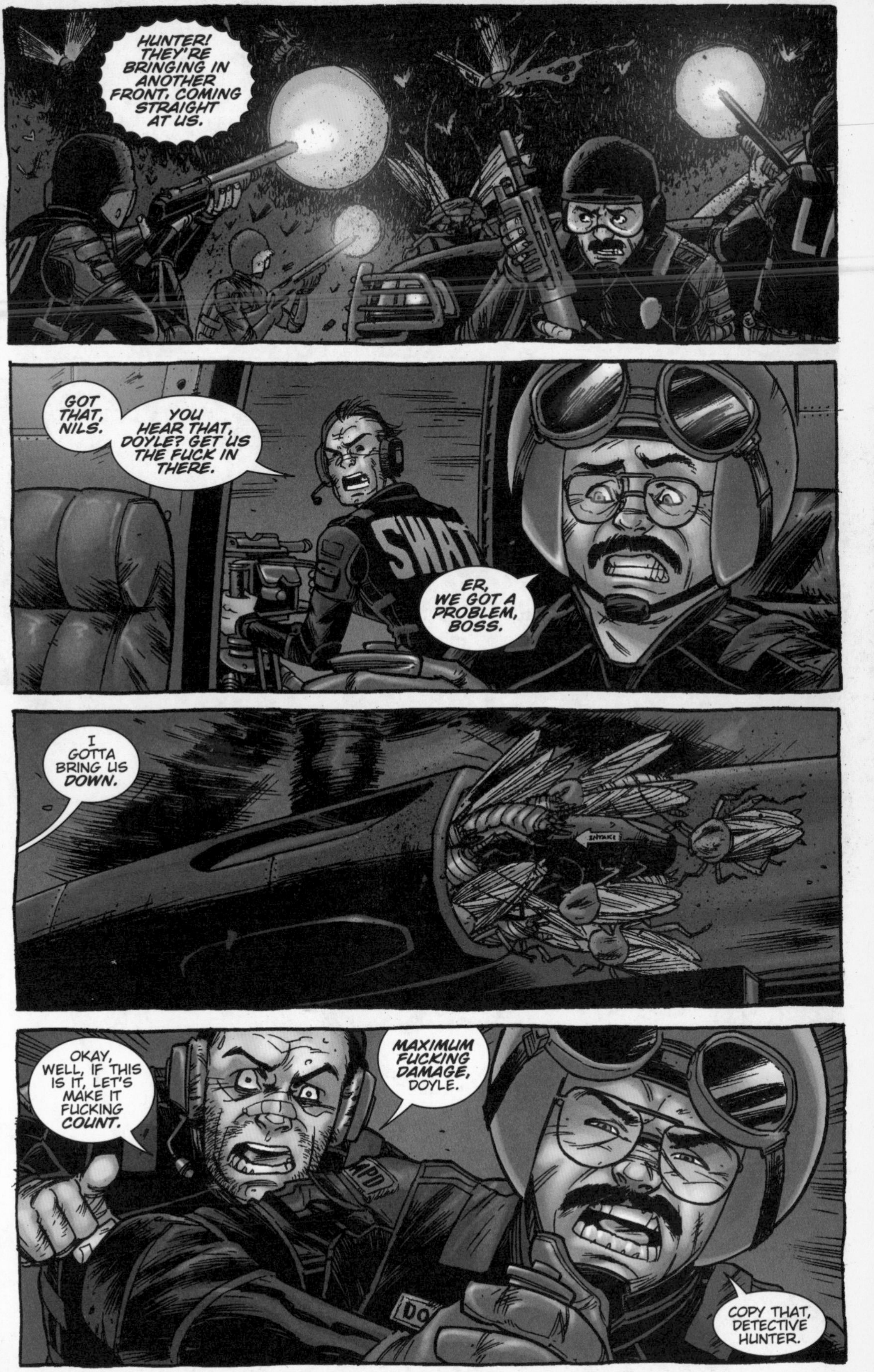
HUNTER! THEY'RE BRINGING IN ANOTHER FRONT, COMING STRAIGHT AT US.
GOT THAT, NILS.
YOU HEAR THAT, DOYLE? GET US THE FUCK IN THERE.
SWAT
ER, WE GOT A PROBLEM, BOSS.
I GOTTA BRING US DOWN.
INTAKE
OKAY, WELL, IF THIS IS IT, LET'S MAKE IT FUCKING COUNT.
MAXIMUM FUCKING DAMAGE, DOYLE.
COPY THAT, DETECTIVE HUNTER.

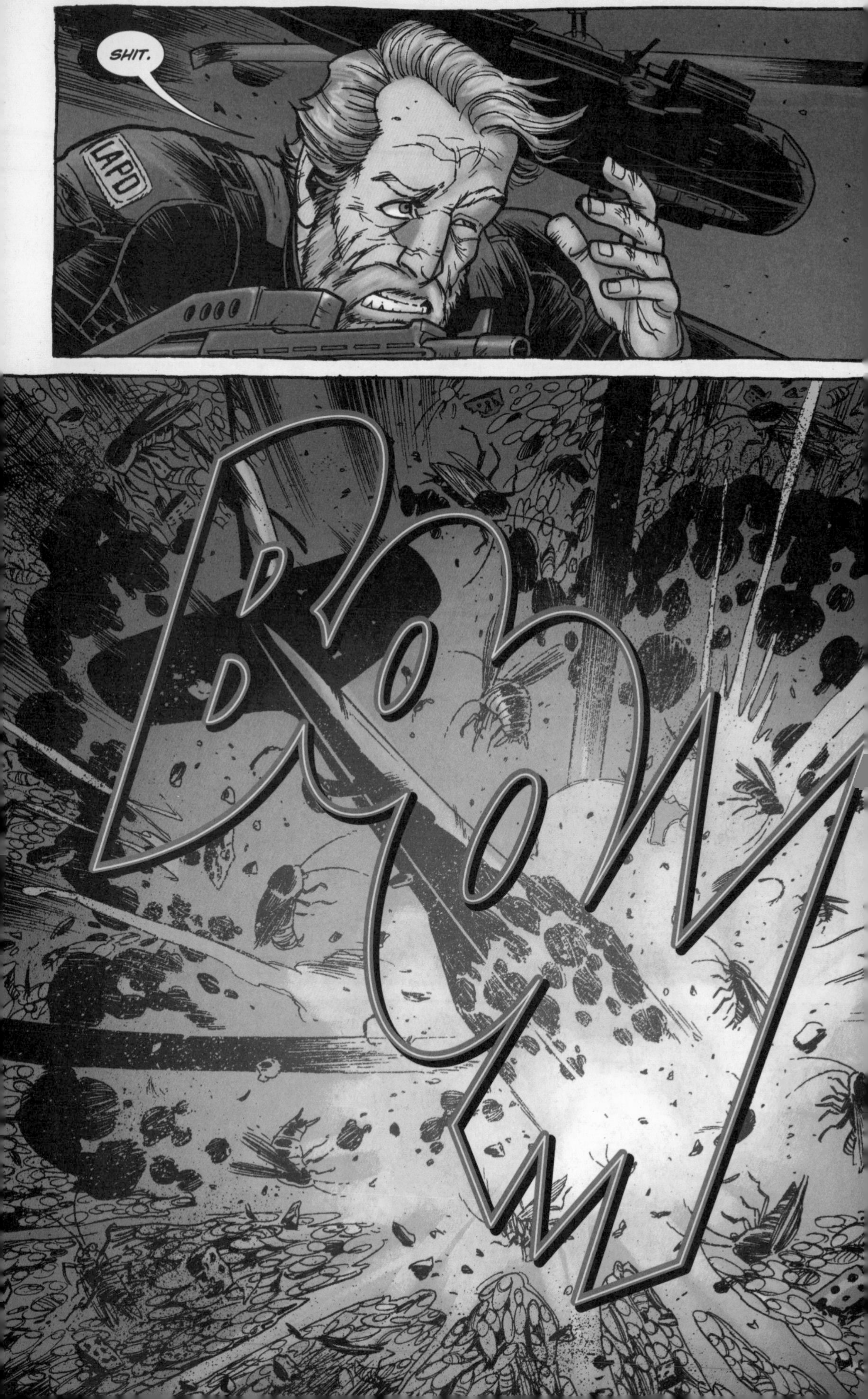
SHIT.
LAPD

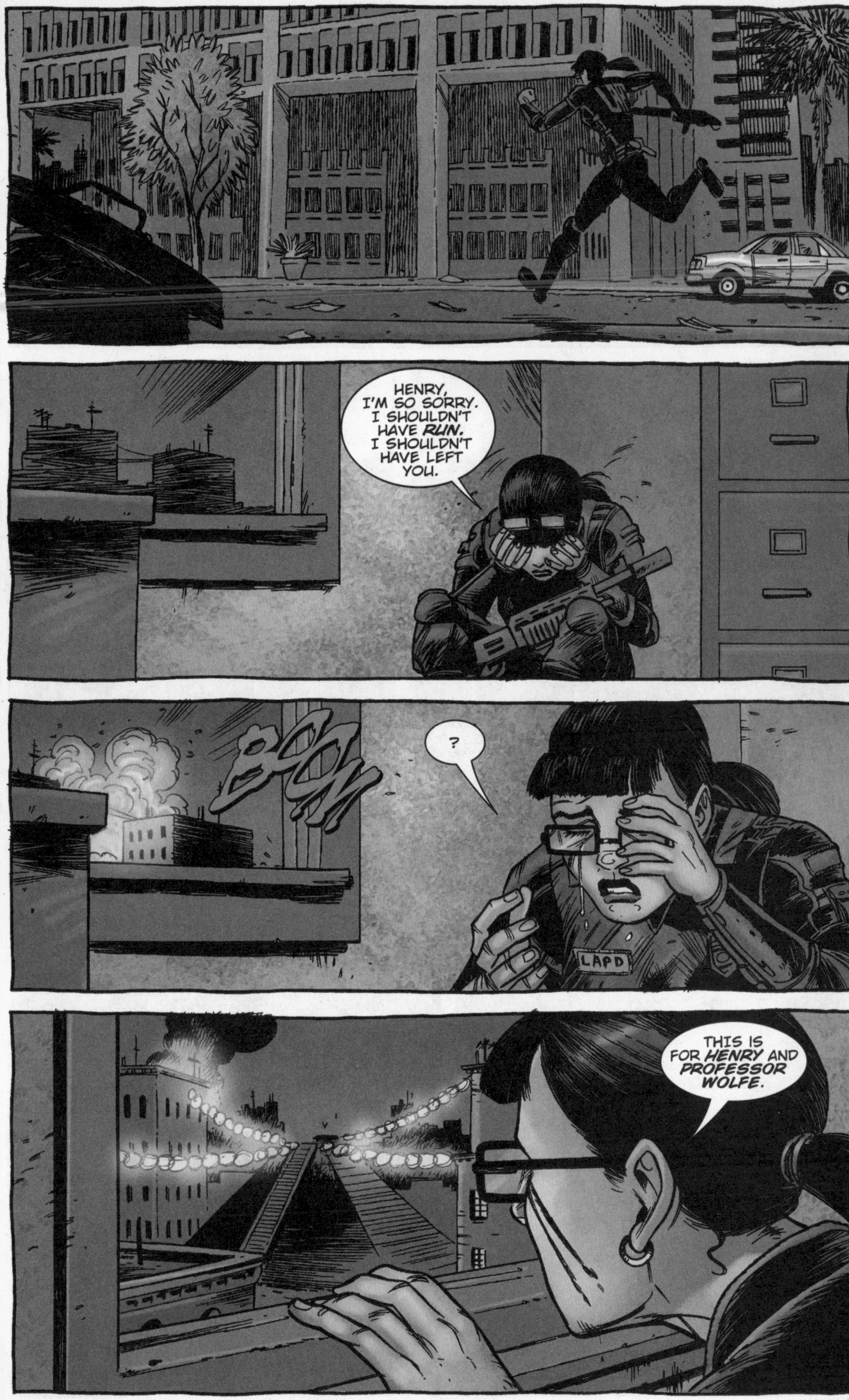
HENRY, I'M SO SORRY. I SHOULDN'T HAVE RUN. I SHOULDN'T HAVE LEFT YOU.
BOOM
?
THIS IS FOR HENRY AND PROFESSOR WOLFE.

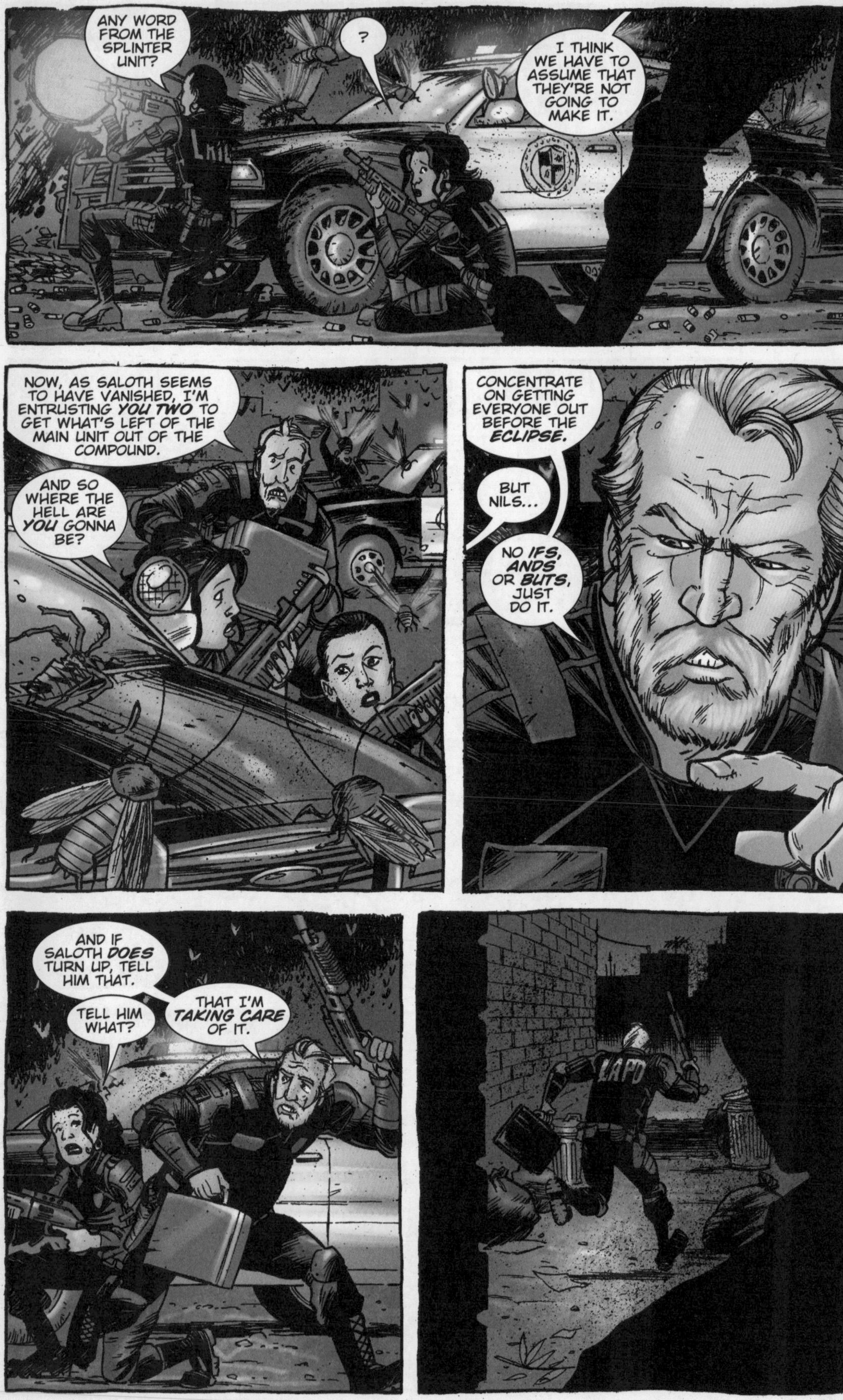
ANY WORD FROM THE SPLINTER UNIT?
?
I THINK WE HAVE TO ASSUME THAT THEY'RE NOT GOING TO MAKE IT.
NOW, AS SALOTH SEEMS TO HAVE VANISHED, I'M ENTRUSTING YOU TWO TO GET WHAT'S LEFT OF THE MAIN UNIT OUT OF THE COMPOUND.
AND SO WHERE THE HELL ARE YOU GONNA BE?
CONCENTRATE ON GETTING EVERYONE OUT BEFORE THE ECLIPSE.
BUT NILS...
NO IFS, ANDS OR BUTS, JUST DO IT.
AND IF SALOTH DOES TURN UP, TELL HIM THAT.
TELL HIM WHAT?
THAT I'M TAKING CARE OF IT.
LAPD

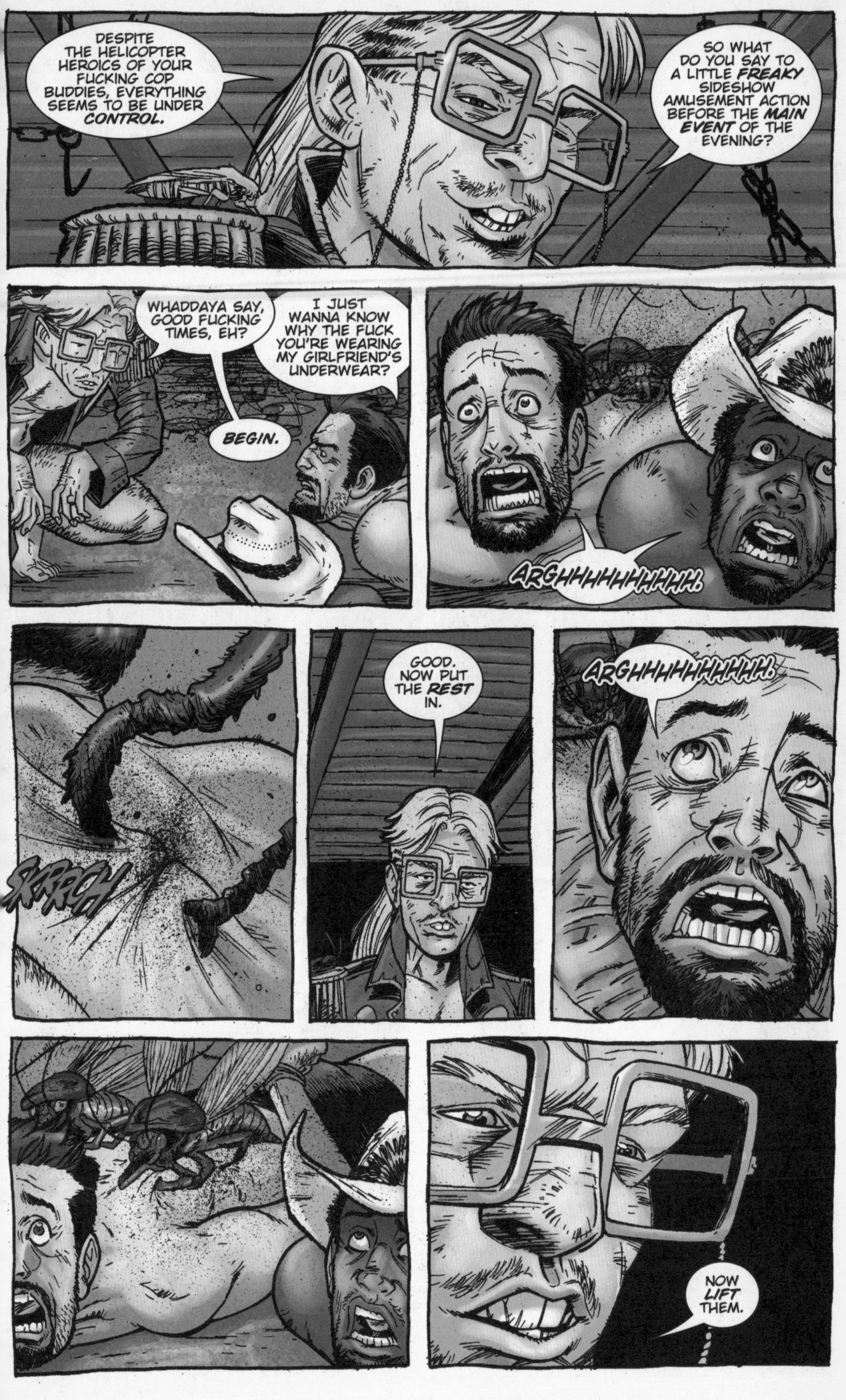

DESPITE THE HELICOPTER HEROICS OF YOUR FUCKING COP BUDDIES, EVERYTHING SEEMS TO BE UNDER CONTROL.
SO WHAT DO YOU SAY TO A LITTLE FREAKY SIDESHOW AMUSEMENT ACTION BEFORE THE MAIN EVENT OF THE EVENING?
WHADDAYA SAY, GOOD FUCKING TIMES, EH?
I JUST WANNA KNOW WHY THE FUCK YOU'RE WEARING MY GIRLFRIEND'S UNDERWEAR?
BEGIN.
ARGHHHHHHHHHH.
SKRRCH
GOOD. NOW PUT THE REST IN.
ARGHHHHHHHHHH.
NOW LIFT THEM.

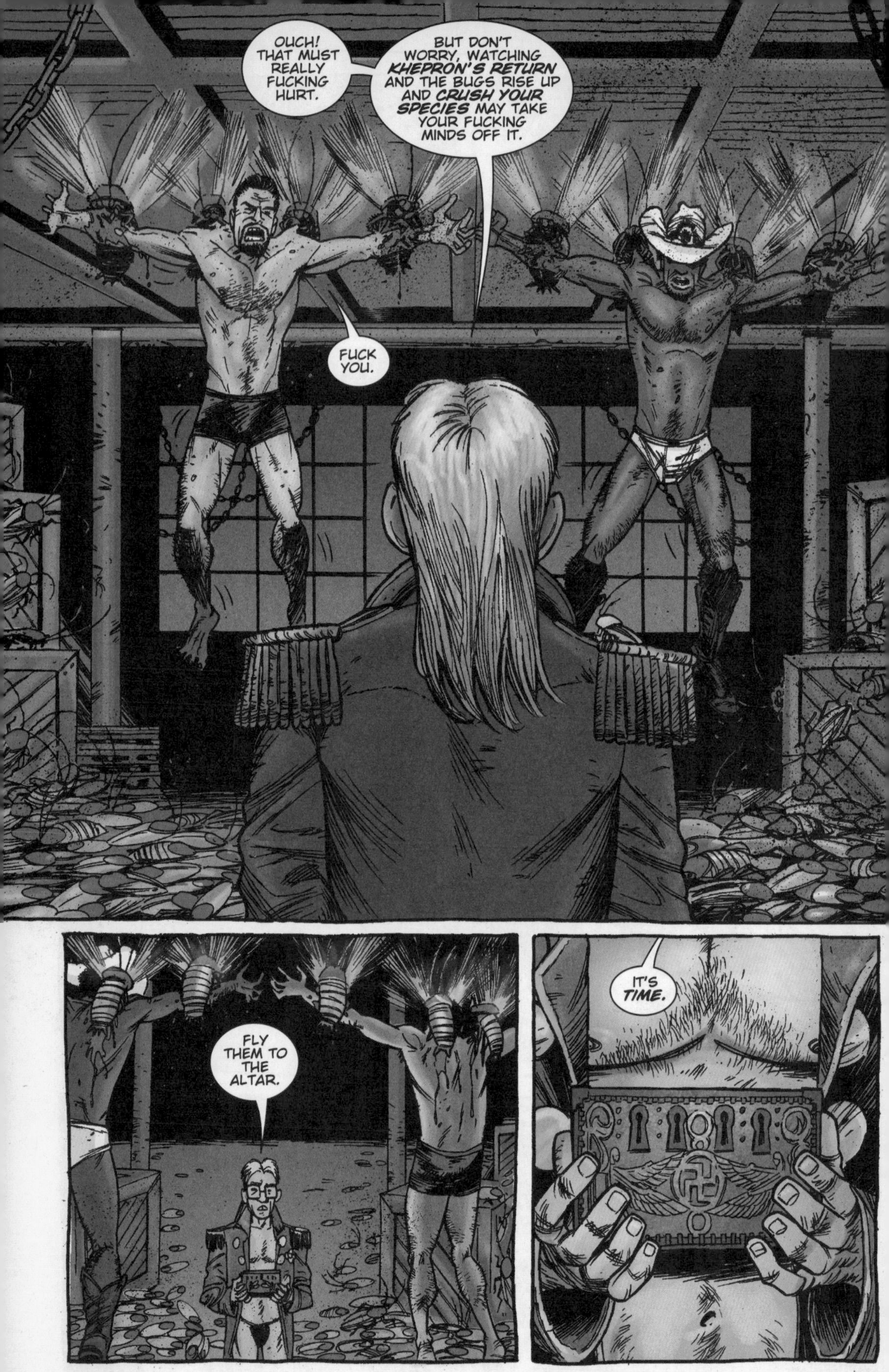
OUCH! THAT MUST REALLY FUCKING HURT.
BUT DON'T WORRY, WATCHING KHEPRON'S RETURN AND THE BUGS RISE UP AND CRUSH YOUR SPECIES MAY TAKE YOUR FUCKING MINDS OFF IT.
FUCK YOU.
FLY THEM TO THE ALTAR.
IT'S TIME.

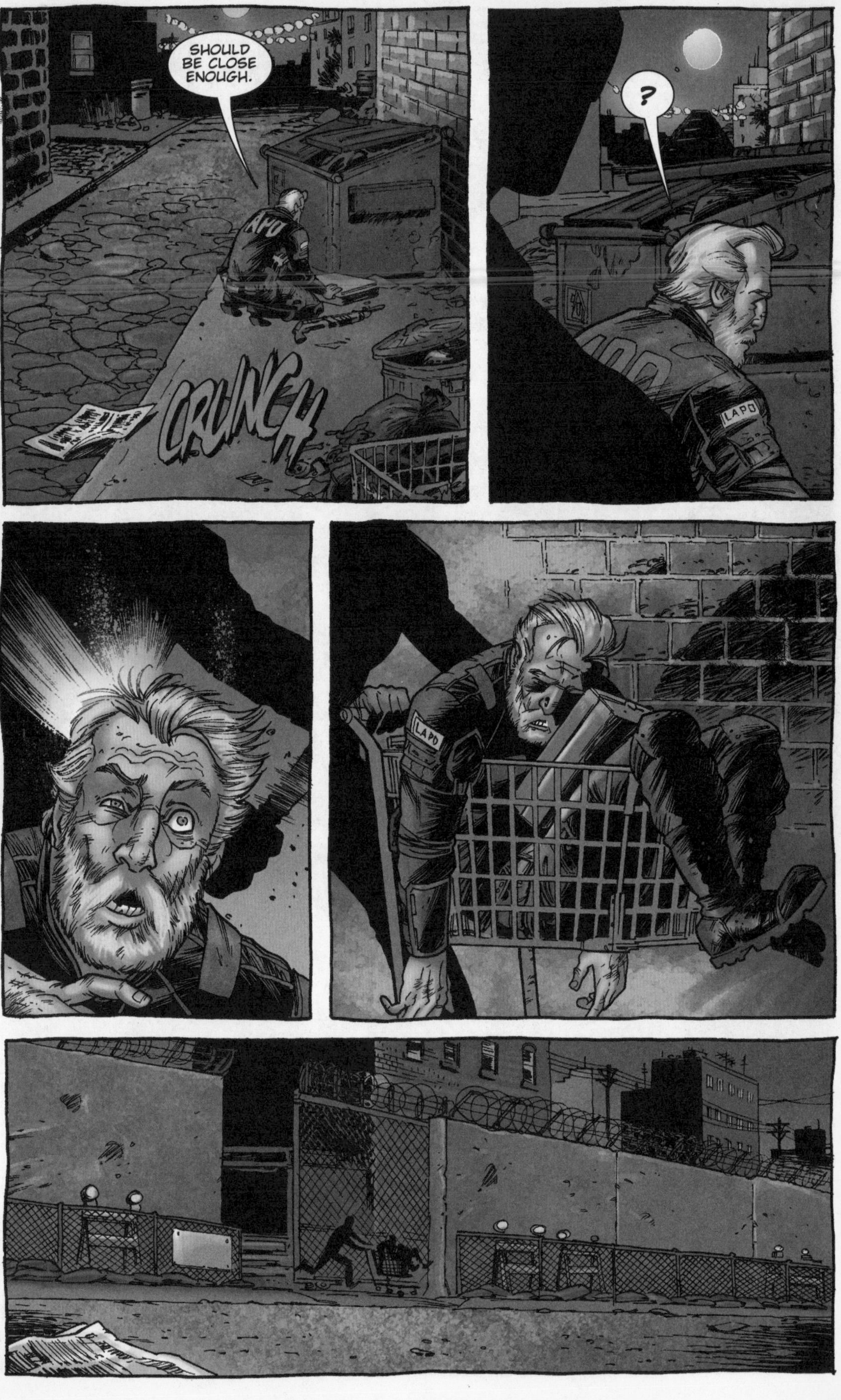
SHOULD BE CLOSE ENOUGH.
CRUNCH
?
LAPD
LAPD

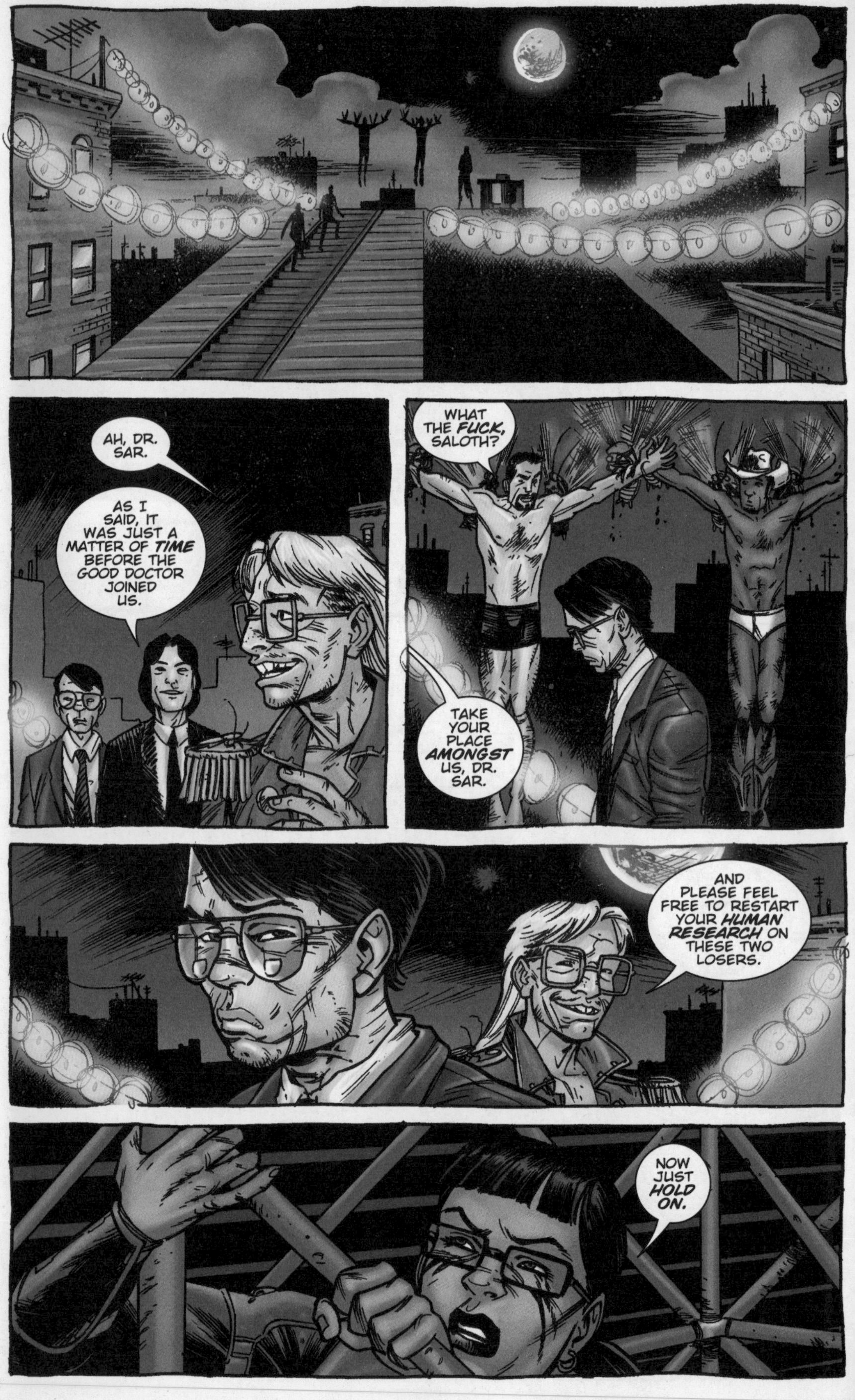
AH, DR. SAR.
AS I SAID, IT WAS JUST A MATTER OF *TIME* BEFORE THE GOOD DOCTOR JOINED US.
WHAT THE *FUCK,* SALOTH?
TAKE YOUR PLACE *AMONGST* US, DR. SAR.
AND PLEASE FEEL FREE TO RESTART YOUR *HUMAN RESEARCH* ON THESE TWO LOSERS.
NOW JUST *HOLD ON.*

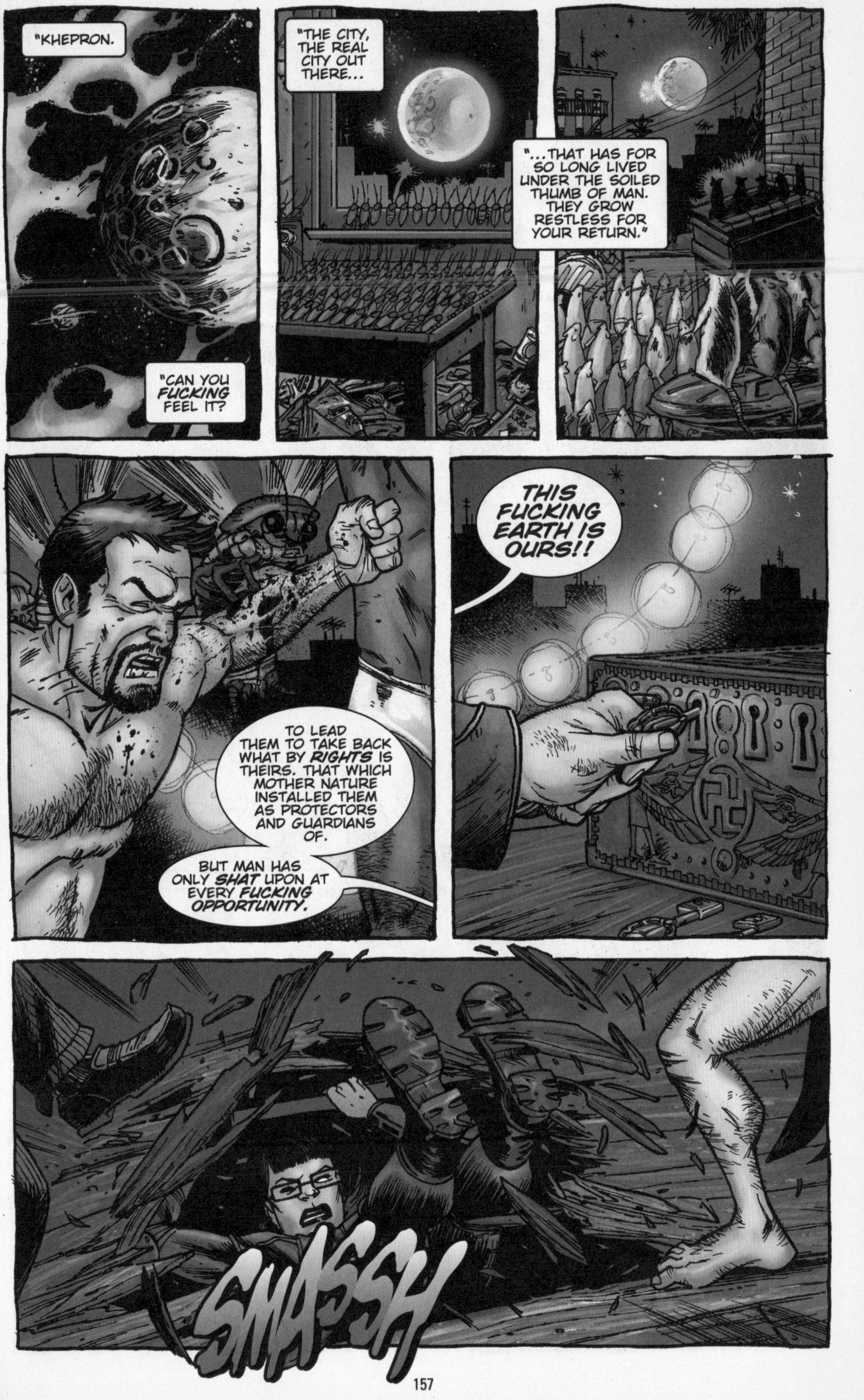
"KHEPRON.
"CAN YOU FUCKING FEEL IT?
"THE CITY, THE REAL CITY OUT THERE...
"...THAT HAS FOR SO LONG LIVED UNDER THE SOILED THUMB OF MAN. THEY GROW RESTLESS FOR YOUR RETURN."
TO LEAD THEM TO TAKE BACK WHAT BY RIGHTS IS THEIRS. THAT WHICH MOTHER NATURE INSTALLED THEM AS PROTECTORS AND GUARDIANS OF.
BUT MAN HAS ONLY SHAT UPON AT EVERY FUCKING OPPORTUNITY.
THIS FUCKING EARTH IS OURS!!
SMASSH

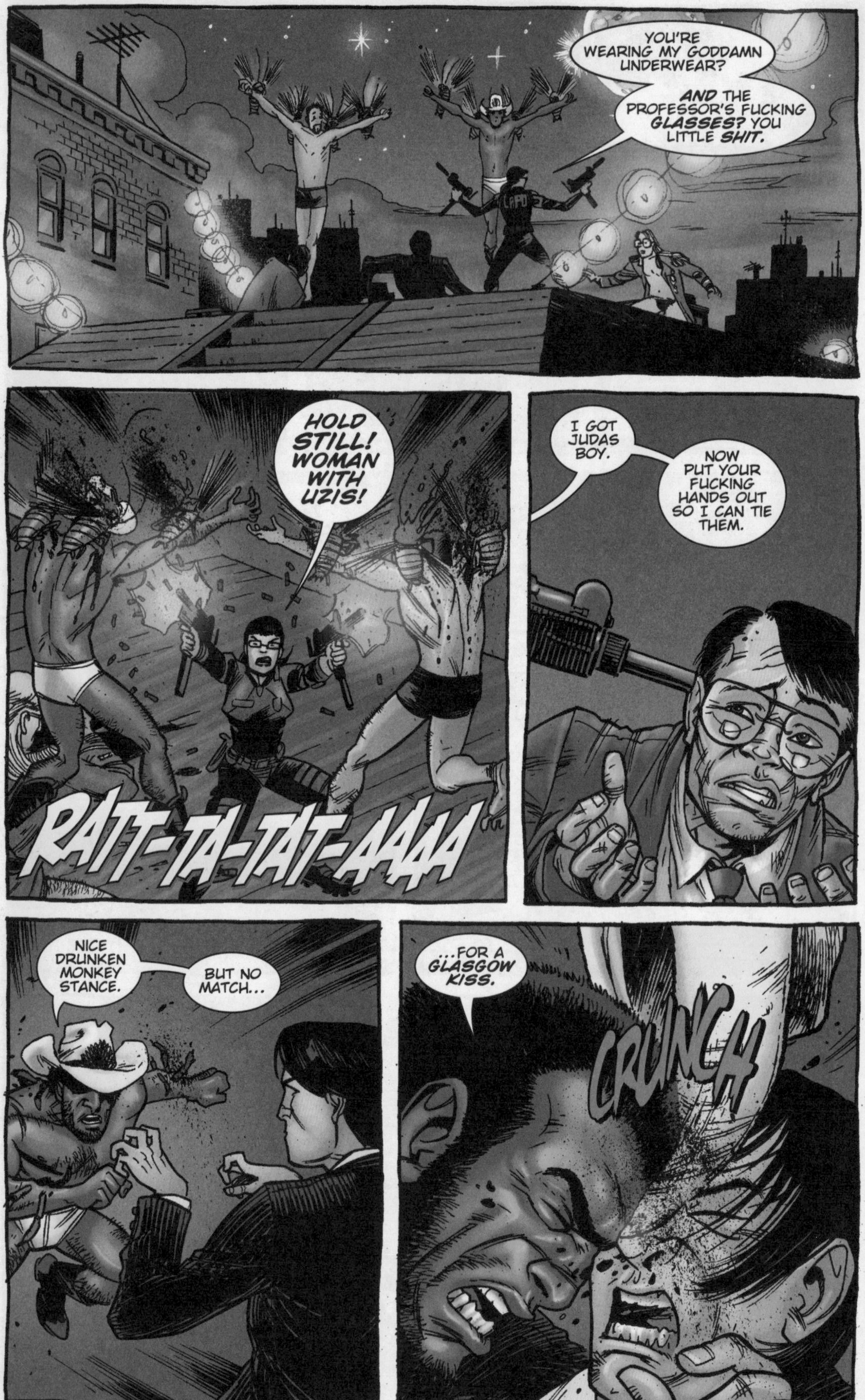

YOU'RE WEARING MY GODDAMN UNDERWEAR?
AND THE PROFESSOR'S FUCKING GLASSES? YOU LITTLE SHIT.
HOLD STILL! WOMAN WITH UZIS!
RATT-TA-TAT-AAAA
I GOT JUDAS BOY.
NOW PUT YOUR FUCKING HANDS OUT SO I CAN TIE THEM.
NICE DRUNKEN MONKEY STANCE.
BUT NO MATCH...
...FOR A GLASGOW KISS.
CRUNCH

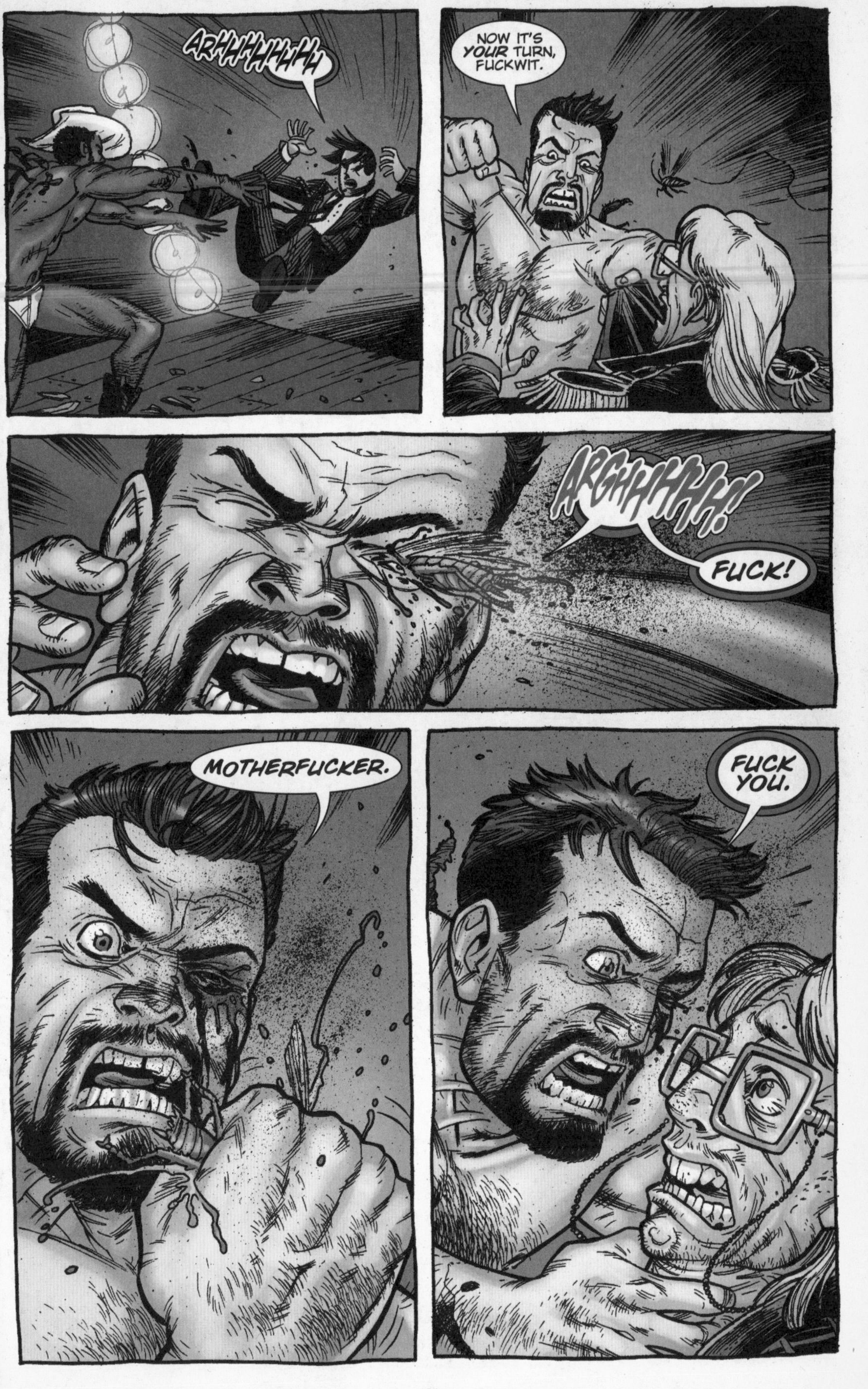
ARHHHHHHHH
NOW IT'S YOUR TURN, FUCKWIT.
ARGHHHHHH!
FUCK!
MOTHERFUCKER.
FUCK YOU.

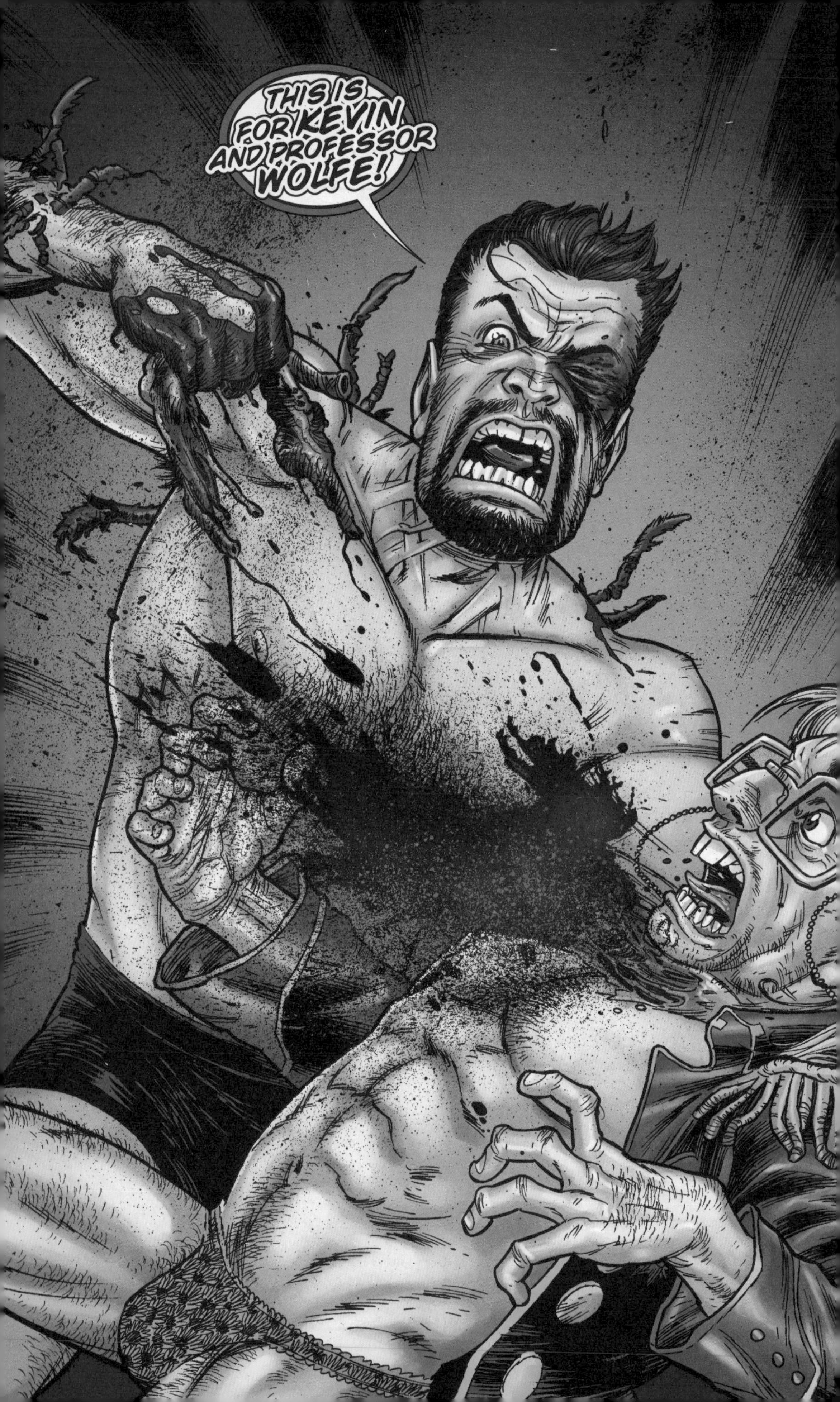
THIS IS FOR KEVIN AND PROFESSOR WOLFE!

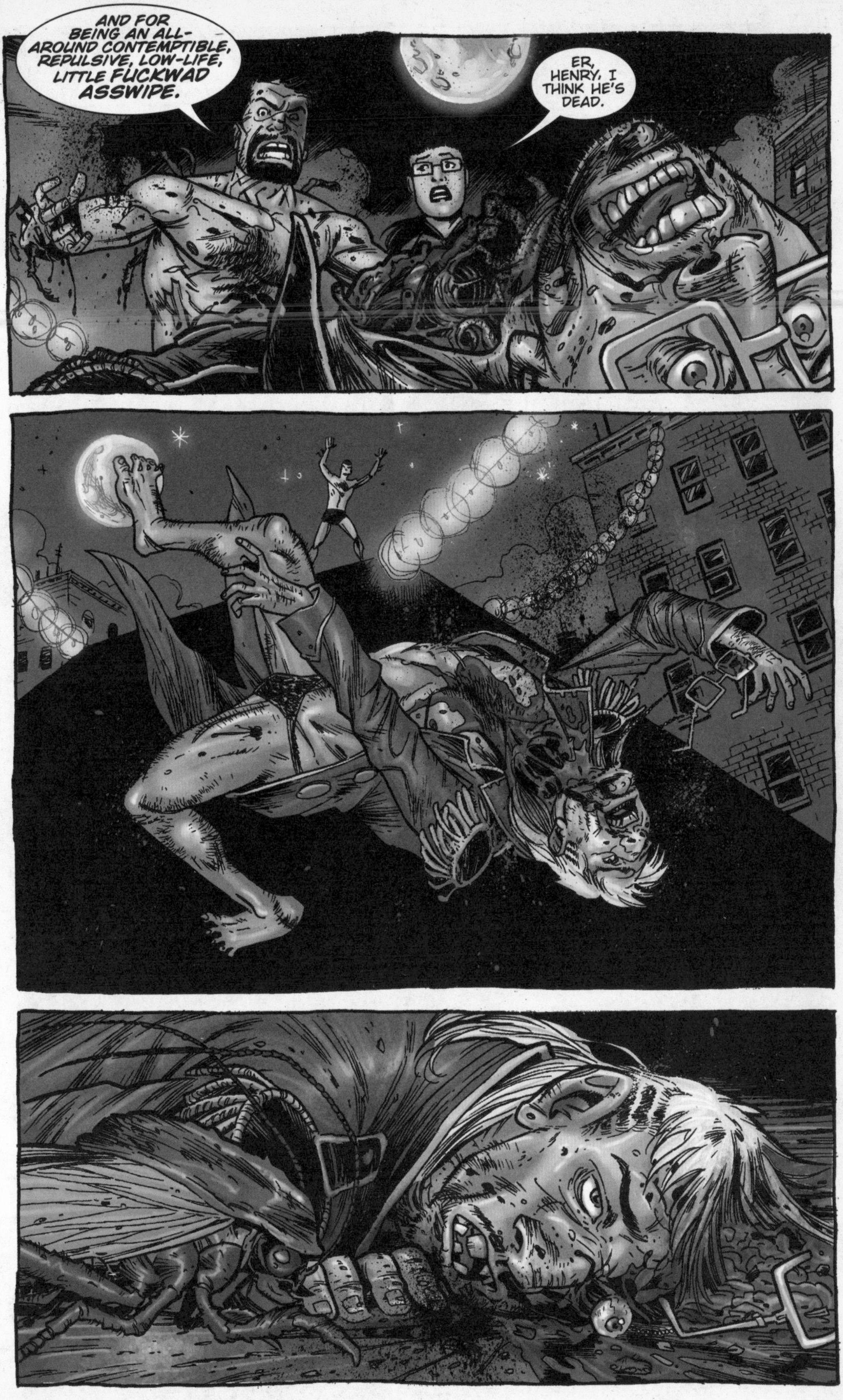
AND FOR BEING AN ALL-AROUND CONTEMPTIBLE, REPULSIVE, LOW-LIFE, LITTLE FUCKWAD ASSWIPE.
ER, HENRY, I THINK HE'S DEAD.

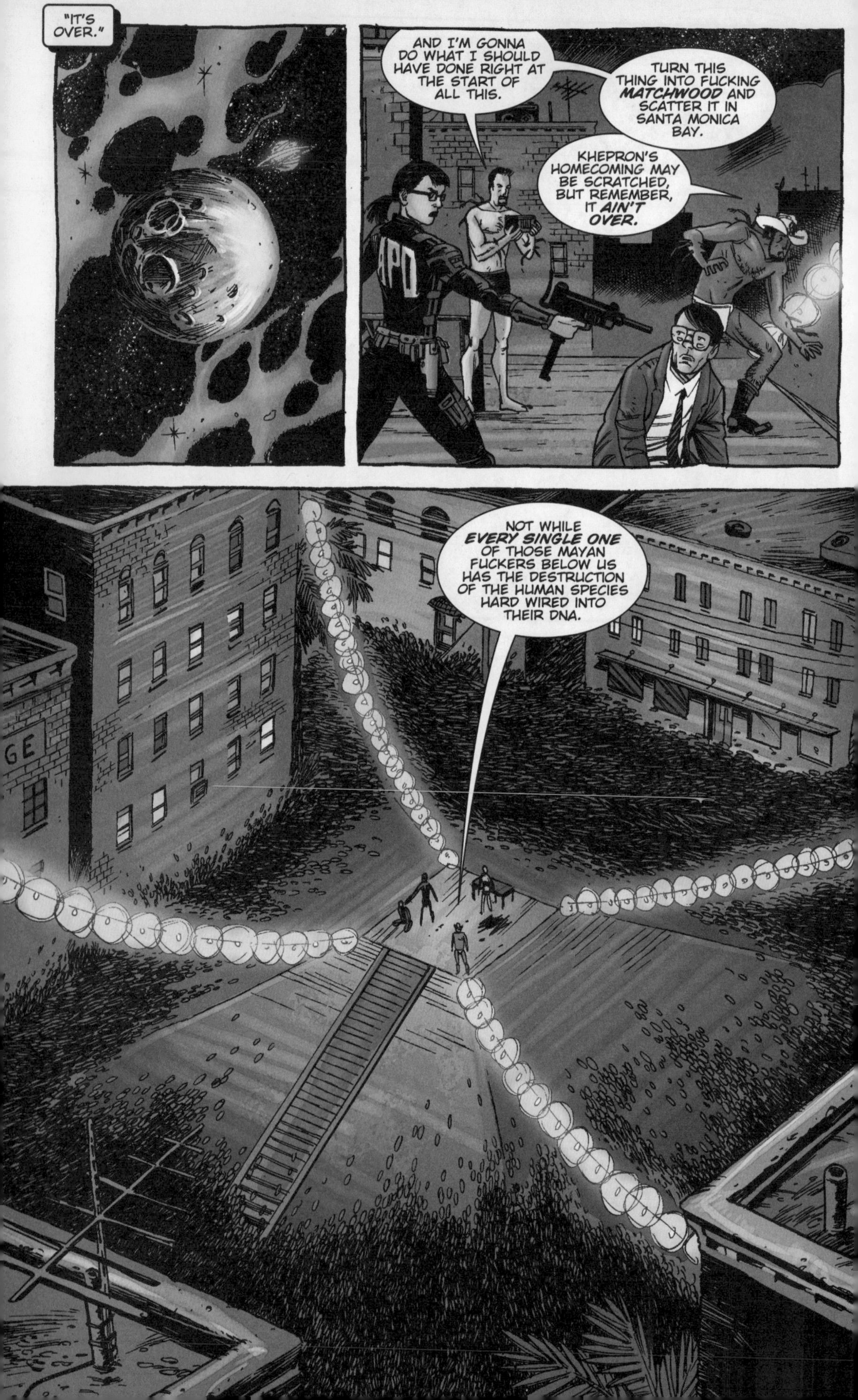

"IT'S OVER."
AND I'M GONNA DO WHAT I SHOULD HAVE DONE RIGHT AT THE START OF ALL THIS.
TURN THIS THING INTO FUCKING MATCHWOOD AND SCATTER IT IN SANTA MONICA BAY.
KHEPRON'S HOMECOMING MAY BE SCRATCHED, BUT REMEMBER, IT AIN'T OVER.
NOT WHILE EVERY SINGLE ONE OF THOSE MAYAN FUCKERS BELOW US HAS THE DESTRUCTION OF THE HUMAN SPECIES HARD WIRED INTO THEIR DNA.

HENRY, THERE'S A STORM DRAIN COVER UNDER THE PYRAMID. WE COULD *MAKE IT*.

I'M TALKING ABOUT RUNNING TO FIGHT ANOTHER DAY, HENRY.

NO, STRETCH IS RIGHT. WE *CAN'T* JUST RUN.

THE SUITCASE.

WHAT THE FUCK?

IT'S BIG ENOUGH TO TAKE OUT A TEN CITY-BLOCK RADIUS.

NILS' BACKUP PLAN?

YES. YOU THREE CAN STILL MAKE IT.

AND YOU?

LONG AGO I ABANDONED MY HUMANITY FOR SCIENTIFIC VANITY. THIS IS MY CHANCE AT REDEMPTION.

ARE YOU *SURE?*

VERY. UNTIE ME, AND LET ME FINISH THIS.

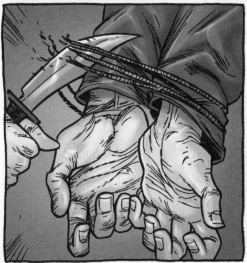

AND YOU SHOULD PROBABLY KEEP A HOLD OF THIS.

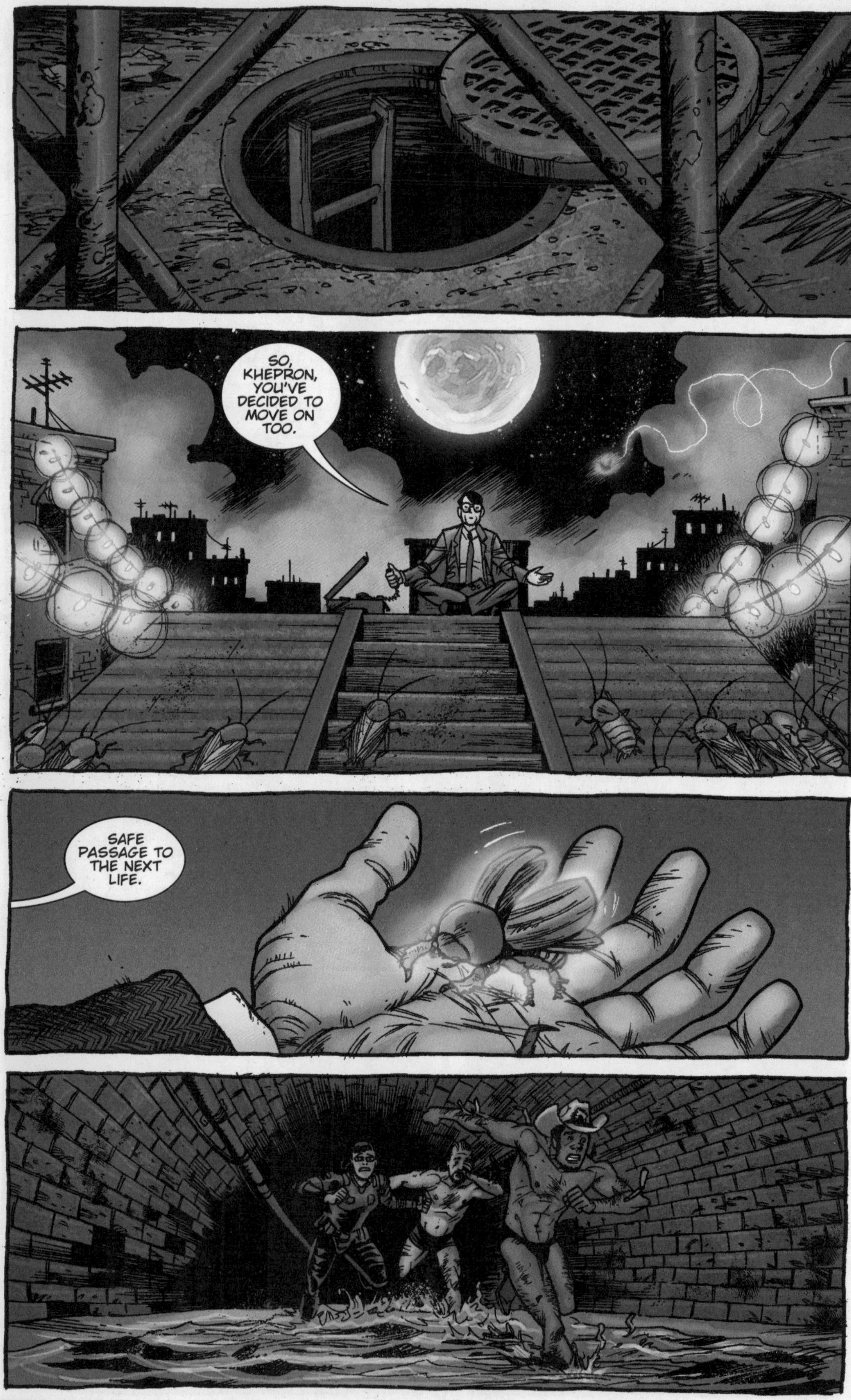
SO, KHEPRON, YOU'VE DECIDED TO MOVE ON TOO.
SAFE PASSAGE TO THE NEXT LIFE.

KLIK

ARHHHHHHH!

BOOMMMMMMMMMMMMMMMMMMMMMM

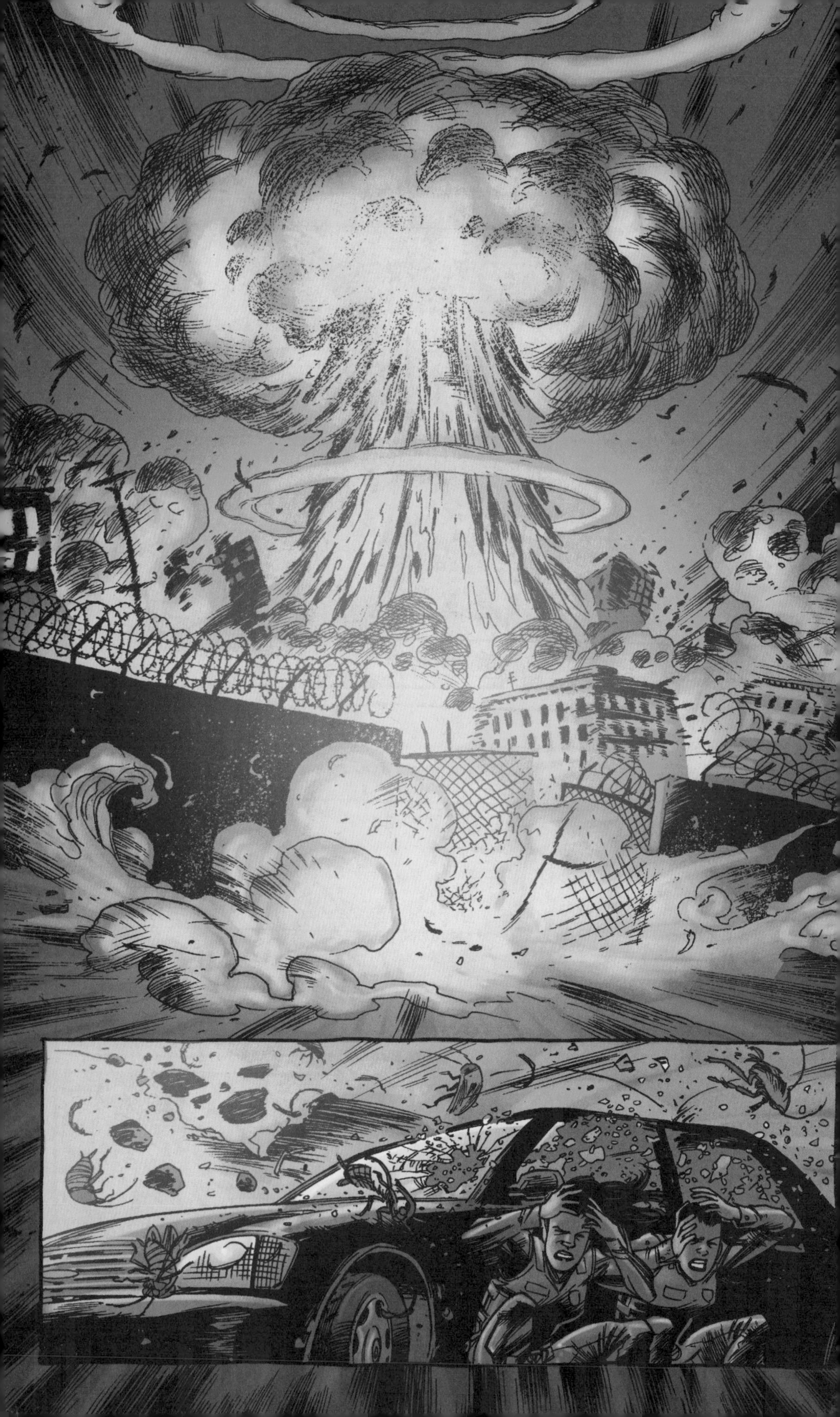

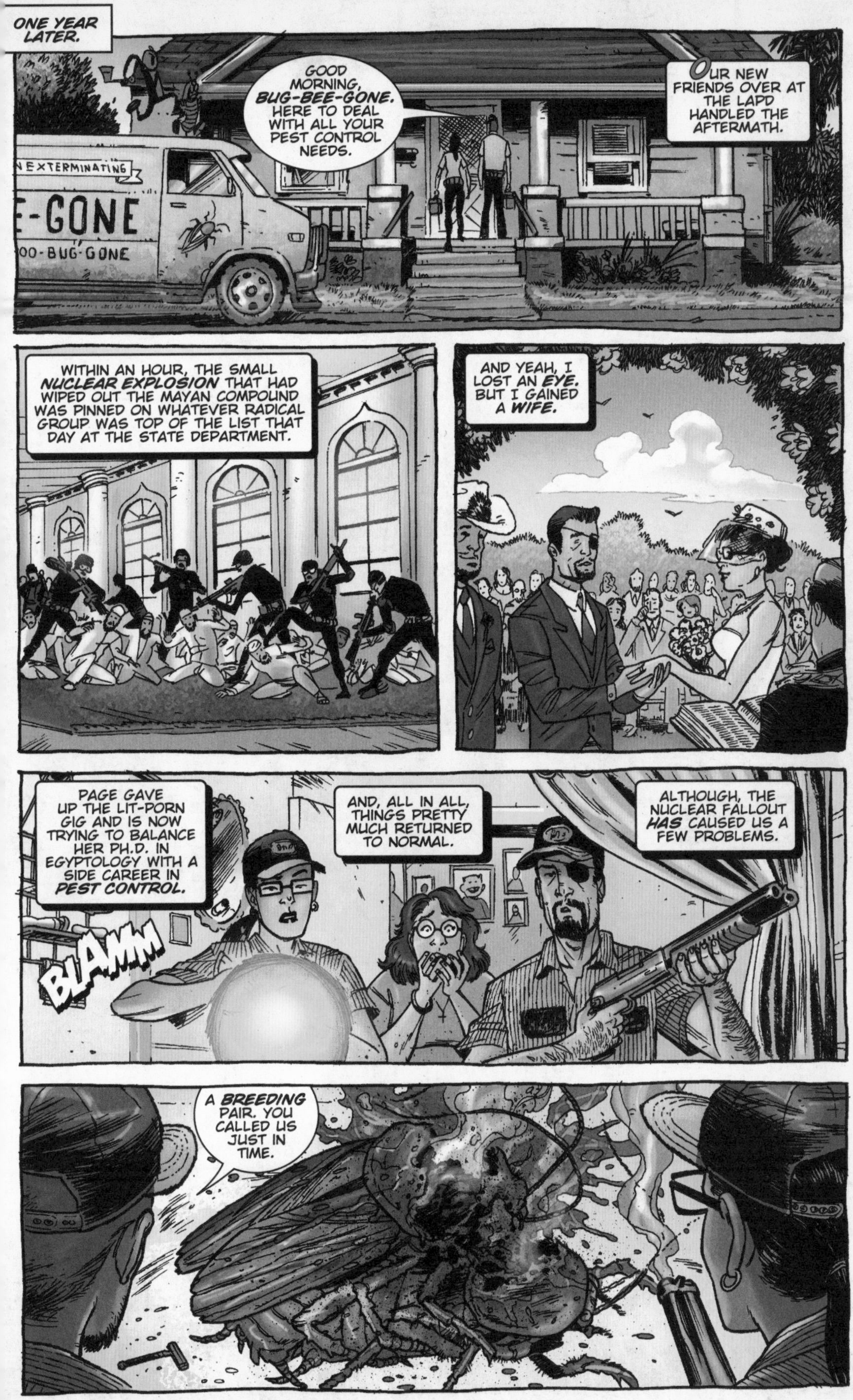
ONE YEAR LATER.
GOOD MORNING, BUG-BEE-GONE. HERE TO DEAL WITH ALL YOUR PEST CONTROL NEEDS.
OUR NEW FRIENDS OVER AT THE LAPD HANDLED THE AFTERMATH.
EXTERMINATING
-GONE
00-BUG-GONE
WITHIN AN HOUR, THE SMALL NUCLEAR EXPLOSION THAT HAD WIPED OUT THE MAYAN COMPOUND WAS PINNED ON WHATEVER RADICAL GROUP WAS TOP OF THE LIST THAT DAY AT THE STATE DEPARTMENT.
AND YEAH, I LOST AN EYE. BUT I GAINED A WIFE.
PAGE GAVE UP THE LIT-PORN GIG AND IS NOW TRYING TO BALANCE HER PH.D. IN EGYPTOLOGY WITH A SIDE CAREER IN PEST CONTROL.
AND, ALL IN ALL, THINGS PRETTY MUCH RETURNED TO NORMAL.
ALTHOUGH, THE NUCLEAR FALLOUT HAS CAUSED US A FEW PROBLEMS.
BLAMM
A BREEDING PAIR. YOU CALLED US JUST IN TIME.

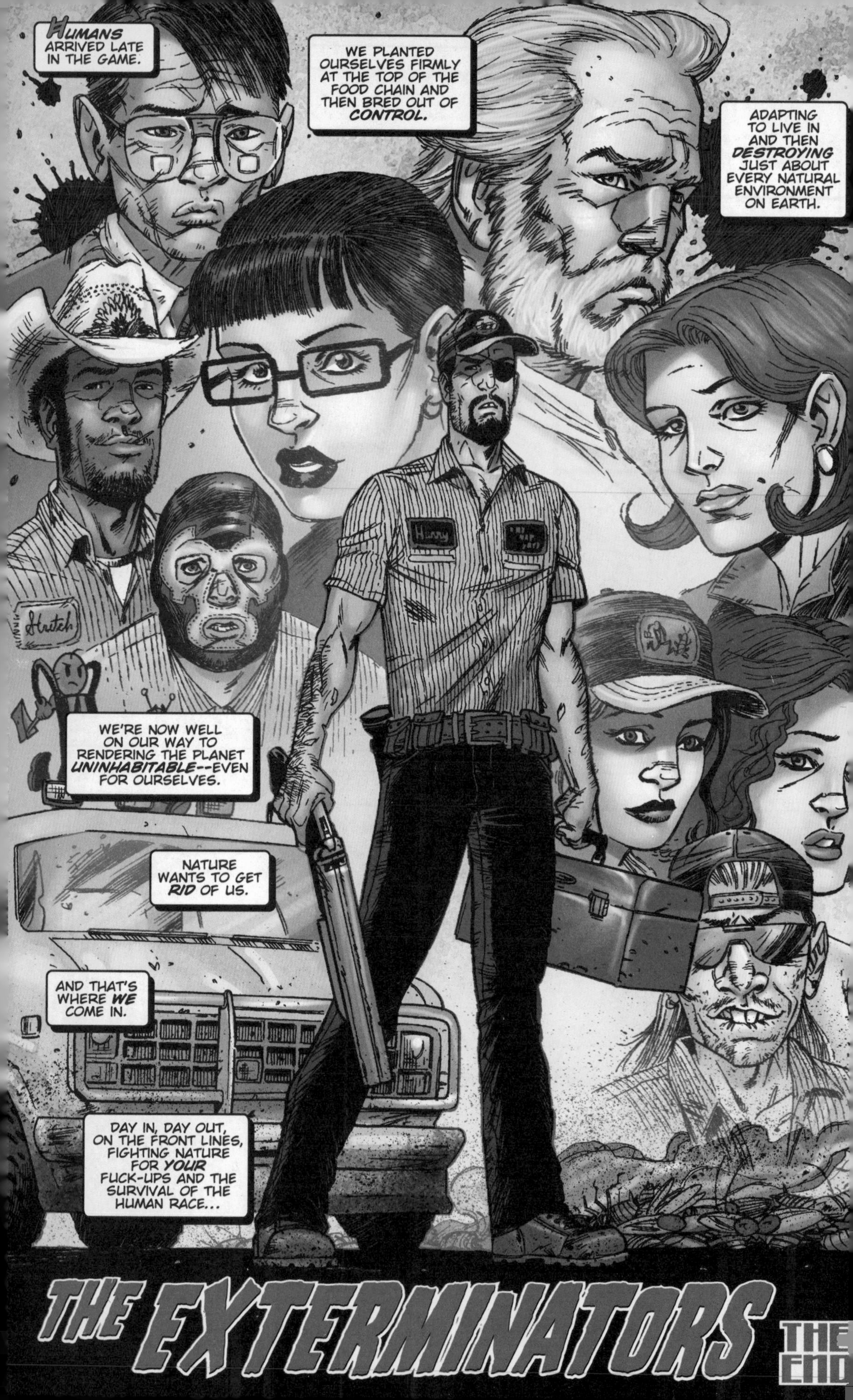
HUMANS ARRIVED LATE IN THE GAME.
WE PLANTED OURSELVES FIRMLY AT THE TOP OF THE FOOD CHAIN AND THEN BRED OUT OF CONTROL.
ADAPTING TO LIVE IN AND THEN DESTROYING JUST ABOUT EVERY NATURAL ENVIRONMENT ON EARTH.
Henry
Stretch
WE'RE NOW WELL ON OUR WAY TO RENDERING THE PLANET UNINHABITABLE--EVEN FOR OURSELVES.
NATURE WANTS TO GET RID OF US.
AND THAT'S WHERE WE COME IN.
DAY IN, DAY OUT, ON THE FRONT LINES, FIGHTING NATURE FOR YOUR FUCK-UPS AND THE SURVIVAL OF THE HUMAN RACE...
THE EXTERMINATORS
THE END

SURVIVING THE GREAT CHICAGO FIRE

By Jo Cleland

Illustrated By Pete McDonnell

ROURKE PUBLISHING

Vero Beach, Florida 32964

www.rourkepublishing.com

Photo Credits: © Tomograf: page 28

Edited by Meg Greve
Illustrated by Pete McDonnell
Art Direction and Page Layout by Renee Brady

Library of Congress Cataloging-in-Publication Data

Cleland, Joann.
  Surviving the Great Chicago Fire / Jo Cleland.
     p. cm. -- (Eye on history graphic illustrated)
  Includes bibliographical references and index.
  ISBN 978-1-60694-440-0 (alk. paper)
  ISBN 978-1-60694-549-0 (soft cover)
1. Great Fire, Chicago, Ill., 1871--Juvenile literature. 2. Fires--Illinois--Chicago--History--19th century--Juvenile literature. 3. Chicago (Ill.)--History--To 1875--Juvenile literature. I. Title.
  F548.42.C68 2010
  977.3'11041--dc22
                                        2009020501

Printed in the USA
CG/CG

www.rourkepublishing.com - rourke@rourkepublishing.com
Post Office Box 643328 Vero Beach, Florida 32964

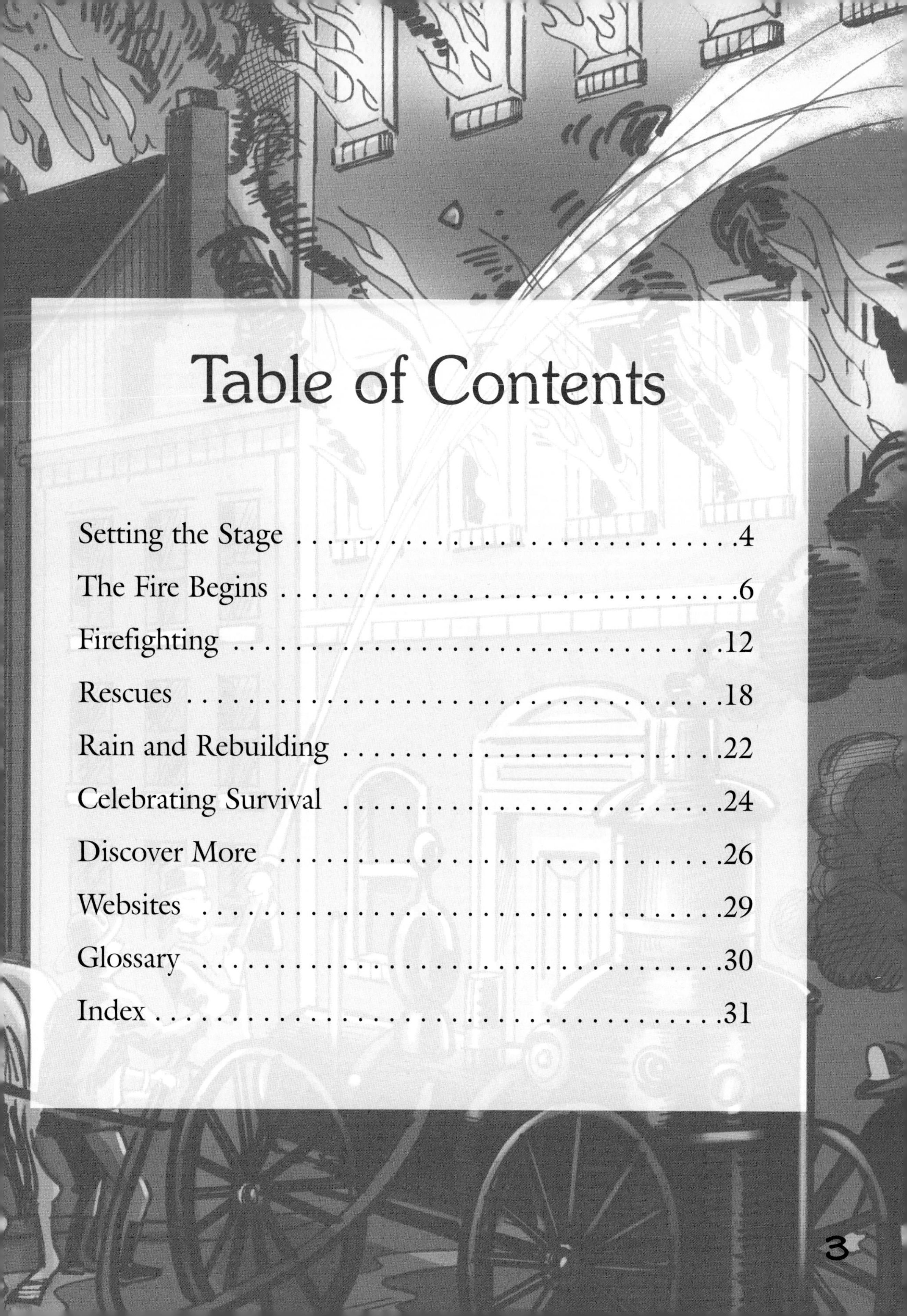

Table of Contents

Setting the Stage

Chicago Daily News

Thursday — Issue 7 Volume 11 — October 12, 1871

Fire Destroys Four Square Miles

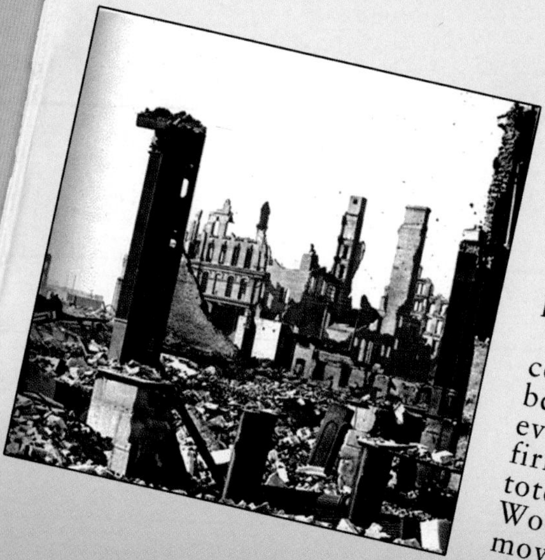

On Sunday, October 8, people in downtown Chicago awoke to see flames leaping at their homes. Grabbing anything they could, they fled toward Lake Michigan. Hundreds did not escape in time, and many suffered serious burns. All lost their homes.

Rumor has it, Mrs. O'Leary's cow kicked over a lantern in her barn, starting this disaster. However, the story has not been confirmed. What is known is that fire totally destroyed four square miles. Wooden buildings fueled the fires moving across the area. The city is pulling together to aid those suffering great losses.

One star on Chicago's official flag stands for the building of Fort Dearborn, the next star stands for the Great Chicago Fire, and the last two stand for the World's Fairs in 1893 and 1933. The top and bottom blue stripes represent Lake Michigan and the Chicago River.

One of the largest fires of the 19th century burned for two days and destroyed four square miles (10 square kilometers) in Chicago. More than 300 people lost their lives, and 100,000 lost their homes.

Several different reasons for the start of the fire have been suggested. The most well-known is that it began when a cow kicked over a lantern in Mrs. O'Leary's barn. Regardless of the reason, Chicago was devasted by the fire. The citizens, however, were commited to rebuilding this great city. Within just four years, workers rebuilt what was lost. Chicago was better than ever.

The Fire Begins

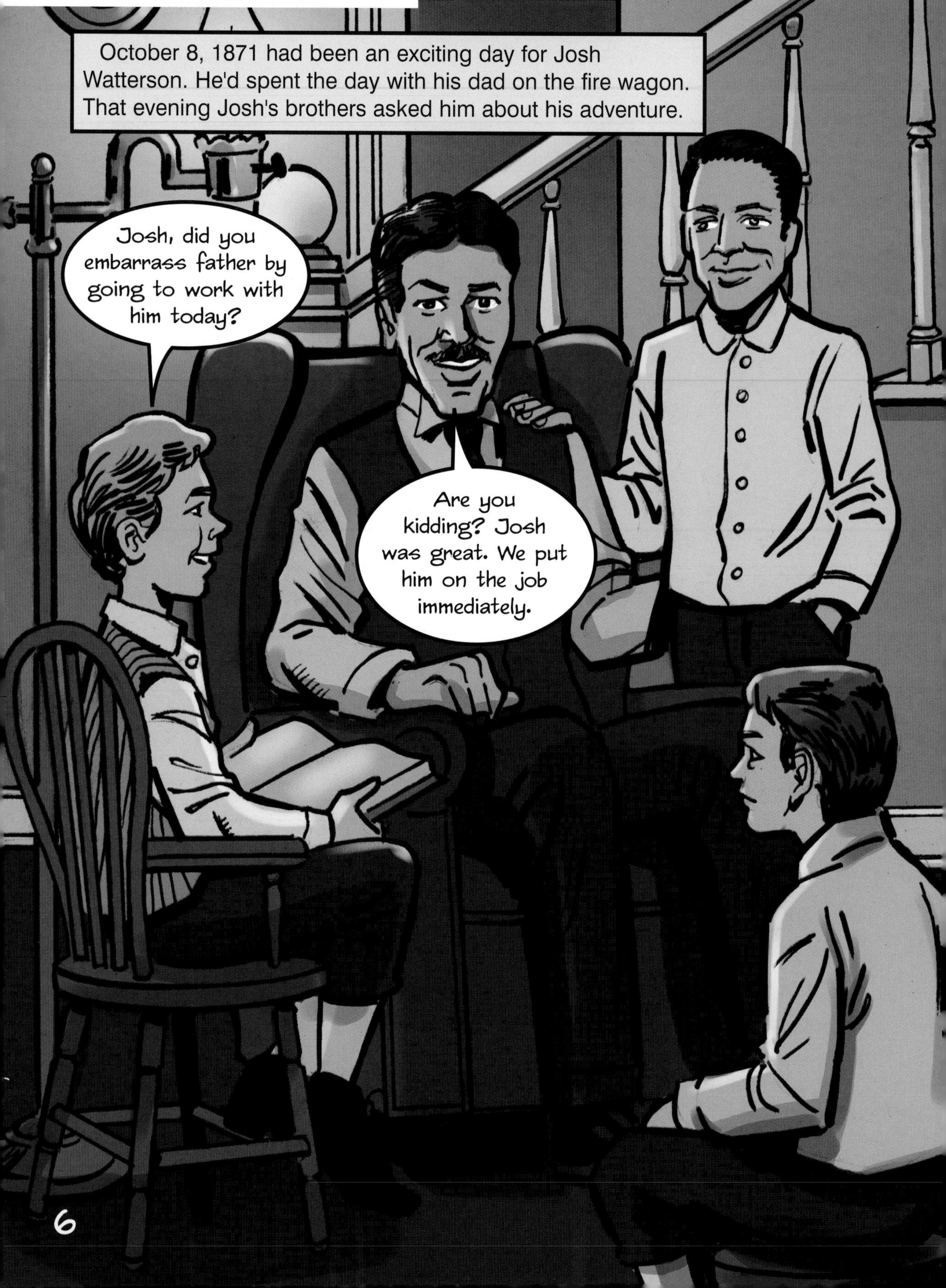

October 8, 1871 had been an exciting day for Josh Watterson. He'd spent the day with his dad on the fire wagon. That evening Josh's brothers asked him about his adventure.
Josh, did you embarrass father by going to work with him today?
Are you kidding? Josh was great. We put him on the job immediately.

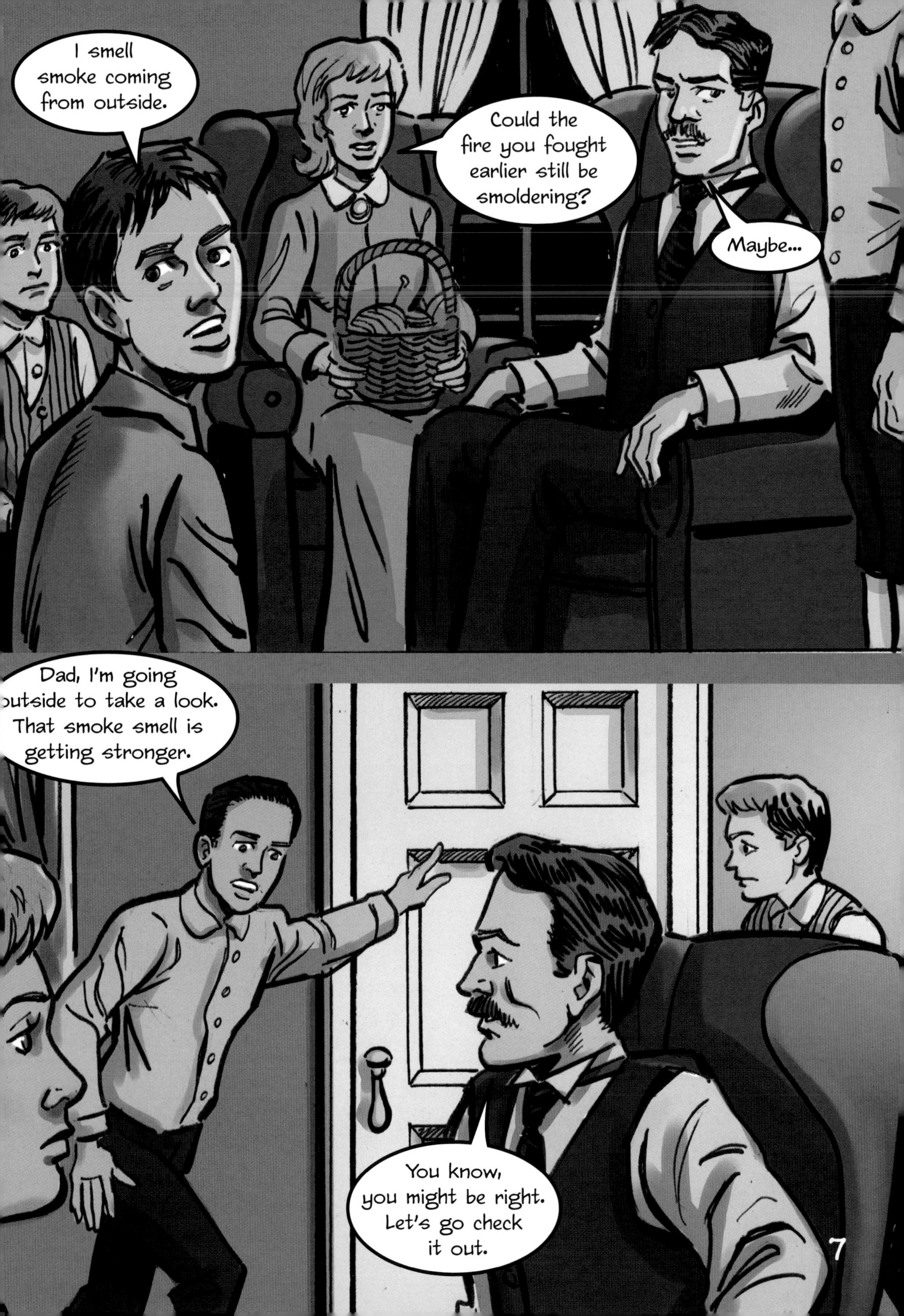
I smell smoke coming from outside.
Could the fire you fought earlier still be smoldering?
Maybe...
Dad, I'm going outside to take a look. That smoke smell is getting stronger.
You know, you might be right. Let's go check it out.

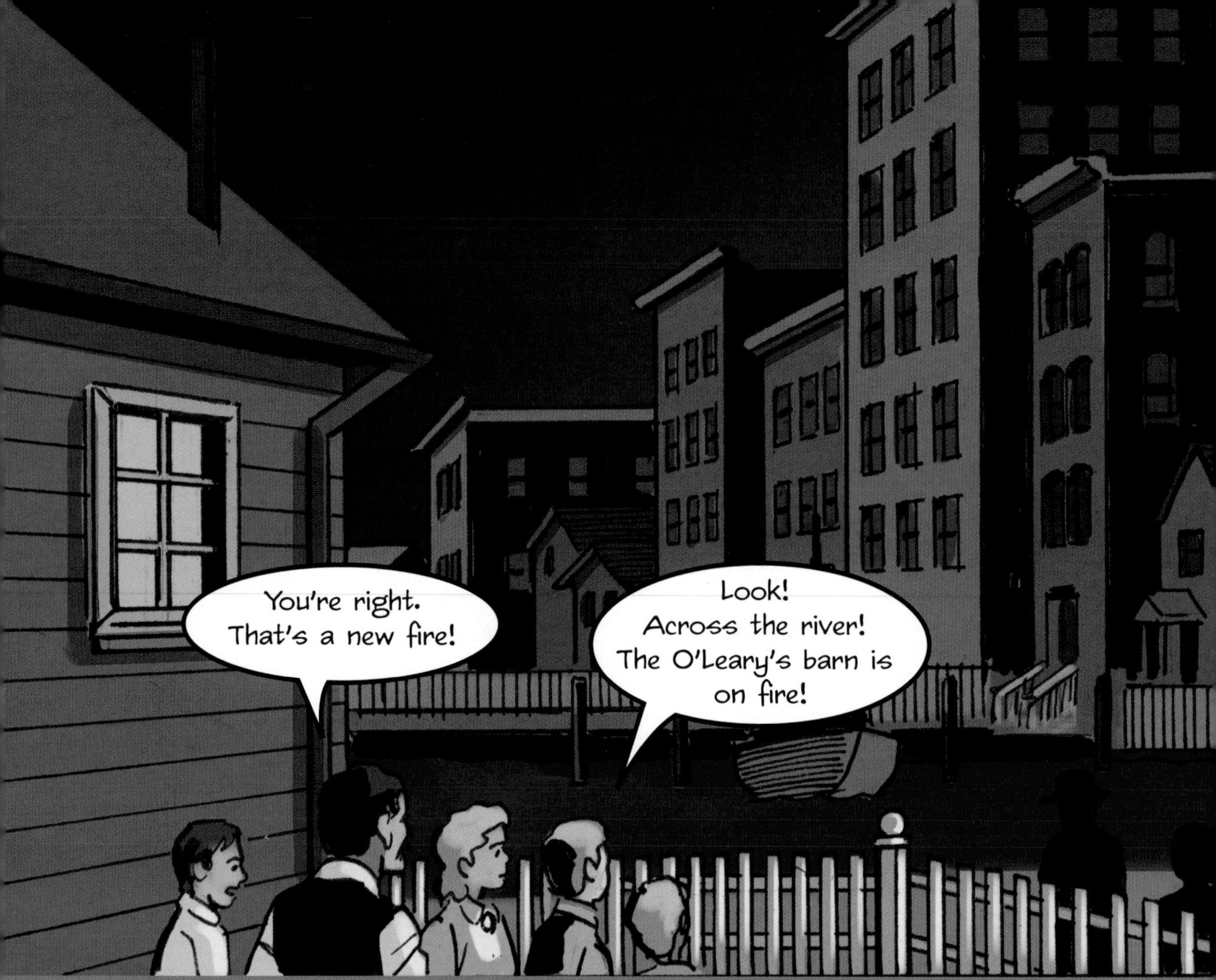
You're right. That's a new fire!
Look! Across the river! The O'Leary's barn is on fire!

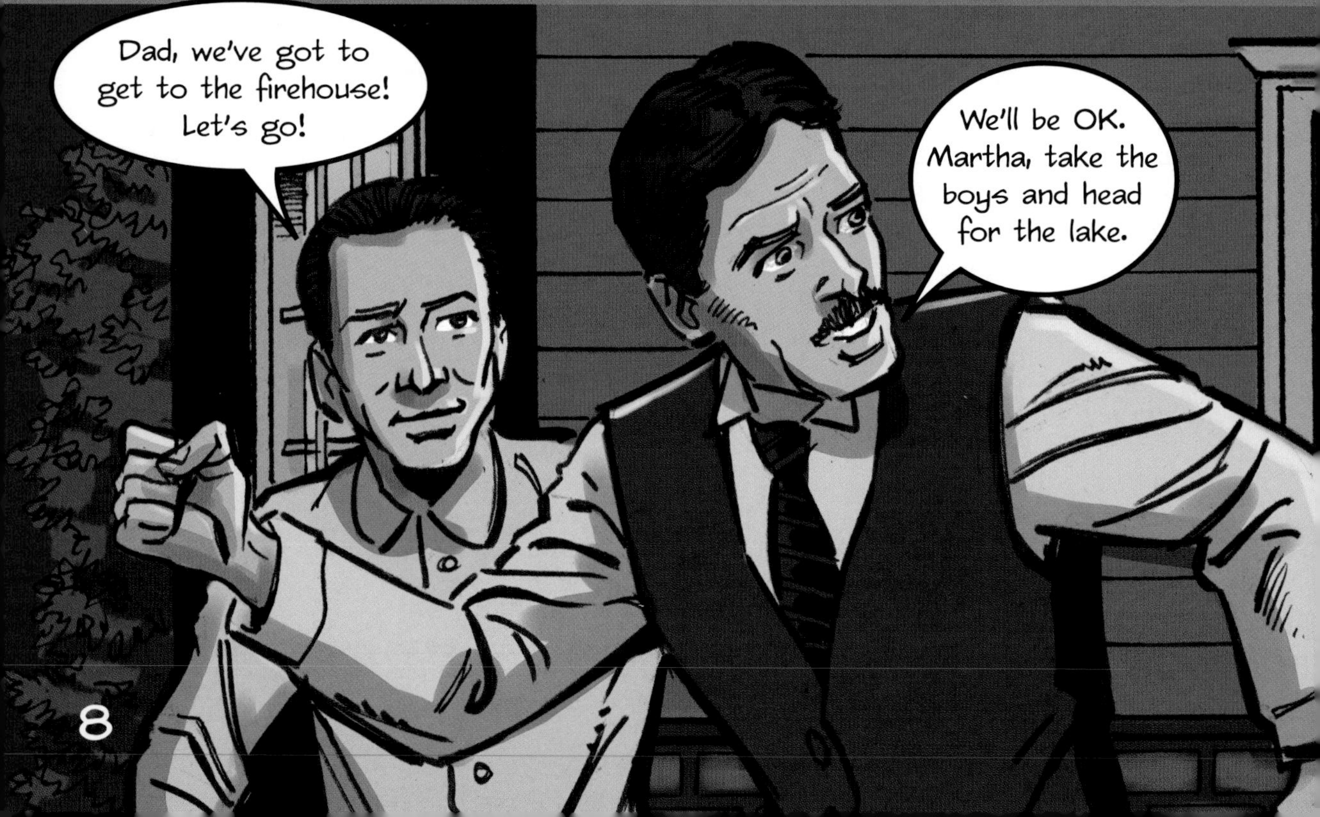
Dad, we've got to get to the firehouse! Let's go!
We'll be OK. Martha, take the boys and head for the lake.

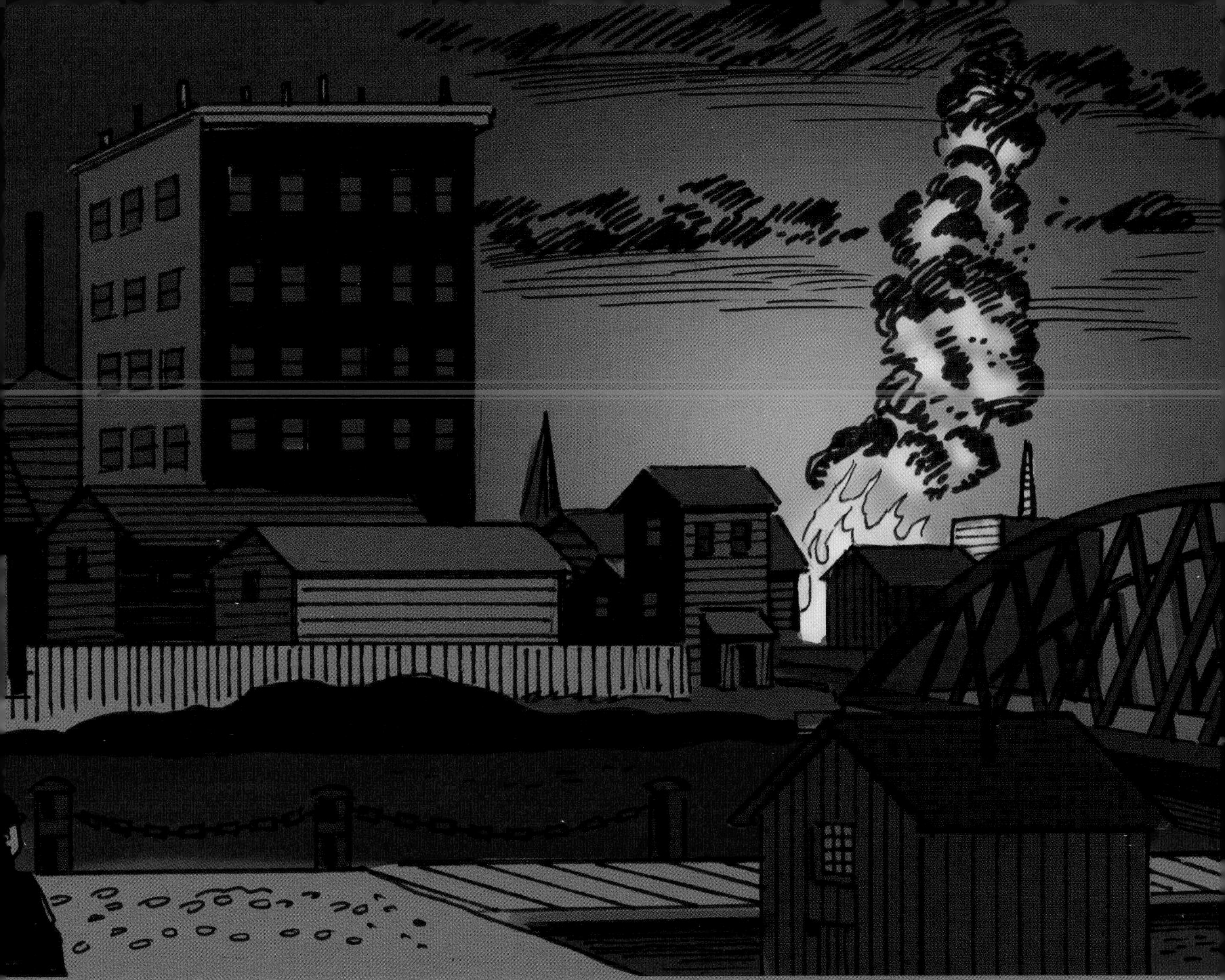

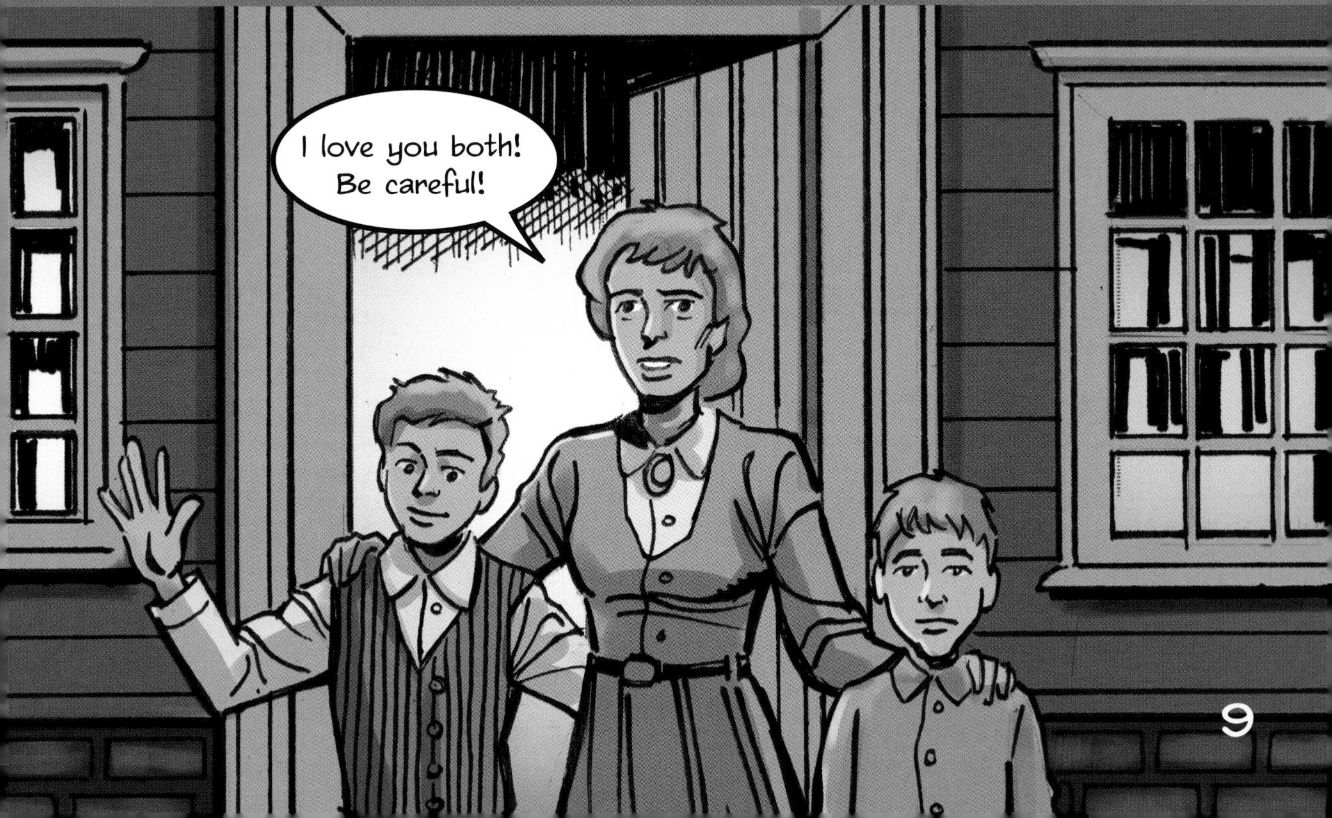
I love you both! Be careful!

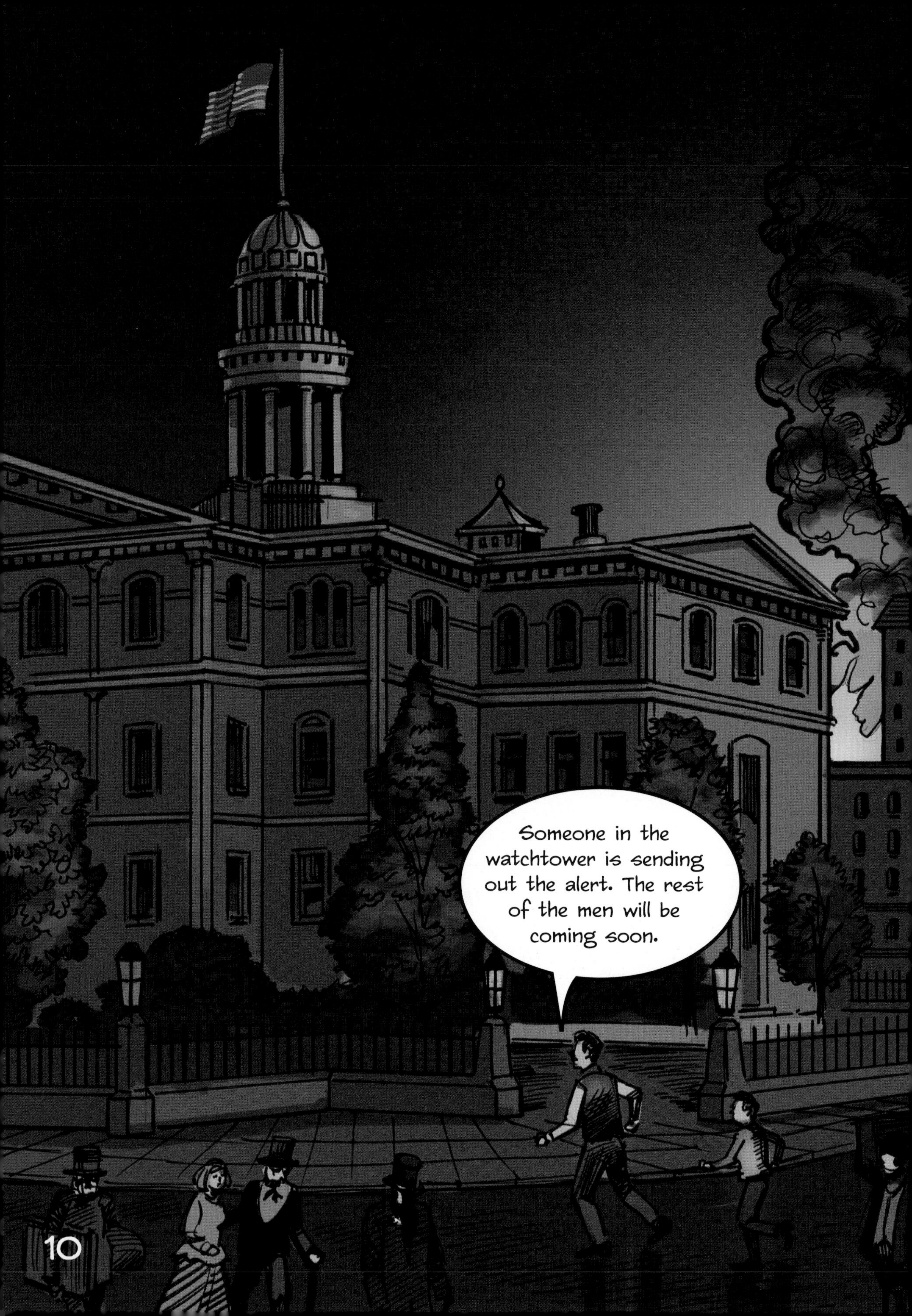
Someone in the watchtower is sending out the alert. The rest of the men will be coming soon.

As Josh and his dad rush on, a wind whips the fire into raging tongues of fire.

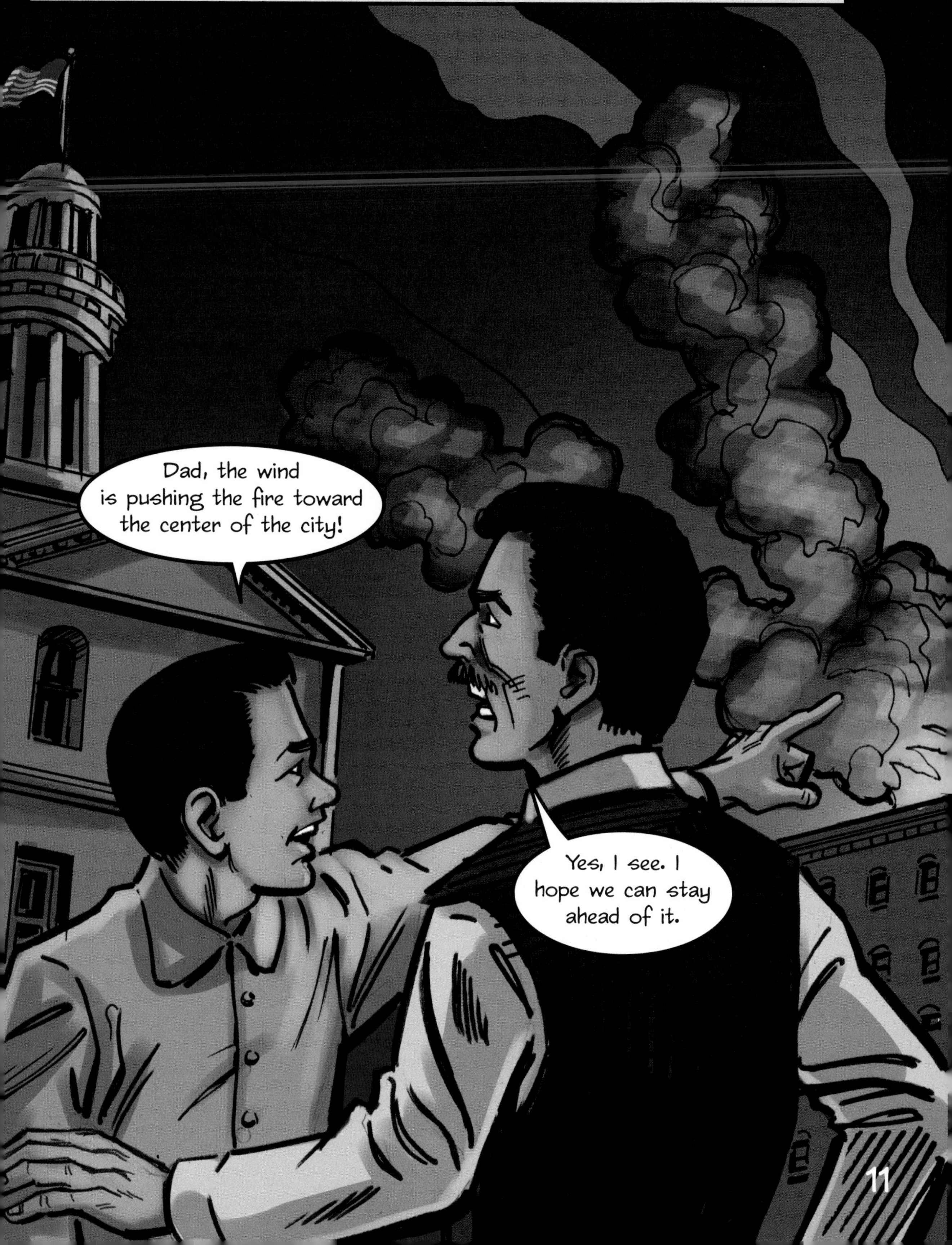
Dad, the wind is pushing the fire toward the center of the city!
Yes, I see. I hope we can stay ahead of it.

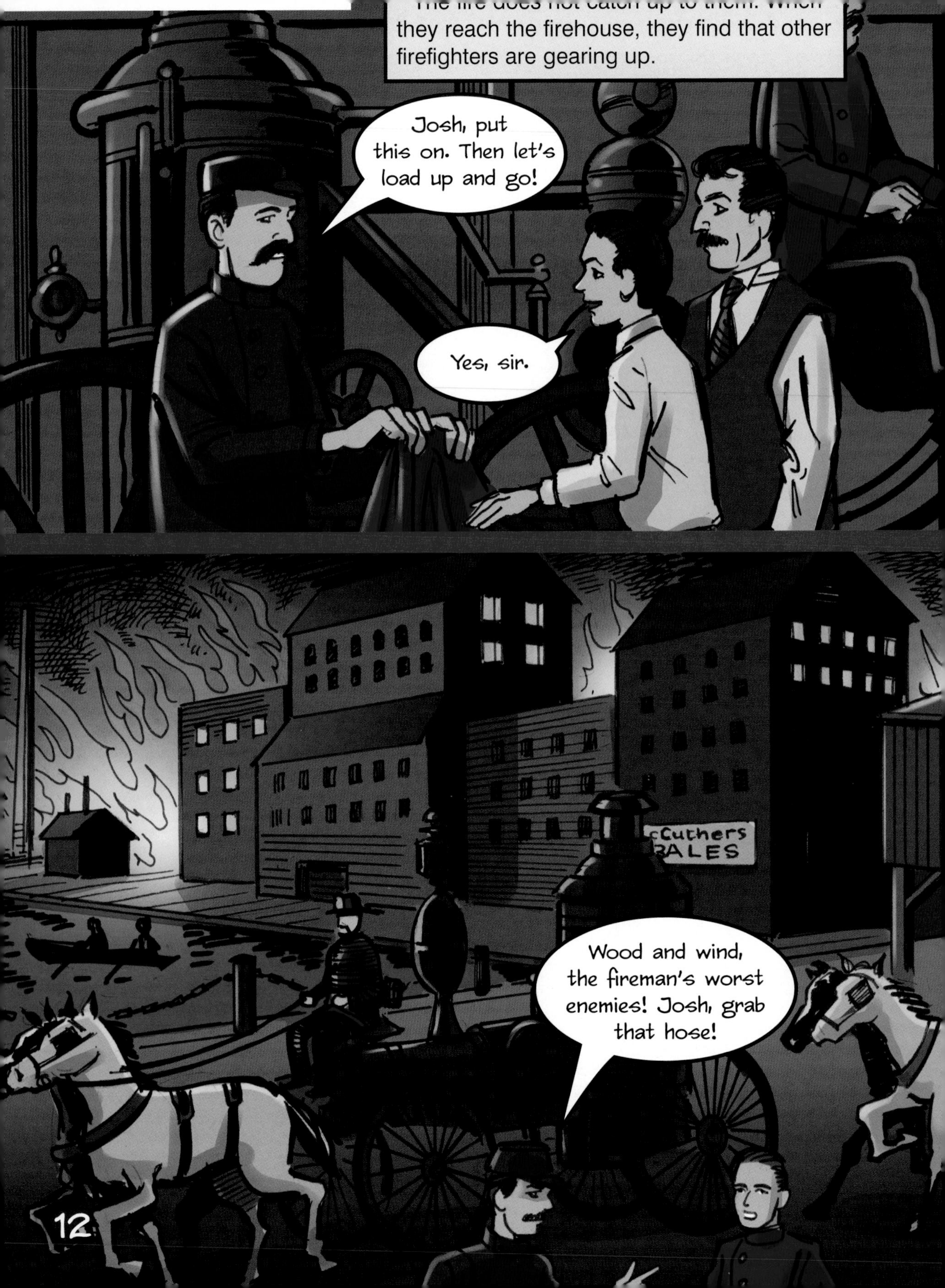
The fire does not catch up to them. When they reach the firehouse, they find that other firefighters are gearing up.
Josh, put this on. Then let's load up and go!
Yes, sir.
cCuthers
ALES
Wood and wind, the fireman's worst enemies! Josh, grab that hose!

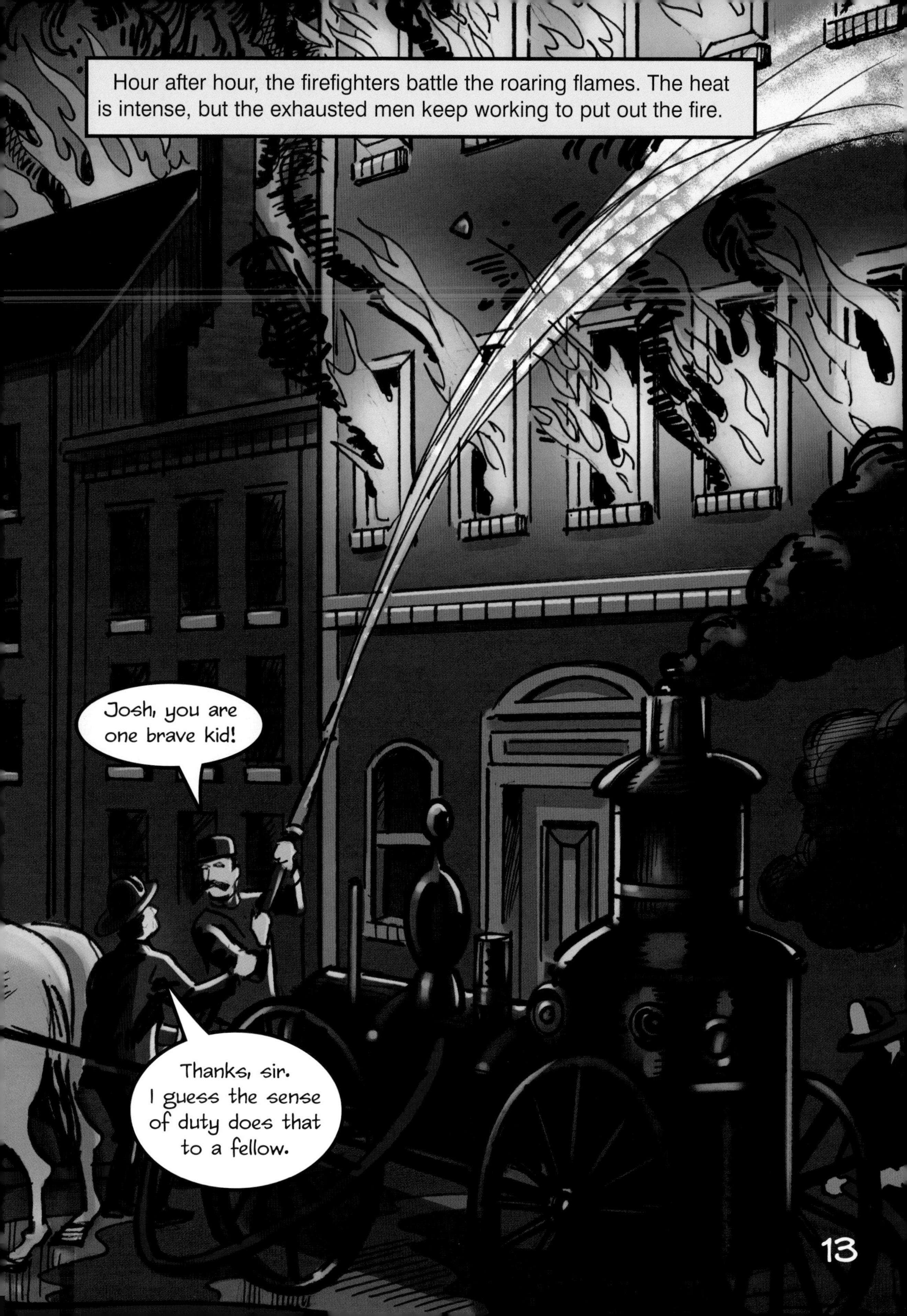

Hour after hour, the firefighters battle the roaring flames. The heat is intense, but the exhausted men keep working to put out the fire.
Josh, you are one brave kid!
Thanks, sir. I guess the sense of duty does that to a fellow.

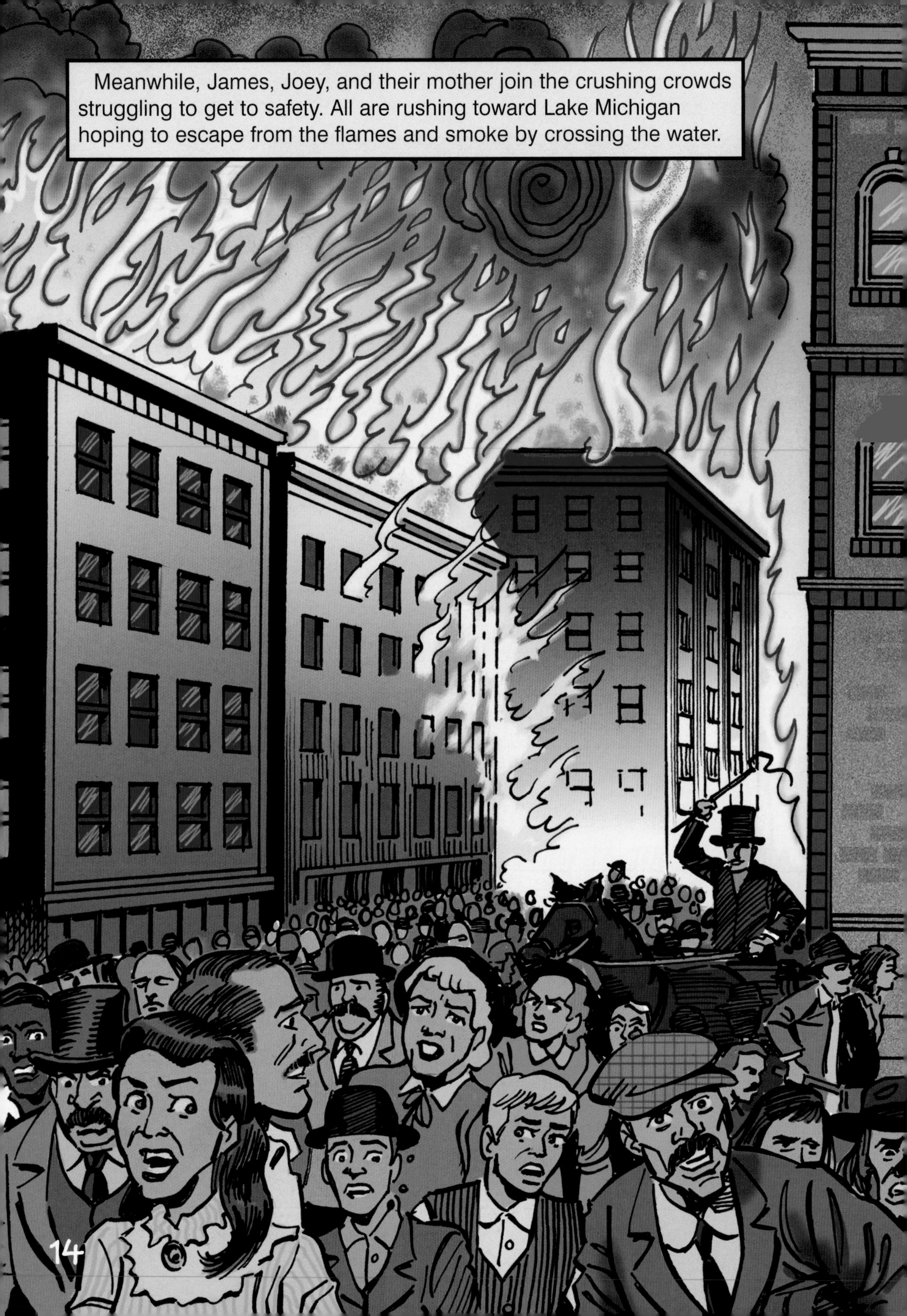
Meanwhile, James, Joey, and their mother join the crushing crowds struggling to get to safety. All are rushing toward Lake Michigan hoping to escape from the flames and smoke by crossing the water.

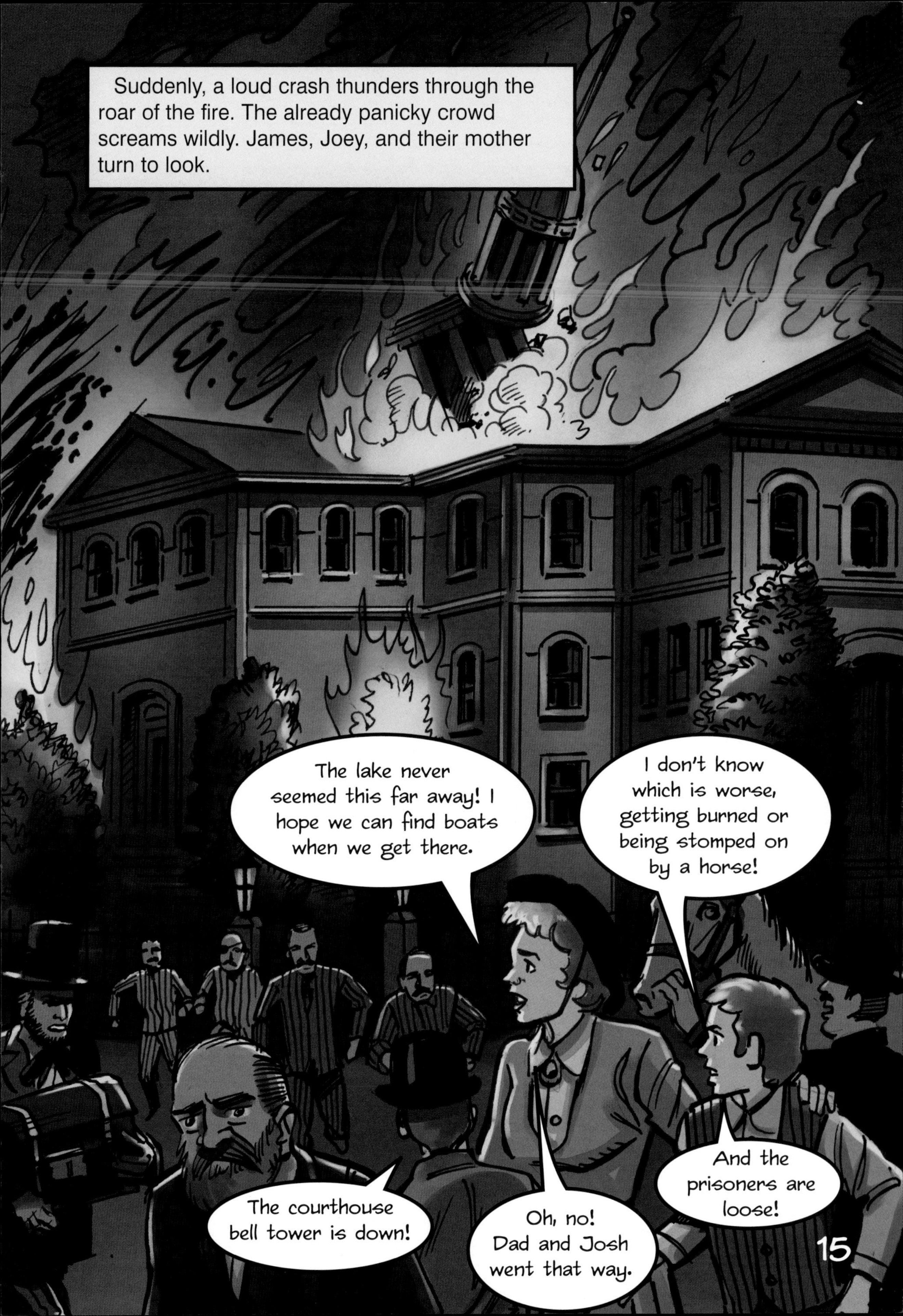
Suddenly, a loud crash thunders through the roar of the fire. The already panicky crowd screams wildly. James, Joey, and their mother turn to look.
The lake never seemed this far away! I hope we can find boats when we get there.
I don't know which is worse, getting burned or being stomped on by a horse!
The courthouse bell tower is down!
Oh, no! Dad and Josh went that way.
And the prisoners are loose!

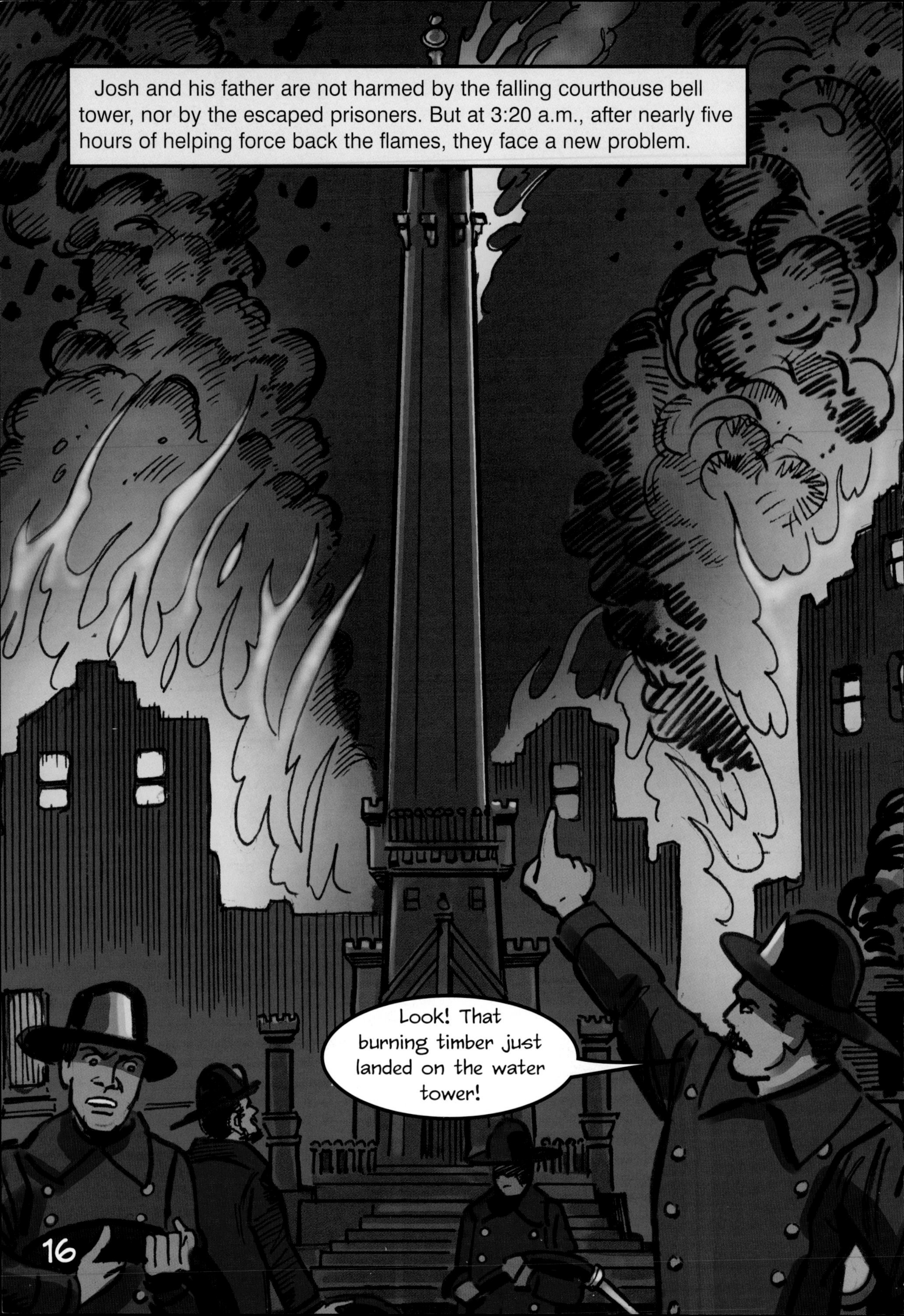
Josh and his father are not harmed by the falling courthouse bell tower, nor by the escaped prisoners. But at 3:20 a.m., after nearly five hours of helping force back the flames, they face a new problem.
Look! That burning timber just landed on the water tower!

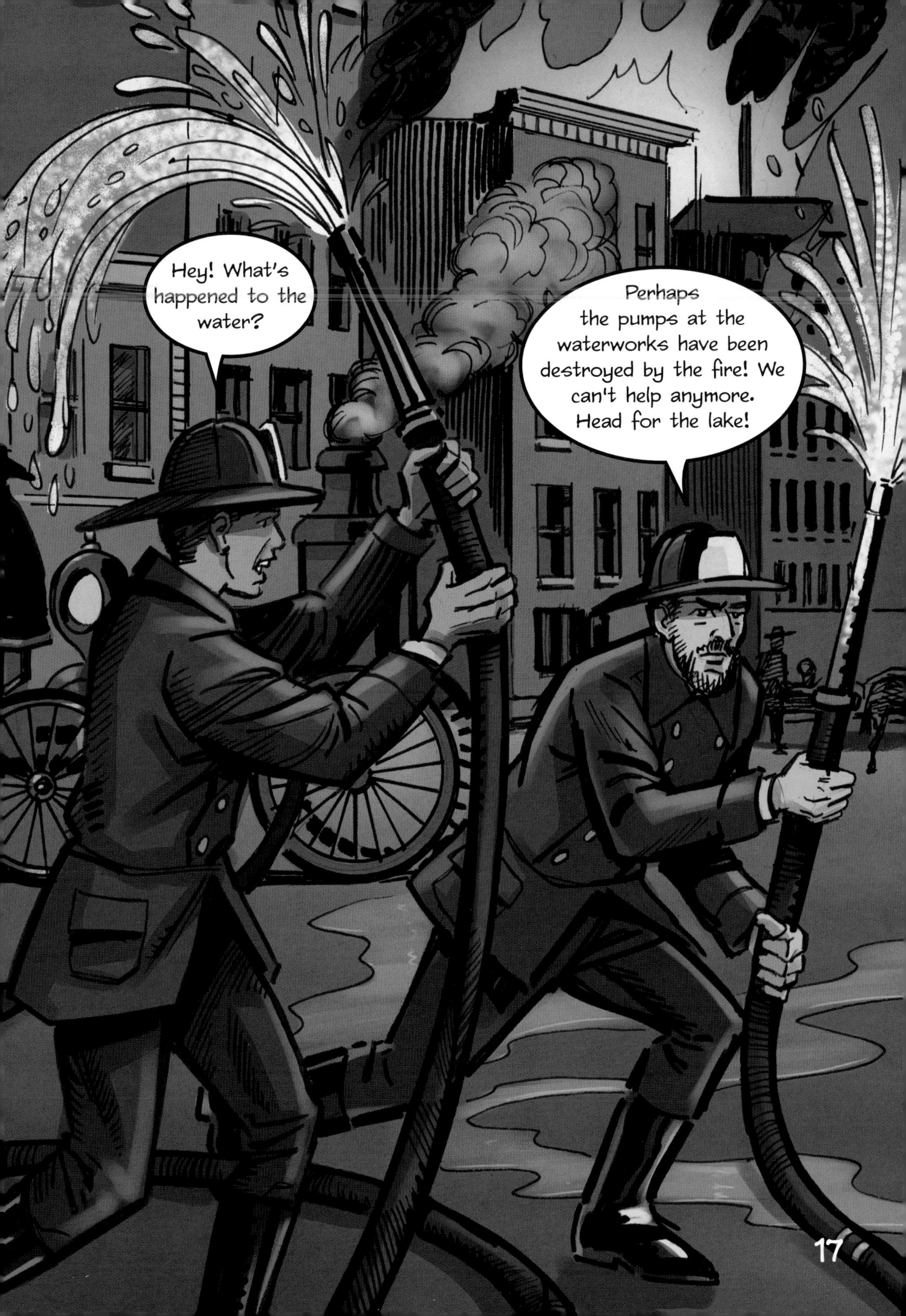
Hey! What's happened to the water?
Perhaps the pumps at the waterworks have been destroyed by the fire! We can't help anymore. Head for the lake!

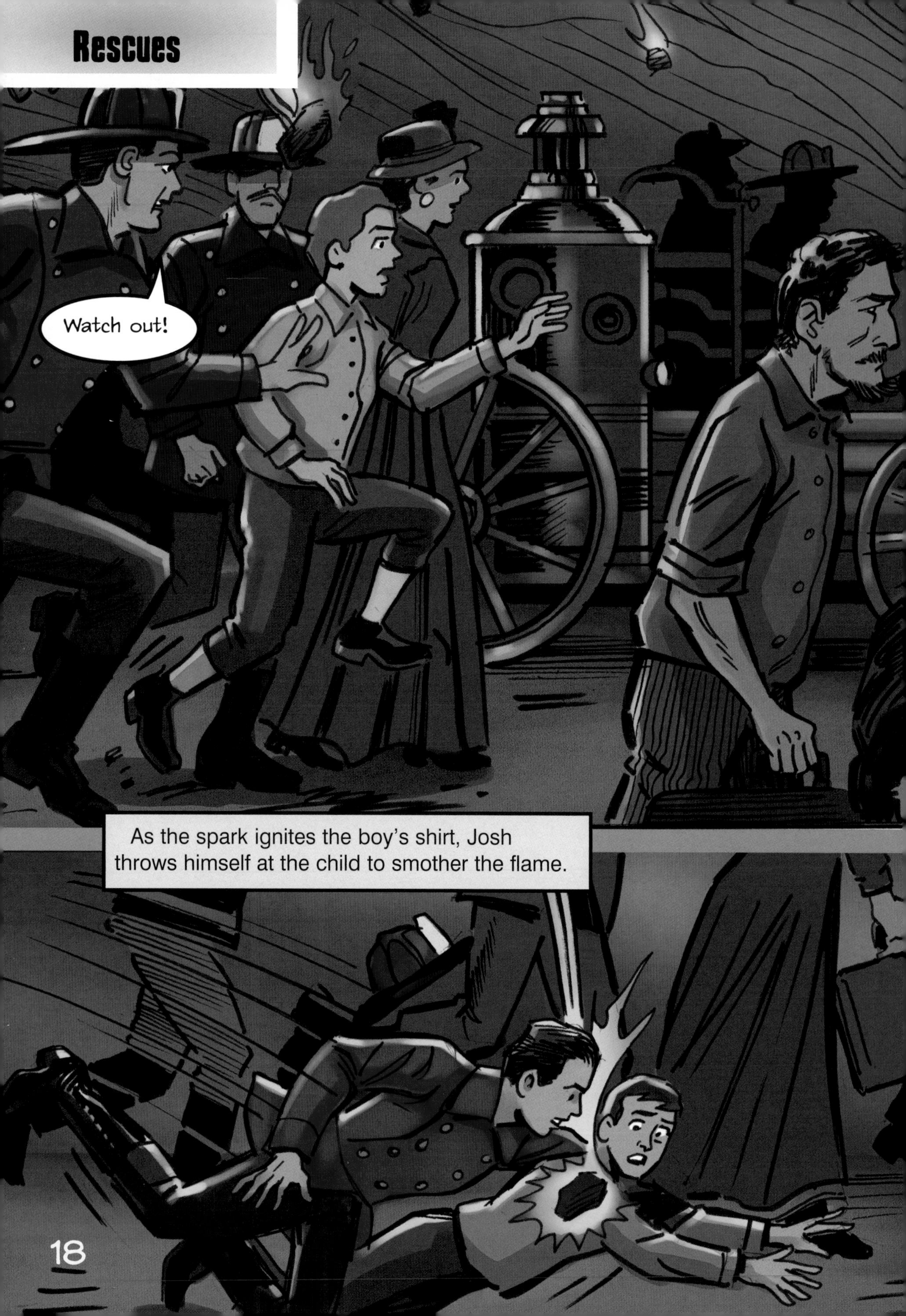
Watch out!
As the spark ignites the boy's shirt, Josh throws himself at the child to smother the flame.

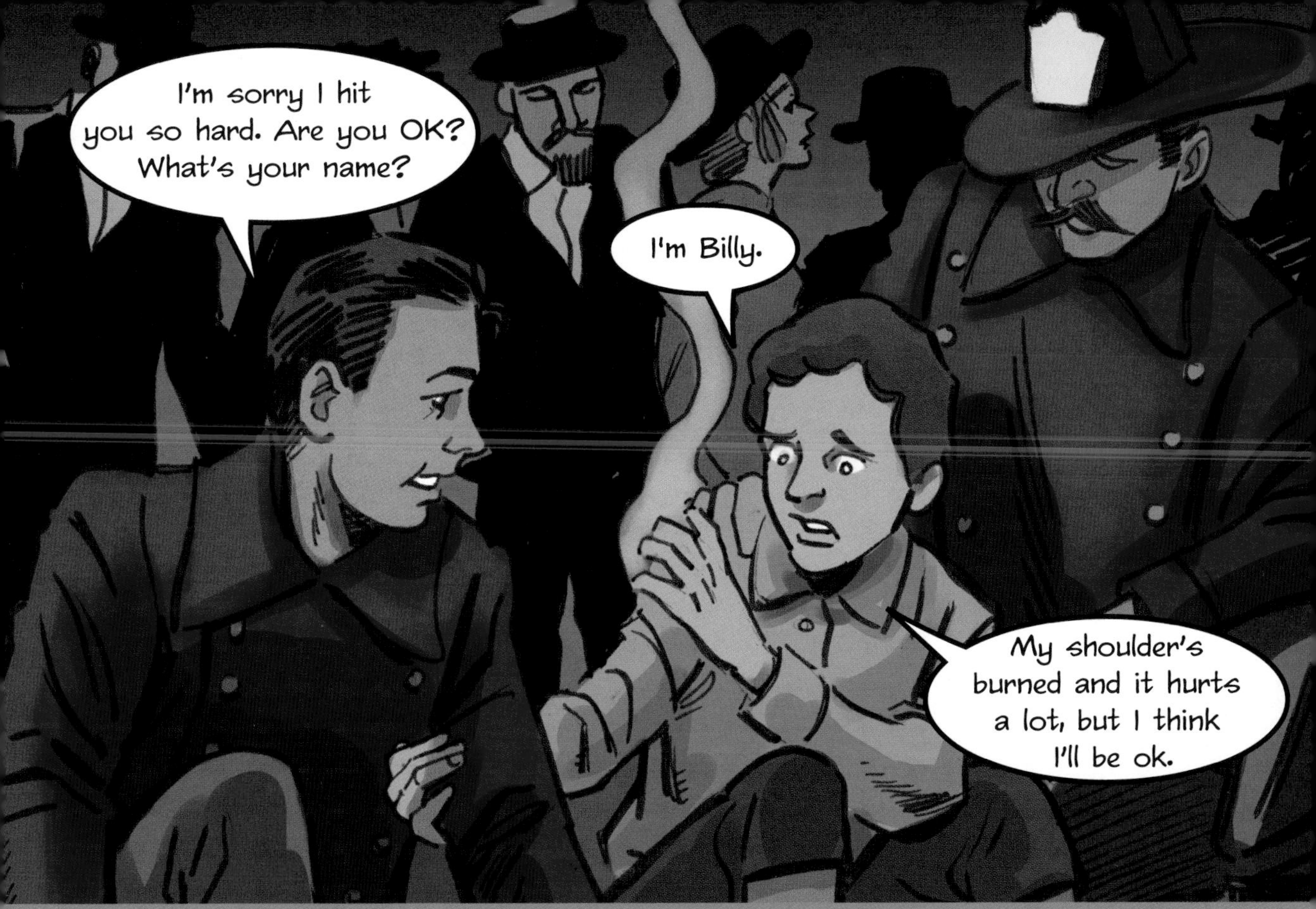
I'm sorry I hit you so hard. Are you OK? What's your name?
I'm Billy.
My shoulder's burned and it hurts a lot, but I think I'll be ok.

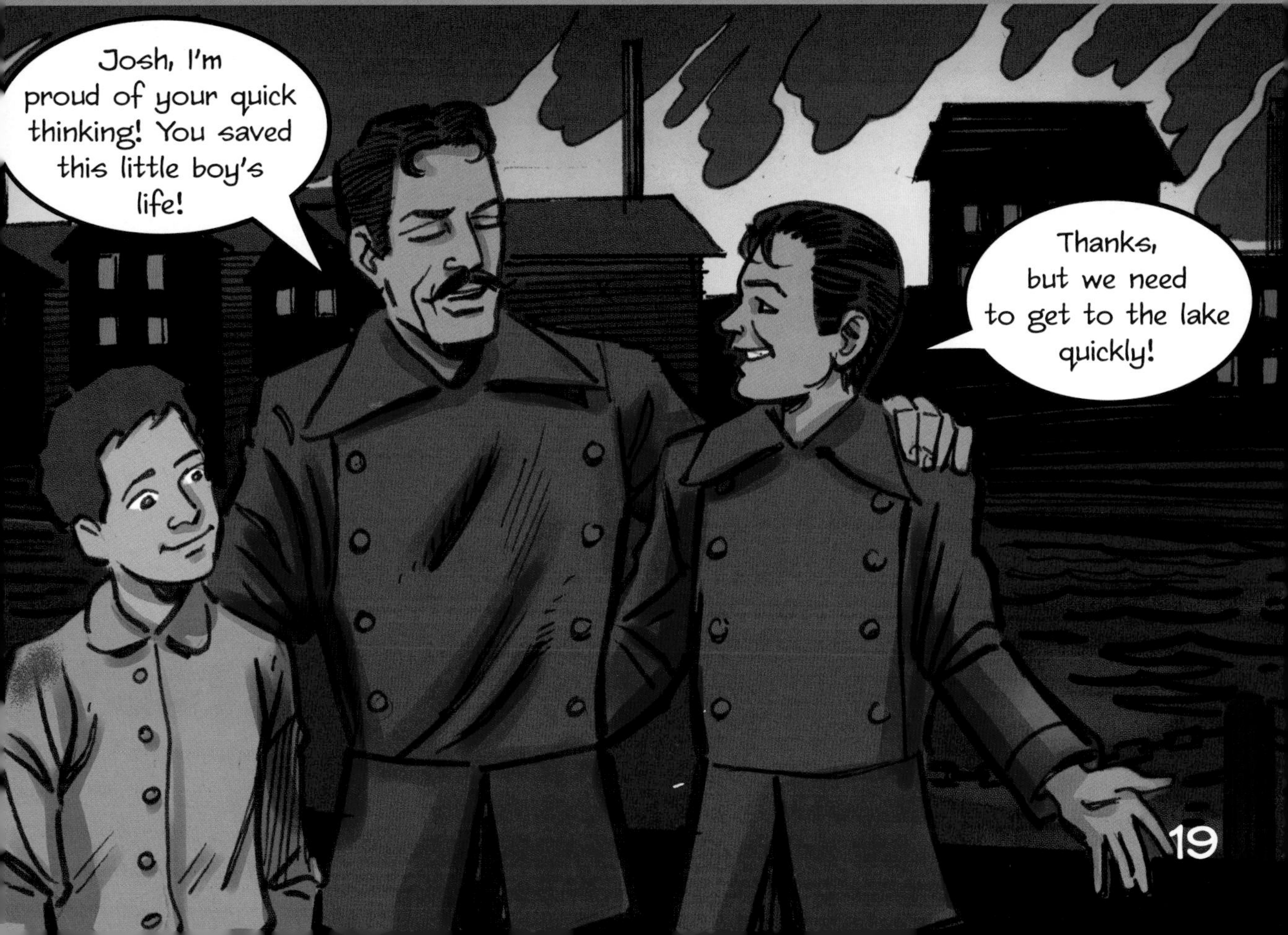
Josh, I'm proud of your quick thinking! You saved this little boy's life!
Thanks, but we need to get to the lake quickly!

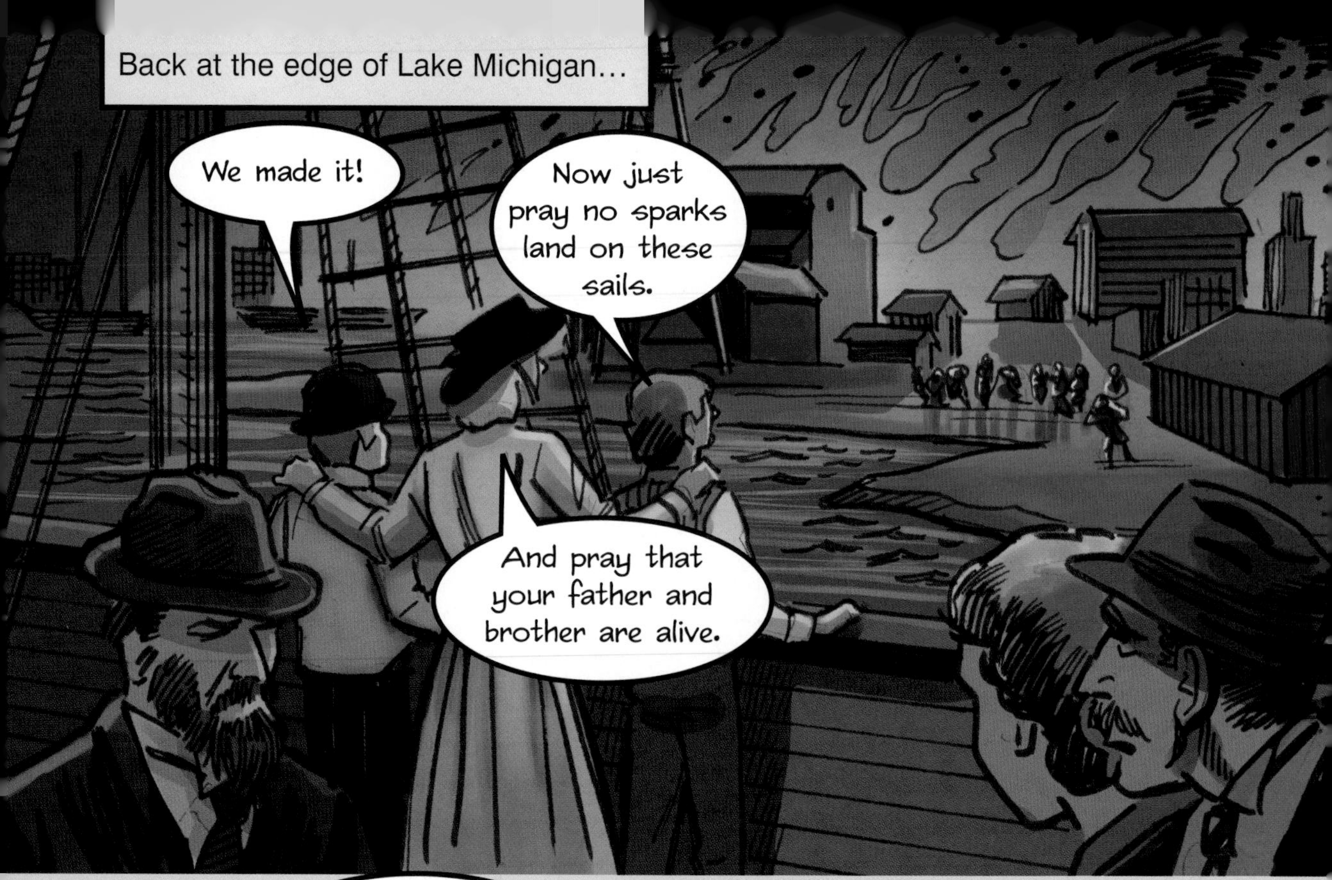
Back at the edge of Lake Michigan…
We made it!
Now just pray no sparks land on these sails.
And pray that your father and brother are alive.

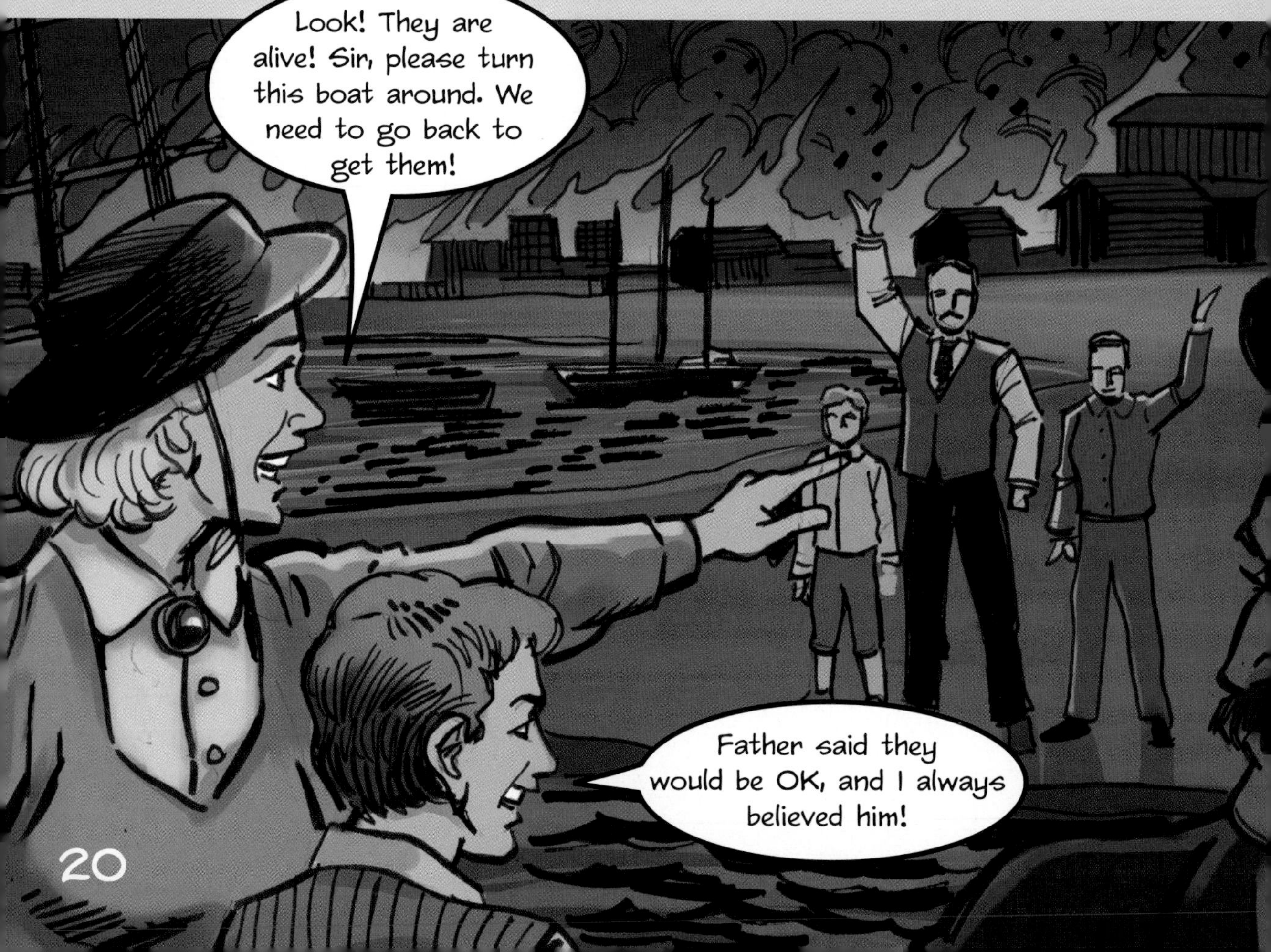
Look! They are alive! Sir, please turn this boat around. We need to go back to get them!
Father said they would be OK, and I always believed him!

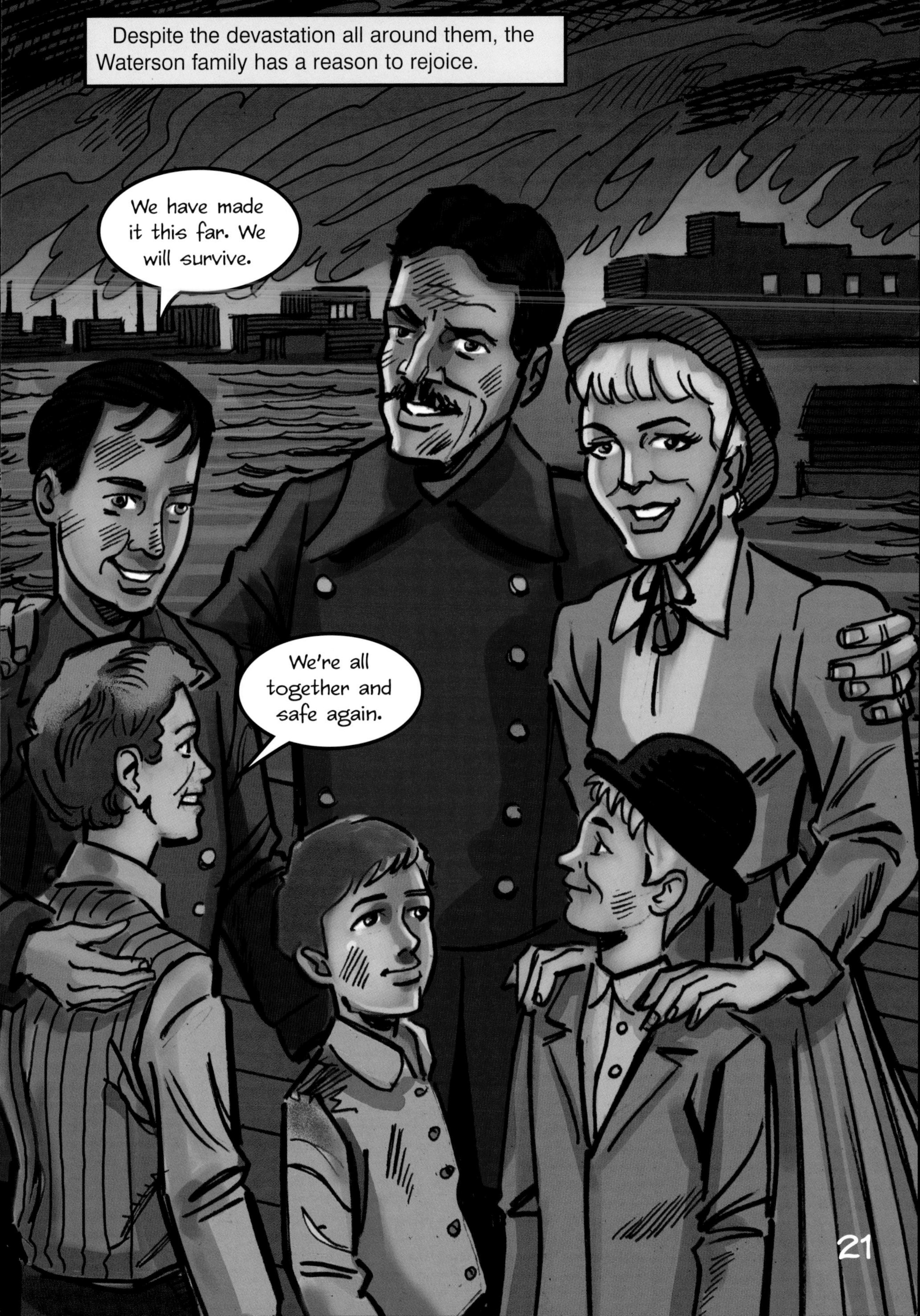
Despite the devastation all around them, the Waterson family has a reason to rejoice.
We have made it this far. We will survive.
We're all together and safe again.

Rain and Rebuilding

After 24 hours, pouring rains bring welcome relief. Boats return to the city. People crawl out from hiding places.

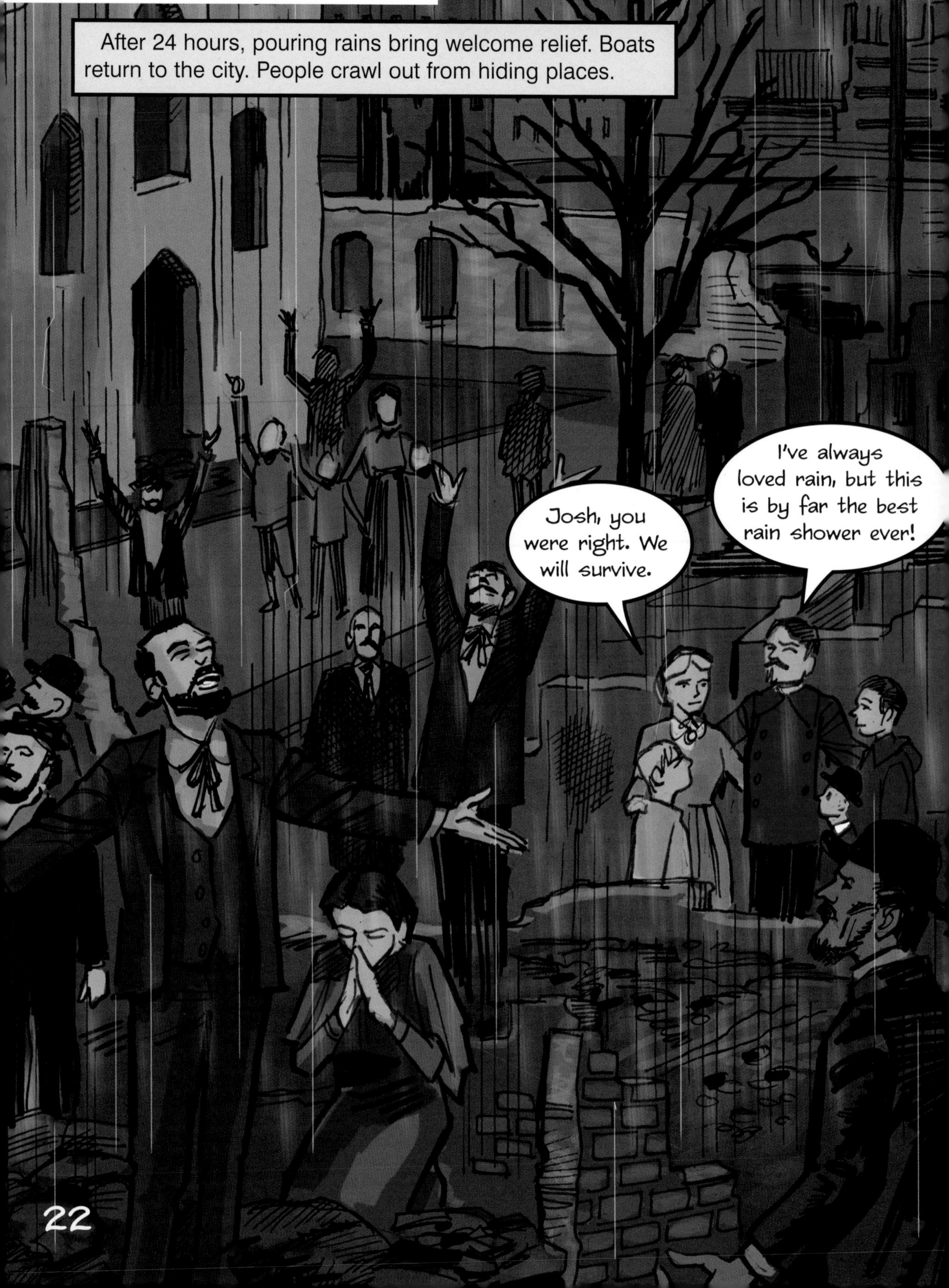
Josh, you were right. We will survive.
I've always loved rain, but this is by far the best rain shower ever!

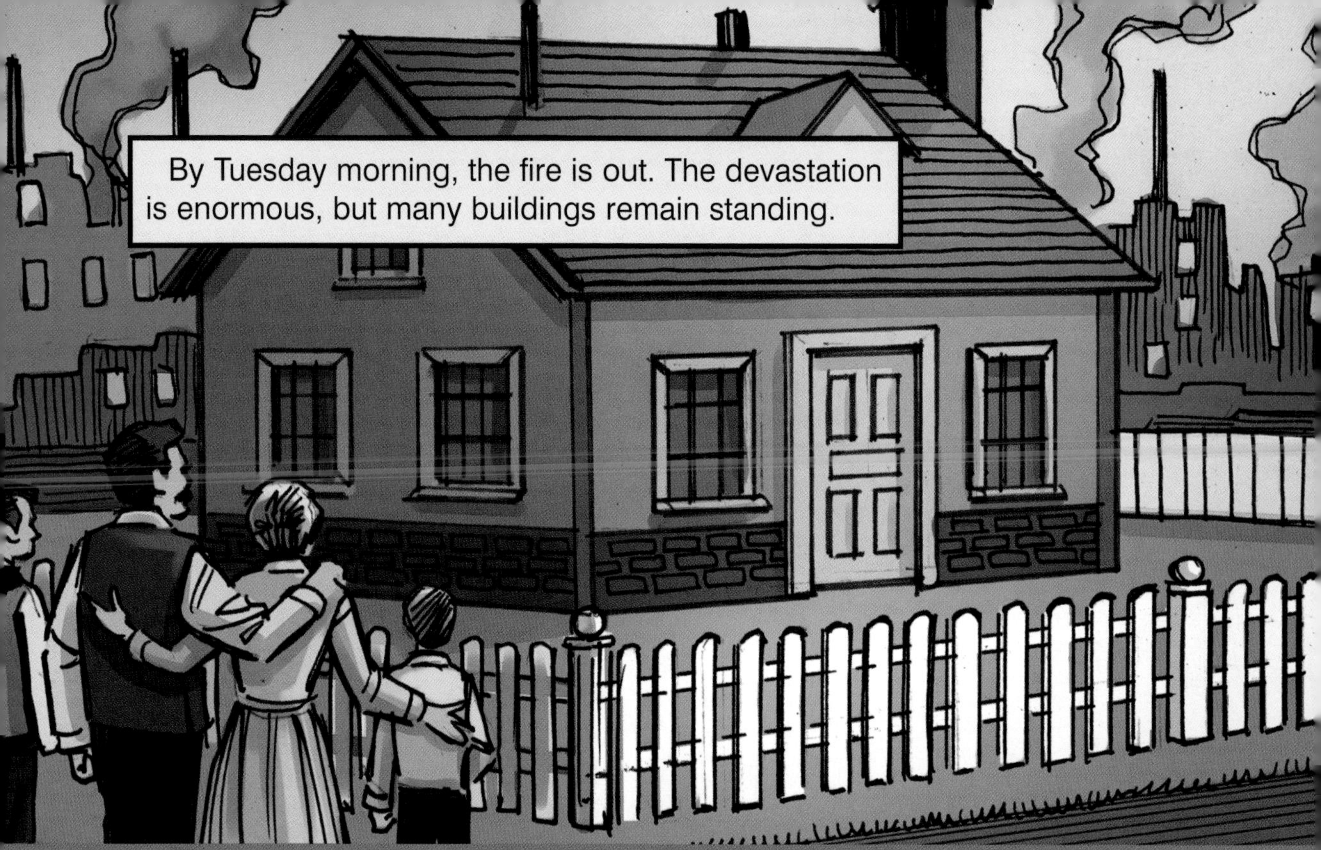
By Tuesday morning, the fire is out. The devastation is enormous, but many buildings remain standing.

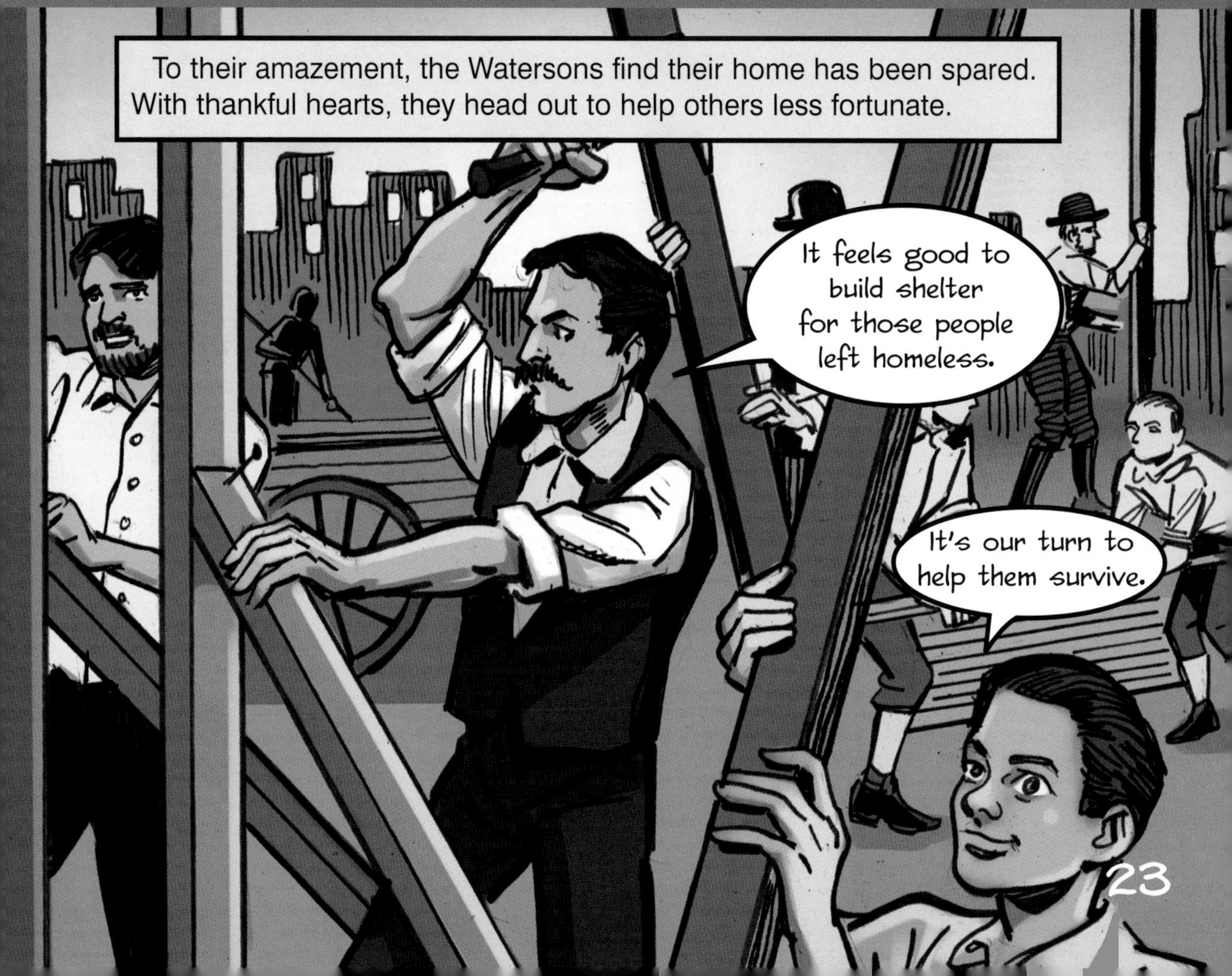
To their amazement, the Watersons find their home has been spared. With thankful hearts, they head out to help others less fortunate.
It feels good to build shelter for those people left homeless.
It's our turn to help them survive.

Celebrating Survival

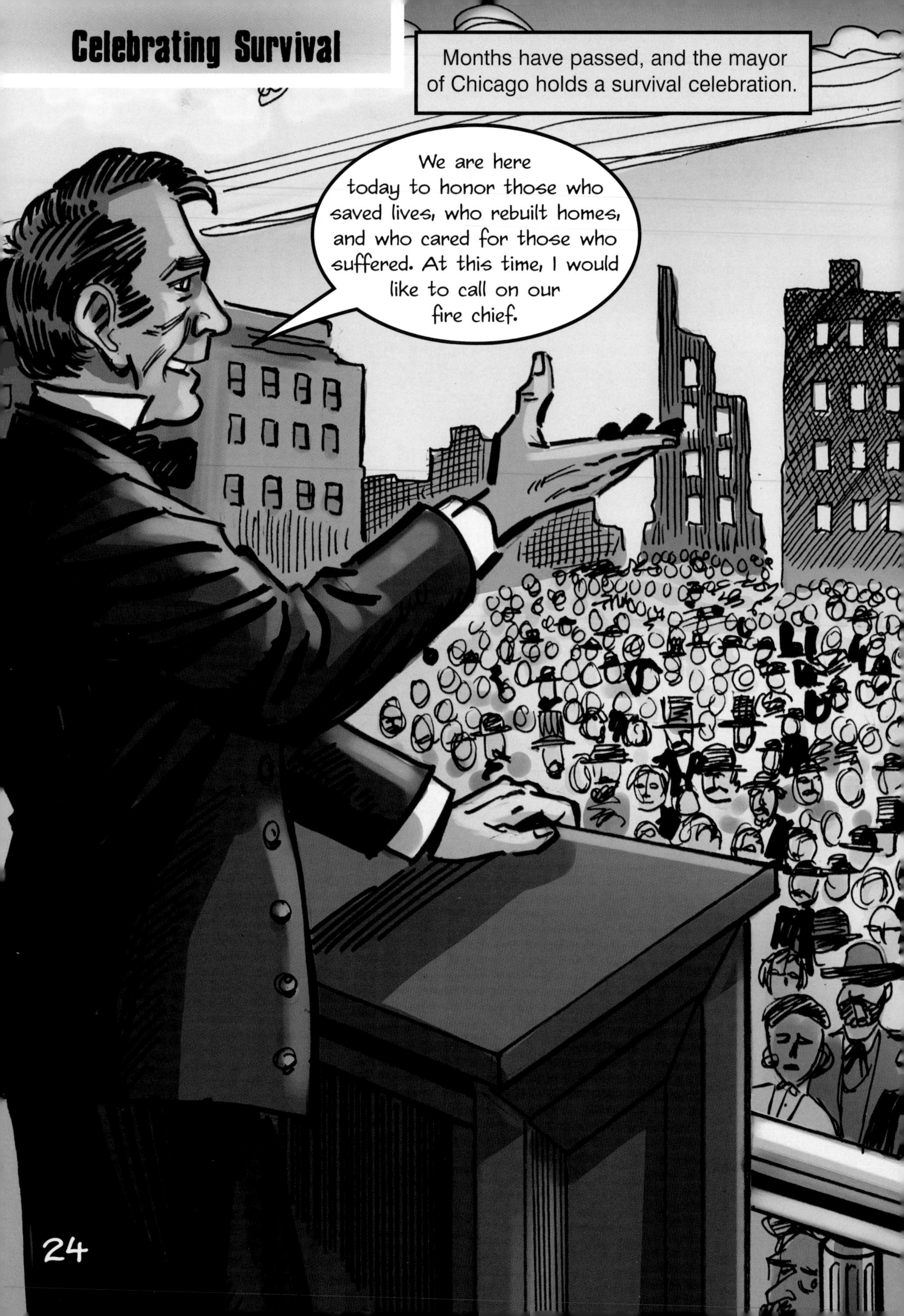
Months have passed, and the mayor of Chicago holds a survival celebration.
We are here today to honor those who saved lives, who rebuilt homes, and who cared for those who suffered. At this time, I would like to call on our fire chief.

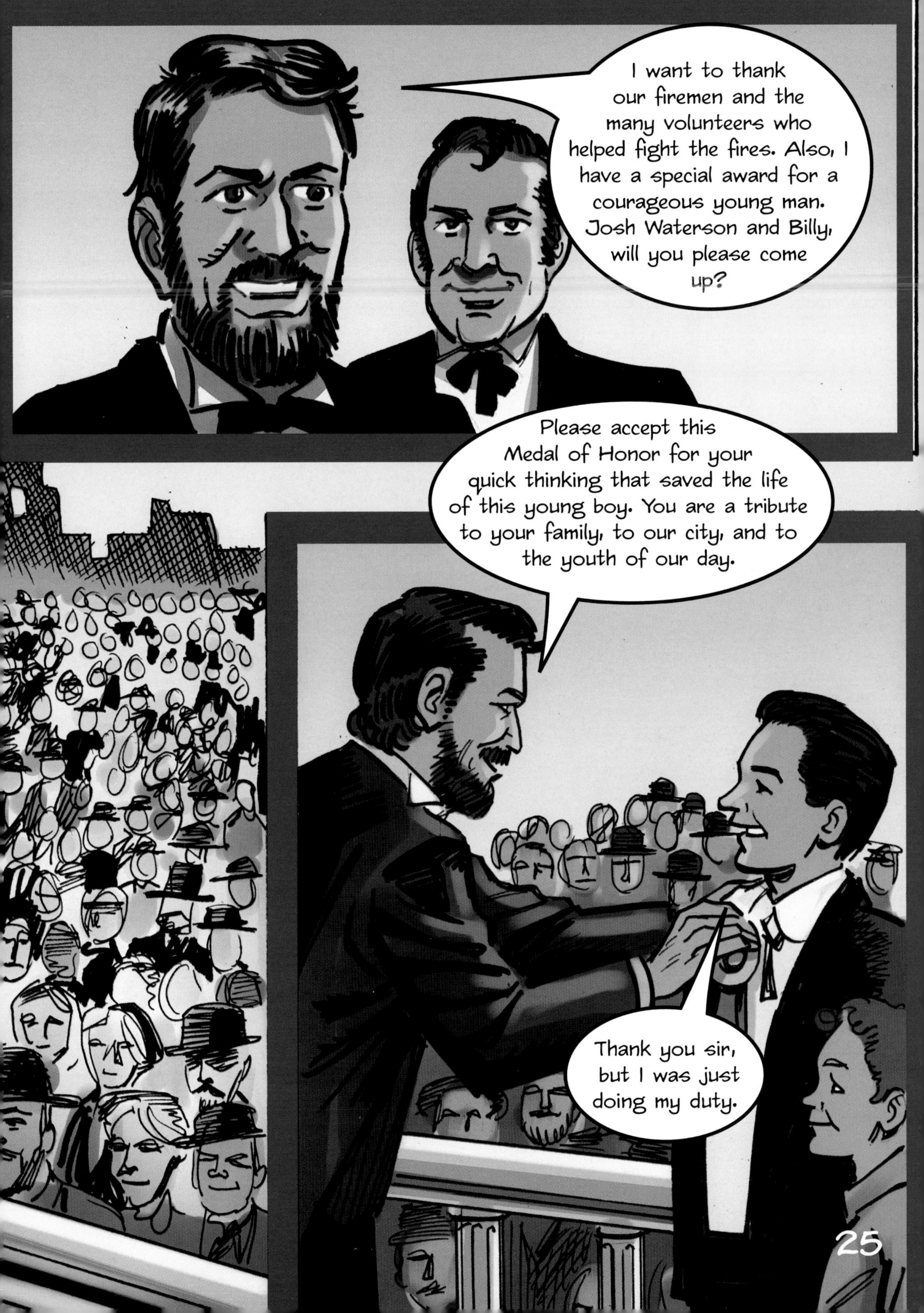
I want to thank our firemen and the many volunteers who helped fight the fires. Also, I have a special award for a courageous young man. Josh Waterson and Billy, will you please come up?
Please accept this Medal of Honor for your quick thinking that saved the life of this young boy. You are a tribute to your family, to our city, and to the youth of our day.
Thank you sir, but I was just doing my duty.

What was the real cause of the Great Chicago Fire of 1871?

No one knows for sure what really started the fire. One **legend** is that Mrs. O'Leary's cow kicked over a lantern inside the barn, which caught nearby straw on fire. It is true that flames were first seen

Thousands ran to escape the intense heat and raging fires.

near the O'Leary barn; however in 1911, the newspaper reporter who submitted that explanation admitted he made up the story.

The most accepted explanation seems well-founded. Mr. O'Leary told officials that on October 8, 1871, Mr. Daniel Sullivan came to Mr. O'Leary's door to alert the family that there was a fire in their barn. Decades later, just before he died, Mr. Sullivan confessed that he had sneaked into the O'Leary's barn to steal milk, and that he had started the fire.

Some scientists had an interesting idea. Two other fires broke out at exactly the same time in nearby cities. One was in Peshtigo, Wisconsin and another was in Holland, Michigan. They wondered if **splintering** comets might have set off all three fires.

Lake Michigan
Chicago River
Grant Park

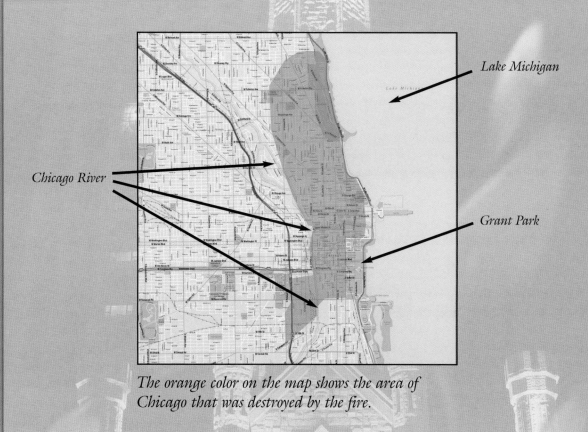

The orange color on the map shows the area of Chicago that was destroyed by the fire.

In the 19th century, was it common for boys to take the same jobs as their fathers?

Yes, most boys entered the same line of work as their fathers. They left school to become **apprentices** at their fathers' places of work to learn a trade or skill. Josh Waterson, the fictional character in this book, is still in school at age 16, which is unusual.

How long did it take to rebuild Chicago?

Within four years, Chicago looked even better than it had before the Great Fire.

Workers began **reconstruction** immediately. They made temporary shelters for the homeless, repaired damaged buildings, constructed new city facilities, and fixed streets and railroad lines. Volunteers included both the young and the old, and the rich and the poor. There were people from the Chicago area and from other cities, and even prisoners whose lives were spared when their courthouse cells were unlocked.

City officials paid close attention to ways of preventing future fire disasters, by replacing wooden structures with stone, adding sprinkler systems, and installing other fire safeguards that were not present in 1871.

To this day, Chicago is one of the most visited cities in the United States.

Parts of Grant Park are built upon debris from structures that burned during the fire.

If you visit Chicago, there are lots of attractions for you to see, including areas where the fire occurred. The old Water Tower and Chicago Pumping Station are the only public buildings that were left standing after the fire. You can tour the tower and learn about its history. You might even get a glimpse of a ghost that is rumored to haunt the upstairs! Other places of interest include an architectural boat tour along the Chicago River, Lincoln Park and its free zoo, and Grant Park with all of its lovely gardens and walkways. When you get hungry, be sure to stop along the way and enjoy Chicago's world-famous hotdogs and deep-dish pizzas.

Websites

www.americaslibrary.gov/cgi-bin/page.cgi/jb/ recon/chicago_l

www.chicagohs.org/fire/intro/gcf-index.html

www.chicagohs.org/history/fire.html

en.wikipedia.org/wiki/Great_Chicago_Fire

alert (uh-LURT): An alert is a signal warning of danger.

apprentices (uh-PREN-tiss-ez): Apprentices are unpaid workers who work to learn a skill or job. Usually, they work beside someone who is already an expert to learn the necessary skills.

devastation (dev-uh-STAY-shuhn): Devastation is complete ruin.

intense (in-TENSS): If a fire is intense, it is very, very hot.

legend (LEJ-uhnd): A legend is a story that has been told many times over the years. It is often based on fact, but is not entirely a true story.

panicky (PAN-ik-ee): When people are panicky, they are so frightened they can't think straight.

raging (RAYJ-ing): A raging fire is very, very strong. It is so strong that it makes a roaring sound.

reconstruction (ree-kuhn-STRUHKT-shun): Reconstruction is the rebuilding of areas that have been destroyed. Workers repair or replace homes, schools, hotels, churches, stores, factories, and other buildings that have been damaged.

smoldering (SMOHL-dur-ing): Something is smoldering if it is still giving off smoke and heat after the flames of a fire have been put out.

splintering (SPLIN-tur-ing): If something starts splintering, it begins to break apart.

stomped (STOMPT): Slammed feet hard on the ground. If someone is stomped on by a horse, it ran right on top of that person.

survive (sur-VIVE): To survive is to live through a very dangerous time.

timber (TIM-bur): Timber is wood.

watchtower (WOCH-tou-ur): A watchtower is a tall building from which workers keep looking all the time for possible trouble. If a watchman sees a fire, he sends out a danger signal.

Index

About the Author

Jo Cleland, Professor Emeritus of Reading Education, taught in the College of Education at Arizona State University for 11 years. Prior to entering university teaching, Jo spent 20 years in public education and continues to work with children through her storytelling and workshops. She has presented to audiences of teachers and students across the nation and the world, bringing to all her favorite message: **what we learn with delight, we never forget**.

About the Illustrator

Pete McDonnell is an illustrator who has worked in his field for twenty-four years. He has been creating comics, storyboards, and pop-art style illustration for clients such as Marvel Comics, the History Channel, Microsoft, Nestle, Sega, and many more. He lives in Sonoma County, California with his wife Shannon (also an illustrator) and son Jacob.